FROM THE ASHES OF ANGELS

Do angels and fallen angels exist outside the realms of myth? What were their true origins, and what impact might they have had on the rise of civilization? Andrew Collins reveals disturbing new evidence to show that:

- angels, demons and fallen angels were flesh and blood human beings responsible for the foundations of Western civilization
- Eden, Heaven and Paradise were once earthly realms placed amid the mountains of Kurdistan
- these human angels, known in ancient Judaic texts as Watchers and Nephilim, came originally from Egypt and were responsible for the construction of the Great Sphinx and other cyclopean monuments
- both Egypt's high civilization and the Watchers of Kurdistan have left as a legacy to humanity a chilling warning that the world ignores at its peril

ABOUT THE AUTHOR

Andrew Collins was born in 1957. He began his journalistic career with the magazine *Strange Phenomena* in 1979 and has penned a series of popular books on historical and landscape quests, including the cult classic *The Black Alchemist*, *The Seventh Sword* and *The Second Coming*. He has also spent twenty years scientifically investigating the relationship between paranormal phenomena, ancient sites and the human mind, the culmination of which has been the publication of influential works such as *The Circlemakers* and *Alien Energy*.

From the Ashes of Angels is the result of a ten-year study by the author into the historical reality of an advanced civilization in Egypt and the Near East during prehistoric times.

From the Ashes of Angels

The Forbidden Legacy of a Fallen Race

ANDREW COLLINS

Additional research by Richard Ward

Bear & Company
Rochester, Vermont

Bear & Company
One Park Street
Rochester, Vermont 05767
www.InnerTraditions.com

Library of Congress Cataloging-in-Publication Data
Collins, Andrew
From the ashes of angels : the forbidden legacy of a fallen race / Andrew Collins ; additional research by Richard Ward.
p. cm.
Includes bibliographical references and index.
Originally published: London ; New York : Signet Book, 1996.
ISBN 978-1-879181-72-4
1. Angels—Miscellanea. 2. Near East—Antiquities—Miscellanea. I. Title.
BF1999 .C683 2001
001.94—dc21
2001043091

Printed and bound in the United States

13

This book is dedicated

to the People of Kurdistan,

Keepers of the Cradle of Civilization

*

May you eventually find the peace and independence

you so sorely deserve

Contents

Author's Note

Unless otherwise stated, all historical dates in this book have been taken from H. E. L. Mellersh, *Chronology of the Ancient World – 10,000 BC to AD 799*, Helicon, Oxford, 1976. All biblical quotations, unless otherwise stated, are taken from the Revised Version of the Authorized (King James) Bible of 1884. Any interpolations by the author within quoted texts are printed in italic within square brackets (or in roman within square brackets in longer italic extracts), to distinguish them from interpolations existing in the originals.

List of Figures

List of Charts

List of Maps

Acknowledgements

First I would like to thank Debbie Benstead, for her five years of inspiration and guidance. Our world together did not survive this book, but nothing is ever forgotten. Thanks also go out to David Southwell, for providing me with his enthusiastic intuition and extraordinary insights into the Watchers' lost history, as well as for offering editorial comments on chapters; to John Day, who encountered the Watchers as early as 1974 and set me on the path; to Bernard, without whom I would never have believed such a forgotten race had ever inhabited this world; to the staff at Leigh Library, for their continued help and support, and for securing books and papers that seemed at first to be a near impossible task; to Professor Philip Alexander, for his help and advice on Judaeo-Christian angelology; to Rodney Hale, for his vital astronomical calculations and for his valued support; to Gareth Medway, for continuing to find obscure references on any subject I put to him; to Steve Wilson, Caroline Wise, Johnny Merron, John and Kerry Horrigan, Jason Digby, Lisa and Karl 'Shem' Dawkins, for their constant friendship and for reading the manuscript in its later stages; and to Richard Ward for his exhaustive research into the Watcher tradition, and for the weekly 'Morphochats' that helped to establish this book.

Thanks also go out to Storm Constantine, for her deep friendship, her constant support, and for her valued editorial comments on the construction of *From the Ashes of Angels*; to Luigi Bonomi and Susan Watt of Michael Joseph, for taking the risk; Simon Trewin of Sheil Land Associates, for his faith in me as a writer; Billie Walker-John for her wonderful illustrations and dedication; Peter Ford for correcting my colloquialisms; Niven Sinclair for his never-ending support; Moira for her constant friendship; Graham Hancock, for setting the scene with his own essential books, and for his invaluable advice, opinions and support; Lynn and Carl McCoy of Sheer Faith for their advice and offer of help on the book jacket; and to Fields of the Nephilim/Nefilim, whose dark, brooding music has helped to resurrect the spirit of the Watchers and has been a constant inspiration during the writing of this book. Lastly, I would like to thank Ennio Morricone for making the music that kept me strong during these troubled times.

Illustration Credits

The publishers wish to thank the following for permission to reproduce copyright material:

the Hebrew University, Jerusalem, for 'James Biberkraut working on the Dead Sea Scroll known as the Genesis Apocryphon', from *A Genesis Apocryphon* by Nahman Avigad and Yigael Yadin (Hebrew University Press, 1956); the Kunsthistorisches Museum, Vienna, for Hugo van der Goes: *Sündenfall* (GG 5822 A), from *Hebrew Myths: The Book of Genesis*, by R. Graves and R. Patai (Cassell, 1964); the British Library (Ref: OR 8761 Folio 52V) for a painting from *Persian Myths* by Vesta Sarkhosh Curtis (British Museum Press, 1993); the Réunion des musées nationaux for the victory stela of Nâram-Sim, in the Musée du Louvre, Paris; the Mithraic lion-head deity (CIMRM 545) printed by kind permission of Kluwer Academic Publishers, Dordrecht, The Netherlands, and M. J. Vermaseren; Mrs B. Walker-John for her drawing and painting of a 'Watcher'.

Every effort has been made to trace and contact all copyright holders. The publishers will be glad to rectify any omissions at the earliest opportunity.

One

I HAVE BEGOTTEN A STRANGE SON

And after some days my son, Methuselah, took a wife for his son Lamech, and she became pregnant by him and bore him a son. And his body was white as snow and red as a rose; the hair of his head as white as wool and his demdema *('long curly hair'[1]) beautiful; and as for his eyes, when he opened them the whole house glowed like the sun . . . And his father, Lamech, was afraid of him and fled and went to Methuselah his father; and he said to him, 'I have begotten a strange son. He is not like an (ordinary) human being, but he looks like the children of the angels of heaven to me, his form is different, and he is not like us . . . It does not seem to me that he is of me, but of angels . . .'*[2]

These words form the opening lines to what must be one of the most astonishing yet chilling fragments of religious text ever written. They are the assertions of the antediluvian patriarch Enoch as he describes the sheer distress and horror that accompanied the miraculous birth of a son to his grandson, Lamech. The passage is taken from the Book of Noah, an ancient script of Hebrew origin appended to the more famous Book of Enoch, a pseudepigraphal (i.e. falsely attributed) work, considered by scholars to have been put together in stages during the first half of the second century BC.[3]

The predicament conveyed by these revealing lines seems manifestly clear: Lamech has recently taken the hand of a woman who has given birth to a child that bears no resemblance whatsoever to its immediate family. His appearance is entirely unlike other 'human beings', for his skin is white and ruddy, his long curly hair is white and 'beautiful', while his eyes mysteriously enable the whole house to 'glow like the sun'. From this specific appearance

Lamech can only conclude that his wife has been unfaithful, since the infant resembles 'the children of the angels' who are 'not like us'.

This seems an extraordinary conclusion on the part of Lamech, and a very strange subject for a religious scribe to invent without good reason. If it can, for a moment, be accepted that this account records an actual event in the history of human kind, then it implies that the strange appearance of this child matched the offspring of angels, and must by inference have been the product of the union between a mortal woman and a divine 'messenger', a 'heavenly intelligence' in the service of God himself.[4]

Surely this is impossible, for according to Judaeo-Christian tradition angels are incorporeal, having neither form nor substance. They are certainly unable to reproduce by immaculate conception. If this is correct, then the story of the birth of Lamech's strange son is in direct contradiction to the rabbinical teachings of Judaism and the creed of the Christian faith. Yet here it is, in print for all to see – heretical words implying that angelic beings were able to produce children by cohabiting with mortal women.

For any reader with an open mind, this is a perplexing enigma further deepened by a more personal portrayal of the birth of Lamech's son, which is to be found in a poorly preserved fragment of religious text, discovered with many other rolled-up brittle scrolls inside a cave overlooking the Dead Sea in 1947. Known to scholars today as the Genesis Apocryphon, this unique work was written in Aramaic, the Syriac language adopted by the Hebrew scribes following the Jews' exile in Babylon during the sixth century BC. Dating back to a similar age as the Book of Enoch, the Dead Sea Scroll in question would have originally contained an alternative, fuller account of the events featured in the Book of Genesis; however, it was so badly damaged when found that only the birth of Lamech's son, an account of Noah's Ark and the biblical Flood, along with the wanderings of the patriarch Abraham, have been preserved.

The fragmentary text was translated by Nahman Avigad and Yigael Yadin in 1954 and published under the title *A Genesis Apocryphon* two years later by the Hebrew University, Jerusalem.[5] With respect to the account of the strange birth of Lamech's son, it differs principally from the version given in the Book of Enoch, in that the narrator has altered from the patriarch Enoch to Lamech himself – it is he who recalls the scene in his own words. The narrative begins just after the strange birth as Lamech starts voicing his suspicions concerning the suspected infidelity of his wife, here named as Bathenosh[6] – and referred to also as his sister – for he says:

Behold, I thought then within my heart that conception was (due) to the Watchers and the Holy Ones . . . and to the Nephilim . . . and my heart was troubled within me because of this child.[7]

Turning to his obviously distraught wife, Lamech makes her swear by the Most High that she will tell him the truth and admit if she has lain with anyone else. In reply she beseeches him to accept her word, saying:

'O my lord, O my [brother, remember] my pleasure! I swear to thee by the Holy Great One, the king of [the heavens] . . . that this seed is yours and that [this] conception is from you. This fruit was planted by you . . . and by no stranger or Watcher or Son of Heaven . . . I speak to you truthfully.[8]

It is clear that Lamech is accusing his wife of sleeping not with angels in general, but with having had relations with a specific race of divine beings known in Hebrew as עירין, *'îrin* (עיר, *'îr* in singular), meaning 'those who watch' or 'those who are awake', which is translated into Greek as 'Εγρήγοροι, *egregoris* or *grigori*, meaning 'watchers'. These Watchers feature in the main within the pages of pseudepigraphal and apocryphal works of Jewish origin, such as the Book of Enoch and the Book of Jubilees. Their progeny, according to Hebrew tradition, are named as ולנפילין, *nephilim*, a Hebrew word meaning 'those who have fallen' or 'the fallen ones', translated into Greek as γίγαντες, *gigantes*, or 'giants' – a monstrous race featured in the *Theogony* of the hellenic writer Hesiod (*c.* 907 BC). As in the biblical account, this ancient Greek work focuses on the creation of the world, the rise and fall of a Golden Age, the coming of the giant races and finally a universal flood.

Bathenosh's touching plea of innocence to her husband and brother Lamech comes across as most convincing, and provides tantalizing evidence that this ancient account may contain some grain of truth. Somehow it could just be based on a real-life event that occurred in a past age of mankind. If so, then exactly who, or what, were these Watchers and Nephilim who could lie with mortal women and produce offspring recognizable by their physiological traits alone? Are there any grounds whatsoever on which to consider that these apocryphal stories were based on the miscegenation between two different races of human beings, one of whom has been misidentified or falsely equated with the angels of heaven? If not, then exactly what were such stories meant to convey to the reader?

The Book of Enoch seems to provide an answer. Lamech, fearful of his predicament, consults his father, Methuselah, who, unable to alleviate the situation, embarks upon a journey to find his own father Enoch, who has withdrawn from the world and now lives 'among the angels'.[9] After Methuselah has tracked him down in a far-off land (referred to in the Genesis Apocryphon as 'Parwain' or Paradise) and conveying the fears of his son Lamech, the ever-righteous Enoch throws light on the situation when he states:

'I have already seen this matter in a vision and made it known to you. For in the generation of Jared, my father, they [the angels] transgressed the word of the Lord, (that is) the law of heaven. And behold, they commit sin and transgress the commandment; they have united themselves with women and commit sin together with them; and they have married (wives) from among them, and begotten children by them . . . And upon the earth they shall give birth to giants, not of the spirit but of the flesh. There shall be a great plague . . . and the earth shall be washed clean (by "a deluge") from all the corruption. Now, make known to your son Lamech that the son who has been born is indeed righteous, and call his name Noah, for he shall be the remnant for you; and he and his sons shall be saved from the corruption which shall come upon the earth . . .'[10]

So the lid is finally lifted as the reader of the Book of Enoch is told that some of the angels of heaven have succumbed to carnal sin and taken wives from among mortal women. From this unholy union have come flesh-and-blood offspring, giant in stature, who, it must be presumed, match the description of the child born to

Bathenosh. This betrayal of the heavenly laws of God was seen as an abomination that would bring only corruption and evil to the human race, the punishment for which was to be a deluge to cleanse the world of its wickedness.

The Sons of God

Theologians are more or less united in their opinion that the widespread accounts of fallen angels cohabiting with mortal women, like those included in the Book of Enoch, the Genesis Apocryphon and similar texts, are no more than fanciful expansions of three verses to be found in Chapter 6 of the Book of Genesis, squeezed between a genealogical listing of the antediluvian patriarchs and a brief account of Noah's Ark and the coming of the Flood.

The first lines in question, making up Chapter 6, verses 1–2, are indelibly imprinted in my mind and read as follows:

And it came to pass, when men began to multiply on the face of the ground, and daughters were born unto them, that the sons of God saw the daughters of men that they were fair; and they took them wives of all that they chose.[11]

By 'sons of God' the text means heavenly angels, although the Hebrew original, בני אלהים, *bene ha-elohim*, should really be translated as 'sons of the gods', a much more disconcerting prospect (and something to be returned to in a subsequent chapter).

In verse 3 of Chapter 6, God unexpectedly pronounces that his spirit cannot remain in men for ever, and that since humanity is a creation of flesh, its lifespan will be shortened to 'an hundred and twenty years'. Yet in verse 4 the tone suddenly reverts to the original theme of the chapter, for it says:

The Nephilim were in the earth in those days, and also after that, when the sons of God came in unto the daughters of men, and they bare children to them: the same were the mighty men which were of old, the men of renown.[12]

In the hundreds of times I have read these isolated words out aloud I have wondered to myself: what could they possibly mean?

There is no consensus in answer to this question, and scholars, mystics and speculative writers have all given their own interpretations over the past two thousand years. Theologians agree in general that such accounts are not to be taken as literal fact, but only as a symbol of humanity's fall from a state of spiritual grace to one of conflict and corruption in the days prior to the Great Flood.

What the texts are saying, the theologians would argue, is that if evil and corruption on this scale does occur in the world, then only those of the purest heart and spirit – individuals exemplified by Noah and his righteous family – will be spared the wrath of God. It is therefore a purely allegorical teaching intent on conveying to the reader the inevitable consequences of wickedness.

The references in verses 2 and 4 to 'the sons of God' coming 'unto the daughters of men', so the scholars believe, demonstrate how even those closest to the purity of God can become infected by corruption and evil. It was usually accepted among religious teachers that any such unholy union between angels and mortal women could only, because it was against God's will, lead to the creation of monstrous offspring. It was this thought-provoking concept which had, according to the early Church Fathers, inspired the creation of various apocryphal and pseudepigraphal works dealing with the fall of the angels and the corruption of mankind before the time of the Great Flood.

Celestial Mafia

So much for the theological debate, but is it correct? Is this all there is to know about the origins of fallen angels? And what about the adherents of the Jewish and Christian faiths? How were they able to interpret such 'myths'? The majority would probably have been unaware that these problematical verses even existed in the Book of Genesis. Others, who did have some knowledge of the matter, are unlikely to have been able to expand on it, while only a very small minority would have believed in the actual existence of fallen angels. Many commentators would have been unable to explain exactly how such stories related to the physical world we live in, while other more fundamentalist Jews or Christians have seen such corruption and wickedness as the actions of blood-line descendants of those first fallen angels who cohabited with mortal women before the time of the Flood. Such suggestions may seem far-fetched, but in the United States there is an organization known as the Sons of Jared, who take their name from the patriarch Jared, the father of Enoch, during whose age the Watchers were said to have been 'cast down' from 'heaven'. In their manifesto, the Sons of Jared vow 'implacable war against the descendants of the Watchers', who, they allege, 'as notorious Pharaohs, Kings and Dictators, have throughout history dominated mankind'. *The Jaredite Advocate*, the voice of the Sons of Jared, quotes lavishly from the Book of Enoch and sees the Watchers as 'like super-gangsters, a celestial Mafia ruling the world'.[13]

Is this simply a view gained from dogmatically accepting the fall of flesh-and-blood angels of heaven? How many individuals have the Sons of Jared accused or persecuted; believing them to be modern-day descendants of the Watchers?

Some academic scholars, on the other hand, while unable to accept any basis in fact behind the concept of fallen angels and their monstrous offspring, the Nephilim, would be willing to admit that the original authors of the Book of Genesis (traditionally accredited to Moses the lawgiver) based their material on previously existing folk legends, probably from Mesopotamia (the country known today as Iraq). The historian S. H. Hooke, for instance, in his book *Middle Eastern Mythology*, accepts that:

Behind the brief and probably intentionally obscure reference in (Genesis) *6:1–4 there lies a more widely known myth of a race of semi-divine beings who rebelled against the gods and were cast down into the underworld . . . The fragment of the myth here preserved by the Yahwist was originally an aetiological myth explaining the belief in the existence of a vanished race of giants . . .*[14]

This might well be so, but accepting Genesis 6:1–4 as the product of far older Middle Eastern myths allows for the possibility that, sometime during a bygone age of mankind, there existed on earth, presumably in the bible lands themselves, an élite and probably superior race of human beings. These people presumably achieved a state of high civilization before degenerating into a corruption and wickedness that included the taking of wives from among the less civilized races and the creation of monstrous offspring of disproportionate size to their immediate family. It might also be suggested that a series of global cataclysms thereafter brought fire, flood and darkness to the earth and ended the reign of this race of 'giants'.

Should we see accounts like Lamech's torment at the miraculous birth of his son Noah, and untold others like it, as tantalizing evidence for the idea that fallen angels were something far more than simply incorporeal beings cast out of heaven by the archangel Michael, as the theologians and propagators of the Christian, Islamic and Jewish faiths have taught during the last two thousand years? Could their very existence be confirmed by making an in-depth study of Hebrew myths and legends and then comparing these with other Near Eastern and Middle Eastern religions and traditions? Most important of all, might evidence of their physical existence on earth be incidentally preserved in the records of modern-day archaeology and anthropology?

Such thought-provoking possibilities were worth further consideration. If, at the end of the day, it was found that no such evidence for the existence of a now lost race in the bible lands could be discovered, then at least an age-old enigma would have been investigated thoroughly. On the other hand, if there really was firm evidence that angels and fallen angels once walked among mankind as beings of flesh and blood, no different from you or me, then it could change our perspective of world history for ever.

Fear of Fallen Angels

There are clear signs that the concept of angels and fallen angels as corporeal beings of flesh and blood, who lived in a distant antediluvian age and left as a legacy an intimate knowledge of many things forbidden to humanity, was once widely accepted by certain elements of the Jewish population. These included the devout religious communities that lived a pious existence in the hot, rugged terrain on the west bank of the Dead Sea from about 170 BC to AD 120.

Known to history as the Essenes, their main centre is thought to have been at Qumrân, where archaeologists have uncovered extensive evidence of occupation, including a massive library room where many of the Dead Sea Scrolls are thought to have been written.

Historical works from this period suggest that the Essenes not only accepted the Book of Enoch as part of their canon, but also used its listing of angels to perform rites of exorcism and healing.[15] Recent studies of the Dead Sea Scrolls have also shown that the Essenes possessed an almost unhealthy interest in Enochian-style material featuring the Watchers and Nephilim.[16] Although many of these works date only to the second century BC, the hidden teachings found among the Qumrân community and known as Kabbalah imply that the Enochian and Noahic scriptures were passed on by word of mouth for thousands of years before finally being set down in written form by the Essenes themselves.[17]

With the advent of Christianity, the Book of Enoch and other such similar works became generally available for the first time. Many of the Early Church leaders, from the first to the third centuries AD, used and quoted openly from their pages.[18] Some Christian scholars held that mortal women had been responsible for the fall of the angels, while Paul in Corinthians 11:10 advocated – according to the Church Father Tertullianus (AD 160–230) – that women cover their heads so as not to incite wantonness in the fallen angels who liked unveiled women with beautiful hair.[19] Even more remarkable was the general acceptance among many prominent theologians that fallen angels possessed corporeal bodies.[20] Indeed, it was not until the age of the Church Fathers, from the fourth century onwards, that such matters were seriously questioned. For these people, fallen angels were *not* flesh-and-blood beings, and any suggestion that they might have been became tantamount to heresy. This attitude led to the suppression of the Book of Enoch, which quickly fell out of favour. Most bizarre of all were the comments of St Augustine (AD 354–430) in respect of the antiquity of this pseudepigraphal work. He claimed that on account of it being *too old* (*ob nimiam antiquitatem*), the Book of Enoch could not be included in the Canon of Scripture.[21] What ever could he have meant by suggesting it was 'too old'? It was a most extraordinary statement to be made by a respected Church father.

Curiously enough, the Book of Enoch had also fallen out of favour among the Jews, after Rabbi Simeon ben Jochai, in the second century AD, cursed all those who believed that the Sons of God mentioned in Genesis 6 were truly angels. This was despite the fact that the Septuagint, the Greek version of the Old Testament, uses the term *angelos* in place of 'sons of God'.[22]

The Church Fathers then went further in their attempts to stamp out the strange fascination with fallen angels among early Christians by condemning as heresy the use of the many hundreds of names given both to angels and fallen angels in various religious works.[23] No longer was the Book of Enoch copied by Christian scribes, and those copies remaining in libraries and churches were either lost or destroyed, denying the world any knowledge of the work's true contents for over a thousand years.

Subsequently, on top of all this, it became the policy of Catholic theologians to eradicate firmly from the teachings of the Church any notion that fallen angels had once been seen as material beings, a situation typified by this quote from the *New Catholic Encyclopedia*: 'In the course of time theology has purified the obscurity and error contained in traditional views about angels (i.e. the belief that they were corporeal in nature and cohabited with mortal women).'[24]

Yet why should such beliefs have become so abhorrent to the Christian faith after the great leaders of the Early Church of Jerusalem had preached so openly on this very controversial subject? It simply did not make sense, and suggested there must have been extremely good reasons for forcing this strain of thought underground, for that was exactly where it went – underground.

From the extraordinary evidence collected together by the author, and presented in this book for the first time, there emerge firm grounds to suggest that initiates and secret societies preserved, revered, even celebrated the forbidden knowledge that our most distant ancestors had gained their inspiration and wisdom, not from God or from the experiences of life, but from a forgotten race remembered by us today only as fallen angels, demons, devils, giants and evil spirits. Should such a view prove in any way correct, then it must indicate one of the greatest secrets ever kept from mankind.

But where was I to start? How was I even to begin the quest to unveil the forbidden legacy of this apparently fallen race? The answer lay with its main sourcebook, the Book of Enoch, for only by understanding its obscure origins and absorbing its bizarre contents could I ever hope to uncover the true picture behind humanity's lost heritage.

Two

THE SEARCH FOR THE SOURCE

My quest to understand the importance of the Book of Enoch began with the man who single-handedly revived the scholarly world's interest in this previously lost piece of Judaic religious literature. His name is James Bruce of Kinnaird, and in 1768 he left England *en route* for Abyssinia, modern-day Ethiopia, in search of something, and it was certainly not the source of the Blue Nile, as he claimed at the time.[1]

Bruce was a Scottish nobleman, a direct descendant of one of the most powerful families of Scottish history. He was also an initiate of Freemasonry,[2] which in Scotland could trace its roots back to the so-called Rite of Heredom, first instituted in early medieval times and later incorporated into the Royal Order of Scotland.[3] This in itself was a chivalric military order of honour and valour founded on the rites of the Knights Templar by James Bruce's own illustrious ancestor, Robert the Bruce, following the celebrated defeat of the English at the battle of Bannockburn in 1314.[4] James Bruce himself was a member of the Canongate Kilwinning No. 2 lodge of Edinburgh, known to be one of the oldest in Scotland, with side-orders and mystical teachings entrenched in Judaeo-Christian myth and ritual.[5]

Freemasonry is an organization with innumerable secrets, and many of these would have been known to the extremely knowledgeable James Bruce. For instance, he would have been aware that in Scottish Masonic tradition the patriarch Enoch, Noah's great-grandfather, was looked upon as one of the Craft's legendary founders, since he was accredited with having given mankind the knowledge of books and writing and, most important of all to Freemasons, to have taught mankind the art of building.[6]

The Antediluvian Pillars

Enoch had many associations with early modern Freemasonry, or speculative Masonry as it is known. According to one legend,[7] Enoch, with foreknowledge of the coming Deluge, constructed, with the help of his son Methuselah, nine hidden vaults, each stacked one on top of the other. In the lowest of these he deposited a gold triangular tablet (a 'white oriental porphyry stone' in one version) bearing the Ineffable Name, the unspoken name of the Hebrew God, while a second tablet, inscribed with strange words Enoch had gained from the angels themselves, was given into the safe-keeping of his son. The vaults were then sealed, and upon the spot Enoch had two indestructible columns constructed – one of marble, so that it might 'never burn', and the other of *Laterus*, or brick, so that it might 'not sink in water'.[8]

On the brick column were inscribed the 'seven sciences' of mankind, the so-called 'archives' of Masonry, while on the marble column he 'placed an inscription stating that a short distance away a priceless treasure would be found in a subterranean vault'.[9] Enoch then retired to Mount Moriah, traditionally equated with the Temple Mount in Jerusalem, where he was 'translated' to heaven.

In time, King Solomon uncovered the hidden vaults while constructing his legendary temple and learned of their divine secrets. Memory of these two ancient pillars of Enoch was preserved by the Freemasons, who set up representations of them in their lodges. Known as the Antediluvian Pillars, or Enoch's Pillars, they were eventually replaced by representations of the two huge columns named 'Jachin' and 'Boaz', said to have stood on each side of the entrance porch to Solomon's Temple.[10]

What exactly the nine hidden vaults constructed by Enoch were meant to represent is completely unknown. They might well refer to the nine levels of mystical initiation contained in the hidden teachings of the Kabbalah, accepted among the Dead Sea communities. On the other hand, perhaps the legends of the hidden vaults referred to actual underground chambers located somewhere in the Holy Land and constructed to hide sacred objects of importance to the future of mankind.

Walked with God

The patriarch Enoch's legendary status among both Jewish mystics and modern-day Freemasons stems from a very strange assumption. In the Bible, Chapter 5 of Genesis contains a genealogical listing of the ten antediluvian patriarchs, from Adam down to Noah. In each case it gives only their names, their age when they 'begat' their first son, and the age at which they died, with one notable exception – Enoch. In his case, he is twice said to have 'walked with God', an obscure statement elaborated only in the second instance with the enigmatic words: 'and he was not, for God took him'.[11] Whatever the writer of Genesis had been attempting to convey by these words, they were taken to mean that Enoch did not die like the other patriarchs, but was instead 'translated' to heaven with the aid of God's angels. According to the Bible, only the prophet Elijah had been taken by God in a similar manner, so Enoch (whose name means 'initiated') had always been accorded a very special place in Judaeo-Christian literature. Indeed, Hebrew mysticism asserts that on his 'translation' to heaven Enoch was transformed into the angel Metatron.[12]

What does it mean: 'translated to heaven'? As we know, people are not carried off to heaven by angels while still living their life on earth. Either these words are metaphorical or else they need drastic reappraisal. Might Enoch have been simply taken away from his people by visitors from another land who were looked upon as angels by the rest of the community? And where was heaven, anyway? We know it is deemed to be a place 'in the clouds', but did this literally mean somewhere beyond the physical world in which we live?

Once in this place called heaven, Enoch would appear to have made enemies immediately, for according to one Hebrew legend, an angel named Azza was expelled from Paradise – the alternative name for the heavenly domain – for objecting 'to the high rank given to Enoch' when he was transformed into Metatron.[13]

Fig. 1. The patriarch Enoch being 'translated' to heaven by two angels, after an eleventh century English manuscript. Enoch was said to have been the first mortal to enter Eden since the expulsion of Adam and Eve after the Fall of Man. Are heaven and Eden ethereal realms of our creation or actual geographical locations in the Near East?

All these legends and traditions concerning Enoch show that the patriarch was highly venerated in Jewish mythology because of his trafficking with the angels. This position led many scholars to believe that apocryphal works, such as the Book of Enoch, were imaginative stories based on his much celebrated translation to heaven, where he now lives in the presence of God.

The Search for the Book of Enoch

James Bruce of Kinnaird was one giant of a man, 'the tallest man you ever saw in your life – at least gratis', or so said one woman who met him.[14] He was fluent in several different languages, including some no longer spoken. These included Aramaic, Hebrew and *Ge'ez*, the written language of the Ethiopian people. Even before his travels in Abyssinia, Bruce had journeyed far and wide, visiting Europe, North Africa and the Holy Land, exploring ancient monuments and searching out old manuscripts ignored by all but a few inquisitive Westerners. In spite of his Blue Nile story, the noble Scotsman would appear to have spent much of his time in Ethiopia within the libraries of ramshackle monasteries, fingering through dusty volumes of neglected religious works, many hoary with age and in a state of advanced disintegration.[15]

So what had he been looking for?

After nearly two years of constant travelling, Bruce arrived at the sleepy monastery of Gondar, on the banks of the vast inland sea named Lake Tana. Having convinced the abbot of his integrity, he was admitted into the dark, dingy library room, where he found, and was finally able to secure, a very rare copy of the *Kebra Nagast*, the sacred book of the Ethiopians. It told of a romantic love affair between King Solomon and the Queen of Sheba, the legendary founder of the kingdom of Abyssinia, and of the birth of their illicit son Menelik, who had conspired with his mother to abduct the fabled Ark of the Covenant from Solomon's Temple. According to the story, the Ark had been carried off to Ethiopia, where it remained to that day.[16]

Had Bruce in fact been searching for a copy of this obscure but very sacred book to take back with him to Europe?

Despite its rarity, the *Kebra Nagast* (or 'Book of the Glory of Kings') had long been known to exist, while its wild claims concerning the Queen of Sheba and the Ark of the Covenant were seen by Western scholars as having been concocted to give Ethiopian Christians an unbroken lineage and national identity stretching back to the time of Adam and Eve. Even so, there is compelling evidence to suggest that the Ark really did reach Ethiopia[17] (although not at the time of King Solomon) and that James Bruce was well aware of this fact and even entered Ethiopia in 1768 with the express intent of bringing it back to Britain.[18]

So was this the answer – a quest for the lost Ark of God? Had Bruce been the Indiana Jones of his day?

Perhaps.

Yet beyond his interests in the *Kebra Nagast* and the Ark of the Covenant, Bruce could hardly have been unaware of the rumours circulating Europe regarding the existence in Ethiopia of the forbidden Book of Enoch. Indeed, during the early 1600s a Capuchin monk visiting Ethiopia had secured a religious text written in *Ge'ez* which was at first believed to be a long-lost copy of this very book. The find caused much excitement in European academic circles. Yet when it was finally studied by an Ethiopian scholar in 1683, the manuscript was identified, not as the missing Book of Enoch, but as a previously unknown text entitled the Book of the Mysteries of Heaven and Earth.[19]

No one really knew what the Book of Enoch might contain. Until the 1600s, its contents were almost entirely unknown. Yet its title alone was so powerful that at least one person attempted to learn its secrets from the angels themselves. This was the Elizabethan astrologer, magus and scientist, Dr John Dee, who, working with an alleged psychic, Edward Kelley, used crystal balls and other scrying paraphernalia to invoke the presence of angels. The spirits told Kelley they would provide him with the contents of the Book of Enoch, and there is evidence to suggest that Dee did actually possess a 'Book of Enoch' dictated through Kelley's mediumship.[20] It is not, however, thought to have in any way resembled the actual work of this name. In addition to this, Dee and Kelley developed a whole written language, complete with its own 'Enochian' script or cipher, from their trafficking with angels. This complex system of magical invocation survives to this day and is still used by many occultists to call upon the assistance of a whole hierarchy of angelic beings.[21]

Scaliger's Discovery

At the beginning of the seventeenth century, a major breakthrough occurred in the search for the lost Book of Enoch. A Flemish scholar named J. J. Scaliger, having decided to study obscure Latin literature in the dimly lit vaults of European libraries, sat down one day to read an unpublished work entitled *Chronographia*, written in the years AD 808–10 by a learned monk named George Syncellus. Having ploughed through lengthy pages of quite mundane sayings and quotes on various matters appertaining to the early Christian Church, he then came upon something quite different – what appeared to be extensive tracts from the Book of Enoch. Handwritten in Greek, these chapters showed that Syncellus had obviously possessed a copy of the forbidden work and had quoted lavishly from its pages in an attempt to demonstrate the terrible transgressions of the fallen angels. Scaliger, realizing the immense rarity of these tracts, faithfully reproduced them in full, giving the world its first glimpse at the previously unknown contents of the Book of Enoch.[22]

The sections quoted by Syncellus and transcribed by Scaliger revealed the story of the Watchers, the Sons of God, who were here referred to by their Greek title *Grigori*. It told how they had taken wives from among mortal women, who had then given birth to Nephilim and *gigantes*, or 'giants'. It also named the leaders of the rebel Watchers and told how the fallen angels had revealed forbidden secrets to mankind, and how they had finally been imprisoned until the Day of Judgement by the archangels of heaven.[23]

We may imagine the conflicting emotions experienced by Scaliger – on the one hand excitement, and on the other horror and revulsion. As a God-fearing Christian of the seventeenth century, when people were being burnt as witches with only the most petty charges brought against them, what was he to make of such claims? What, moreover, was he to do with them? Angels lying with mortal women and the conception of giant babies? What could this all mean? Was it true, or was it simply an allegorical story concerning the consequences of trafficking with supernatural beings such as angels? Merely by making copies of this forbidden text, he ran the risk of being accused of practising diabolism.

Yet this incredible chance discovery begged the question of what the rest of the book might contain. Would it be as shocking as these first few chapters appeared to suggest?

Bruce must have been aware of the controversial nature of the sections of the book preserved for posterity by Syncellus in the ninth century. He must also have been aware of the enormous implications of retrieving a complete manuscript of the Book of Enoch. It was perhaps for this very reason that he spent so long talking to the abbots and monks at the Ethiopian monasteries. In the light of this supposition it becomes crystal clear that one of the primary objectives of Bruce's travels must have been to secure and bring back to Europe a copy of the Book of Enoch.

And Bruce's efforts did not go unrewarded, for he managed to track down and obtain not one but *three* complete copies of the Book of Enoch, with which he returned to Europe in 1773.[24] One was consigned to the National Library of Paris, one he donated to the Bodleian Library in Oxford; and the third he placed 'amongst the books of Scripture, which I brought home, standing immediately before the Book of Job, which is its proper place in the Abyssinian Canon'.[25]

The earth-shaking consequences of these gracious acts of literary dedication can scarcely have been realized by Bruce himself during his lifetime, for they would ultimately lead to the recirculation of heretical stories concerning humanity's forbidden trafficking with the fallen race. And yet from the very moment of Bruce's return to Europe with his precious Ethiopian manuscripts, strange events were afoot. Having deposited the copy with the Paris library, Bruce made tracks to return to England, where he planned to visit the Bodleian Library at his earliest convenience. Even before he had a chance to leave France, however, he learnt that an eminent scholar in Egyptian Coptic studies, Karl Gottfried Woide, was already on his way from London to Paris, carrying letters from the Secretary of State to Lord Stormont, the English Ambassador, desiring that the latter help him gain access to the Paris manuscript of the Book of Enoch, so that a translation could be secured immediately. Permission was duly granted to Woide, who after admission into the National Library wasted no time in making the necessary translation of the text. Yet as Bruce was to later admit in his *magnum opus* on his travels to Ethiopia 'it has nowhere appeared'.[26]

What therefore were the motives behind this extraordinary urgency in translating the Book of Enoch, before even the Bodleian Library had received its own copy? The absurdity of the situation lies in the fact that no outright translation of the valuable *Ge'ez* text was to appear in any language whatsoever *for another forty-eight years*.

Why this delay? Why should such an important piece of lost religious literature have been ignored for so long, especially since there were now not one but two extant copies available to the theological world? This ridiculous situation must have infuriated James Bruce after he had gone to all the trouble of finding and securing these manuscripts in the belief that they would be presented to the public domain in a translated form before the expiry of his own life (he died in 1794).

Tempting as it may be to evoke the idea of some kind of organized conspiracy behind these extraordinary actions on the part of Woide and the English Secretary of State, the truth of the matter was far more mundane and lay in the economical and political climate of the time. The late eighteenth and early nineteenth centuries saw a massive decline in the popularity of the Christian Church in many parts of Protestant Europe. Attendance at church services was dwindling, and churches everywhere were being neglected and left to fall into ruin under the impact of Newtonian science and the arrival of the Industrial Revolution. In an age of reason and learning, there was little place for the alleged transgressions of angels, fallen or otherwise. Most of the general public were simply not interested in whether or not angels had fallen through grace or lust, while any theological debate as to whether or not fallen angels possessed corporeal bodies was simply not a priority in most people's minds.

Fuelled by Fallen Angels

The Book of Enoch remained in darkness until 1821, when the long years of dedicated work by a professor of Hebrew at the University of Oxford were finally rewarded with the publication of the first ever English translation of the Book of Enoch. The Reverend Richard Laurence, Archbishop of Cashel, had laboured for many hundreds of hours over the faded manuscript in the hands of the Bodleian Library, carefully substituting English words and expressions for the original *Ge'ez*, while comparing the results with known extracts, such as the few brief chapters preserved in Greek by Syncellus during the ninth century.[27]

It is fair to say that the publication of the Book of Enoch caused a major sensation among the academic and literary circles of Europe. However, its disturbing contents were not simply being read by scholars, but also by the general public. Churchmen, artists, writers, poets all sampled its delights and were able to form their own opinions on the nature of its revelations. The consequences of this knowledge passing into the public domain for the first time were to be enormous in many areas of society.

Romantic writers, for instance, became transfixed by the stories of the Sons of God coming unto the Daughters of Men, and began to feature these devilish characters in their poetic works.[28,29] A little later, Victorian painters started portraying this same subject matter on canvas.[30] One might even be tempted to suggest that the Book of Enoch was a major inspiration behind the darker excesses of the so-called Gothic revival, which culminated in such literary works as Bram Stoker's *Dracula*, in which the eponymously named character is himself a fallen angel.[31]

Why should such satanic subjects have inspired or repulsed people to this extent? Why are people so fuelled by stories of fallen angels?

It also seems certain that the Book of Enoch was readily accepted as a work of great merit among the Freemasons, who used it to revive their ancient affiliation with the antediluvian patriarch; indeed, my own 1838 copy of Laurence's translation once belonged to the library of the Supreme Council 33°, the highest ranking enclave of Royal Arch Freemasons in Britain. There is even a rumour that the third copy brought back to Europe was presented by Bruce to the Scottish Grand Lodge in Edinburgh.[32]

Gradually, as the Oxford University edition of the Book of Enoch reached wider and wider audiences, scholars began checking in library collections across Europe, the result being that many more fragments and copies of the Enochian text in Ethiopian, Greek and even Latin were found tucked away in neglected corners. New translations were made in German and English, the most authoritative being that achieved in 1912 by Canon R. H. Charles.[33] Even a sequel to the original text entitled the Book of the Secrets of Enoch was found in Russia and translated in 1894.[34]

Since that time, the authenticity of the Book of Enoch has been amply verified with the discovery of the Dead Sea Scrolls. Many fragments of copies written in Aramaic have been identified among the hundreds of thousands of brittle scraps retrieved over the years from the caves on the Dead Sea, where they were placed in around AD 100 by the last survivors of the Essene communities at Qumrân and nearby En-Gedi.[35] The Ethiopian copyists had kept true to the original Aramaic text, which had probably passed into their country in its Greek translation sometime during the second half of the fourth century AD.[36] For generation after generation, the Book of Enoch had been copied and recopied by Ethiopian scribes, the old battered and torn manuscripts being either cast away or destroyed during the many bloody conflicts that took place in Abyssinia over a period of fifteen hundred years.

The fact was that somehow the Book of Enoch had survived intact, despite its heavy suppression by the Christian Church, and it was to the authoritative English translation made by Canon R. H. Charles in 1912 that I would next turn to discover for myself the dark secrets within its pages. Only by absorbing the obscure contents of this unholy treatise could I begin to understand why its forbidden text had become abhorrent to so many over the previous centuries.

Three
DEMONIC DOCTRINE

Reading the Book of Enoch for the first time was quite an unnerving experience, which on more than one occasion sent unexpected shivers down my spine. Here was perhaps one of the oldest accounts of mankind. It had been passed down orally from one storyteller to the next over thousands of years. Finally it became a book in its own right sometime after 200 BC, almost certainly at the hands of the Essene community at Qumrân on the Dead Sea. Yet what were its contents, and why had it caused so much consternation to the Jewish rabbis and the Early Church of Christianity?

I found the Book of Enoch to be a colourful but often confusing and contradictory patchwork of material that required extensive disentanglement before any cohesive picture could be gleaned from its contents. Much of it appears to have been written – originally on sheets of fine animal skin – during or shortly after the reign of Antiochus Epiphanes, the Syrian king who ruled Judaea at the time of the Maccabean revolt of 167 BC.[1] Among its 108 short chapters is irrefutable evidence of the battles fought and won against the hated Syrian ruler by the Jewish reactionary movement, the Zadokite Hassidaeans, under the leadership of Judas Maccabeaus.[2] Other parts were written shortly after this period, while some passages even reflect an age postdating the commencement of the Christian era.

So what does it contain? What element is it that so offends its opponents?

In the opening chapters the narrator reiterates the story told in Genesis 6 concerning the Sons of God coming unto the Daughters of Men and taking wives from among their number. The reader then learns how, 'in the days of Jared', two hundred Watchers 'descended' on 'Ardis', the summit of Mount Hermon – a mythical location equated with the triple-peak of Jebel esh Sheikh (9,200 feet), placed in the most northerly region of ancient Palestine. In Old Testament times its snowy heights had been revered as sacred by various peoples who inhabited the Holy Land; it was also the probable site of the Transfiguration of Christ when the disciples witnessed their Lord 'transfigured before them'.[3]

On this mountain the Watchers swear an oath and bind themselves by 'mutual imprecations', apparently knowing full well the consequences their actions will have both for themselves and for humanity as a whole.[4] It is a pact commemorated in the name given to the place of their 'fall', for in Hebrew the word Hermon, or *herem*, translates as 'curse'. Why the two hundred angels should have picked this location as opposed to any other to make their descent into the lowlands is never made clear. Yet this is what they do, travelling down to mix and mingle among humanity in the hope of sampling the delights of mortal women.

The reader is then introduced to Shemyaza, the leader of the Watchers, while nineteen of his minions are also named; these, it says, are 'their chiefs of tens'.[5] At this stage I will not question the authenticity, origin or reality of this curious narrative, but simply continue with the story as told in the Book of Enoch.

After the Watchers find themselves wives and 'go unto them', the women give birth to the enormous Nephilim babies, who grow up to become barbaric in every way possible. The words here are pertinent and must be quoted in full:

> *And they* [the mortal women] *became pregnant, and they bare great giants, whose height was three thousand ells: who consumed all the acquisitions of men. And when men could no longer sustain them, the giants turned against them and devoured mankind. And they began to sin against birds, and beasts, and reptiles, and fish, and to devour one another's flesh, and drink the blood. Then the earth laid accusation against the lawless ones.*[6]

The height of the Nephilim, here given as 3,000 ells, with one English ell being the equivalent of forty-five inches, is an exaggeration of the sort so often found in Jewish myth. It is used only to emphasize a specific point, which is to record that these *gibborim*,[7] or 'mighty men', were of great height and possessed enormous appetites. More disconcerting is the suggestion that the Nephilim turned against their mortal families and engaged in what can only be described as cannibalism.

'Sinning' against 'birds, and beasts, and reptiles, and fish' could either mean that they were consumed by the Nephilim as food, or that the giants committed barbaric sexual acts with them, perhaps both. Whatever the answer, they would appear to have developed a lust for drinking blood, which must also have been viewed as abhorrent by the communities in which they were born and raised.

The Secrets of Heaven

The narrative then tells how the rebel Watchers who walked among humanity revealed the forbidden secrets of heaven. One of their number, a leader named Azazel, is said to have 'taught men to make swords, and knives, and shields, and breastplates, and made known to them the metals (of the earth) and the art of working them', indicating that the Watchers were the first to bring the use of metal to mankind. He also instructed them on how they could make 'bracelets' and 'ornaments' and showed them how to use 'antimony', a white brittle metal employed in the arts and medicine. To the women he taught the art of 'beautifying' the eyelids, and the use of 'all kinds of costly stones' and 'colouring tinctures', indicating that before this time the wearing of make-up and jewellery was unknown.[8]

Through this unforgivable act, the Daughters of Men were believed to have been 'led astray', and because of it they became 'corrupt', committing fornication not only with the Watchers themselves, but also, it must be assumed, with men who were not their regular partners. Azazel also stood accused of teaching women how to enjoy sexual pleasure and indulge in promiscuity – a blasphemy seen as 'godlessness' in the eyes of the Hebrew story-tellers.

Linguistic experts believe that the names Azazel and Shemyaza probably derive from the same source, but were made into two separate fallen angels before their introduction to the Book of Enoch; however, since they both have quite independent legends attributed to them, each will be dealt with separately as and when they appear.

Other Watchers stand accused of revealing to mortal kind the knowledge of more scientific arts, such as the knowledge of the clouds, or meteorology; the 'signs of the earth', presumably geodesy and geography; as well as astronomy and the 'signs', or passage, of the celestial bodies, such as the sun and moon. Shemyaza is accredited with having taught men 'enchantments, and root-cuttings',[9] a reference to the magical arts shunned by most orthodox Jews, but accepted to some degree by the Dead Sea communities. One of their number, Pênêmûe, taught 'the bitter and the sweet', surely a reference to the use of herbs and spices in foods, while instructing men on the use of 'ink and paper', implying that the Watchers introduced the earliest forms of writing.[10] Far more disturbing is Kâsdejâ, who is said to have shown 'the children of men all the wicked smitings of spirits and demons, and the smitings of the embryo in the womb, that it may pass away'.[11] In other words, he taught women how to abort their babies.

These lines concerning the forbidden sciences handed to humanity by the rebel Watchers raise the whole fundamental issue of why angels of heaven should have possessed any knowledge of such matters in the first place. Why should they have needed to work with metals, use charms, incantations and writing; beautify the body; employ the use of antimony, and know how to abort an unborn child? None of these skills are what one might expect heavenly messengers of God to possess, unless, that is,they were human in the first place.

In my opinion, this revelation of previously unknown knowledge and wisdom seems more like the actions of a highly advanced race passing on some of its closely guarded secrets to a less evolved culture still striving to understand the basic principles of life. A comparison might be drawn with the way in which supposedly civilized cultures of the Western world have introduced everything from whisky to clothes, firearms, rigid thinking and religious dogma to indigenous races in remote regions of the world. If such ancient texts are to be taken at face value, then could it be that this is what really happened – members of one highly advanced race passing on its knowledge to a less evolved culture still struggling for survival?

Plight of the Watchers and Nephilim

One by one the angels of heaven are appointed by God to proceed against the Watchers and their offspring the Nephilim, described as 'the bastards and the reprobates, and the children of fornication'.[12] Azazel is bound hand and foot, and cast for eternity into the darkness of a desert referred to as Dûdâêl. Upon him are placed 'rough and jagged rocks' and here he shall forever remain until the Day of Judgement, when he will be 'cast into the fire' for his sins.[13] For their part in the corruption of mankind, the Watchers are forced to witness the slaughter of their own children before being cast into some kind of heavenly prison, an 'abyss of fire'.[14] Although the Watchers' leader, Shemyaza, is cast into this abyss alongside his brothers, in other versions of the story he undergoes a more dramatic punishment. Since he was tempted by a beautiful mortal maiden named Ishtahar to reveal the Explicit Name of God in exchange for the offer of carnal pleasure, he is to be tied and bound before being made to hang for all eternity between heaven and earth, head down, in the constellation of Orion.[15]

The suggestion that the rebel Watchers had to look on as their children were murdered hints at a form of infanticide in which those born of the union between fallen angels and mortal women were systematically rounded up and slaughtered as their fathers watched helplessly. If this supposition is correct, then it could explain the fear and revulsion instilled in Lamech and Bathenosh at the birth of their son Noah, who apparently resembled a Nephilim baby; their horror being connected not simply to their own son's strange appearance, but to the fact that the offspring of the Watchers were being murdered by those angels still loyal to heaven.

Following the incarceration of the rebel Watchers, Enoch is summoned to 'heaven' and addressed by the archangels, who are also, confusingly, referred to as Watchers. They request that he intercedes on their behalf and puts to the rebel angels the crimes they have committed against mankind. Enoch accepts this task and goes to see them in their place of incarceration. On his approach, he finds them 'all afraid, and fear and trembling seized them'.[16] Fear of punishment is surely a human tendency, not the emotions one might expect of incorporeal messengers of God, and where was this prison, so accessible to Enoch? The text suggests it was near 'the waters of Dan, to the south of the west of Hermon.'[17] The 'waters of Dan' refers to one of the tributaries of the river Jordan in northern Palestine. The root of the Hebrew word *dan* means 'to judge', and Canon R. H. Charles in a footnote to this particular reference in his widely accepted translation of the Ethiopian text, concedes that this location was specifically chosen 'because its name is significant of the subject the writer is dealing with, i.e the *judgement* of the angels [*author's italics*].'[18] The geographical positioning of this story is therefore symbolic and not actual. Clearly the author of the Book of Enoch is attempting to create some kind of sound geographical perspective to the narrative, in this case establishing the rebel Watchers' place of incarceration close to the location of their original descent upon Mount Hermon. In other words, many of the sites given in the Book of Enoch were chosen simply to give credence to the stories it contains.

The corruption still left in the world after the imprisonment of the Watchers, and the death of their Nephilim offspring, is to be swept away by a series of global catastrophes, ending in the Great Flood so familiar within biblical tradition.[19] In a separate account of the plight of the Nephilim,[20] this mass-destruction is seen in terms of an all-encompassing conflagration sent by the angels of heaven in the form of 'fire, naphtha and brimstone'.[21] No one will survive these cataclysms of fire and water save for the 'seed' of Noah, from whose line will come the future human race.[22]

This is how the Dead Sea communities and the earliest Christians understood the Book of Enoch, yet never is there any insinuation that the rebel Watchers were beings of flesh and blood, only that they assumed physical form in order to lie with mortal women. Having read and reread the story of the fall of the Watchers several times over, I began to realize that such a view of events could be seriously challenged, for there seemed compelling evidence to suggest that the rebel Watchers – and, by virtue of this, the angels of heaven themselves – might originally have been a race of human beings who existed in the Middle East at a distant point in history. If this were so, then memories of these monumental and quite horrendous events would appear to have been distorted and mythologized across the passage of time, until they became simply moralistic folk-tales in a slowly evolving religious history adopted by the Jewish race during Old Testament times.

Did this provide a valid answer? To me it appeared as credible as any. Yet if my solution was incorrect, then what were the alternatives?

There were two. Either the reader can accept that religious literature of this nature is pure fantasy, based on the deep psychological needs and values of a God-fearing society. Or he or she can accept that incorporeal angels not only exist, but that they can also descend to earth, take on human form and then couple with mortal women, who afterwards give birth to giants that grow up to become ruthless barbarians of the sort portrayed in the Book of Enoch.

Which of these solutions seems easiest to accept?

Which of these choices feels most right to accept?

And even if the rebel Watchers *were* once human beings of flesh and blood, where did they come from, in what time-frame did they live, and what was the *true* fate of their progeny? Did they all either perish in the mass genocide orchestrated by the angels still loyal to heaven or die in the cataclysms which culminated in the Great Flood? Did any survive? The Book of Enoch provided no immediate answers, though my mind lingered over one particular passage in Chapter 15 concerning the final fate of the Nephilim:

. . . because they are born from men (and) from the holy watchers in their beginning and primal origin; they shall be evil spirits on earth, and evil spirits shall they be called . . . And the spirits of the giants (will) afflict, oppress, destroy, attack, do battle, and work destruction on the earth, and cause trouble; they (will) take no food, [but nevertheless hunger] and thirst, and cause offences. And these spirits shall rise up against the children of men and against the women, because they have proceeded (from them).[23]

The text here speaks of 'evil spirits' – demons and devils might be more appropriate terms. Yet if it could for one moment be assumed that 'blood descendants' is what was originally intended, then these enigmatic lines imply that those born of Nephilim blood are, by virtue of their ancestral 'spirit', destined to 'afflict, oppress, destroy, attack, do battle, and work destruction on the earth'.

These are chilling thoughts indeed, yet in the puritanical words of the Book of Enoch these corrupted souls are also destined to become the damned, who will 'take no food, [but nevertheless hunger] and thirst'. The djinns, the malevolent spirits of Islamic tradition, are said to 'suffer from a devouring hunger and yet cannot eat',[24] while in East European folklore, as well as in popular romance, there are likewise supernatural denizens that drink blood yet can 'take no food, [but can nevertheless hunger] and thirst', and these are, of course, *nosferatu* – vampires. Whatever the reality of such beings in anthropological terms, vampires live on in the dark, sinister world of Gothic horror, which, as I had already realized, owes much of its character to the way in which the initial publication of the Book of Enoch in 1821 influenced the inner visions of the poets and artists of the romantic movement.

Perhaps the 'spirit' of the fallen race does therefore live on in the collective unconscious of modern-day society. Perhaps the descendants of the Nephilim, the hybrid offspring of the two hundred rebel Watchers, are still inside us, their presence hinted at only by the unsettling knowledge that our dark past holds hidden truths which are now beginning to reveal themselves for the first time – secrets that only a few enlightened souls have ever realized are preserved in the heretical Book of Enoch, this 'demonic doctrine', as it was aptly described by the Canon R. H. Charles.[25]

Descendants of Noah

Despite the Book of Enoch's extraordinary material concerning the story of the Watchers, much of its later chapters appeared to be unconnected with my search to discover the origins of the fallen race. Indeed, they seemed to have been written by a different hand altogether. This supposition was confirmed when I realized that the chapters featuring the fall of the Watchers, the birth of Noah and the Flood narrative had all been taken from the much earlier, now lost, apocalyptic work known as the Book of Noah.[26] It would simply confuse matters if I were to start referring to the Book of Noah instead of the Book of Enoch, but knowledge that Noah, not Enoch, was the original narrator of this story is important indeed and may well provide the key to understanding the reasons behind the Essenes' interest in this demonic literature.

Because of the covenant Noah had made with God at the time of the Great Flood, the Dead Sea communities accredited him with having been God's first bringer of rain, or rainmaker, and saw themselves as direct lineal descendants of this rain-making line – a point emphasized again and again in their religious literature. Many Jews in the last two centuries before Christ actually believed that wandering holy men, or *zaddiks*, 'the righteous', were direct descendants of Noah and could therefore perform rain-making feats – a divine virtue bestowed upon them by birthright.[27] Most renowned of the rainmakers in Jewish tradition was Onias the Righteous, also known as Honi the Circle-drawer. His daughter's son, Hanan the Hidden, and another grandson named Abba Hilkiah, were also able to repeat their grandfather's rain-making feats.

From research into rain-making traditions, it seems probable that the priests would achieve these inexplicable weather changes by retiring from the community and drawing rings of sand on the ground. They would then stand in the centre of this magic circle and perform their supernatural conjuration – the effectiveness of such wild talents never being doubted.[28] When they were not drawing down rain, the *zaddiks* would live wild existences, crossing great distances on foot and spending long periods among the harsh, rugged hills on the west bank of the Dead Sea. Here they would enter into the isolated caves and spend long periods deep in meditation and contemplation.

More important, however, was the knowledge that these wandering *zaddik*-priests, who walked freely among the Dead Sea communities, were the teachers of the Kabbalah, the arcane knowledge passed on orally from person to person.[29] With their great understanding of the Kabbalah, and their claimed descent from Noah, it seemed extremely likely that it was these wandering holy men who had first conveyed knowledge of the Watchers' story to the Essenes.

If this theory was correct, then who were these wandering *zaddiks*? Why did they believe themselves to be direct descendants of Noah? And where and when did they obtain these stories concerning the fall of the Watchers? Until I could answer these questions, the authenticity of the Book of Enoch must inevitably remain difficult to assess as historical fact. For the moment, I needed to understand more about the roots behind the story of the Watchers, how their 'fall' came about and, most important of all, its point of origin.

Four

INSANE BLASPHEMY

Not everyone agreed on what the Sons of God coming unto the Daughters of Men actually represented so far as the accepted history of the Bible was concerned. By the late fourth century, the Syrian Church had begun to circulate a brand-new religious text claiming to give a true rendition of the lines in Genesis 6. In this variation of the story, the Sons of God are no longer dark angels but the Sons of Seth, a righteous community of men and women who reside in peace on the Mountain of God. This mythical location lies beyond the Gates of Paradise, out of which humanity's First Parents, Adam and Eve, had been cast many generations before.

Living among the Sons of Seth are the now familiar antediluvian patriarchs, such as Jared, his son Enoch, his grandson Methuselah and his great-grandson Lamech. In their midst is the entrance to the so-called Cave of Treasures, within which lie the earthly remains of the first men and women, including Adam and his wife Eve, as well as the Three Gifts of God. These latter are caskets containing the frankincense, gold and myrrh destined to remain in the possession of Israel and Judah until they are finally presented to Christ at the time of the Nativity. Elsewhere in the enormous cave burns a perpetual flame symbolizing the light of God given to Adam in his darkest hour.

Down in the lowlands lives a somewhat more primitive culture that, without the just guidance of God, leads depraved lifestyles of sin and corruption. Among them are the Daughters of Cain, the progeny of Adam's first son, Cain, who, according to Genesis 4, slew his brother Abel and was cursed and 'sent out' by God to dwell 'in the land of Nod on the east of Eden'.[1]

The Daughters of Cain are easily led into unbridled debauchery, a vice that conjures the manifestation of Satanail, i.e. Satan or the Devil. Convinced that he can take advantage of their wicked ways to lead astray the Sons of God, the arch-fiend hatches a cunning plan. He convinces the naïve Daughters of Men to wear make-up and adorn themselves with fine jewellery and exotic garments. Satanail then directs them towards the Mountain of God, where the Sons of Seth lead their pious existence in the presence of the Most High. The women try to convince the religious men to come down from the heights so that they may be tempted to commit gross acts of fornication and indecency. To this end the Daughters of Cain approach the base of the mountain and begin playing musical instruments, dancing wildly, singing loudly and calling to the 520 Sons of God[2] to come and join them in sweet pleasure. Hearing the women's enticing voices, many of the men descend the holy mountain and indulge in carnal delights. Only the most righteous – in other words, figures such as Jared, Enoch, Methuselah, Lamech and his son Noah – refuse to be tempted by this gross iniquity.

As a result of their unholy union, giants are inevitably born unto the godless women, and the 'fallen' Sons of Seth are prevented by God from returning to their mountain retreat close to the Cave of Treasures. The Most High then unleashes a great tempest and deluge to purge the world of all wickedness and corruption, as in Enochian and Old Testament tradition.[3]

This alternative rendering of the enigmatic lines of Genesis 6 appears at first to provide a major breakthrough in their interpretation, and this was the opinion shared by a great number of biblical scholars right down to the Middle Ages. Removing any reference to fallen angels nullified the story of the fall of the Watchers as it was portrayed in a convincing and quite unnerving manner within the Book of Enoch.

No fallen angels – no truth to the Book of Enoch; this was the philosophy of those who believed in the reality of the story of the Daughters of Cain coming to the Sons of Seth. It was an easy demolition of the ancient text, if it could be accepted that the Cave of Treasures story was the word of God. Unfortunately, however, these early Church Fathers, who mostly belonged to the Syrian Church, overlooked one tiny point. The Book of the Cave of

Treasures, as it became known, was almost entirely the creation of an early Christian writer named Julius Africanus (AD 200–245), and written more out of pure ignorance than deliberate design. He observed that the term *elohim* was used in the Old Testament, as well as in other apocryphal works, to denote 'foreign rulers' and 'judges'.[4] From this it was concluded that the *bene ha-elohim*, the Sons of the Elohim, were none other than the early patriarchs, the descendants of Adam's third son, Seth. The deduction was made despite the more obvious fact that the term *bene ha-elohim* was also used with reference to heavenly hosts, or angels.

In spite of the text's clear failings, the early Church Fathers quickly adopted Africanus' concept of the fall of the Sons of God and pronounced it the only true and authentic interpretation of the Genesis text. Yet even this did not stop the spread of wild accounts concerning the deeds of the fallen angels. The story of the Daughters of Cain coming unto the Sons of Seth was very often placed alongside alternative material concerning the fall of the Watchers, taken either directly or indirectly from the Book of Enoch. An outstanding example of this is the account of the fall of the angels contained in the Ethiopian *Kebra Nagast*. Here, next to a précis of the Cave of Treasures story, is a somewhat shocking reference to the enormous size of the Nephilim babies and the way in which they entered the world:

And the daughters of Cain with whom the angels had companied conceived, but they were unable to bring forth their children, and they died. And of the children who were in their wombs some died, and some came forth: having split open the bellies of their mothers they came forth by their navels . . .[5]

Sir E. A. Wallis Budge, the eminent Egyptologist and literary scholar who translated the *Kebra Nagast* into English, openly admitted that this gruesome passage showed that the unborn babies 'were so large that they could not be born in the ordinary way, but had to be removed from the mothers by the umbilicus'.[6] In other words, because of their immense size, the Nephilim children could only be born by using the surgical operation we know today as Caesarian section. This was a disconcerting thought, which, although not confirmed anywhere else in Hebrew literature, will be encountered again in connection with the birth of giant children in another Middle Eastern country (see Chapter 9).

Mani the Ignorant

Even though the Book of Enoch had fallen foul of the developing Christian Church during the early fourth century, there are firm indications that some individuals had studied its contents and had, as a consequence, begun extolling its dire consequences for mankind. One such indication of this situation comes from a tract on the Book of Enoch written by St Jerome (AD 342–420), a Syriac Church Father of renown and scholarship, who had this to say on the subject:

> *We have read in a certain apocryphal book* [i.e. the Book of Enoch] *that when the sons of God were coming down to the daughters of men, they descended upon Mount Hermon and there entered into an agreement to come to the daughters of men and make them their wives. This book is quite explicit and is classified as apocryphal. The ancient exegetes have at various times referred to it, but we are citing it, not as authoritative, but merely to bring it to your attention . . . I have read about this apocryphal book in the work of a particular author who used it to confirm his own heresy . . . Do you detect the source of the teachings of Manichaeus, the ignorant? Just as the Manichaeans say that the souls desired human bodies to be united in pleasure, do not they who say that angels desired bodies – or the daughters of men – seem to you to be saying the same thing as the Manichaeans?*[7]

Manichaeus 'the ignorant', or Mani as he is more commonly known, was a much-hated prophet of Parthian stock who had a huge impact on the development of Christian heresy from the third century right through till the end of the Middle Ages. And St Jerome was right. There *is* firm evidence to show that Mani devised his holy scriptures and teachings after studying the Book of Enoch.

Mani was born in the Babylonian town of Ctesiphon, near modern-day Baghdad, in the year AD 215. Both his mother and father appear to have been directly related to the exiled Parthian dynasty of princes who, before being deposed in AD 224, had ruled the Persian Empire unhindered since 247 BC.[8] Their national religion had featured many elements of Zoroastrianism, a monotheistic (and partially dualistic) faith founded, according to early Iranian tradition, by the prophet Zarathustra, the Greek Zoroaster, sometime during the sixth century BC (see Chapter 8).

Perhaps influenced by the knowledge that Zoroastrianism acknowledged whole hierarchies of angels and demons, or *daęvas*, Mani appears to have fully accepted the Enochian account of the fall of the Watchers. As a consequence, he formulated his own dualistic, gnostic creed, complete with its own holy scriptures and creation myths. In his sacred books he portrayed the material world not as the dominion of God, but as the domain of the Rulers of Darkness, in other words of Satan and his fallen angels. All that remained of God was the divine spirit trapped inside the physical body, and only by striving to find oneness with God could humanity hope to achieve a promised afterlife in the heavenly paradise.

According to an anathema of Manichaeism written by its Christian opposers, Mani believed Adam to have been the outcome of a fertilized embryo, produced by the intercourse of male and female fallen angels, then swallowed by Satan, who subsequently coupled with his spouse to bring forth the First Man.[9] Such a pessimistic view of life meant that Mani and his followers saw the very roots of humanity not just as evil, but as rotten to the core.

Mani preached a synthesis of different faiths, including aspects of Buddhism, Christianity, Zoroastrianism and Mandaism, a strange religion native to Iraq and Iran. His faith became extremely popular for several centuries and was carried by his dedicated disciples and followers across the Orient, reaching as far east as India and Tibet.[10]

Manichaeism was quite obviously seen as a huge threat to the other major religions of the age. It was therefore condemned as outright heresy by the ruling Sassanian dynasty of Persian kings as well as by the early Church Fathers of Asia Minor. Followers of the faith were denounced as heretics and put to death, while a more horrific fate awaited Mani himself at the hands of fanatical Zoroastrians at Jund-i-Shapur, in south-west Persia. In AD 277 he was accused of preaching false doctrines, and as a consequence was thrown in prison, where he was bound by chains, tortured to the point of death and left to die. His exhausted body was then publicly humiliated in the most gruesome manner: his skin was flayed and stuffed with straw before being strung up on the gates of the town as blood still issued from his warm carcass, which was decapitated and erected on a pole for all to see. Instead of quelling the growing unrest against Manichaeism by the Persian people, the death of Mani incited a sanguine crusade against his followers, who were rounded up throughout the empire and slaughtered by Zoroastrians – the price, it seems, for believing in the fall of the angels and their corruption of mankind.[11]

Unorthodox Thoughts

The existence of heresies such as Manichaeism and other forms of Christian gnosticism once again raised the whole fundamental issue of the corporeal nature of fallen angels and the Sons of God in the minds of the most eminent theologians and churchmen of the day. One Church Father, St John Chrysostom (AD *c.* 347–407), an archbishop of Constantinople, spoke out vehemently against the Book of Enoch, stating indignantly that it would be 'folly to accept such insane blasphemy, saying that an incorporeal and spiritual nature could have united itself to human bodies'.[12] It had become blasphemous and highly heretical to preach, circulate or support the doctrine contained within the Book of Enoch, or indeed any other apocryphal or pseudepigraphal work. In no way did the Church want the spread of Jewish traditions completely at variance with its gradually emerging corpus of scripture, especially if these concerned alternative views on the fall of mankind and the descent of the angels. Such subjects needed to be kept strictly out of bounds.

Is it possible for us to understand this fanatical zeal towards the unorthodox – a zeal that persisted in the name of religion throughout the Middle Ages and probably cost the lives of countless hundreds of thousands of individuals accused of heresy and witchcraft? Why should the Christian Church have been so paranoid about a narrative concerning a group of two hundred angels who fell from grace and lusted after the Daughters of Men? Surely not all the heavenly messengers of God were perfect, so why has there been this blanket suppression of anything even remotely promoting such radical ideas even through to the present day?

Serpents that Walked

Part of the answer lies in the fact that there seems to be a clear overlap between the story of the fall of the Watchers and the account of the temptation of Eve by the Serpent as portrayed in the Book of Genesis. Since this is such an important subject in our quest to understand the origins of fallen angels, it will be worth recalling exactly what happened on that day in the Garden of Eden.

Adam and Eve, the idealized first man and woman in Christian, Islamic and Judaic mythology, live in a state of innocence and grace within the garden until the Serpent of Eden questions God's authority by telling Eve she will not die if she eats the forbidden fruit of the 'tree which is in the midst of the garden',[13] for, it says: 'God doth know that in the day ye eat thereof, then your eyes shall be opened, and ye shall be as gods, knowing good and evil.'[14]

Accordingly, so Genesis informs us, Eve saw that the fruit of the tree 'was good for food' and pleasant to the eyes, and that it was 'a tree to make *one wise* [*author's emphasis*]'. She then picked and ate of the fruit, giving it also to her partner Adam to eat; the result being that their eyes were 'opened', enabling them to realize that they were naked. In other words, eating the fruit of the tree had somehow managed to allow them to gain the knowledge and wisdom to understand their predicament in the idealized world – all thanks to the 'subtil' serpent who 'beguiled' Eve into eating of the Tree of Knowledge of Good and Evil.

For this heinous crime against mankind the Serpent is then:

> *cursed* [by God] *above all cattle, and above every beast of the field; upon thy belly shalt thou go, and dust shalt thou eat all the days of thy life: and I will put enmity between thee and the woman, and between thy seed and her seed; it shall bruise thy head, and thou shalt bruise his heel.*[15]

Adam and Eve are also cursed by God, for to Eve he says: 'I will greatly multiply thy sorrow and thy conception; in sorrow thou shalt bring forth children; and thy desire shall be to thy husband, and he shall rule over thee' – mortifying words which have loomed over the heads of Western women ever since. In Adam's case, God rules that 'in sorrow shalt thou eat of it all the days of thy life', referring, of course, to the forbidden knowledge the couple have gained through eating of the tree.[16]

In order that Adam and Eve, with their new-found 'wisdom', do not want of the garden's other tree, the 'tree of life', and become immortal like gods, they are cast out of Eden 'to till the ground from whence he (Adam) was taken'.[17]

This is the story of the so-called 'fall of man', as well as the roots of the misery and suffering humanity is forever forced to suffer because of this act of disobedience.[18] As a consequence of the sin committed by our First Parents, we are deemed to have inherited a corrupt nature, with a prevailing tendency towards evil, the very stance adopted by Manichaeism and many of the other more obscure gnostic cults that thrived during the first four centuries of the Christian era.

The fall of mankind was obviously compared by religious scholars with the angels' fall through lust and pride, while the Serpent of Temptation was commonly believed by theologians to have been the form taken by Satan to corrupt mankind.[19] Satan's chosen guise as a serpent to beguile Eve was thought to have been because of its sly and cunning ability to hypnotize its prey into submission. The snake's loathsome and frightful appearance also made it an ideal totem of the darkness, and thus of the Devil himself. All these explanations are, however, somewhat naïve, for the snake is a very ancient symbol that represented the conveyance of sexual desires, hidden wisdom and secret knowledge in many different Middle Eastern faiths and religions.

The serpent makes an appearance in a great number of creation myths featuring the first humans and is often portrayed as a wise benevolent spirit, not a beguiling messenger of temptation and evil. Moreover, the serpent has an intrinsic association with the first woman in these myths, a fact confirmed in the knowledge that the name Eve is synonymous with both the word for 'life' and 'snake'. For instance, in Hebrew *hawwah*, i.e. Eve, means 'she who makes live'. It is also related to the word *hevia*, signifying a female serpent. Furthermore, in Arabic 'serpent' is *hayya*, which is itself cognate with *hayat*, meaning 'life'; the Arabic for Eve being *hawwa*.[20] In other accounts from Jewish lore, Eve is actually seen as the ancestral mother of the Nephilim,[21] who were themselves described in Hebrew myth as *awwim*, meaning 'devastators' or 'serpents'.[22]

Angels, too, are integrally linked with the form of the serpent: one of the principal classes of angelic being in Hebrew lore is the Seraphim, or 'fiery serpents', who are 'sent by God as his instruments to inflict on the people the righteous penalty of sin'.[23] The link is further strengthened by an occasional statement here and there in the Book of Enoch. In Chapter 69, for instance, where it outlines the forbidden arts taught to mankind by the Watchers, one angel known as Kâsdejâ is accused of showing men how to take away 'the bites of the serpent, and the smitings which befall through the noontide heat (i.e. sunstroke . . .) the son of the serpent named Tabâ'et'.[24] Although the exact meaning of these lines is now lost, it clearly mentions 'the son of the serpent named Tabâ'et', a reference, it seems, to a Nephilim born to a 'serpent', or Watcher, named Tabâ'et.

So if the Watchers are intrinsically linked with the symbol of the serpent, the conveyers of sexual desire, hidden wisdom and forbidden knowledge, then how do they relate to the Serpent of Eden? One tantalizing clue to this perplexing enigma is to be found in Chapter 69 of the Book of Enoch, for included among those Watchers who have revealed the heavenly secrets to mankind is Gâdreêl, identified as the fallen angel who 'led astray Eve'.[25]

The fallen angel who 'led astray Eve'?

Here is a very revealing statement. What is it supposed to mean? And how might it be equated with our knowledge of the Fall of Man in the heavenly paradise?

If this particular passage is contemporary with the book's original construction during the first half of the second century BC, then it firmly associates the rebellion of the two hundred Watchers, during the age of the patriarch Jared, with the beguiling of Eve and thus with the corruption of humanity. Despite this realization, it would be foolhardy to accuse one Watcher alone of this most heinous of crimes, for it seems clear that at some point in the distant past the Watchers were collectively seen as 'the Serpent' who divulged the hidden wisdom and knowledge to the First Parents, a metaphorical reference to humanity in general. In doing so, it caused them to commit the first sin, the act of self-awareness. As a consequence of this interference in human affairs, our ancestors were forced into a material existence over and beyond the natural evolution and progression it would presumably have achieved had the Watchers not intervened to change the course of destiny.

That was certainly the way it was beginning to look, and, if correct, then it meant that the story of the 'Fall of Man' in the Garden of Eden was merely a highly abstract expression of the way in which the Watchers supposedly corrupted the minds of human kind. If so, then which story influenced the other? And were we to assume that, because of the Watchers' interference in humanity's affairs, humanity now bears within it the seeds of eternal corruption and evil? And what of the connection with Satan, the Devil, God's greatest adversary? How did he fit into this gradually emerging picture, and what was his association with the Watchers of the Book of Enoch?

The Devil in Disguise

The name Satan comes from the Hebrew *ha-satan*, meaning 'the adversary'. In the Old Testament this term is used exclusively to describe either the enemies of God or the enemies of the Israelite race in general. Never is the Devil referred to as the evil one. Not until the advent of the New Testament, the collection of books and gospels relating to the period subsequent to the birth of the Christian era, does the term *ha-satan* take on this all-important role. At this point Satan becomes an angel fallen from grace and expelled from heaven, along with his fellow-rebels, by the archangel Michael. References to Satan's own fall appear in passages such as Luke 10:18, where Christ is said to have 'beheld Satan fallen as lightning from heaven'. It is, however, only in the Bible's final book, the Revelation of St John the Divine, written during the first century AD, that the full story of Satan's fall is revealed for the first time. In Chapter 12, verse 9, it proclaims: 'And the great dragon was cast down, the old serpent, he that is called the Devil and Satan, the deceiver of the whole world; he was cast down to earth, and his angels were cast down with him.' And then again, in Revelation 20:2–3, it says: 'And he laid hold on the dragon, the old serpent, which is the Devil and Satan, and bound him for a thousand years, and cast him into the abyss, and shut it, and sealed it over him, that he should deceive the nations no more.'

This is all that may be gleaned from the holy scriptures concerning the fall of Satan, although it is clear that St John the Divine based his visions of Satan and his fallen angels on the story of the Watchers contained in the Book of Enoch; an assertion supported by the fact that this apocalyptic work was freely circulating among early Christians around this time. Having established Satan as God's arch-enemy, the Christians adopted him as the root of all evil in the world, and any trafficking with either him or his fallen angels was seen as black magic, heresy, sorcery and, of course, witchcraft – acts that were punishable by death throughout Christendom until comparatively recent times.

In medieval times, theologians, such as Peter Lombard (*c.* 1100–1160), 'saw Satan in the guise of the serpent tempting Eve', while other scholars, such as the ninth-century Bishop Agobard, held that 'Satan tempted Eve through the serpent'.[26] Either way, such ideas became mainstream in the Christian philosophy of the Middle Ages and a general acceptance of this assumption has helped to mould religious thought right through to the present day.

So was Satan behind the story of the Serpent of Eden? Perhaps the medieval scholars actually got it right, realizing that the references in the Book of Revelation to the casting out of heaven of Satan and his adversaries was one and the same story as the pre-Christian account of the fall of the Watchers, alluded to in the story of the Sons of God coming unto the Daughters of Men in Genesis 6. Satan is referred to in Revelation as 'the old serpent', a synonym that seems quite clearly to refer not just to the Serpent of Temptation but also to the rebel Watchers of the Book of Enoch.

Since the revealing to humanity of the hidden secrets of heaven by the Watchers appears to have been the impetus behind the rise of civilization as we know it today, and Satan and his fallen angels

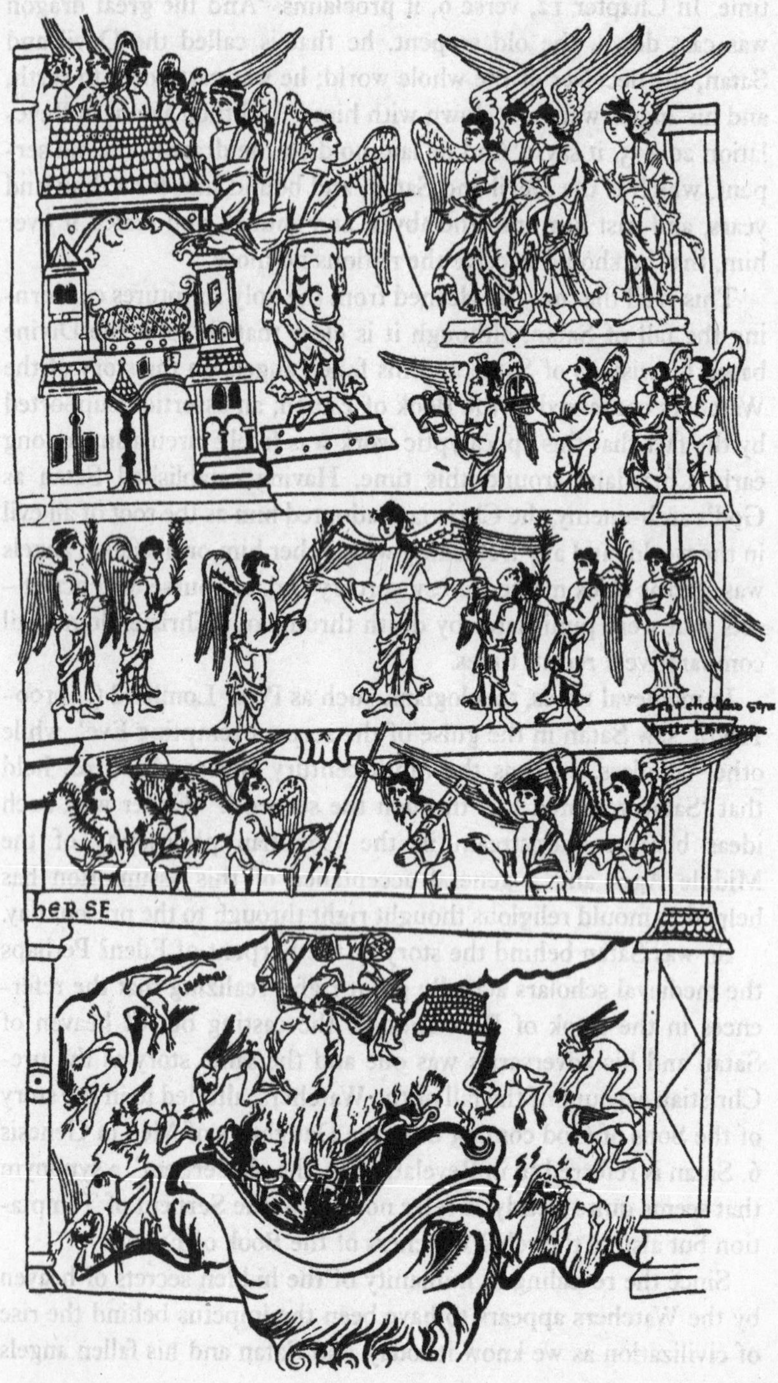
herse

are to be identified with the fallen angels of the Book of Enoch, then it implies that, in Christian terms at least, the genesis of the civilized world can be attributed not to the will of God, but to the intervention of his antithesis – the Devil.

Mani's dualistic world must have been full of contradictions – on the one hand he was preaching the purity of God and the way of the Holy Spirit, and on the other he taught that the roots of evil lay within us all. Was this why the early Church Fathers so vehemently condemned the Book of Enoch's portrayal of the fall of the Watchers as 'insane blasphemy'? The answer is no, since they themselves came to accept this very doctrine that St Augustine named as 'original sin', which placed the blame not on the Watchers but on Eve. It is interesting to note that Augustine, who condemned the Book of Enoch as 'too old' for inclusion in the canon, had himself at one time been a Manichaean. It is more likely that those heretics, such as Mani, who wholeheartedly accepted and preached the demonic doctrine outlined in Enochian literature, were always persecuted in such ghastly ways for this reason alone. What justification could there be for such crimes against humanity, and, more importantly, just what is it the world fears *so much* about fallen angels?

Fig. 2. The expulsion of the angels from heaven after their fall through lust and pride, from an eleventh century English manuscript. Does this event record the forbidden trafficking between two entirely different races or cultures during the protoneolithic age?

Five

VISAGE LIKE A VIPER

Many people believe the Old Testament to be littered with references to the appearance of angels, but this is simply not the case. In fact there are relatively few accounts featuring angels, and when they do crop up there is often no real indication of what exactly is taking place. For instance, in Genesis there are the three 'angels in the guise of men' who approach Abraham as he sits at his tent door by the Oak of Mamre, near the ancient city of Hebron in southern Palestine. They confirm the imminent birth of a son to his elderly wife Sarah and announce their planned destruction of Sodom, the city of iniquity by the Dead Sea. The Bible says that a feast was prepared for them, and that Abraham 'took butter, and milk, and the calf which he had dressed, and set it before them; and he stood by them under the tree, *and they did eat* [*author's emphasis*]'.[1]

'And they did eat . . .' Angels eating food? Surely incorporeal beings would not need to consume earthly sustenance.

Then there are the two angels who visit Lot and his wife in Sodom, immediately prior to the city's destruction. They are said to have entered Lot's house, where he 'made them a feast, and did bake unleavened bread, and', as in the case of the Abraham story, 'they did eat'.[2] Men of Sodom surround Lot's home, calling upon him and shouting out 'where are the men which came in to thee this night? bring them out unto us, that we may know them'.[3] In other words they wanted to have sex with them. It is, of course, from this bible passage that we gain the term sodomy, or anal penetration.

Did the inhabitants of Sodom want sex with all strangers who visited the city, or was there something noticeably different about these 'men'?

Then we have the angel, or 'man', with whom Jacob wrestles in hand-to-hand combat[4] at Penuel, or the whole host of angels whom Jacob sees moving up and down a ladder that stretches between heaven and earth as he rests at a place known as Bethel.[5]

Are these really accounts of angels of heaven, or are they of mortal men?

Angels gain their name from the word *angelos*, the Greek rendition of the Hebrew *mal'akh*, meaning 'messenger', since they act as mediators between God and humanity. They are undoubtedly incorporeal beings, although, to allow for stories such as those concerning Abraham, Lot and Jacob, it has generally been accepted by Judaeo-Christian theologians that angels could take on physical form to carry out specific tasks on earth.

Whatever the actual nature of the angels of the Old Testament, to both the Judaic and Christian faiths they are purely that – angels, messengers of God, unconnected with the fallen angelic race of both Genesis 6 and Hebrew apocryphal tradition. At no time are the angels of the Pentateuch, the first five books of the Bible, ever equated with the Sons of God, the Watchers or the Nephilim, and there is never any insinuation that it was two hundred of *their* heavenly companions who took on physical form to lie with the Daughters of Men in the generations prior to the Great Flood. It is almost as if the writers of the Pentateuch either have no apparent knowledge of the connection between angels and the fall of the Watchers, or else they are deliberately avoiding the subject altogether.

Who, then, were the angels, whether heavenly or fallen? Where did they come from? Where did they live? What did they look like? Only by establishing these facts could I go on to speculate on the true origins of this apparent race or culture – lost to the pages of history. It seemed imperative that if I was to widen my knowledge of the fallen race, then I would need to uncover and study whatever had been written about them, not just in recorded Hebrew folklore and mythology, but also among the more recently translated Dead Sea Scrolls, which contained much new material on the nature of angels and the fall of the Watchers.

The Testament of Amram

It was this last area of study that in 1992 provided me with a vital piece of evidence which altered my whole perspective of the Watchers. In a reconstructed apocalyptic fragment, translated by the Hebrew scholar Robert Eisenman and referred to as the Testament of Amram, there is a rather unnerving account featuring the appearance of two Watchers to Amram, the father of Moses the lawgiver. The relevant section reads as follows:

[I saw Watchers] in my vision, the dream-vision. Two (men) were fighting over me, saying . . . and holding a great contest over me. I asked them, 'Who are you, that you are thus empo[wered over me?' They answered me, 'We] [have been em]powered and rule over all mankind.' They said to me, 'Which of us do yo[u choose to rule (you)?' I raised my eyes and looked.] [One] of them was terr[i]fying in his appearance, [like a s]erpent, [his] c[loa]k many-coloured yet very dark . . . [And I looked again], and . . . in his appearance, his visage like a viper, and [wearing . . .] [exceedingly, and all his eyes . . .].[6]

The ancient text then identifies this Watcher as Belial, the Prince of Darkness and King of Evil, while his companion is revealed as Michael, the Prince of Light, who is also named as Melchizedek, the King of Righteousness. It was, however, Belial's frightful appearance that took my attention, for he is seen as terrifying to look upon and like a 'serpent', the very synonym so often used when describing both the Watchers and the Nephilim. If the textual fragment had ended here, then I would not have known why this synonym had been used by the Jewish scribe in question. Fortunately, however, the text goes on to say that the Watcher possessed a *visage*, or face, 'like a viper'. Since he also wears a cloak 'many-coloured yet very dark', I had also to presume that he was anthropomorphic, in other words he possessed human form.

'Visage like a viper . . .' What could this possibly mean?

How was I to interpret this metaphor used in connection with the terrifying appearance this being must have instilled in the minds of those who originally trafficked with the walking serpents of the Book of Enoch?

How many people do you know with a 'visage like a viper'?

For over a year I could offer no suitable solution to this curious riddle.

Then, by chance, I happened to overhear something on a national radio station that provided me with a simple though completely unexpected explanation.

In Hollywood, Los Angeles, there is a club called the Viper Room. It is owned by actor and musician Johnny Depp, and in October 1993 it hit the headlines when the up-and-coming young actor River Phoenix tragically collapsed and died as he left the club, following a night of over-indulgence. In the media publicity that inevitably surrounded this drugs-related incident, it emerged that the Viper Room gained its name many years beforehand when it had been a jazz haunt of some renown. As the story goes, the musicians would take the stage and play long hours, prolonging their creativity and concentration by smoking large amounts of marijuana. Apparently, the long-term effects of this drug abuse, coupled with exceedingly long periods without food and sleep, caused their emaciated faces to appear hollow and gaunt, while their eyes closed up to become just slits. Through the haze of heavy smoke, the effect was to make it seem as if the jazz musicians had faces like vipers, hence the name of the club.

This diverting anecdote sent my mind reeling and helped me to construct a mental picture of how a person with a 'visage like a viper' might look: their faces would appear long and narrow, with prominent cheekbones, elongated jawbones, thin lips and slanted eyes like those of many East Asian racial types. Was this the solution to why both the Watchers and Nephilim were described as serpents? It seemed as likely a possibility as any, though it was also feasible that their serpentine connection related to their accredited magical associations and capabilities, perhaps even their bodily movements and overall appearance.

Wingless Angels

A separate account of the appearance of two Watcher-like figures, this time to Enoch as he rests in his bed, closely parallels the way in which they appeared to Moses's father, Amram, and seems to throw further light on their apparent descriptions:

And there appeared to me two men very tall, such as I have never seen on earth. And their faces shone like the sun, and their eyes were like burning lamps; and fire came forth from their lips. Their dress had the appearance of feathers: . . . [purple], their wings were brighter than gold; their hands whiter than snow. They stood at the head of my bed and called me by my name.[7]

I knew it was taking an enormous gamble to assume for one minute that these textual accounts from Judaic apocalyptic and pseudepigraphal works actually recorded true-life descriptions of a race that in theory never existed outside the minds of the original storytellers. On the other hand, I felt I would be better able to investigate any historical origin if I could discover a cohesive pattern among the religious literature under study.

So what could be learnt from this second account?

I could begin by stripping away the angels' golden wings, for this part of the text was undoubtedly a very late addition, since angels were rarely deemed to possess wings until well into the Christian era. In the Old Testament, for example, only heavenly hosts such as the Cherubim and Seraphim are ever described as having multiple wings, four or six being the usual number. This feature is thought to have been a borrowing from the iconography of Assyria and Babylonia, where sky genii and temple guardians were depicted with very similar sets of wings.[8] Yet Cherubim and Seraphim were never strictly angels, or 'messengers of God', who almost certainly received their wings at the hands of early Christian artists and scribes influenced by classical iconography, which often portrayed mythological beings with wings.

For most of us our view of angels is typified no better than in the vivid detail of Pre-Raphaelite paintings by such artists as Edward Burne-Jones, Evelyn de Morgan and John William Waterhouse, and by the ornately carved statues of angels found in ecclesiastical buildings, including churches, cathedrals and minsters. These convey to us idealized impressions of angels which contain the notion that they must have had beautiful wings, like those of the finest swans. This vision, however, bears little resemblance at all to accounts of angels that appear either in the Old Testament or in the earliest Judaic religious literature. For confirmation of this, one has only to reread the account of the appearance of the Watchers to Amram – there is no mention of wings. Even in the Book of Enoch itself, there is concrete evidence to show that wings were grafted on to existing accounts of angels sometime after the first century AD, since earlier renditions of the text make no mention of wings at all.

As Tall as Trees

If we take away the wings we are left with two tall men, 'as I have never seen on earth'. Why is there this obsession with height in connection with the fallen race? Was there some deep-rooted psychological need for Judaeo-Christian angels to be of enormous stature? In the stylized art of Ancient Egypt the Pharaohs, considered to be incarnations of the god Horus, were always depicted larger than any other figure around them, including their consorts and courtly entourage. Symbolic art of this nature makes perfect sense, since it instantly elevates the Pharaoh to a position higher than the rest of his subjects. In this way we can understand why divine beings, such as angels, should be portrayed as larger than life in religious iconography, but why were both the rebel Watchers and the Nephilim repeatedly described as giant in stature, or like 'trees' as they are metaphorically referred to in some accounts?[9] Surely their great size must convey something more than simply misappropriate iconography. Could we possibly be dealing with actual human beings of greater stature than their contemporaries? Was this one of the features that made them stand out from other people?

Shining Like the Sun

The skin on the hands of the angels who appear to Enoch is described as 'whiter than snow', which seems to be another feature common to the fallen race. Elsewhere in the Book of Enoch, the Watchers are referred to simply as 'like white men',[10] while, in the account of the birth of Noah, the infant is seen as possessing a body 'white as snow and red as a rose'.[11] This suggests a type of complexion not dissimilar from that of white Caucasians of today, who often experience a ruddiness of the skin when exposed to harsh outdoor weather. Is this a clue to the Watcher's place of origin – an environment that suffered much harsher climatic conditions? Since the Book of Enoch was written by olive-skinned Jews in a hot sunny climate, this type of reference is not to be regarded lightly.

In the same vein, the faces of the two 'men' who visit Enoch are described as shining 'like the sun', a metaphor invoked to denote Watcher-like beings in Hebrew myth and legend. What could the Jewish scribes have meant by using such a term? Was it simply to convey the divine nature of the beings in question, in a similar manner to the way in which saints and holy men are depicted with halos or nimbuses in Christian art, or was there another, more supernatural, explanation for such statements?

Some light is thrown on the matter in one fascinating account that follows shortly after the two men's appearance to Enoch. Having been transported to the various heavenly realms by these angelic beings, the antediluvian patriarch arrives at the seventh and final heaven, where he encounters the Lord seated upon a great throne. In the Lord's company are hosts of Cherubim and Seraphim, and Enoch is greeted by the archangels Gabriel and Michael, who are also described as Watchers in the Book of Enoch. The humble prophet is then made to undergo a form of ceremony in which he is anointed with oil by one of the archangels:

And the Lord said to Michael: 'Go and take from Enoch his earthly robe, and anoint him with My holy oil, and clothe him with the raiment of My glory.' And so Michael did as the Lord spake to him. He [stripped me of my clothes and] anointed me and clothed me, and the appearance of that oil was more than a great light, and its anointing was like excellent dew; and its fragrance like myrrh, shining like a ray of the sun. And I gazed upon myself, and I was like one of His glorious ones. And there was no difference, and fear and trembling departed from me.[12]

Seeing beyond the highly religious overtones of these lines, it is difficult not to question the nature of the ceremony which Enoch undergoes. Stripped of his clothes, he is anointed with an oil that has a fragrance like myrrh. It makes him shine 'like a ray of the sun', so that he appears no different from the archangels, making all fear and trembling depart from him.

Is there any possibility that the archangels, who obviously bore a close resemblance to Enoch in the first place, covered their bodies with a type of oil that made them shine 'like a ray of the sun'? Considering for a moment that we might well be dealing with highly distorted recollections of actual encounters between earthly individuals, then why should these exalted ones need to cover their bodies in oil? Was it simply for aesthetic or ritualistic purposes? Or was there some other more practical reason behind this act? It is too easy to jump to conclusions here, especially in the knowledge that the skin of the Watchers is, when described, almost always spoken of as 'white as snow' and ruddy in appearance. Yet might it be remotely feasible that the body oil was used to protect the skin from harmful ultraviolet (UV) radiation, in much the same way as we use a sun-block today? Such usage would undoubtedly give the skin a shimmering, reflective quality, especially in the presence of a flickering fire. And, as I was aware, the skin of white Caucasians is far more vulnerable to the harmful effects of the sun than that of any other race.

Eyes Like Burning Lamps

More intriguing still is the description of the angels' eyes, for they are said to have been 'like burning lamps' – perhaps the missing words from the terrifying appearance of the Watcher Belial in the Amram text. Yet why 'burning lamps'? Was it simply the way in which the eyes of the Watchers were somehow able to reflect the flickering light of a burning lamp? Or did it mean something more?

Time and time again the eyes of Watchers, and angels in general, are described as appearing 'like the sun', and here, too, the birth of Noah is a prime example, for it is said that 'when he opened them (i.e. his eyes) the whole house glowed like the sun'.[13]

'Glowed like the sun . . .' What did this mean?

Quite obviously, there was no hard-and-fast answer to this perplexing mystery, yet if these accounts recorded distorted memories of an actual Middle Eastern culture living long ago, then their eyes must have been singled out for a specific reason. For the moment all I could conclude was that they either reflected sunlight, or their irises were likened to the sun; in other words, their eyes were perhaps golden or honey-coloured in appearance, a characteristic common among certain tribal cultures of central Asia even today.

As White as Wool

And what can be said about the hair of the Watchers? Since we know that Noah in every way resembled the appearance of the fallen race, then we must assume that the revulsion to his 'thick and bright' white hair 'as pure as wool'[14] also indicates one of their recurring physiological traits. In the account of his birth given in the Ethiopian Book of Enoch, the infant's hair is said to have been like a *demdema*, a *Ge'ez* word similar to the English term 'Afro-cut'. More correctly, this refers to 'long curly hair',[15] which will form dreadlocks if left unkept for any length of time. Applying this information I had therefore to presume that, besides their pale white skin, the Watchers possessed thick, curly white hair, perhaps matted to form long dreadlocks, similar to the style sported by so-called 'travellers' in Britain today. This, too, would have made them appear like white Caucasians, who, it may be assumed, looked quite alien to the indigenous cultures which first began relating stories concerning the presence of these apparently divine beings.

Children of the Angels

A lot of emphasis is placed here on the peculiar appearance of the infant Noah in the belief that he in some way resembled the physical appearance of the fallen angels and, by virtue of this, angels in general. And yet what proof was there that his strange birth could be conceived as an actual event in humanity's long history? Why not accept this account as simply a metaphor for an unholy union between a conceptual being of light and a mortal woman?

One answer is the continued existence of an extraordinary belief, perhaps thousands of years old, that some young children are born 'of the angels', bearing not only their assumed physical characteristics but also their divine personas. I would never have believed such a thing, had it not been for an account given to me by an elderly woman, named Margaret Norman, following a lecture in which I included details of the birth of Noah and the apparent physiological traits of the fallen race.[16]

Today Margaret lives in the English county of Essex, but in her younger years she was a resident of London, and it was here she learnt from her mother the details of a story concerning a so-called 'angel child'. In 1908 a son was born to a German father and English mother in the suburb of Hampstead. It weighed a healthy eleven pounds and possessed blue eyes and golden blond locks. Sadly, it died at the age of three and a half, but while it was alive the infant was apparently adored by everyone for its 'serene and dreamy loving nature'. As Margaret's mother told her, people would stop in the street, place money in the infant's pram for luck and refer to him as an 'angel child'. Most peculiar of all was her mother's insistence that the baby 'just shone', a statement on which Margaret found it very difficult to expand.

I asked Margaret whether it was the pale nature of its skin, the smile on the baby's face or perhaps some kind of inner radiance that had led people to believe this child 'just shone'. She could only shake her head and say: 'I really don't know. It was just something about him.'

'Just shone . . .'

'. . . and as for his eyes, when he opened them the whole house glowed like the sun'. These are the enigmatic words used by the Jewish scribes to describe the infant Noah, who was himself spoken of as 'like the children of the angels'. Perhaps the way in which the Watchers' eyes and faces had shone 'like the sun' really did relate to some kind of intangible radiance no longer known to the world today. Yet the idea that a child in twentieth-century London was seen to have the appearance of a Nephilim baby, and be given money in the hope of receiving good luck, is compelling evidence that the birth of Noah, as well as the many other descriptions of Watchers and angels in general, provides us with eyewitness accounts of an actual race that once walked the earth.

The Shamanic Solution

'Their dress had the appearance of feathers' – this is the final piece of descriptive narrative concerning the two 'men' who appeared before Enoch. In the Testament of Amram, the Watcher Belial is adorned in a cloak 'many-coloured yet very dark'. Despite the habit among medieval artists of portraying angels with bodies covered with feathers, which has no real basis in biblical tradition, I felt this statement concerning feathers to be very important indeed. It also seemed like an oversight on the part of the scribe who conveyed this story into written form, for having added wings to the description of the two 'men', why bother to go on to say they wore garments of feathers? Surely this confusion between wings and feather coats could have been edited to give the Watchers a more appropriate angelic appearance.

Somehow I knew that here was a key to unlocking this strange mystery. It suggested that, if the original fallen race had indeed been human, then they may have adorned themselves in garments of this nature as part of their ceremonial dress. The use of totemic forms, such as animals and birds, has always been the domain of the shaman, the priest-magician of tribal communities. In many early cultures the soul itself was said to have taken the form of a bird to make its flight from this world to the next, which is why it is often depicted as such in ancient religious art. This idea may well have stemmed from the widely held belief that astral flight could only be achieved by using ethereal wings, like those of birds – a view that almost certainly helped to inspire the idea that angels, as messengers of God, should be portrayed with wings in Judaeo-Christian iconography.

To enhance this mental link with a shaman's chosen bird, he or she would adorn their body with a coat of feathers and spend long periods studying the bird's every action. They would enter its natural habitat and watch every facet of its life – its method of flight, its eating habits, its courtship rituals and its movements on the ground. By so doing they would hope to become as birds themselves, an alter-personality adopted by them on a semi-permanent basis. Totemic shamanism is more or less dependent on the indigenous animals or birds present in the locale of a culture or tribe, although in principle the purpose has always been the same – to use this mantle to achieve astral flight, divine illumination, spirit communication and the attainment of otherworldly knowledge and wisdom.

So could the Watchers and Nephilim have been bird-men as well as walking serpents?

The answer is almost certainly yes, for in one Enochian text discovered among the Dead Sea Scrolls[17] the Nephilim sons of the fallen angel Shemyaza, named as 'Ahyâ and 'Ohyâ, experience dream-visions in which they both visit a world-garden and see two hundred trees being felled by heavenly angels.[18] Not understanding the purpose of this allegory, they put the subject to the Nephilim council, who appoint one of their number, named Mahawai, to go on their behalf to consult Enoch, who now resides in an earthly Paradise. To this end Mahawai then:

> *[. . . rose up into the air] like the whirlwinds, and flew with the help of his hands like [winged] eagle [. . . over] the cultivated lands and crossed Solitude, the great desert, [. . .]. And he caught sight of Enoch and he called to him . . .*[19]

Enoch explains that the two hundred trees represent the two hundred rebel Watchers, while the felling of their trunks signifies their destruction in the coming conflagration and deluge. More significant, however, is the means by which Mahawai attains astral flight, for he is said to have used 'his hands like (a) [winged] eagle'. Elsewhere in the same Enochian text, Mahawai is said to have adopted the guise of a bird to make another long journey.[20] On this occasion, he narrowly escapes being burnt up by the sun's heat and is only saved after heeding the celestial voice of Enoch, who convinces him to turn back and not die prematurely – a story that has close parallels with Icarus' fatal flight too near the sun in Greek mythology.

In addition to this evidence, a variation of this same text equates

Shemyaza's sons 'not (with) the . . . eagle, but his wings', while in the same breath the two brothers are described as 'in their nest',[21] statements which prompted the Hebrew scholar J. T. Milik to conclude that, like Mahawai, they too 'could have been bird-men'.[22]

Is it really possible that the Watchers might have belonged to a race or culture which practised an advanced form of bird shamanism? Were they shamans themselves, able to communicate with the spirit world and experience dream-visions through astral flight? All the extant works featuring the legends of the Watchers and Nephilim are primarily concerned with dream-visions, the products of astral flight and journeys to the other world. This strongly supports the view that the original source of these visionary tracts was a race or culture that employed the use of shamanistic practices of the sort expressed within their very pages.

The idea of bird-men acting as the bringers of knowledge and wisdom to mortal kind is not unique to the Middle East. An African tribe called Dan, who live close to the village of Man on the Ivory Coast, say that at the beginning of time, in the days of their first ancestors, a race of 'attractive human birds appeared, possessing all the sciences which they handed on to mankind'. Even today the tribal artists make copper representations of these bird-men, who are shown with human bodies and heads supporting long beaks, like those of birds of prey.[23]

Might these 'attractive human birds' have been what the Book of Enoch describes as Watchers? The bird-men of the Ivory Coast would certainly appear to have played a similar role to that of the rebel angels in Hebraic tradition.

Could this new-found connection between Watchers and shamanism now throw further light on their association with serpents, the bringers of knowledge and wisdom in so many ancient mythologies? In the Book of Enoch, the Watcher named Kâsdejâ is accused of showing men how to take away 'the bites of the serpent',[24] knowledge that would in past ages have gone hand in hand with the magical duties of priest-magicians, or shamans, deemed to have power over snakes. As in the case of bird shamanism, serpent shamans would have adorned themselves with snake relics and carried serpent-related items, such as snake charms and a long rod or pole adorned with serpentine symbols, helping to explain why the

Watchers and Nephilim were referred to as serpents. Furthermore, both birds and snakes were seen by many Middle Eastern cultures as ultimate symbols of transformation of the soul, bringing together these two quite separate forms of totemic practice.

One thing was certain, the ornithomorphic association with both the Watchers and the Nephilim was clearly not meant to convey the idea that they possessed heavenly wings in the traditional sense. It was, however, possible that the repeated usage of bird symbolism in connection with angelic beings may have led early Hebrew and Christian scholars and scribes to *assume* this very thing – a confusion which, like so many other mistranslations or misrepresentations of early religious scriptures, led to the iconographic forms of angels and fallen angels as we know them today.

The Face of a Watcher

It was beginning to appear as if the whole concept of angels had been born out of misconceptions concerning either references to heavenly beings in Old Testament tradition, who may well have had quite earthly origins in the first place, or mythological beings and protective spirits borrowed from other contemporary cultures. Strip these away from the literature and you are left with bizarre yet highly descriptive accounts of anthropomorphic figures, such as the Watchers, who probably only became synonymous with the term *mal'akh*, or 'angel', long after their legends had been accepted into Hebrew mythology. More disconcerting was the knowledge that the world's current perception of angels bore little resemblance to their earliest recorded appearances, whether as physical denizens that once walked this earth or as incorporeal beings of faith alone.

So what did they really look like?

Using the various individual components deduced from the different accounts given of the fallen race found in Enochian and Dead Sea literature, I asked an accomplished artist, the author and illustrator Billie Walker-John, to draw a composite picture of a Watcher. Although this was simply meant to be an interesting exercise, the finished result was stunning to say the least. The striking,

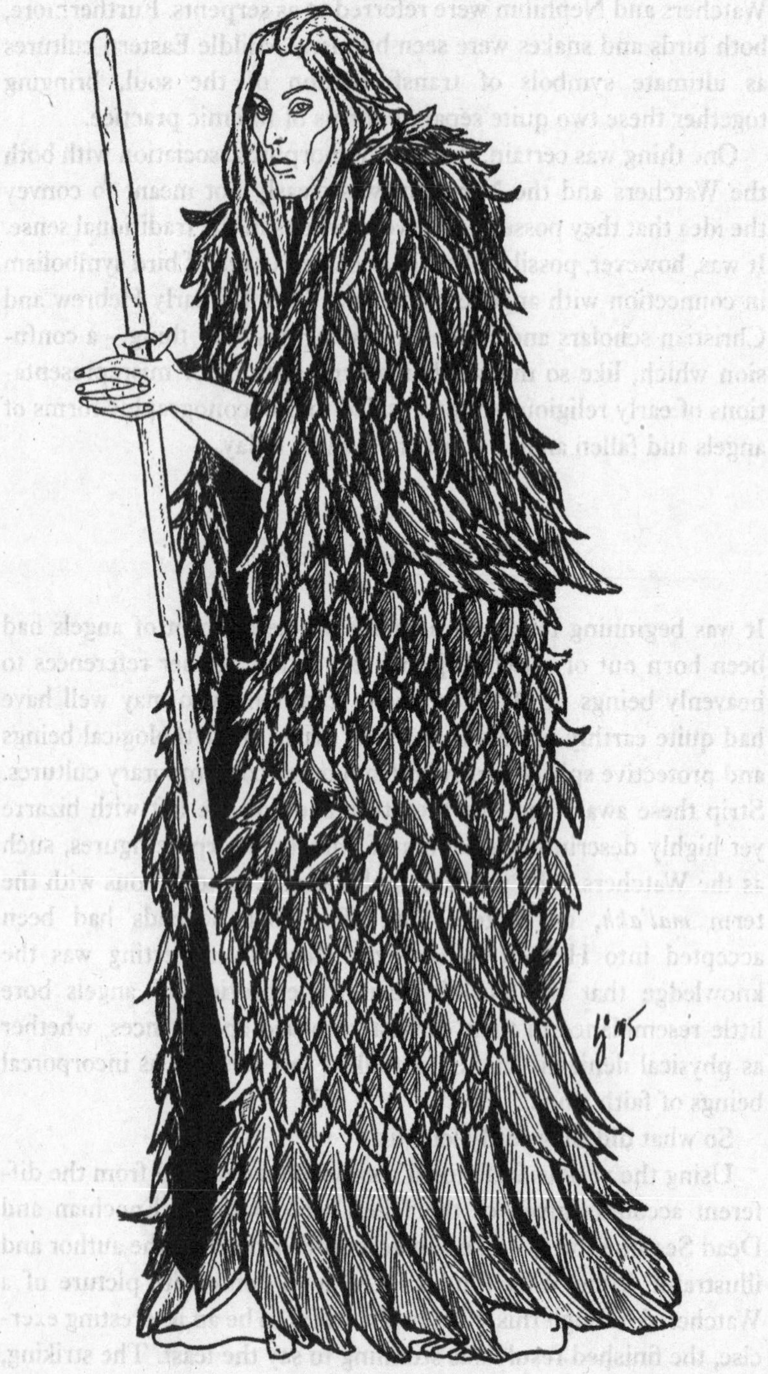

almost amoral face of this walking bird-man with his shaman's staff was utterly mesmerizing, even a little chilling in some respects. Most disturbing was the knowledge that the black-and-white drawing portrayed the most accurate depiction of an angelic being executed in modern times. So who were these people? And why had the world forgotten them?

Fig. 3. Billie Walker-John's composite impression of a Watcher or angelic being based on descriptions given in early Judaic sources such as the Book of Enoch and Dead Sea literature. This most ancient image of a so-called 'angel' contrasts markedly to the more familiar images conveyed by Renaissance art and nineteenth-century Pre-Raphaelite paintings (see also Plate 22).

Six

WHEN GIANTS WALKED THE EARTH

If we read the Book of Genesis, we can see just how out of place the story of the Sons of God coming unto the Daughters of Men appears to be in comparison with the rest of its eclectic contents. Indeed, if it is correct to assume that the account of the Fall of Man and the Serpent of Eden reflect an abstract rendition of the fall of the Watchers, then the whole story is included twice.[1]

Adding to the mysterious nature of Genesis 6 is the fact that there are, neither before nor after these verses, any direct references to the coming of the Sons of God, the Nephilim or the Mighty Men (*gibborim*). Nor are there any references anywhere in the Bible to equate the *bene ha-elohim* with the Watchers. This information comes only from the Enochian literature of the first and second centuries BC. To add to the confusion, the term *bene ha-elohim* actually translates as 'the sons of the *gods*', while the name *elohim* is a female noun with an irregular plural, implying not 'gods' at all, but 'sons of the *goddesses*'. Never is this theological 'hot potato' sufficiently explained, and for my purposes it seemed best to stick simply with the idea that the term referred to fallen angels alone, without evoking a fixed gender.

So what about the rest of the Pentateuch – the first five books of the Old Testament, traditionally accredited to Moses the lawgiver? Could this provide me with additional clues to the origin of the Genesis chapter concerning the Sons of God coming unto the Daughters of Men, along with their subsequent incarceration and the destruction of their offspring, the Nephilim?

Glancing through the chapters of Genesis that immediately follow these enigmatic verses, we read about the generations of Noah and his subsequent role as the saviour of both humanity and the animal kingdom. It is a story that all of us learn in primary school, yet like most of Genesis it is awkwardly worded, confusing, repetitive and highly contradictory in its statements.

The Bible says that God purged the earth of its corruption and iniquity by bringing about a universal deluge, yet nowhere does it say that the Sons of God, the Nephilim or the Mighty Men, were destroyed by these global cataclysms. This fact has to be assumed by the reader simply because Noah, his wife, his three sons and their wives, are the sole survivors of the Great Flood. Moreover, there is much evidence to suggest that some members of the fallen race actually survived these troubled times.

Races of Giants

Scattered throughout the Pentateuch are enigmatic references to the existence of giants living in the bible lands long after the generations of Noah. These terrifying individuals almost invariably feature in wars waged against foreign raiders and the Israelite peoples by indigenous Canaanite tribes; Canaan being the name given to Palestine, Western Syria and Lebanon in Old Testament times.

If we look at the later chapters of Genesis, we will find references to giants living in the age of the prophet Abraham, a date usually fixed at around 2000 BC. Several verses deal with how Chedorlaomer, the king of ancient Elam, a country placed in the highlands of south-west Iran, encounters no less than three tribes of giants, who rise up against him and are defeated by his forces in the land of Canaan. They are listed as 'the Rephaim in Ashteroth Karnaim . . . the Zuzims in Ham; and the Emims in Shaveh Kiriathaim'.[2]

Later, in the Book of Deuteronomy, which deals with the wanderings of the Jewish tribes, following the Exodus out of Egypt at the time of Moses, the text speaks of Canaan as 'a land of Rephaim', or giants, where the 'Rephaim dwelt therein aforetime'. Because of their reported great stature, in many translations of the Bible from the original Hebrew, the word 'giants' is rendered instead of 'Rephaim'. Deuteronomy also tells us that 'the Ammonites call them Zamzummins: a people great, and many, and tall, as the Anakim'.[3]

As tall 'as the Anakim'?

Who then were the Anakim? And how might they relate to the Watchers and Nephilim? Reaching for my weighty, leather-bound edition of *Hitchcock's New and Complete Analysis of the Holy Bible*, I turned to its edition of *Cruden's Concordance* – the complete listing of all names, terms and expressions found in the Bible. There are a number of further entries for the Anakim, the most important of which is found in the Book of Numbers:

And there we saw the Nephilim, the sons of Anak, which come of the Nephilim: and we were in our own sight as grasshoppers, and so we were in their sight.[4]

So the Anakim are specifically cited as the descendants of the legendary Nephilim. Elsewhere the Anakim are referred to as the inhabitants of Canaan, 'a land that eateth up the inhabitants thereof: and all the people that we saw in it are men of a great stature'.[5] Reading on, it actually names the 'sons of Anak', or Anakim, as Ahiman, Sheshai and Talmai, although no further details are given concerning their appearance.[6] They are encountered by the spies sent out by Joshua, Moses' successor, to report back on the inhabitants of Hebron, or Kirjath-arba, 'the chief city of the Anakim', situated in what is today southern Palestine,[7] before they are attacked and finally defeated by one of these 'spies', named Caleb.[8]

So the Anakim were destroyed, but survivors of their race probably lived on, and certainly did so in the minds of the Old Testament chroniclers. They may have been three brothers from the town of Hebron, one of Palestine's most ancient cities, but there is every indication that they were also a powerful race in their own right who inhabited Canaan from very earliest times.

The word Anak is generally taken by Jewish scholars to mean 'long-necked',[9] or 'the men with the necklaces',[10] conjuring an immediate image of the ring collars worn even today by certain tribes of central Africa. Was this yet another physical feature of the original fallen race – long necks bearing ringed necklaces?

The enormous size of the Anakim is, of course, to be taken with a large pinch of salt; yet why were the Anakim seen as direct lineal descendants of the Nephilim, the progeny of the fallen angels who were supposedly wiped out at the time of the Great Flood? No explanation is given, and the reader is left to assume that they must have been linked in some way to the family of Noah, who himself bore the traits of the Watchers and Nephilim.

King Og of Bashan

Most renowned of the giants of Canaan was the legendary King Og of the land of Bashan, who with his brother Sihon controlled vast areas of land that stretched for many hundreds of miles in every direction. Being himself a descendant of the Rephaim,[11] Og is said to have resided 'at Ashtaroth and at Edrei',[12] the latter being a giant city identified with the modern Jordanian town of Der'a, some thirty miles east of the southern end of the Sea of Galilee. Here archaeologists have uncovered a vast subterranean city, cut deep into the bedrock, beneath the existing buildings of the town, although how it might be linked with King Og is uncertain.[13]

The kingdom of Bashan, the so-called 'land of the Rephaim',[14] or giants, supposedly extended from Mount Hermon in the north of Canaan to Gilead in the south, a region geographically placed on the east side of the Jordan river.[15] It was here that almost six hundred years before, according to the Bible, the Elamite king Chedorlaomer apparently 'smote the Rephaim', King Og's own ancestors, in the age of the patriarch Abraham.[16] It is also interesting to note that Og was said to have reigned 'in Mount Hermon',[17] the most northerly point of his kingdom and the location where, according to the Book of Enoch, the rebel Watchers 'descended'.

Various Hebrew myths outside the Bible cite King Og as the progeny of Hiya, a son of the fallen angel Shemyaza, and a woman who subsequently became the wife of Ham, the son of Noah.[18] Og was said to have escaped the Deluge by clinging to a rope ladder attached to the Ark and being daily fed through a port hole by Noah himself. He took pity on the giant after he swore to repent and become his slave! Afterwards, however, Og apparently resumed his wicked ways.[19]

Quaint as the story of Og's survival of the Deluge may seem, it makes nonsense of biblical chronology, for if this giant king *had* existed at the time of the Great Flood – which is seen by theologians as having taken place in '2348 BC'[20] – then he would have been around 1,100 years old at the time of Moses. Stories such as this were almost certainly concocted at a very late stage in the development of Hebrew myth and legend, their purpose being to account for the existence in Canaan of outsized indigenous tribes such as the Anakim, the Emim, the Rephaim, the Zuzim, as well as the peoples under the leadership of King Og, who were encountered by the first Israelites when they entered this foreign land from Mesopotamia at the beginning of the second millenium BC.

Many of these giant races were quite obviously looked upon as actual lineal descendants of the Nephilim, whose existence must still have been entrenched in the minds of the first Israelites. Yet there is very little evidence whatsoever outside Jewish religious literature for the existence of these giant races, either from other contemporary sources of the time or from archaeological discoveries made over the past hundred years or so of biblical exploration. At first sight this may seem a disconcerting realization, and one which has grave implications for the historical reality of the Watchers and Nephilim in more distant times. However, there is no reason why 'giants' should *not* have existed in the bible lands in distant ages. Variations of anything up to eighteen inches between individuals of different races or cultures were not unusual in prehistoric times. Indeed, such differences are still common today. One has only to look at an American basketball team to see that seven-foot tall 'giants' exist, and from a mythological context it is this distinction alone that leads us to evoke terms such as 'giant' and 'dwarf', *not* the specific size of cultures or races as a whole.

Mention must also be made here of the most famous giant of all in biblical tradition, and this is Goliath, David the shepherd boy's gigantic opponent, who is said to have belonged to the tribe of Gath and to have fought alongside the Philistine army. In the well-known story, presented in 2 Samuel, this enormous figure of a man was said to have been ten feet tall and to have worn a copper coat of mail weighing an incredible 120 pounds.[21] He also carried a spear weighing 15 pounds, which apparently possessed a shaft 'like a weaver's beam'.

Could a person of this size and strength ever have walked the earth?

The answer is very possibly yes, for despite the lack of archaeological evidence for the presence in the past of actual giant races, there is compelling evidence to suggest that individuals of this size did once exist. Too many outsized human remains, worked tools and stone coffins have been unearthed in different parts of the world, from ancient times down to the present era, for such traditions to be dismissed out of hand.[22] These accounts, often published in sane and sober journals and books, refer mainly to isolated discoveries and therefore *do not* constitute hard evidence for the existence of whole races of giants.

Despite such shortcomings, it does not follow that the bold accounts of giant races roaming the earth in Old Testament times are completely worthless. Far from it, they appeared vital to my understanding of the roots behind the terms and expressions used by the chroniclers of Genesis to recall the former existence of the angelic race who fell from heaven.

Source of the Nephilim

The Book of Numbers specifically refers to the Anakim as descendants of the Nephilim – not the Watchers, or the Sons of God, but the Nephilim. This is important, for it implies that at the time of Moses, when the core material for the Pentateuch was being established and recorded for the first time, only the term 'Nephilim' was used to denote the giant race who had fallen because of its lust for mortal women in antediluvian times. If, for a moment, we disregard the contentious lines of Genesis 6 as much later interpolations (see below), it would appear that other terms for the fallen race, such as Watchers and Sons of God, were clearly *unknown* to the Israelite tribes at the time of Moses, *c.* 1300 BC.

This implies that *nephilim*, a word meaning the 'fallen ones', or 'those who have fallen', was the *original* name given by the Israelites to the fallen angels. Strange confirmation of this suggestion

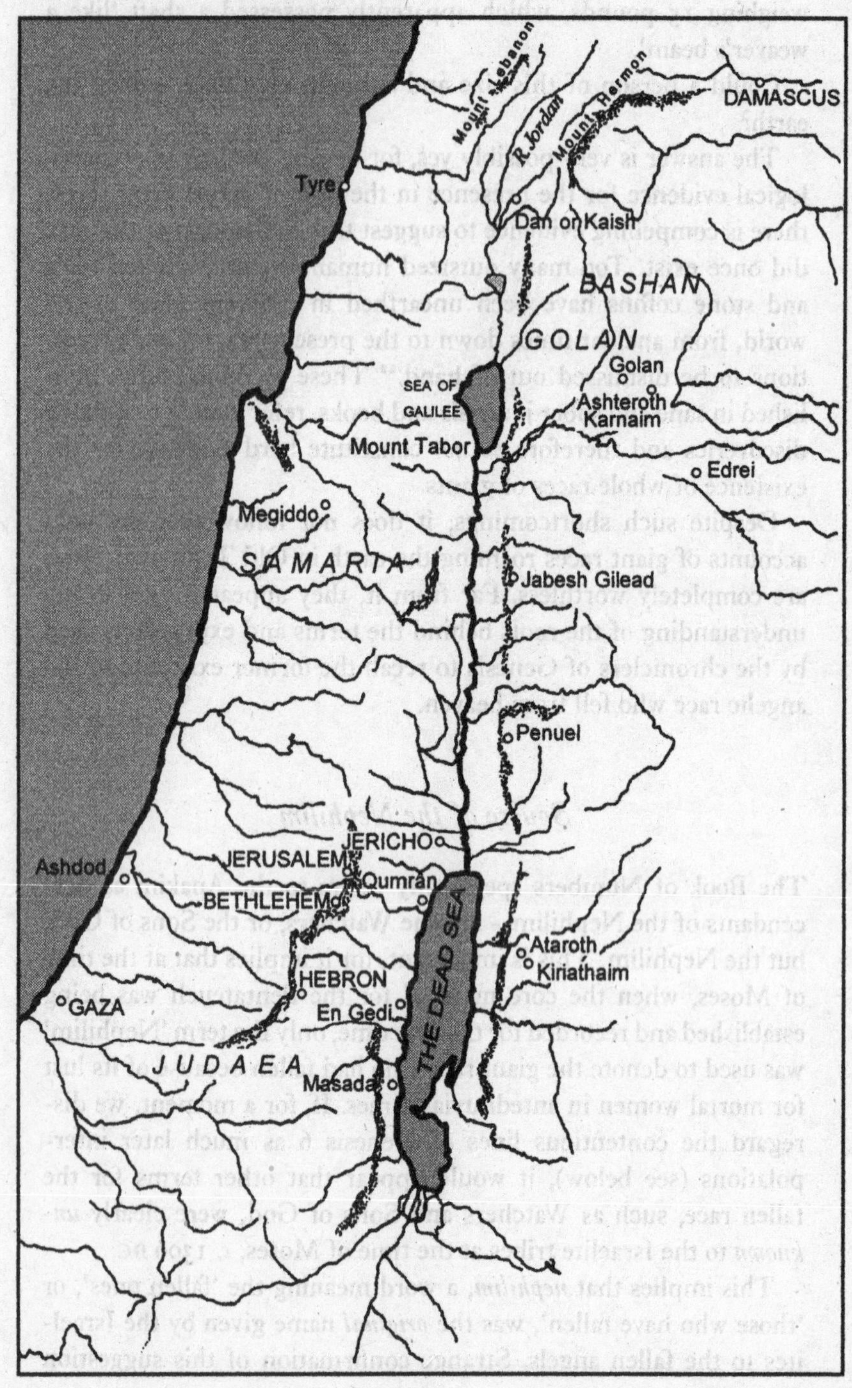
Mount Lebanon
R. Jordan
Mount Hermon
DAMASCUS
Tyre
Dan or Kaish
BASHAN
GOLAN
Golan
SEA OF
GALILEE
Ashteroth
Karnaim
Mount Tabor
Edrei
Megiddo
SAMARIA
Jabesh Gilead
Penuel
JERICHO
JERUSALEM
Ashdod
Qumran
BETHLEHEM
THE DEAD SEA
Ataroth
Kiriathaim
HEBRON
GAZA
En Gedi
JUDAEA
Masada

comes from rereading Genesis 6. Verse 2 speaks of the Sons of God coming unto the Daughters of Men, while in contrast verse 4 states firmly that: 'The Nephilim were in the earth in those days, *and also after that*, when the sons of God came in unto the daughters of men [*author's emphasis*].'

'*And also after that* . . .'

The meaning was clear enough: there were two quite separate traditions entangled here – one concerning the fallen race known to the early Israelites as the Nephilim, and the other concerning the *bene ha-elohim*, the Sons of God, who are identified directly with the Watchers of Enochian tradition.

So was this assumption correct? Could I find some kind of scholastic support for such a contention? Once again, I would not be the first person to point out the seemingly paradoxical reference in Genesis 6:4 to two quite independent fallen races, for theologians have long pondered over this puzzle. Yet only one modern-day Hebrew scholar has attempted to explain its presence. In an important article published in the *Hebrew Union College Annual* of 1939, under the rather uninspiring title of 'The Mythological Background of Psalm 82', Julian Morgenstern came to the quite astonishing conclusion that there must have been two quite separate occasions when the angels fell from heaven – once through lust and a second time through pride.[23]

Despite the originality of this solution, in my view it simply muddies the picture, for the easiest answer would be to accept that two separate renditions of the same story somehow became confusingly joined by the compilers of Genesis. On the one hand, there was the story of the *nephilim*, the fallen race seen by the early Israelites, and perhaps even by the indigenous tribes of Canaan, as the progenitors of the much later giant races of the Bible; while on the other, there were the quite separate stories concerning the *bene ha-elohim*, the Sons of God, the Watchers of the Book of Enoch. In some way the two traditions had become fused as one to form the enigmatic verses of Genesis 6, while in the Enochian literature the Nephilim were demoted to being purely the giant offspring of

Map 1. Principal biblical locations associated with the early patriarchs and giant races of biblical tradition.

the Sons of God. Everything pointed towards the fact that the lines of Genesis 6 had either been added to the Bible at a much later date, or else that they had been seriously tampered with to include the two quite independent origins of the Nephilim and Watchers.

For the moment, it was important to examine the rest of the Pentateuch to see whether it could throw further light on the origins and age of the story of the Watchers.

A Goat for Azazel

Only one other possible reference to the fall of the angels is to be found in the Pentateuch. According to the Book of Leviticus, each year on the feast of Yom Kippur, the Day of Atonement, the Israelites would sacrifice two he-goats. One animal was offered up to God, so that he might absolve the Jews of their sins, while the other was set aside 'for Azazel', who is named as a leader of the Watchers in the Book of Enoch.[24] During this sacrificial rite the priest is said to have placed both hands on the head of the goat 'for Azazel' and to have confessed 'over him all the iniquities of the children of Israel, and all their transgressions in all their sins'. He would then send the animal away 'by the hand of a fit man into the wilderness',[25] where it would plunge to its death over a steep cliff, recalling the plight of the fallen angel Azazel, who was seen as perpetually bound and chained in the wilderness. In much later times, a red or scarlet ribbon was apparently tied to the goat's head to represent these sins, since it states in Isaiah that 'though your sins be as scarlet, they shall be as white as snow'.[26]

Further expanding on the barbaric ritual of the 'scapegoat', as the goat is referred to instead of 'Azazel' in the Authorized Version of the Bible, are the words of rabbi Moses ben Nahmen, who in the twelfth century AD wrote:

> *God has commanded us, however, to send a goat on* Yom Kippur *to the ruler whose realm is in the places of desolation. From the emanation of his power come destruction and ruin . . . His portion among the animals is the goat. The demons are part of his realm and are called in the Bible* seirim *(legendary he-goats fostered by Azazel).*[27]

Whether or not this suggests the survival into the Middle Ages of the scapegoat ritual is not specified, although it does show the importance it must still have held for the Jews of medieval Europe.

The scapegoat was conceived as embodying the spirit of Azazel, and in so doing it was able to carry away the sins of the Jews, a role which Jesus Christ was voluntarily to undertake in much later Christian tradition. The association of the scapegoat with both sin and impurity eventually led to it becoming an animal of Satan and the Devil in early Christianity – a figurative connection it sadly retains to this day. Even the inverted, or reversed, pentagram, seen by Western society as embodying ultimate evil, stems exclusively from this strange association between Azazel and the scapegoat ritual. Since Victorian times, this abhorred symbol has been seen as a sign of the goat of the witches, the two upright points signifying the animal's horns 'attacking the heavens',[28] an empty and meaningless legend that has no basis in ancient religious law, either Jewish or Christian. How so simple a design can have come to be so reviled by so many people is a mystery in itself. Yet knowledge that this association between the Devil and the goat stems back to the punishment administered to Azazel makes the inverted pentagram one of the only symbols actually to preserve the memory of the fall of the Watchers.

To Act Like Angels

Although the scapegoat ritual is no longer practised, the Day of Atonement is still revered as the holiest festival in the Jewish calendar. It forms the climax of a ten-day period that begins with the Jewish New Year – a date that usually falls during either late September or early October in the Gregorian calendar. For Jews worldwide, Yom Kippur is a time when all sin is renounced and everyone has to make the choice between either obeying or disobeying the divine sovereignty of God. The day is marked by a twenty-four hour period of prayer and fasting in which a Jew must not eat, drink, anoint with oil, wear sandals or have sexual intercourse. Instead he or she must continually praise God in emulation of his angels, for it is on this one day of the year that Jews must attempt to serve God '*as if they were angels* [*author's emphasis*]'.[29]

'As if they were angels?'

Was this simply a metaphorical statement, or could there be some more deep-rooted assertion behind this tradition?

Throughout the twenty-four hour period that constitutes Yom Kippur, it has always been believed that Satan possesses no power over the life of a Jew, and because of this God invites his adversary to look in on the homes of Jewish families to see what they are doing. Satan will hopefully find them fasting and praying like angels 'dressed in white garments', upon which he is forced to admit: '"They are like angels and I have no power over them." Whereupon God binds Satan in chains and declares to His people: "I have forgiven you all".'[30]

That Satan should be annually bound and chained while the Jews themselves attempt to emulate angels 'dressed in white garments' is difficult to understand in conventional theological terms. To a non-Jew, such curious and somewhat naïve beliefs and customs are baffling, to say the least, yet since they relate to the very day on which the rite of the scapegoat once took place, it seems likely that the original adversary in this story was not Satan at all but Azazel. Moreover, the practice of becoming 'like angels' on the Day of Atonement is almost certainly a distant echo of the fall of the Watchers and the punishment supposedly suffered by Azazel because of his corruption of humanity, prior to its destruction at the time of the Great Flood. If this theory is correct, it provides solid evidence to suggest that the traditions concerning the fall of the angels existed in both Judaic myth and ritual as far back as the establishment of the Israelite tribes following the Exodus out of Egypt, the period when the scapegoat ritual presumably first entered Mosaic tradition.

Yet are the contents of the Pentateuch really to be trusted? How are we to know that the references to the scapegoat ritual were themselves not much later interpolations?[31] Furthermore, how are we to know that the verses concerning the existence in Canaan of indigenous giant races were also not added at some later date in its construction? For example, much of Deuteronomy, in which these references appear, is thought to have been compiled, not at the time of the Exodus of Moses, but by Jewish scribes living in Jerusalem as late as the seventh century BC.[32]

Moses is supposed to have left the Pentateuch to the Jewish peoples as its Torah, or Holy Law. And yet it was only after the time of the so-called Babylonian Captivity in the sixth century BC that much of what we know today as the Old Testament was first set down in writing.[33] Indeed, other than a small rolled silver amulet,[34] inscribed in Hebrew with a form of the Priestly Blessing found in the Book of Numbers (one of five books of the Pentateuch)[35] and dated to the sixth century BC, there is no hard evidence *whatsoever* for the existence of the Bible before post-exilic times. Emphasizing this rather disconcerting situation may, I realize, look rather cynical, though I certainly accept that large tracts of the Old Testament are not only period set but also contain invaluable information concerning the history of the Middle East from its very earliest times through till the establishment of the Christian era. It was, however, with this more sceptical view at the forefront of my mind that I was going to have to continue my search for the original sources behind the story of the Watchers, for only by establishing how and when this tradition first entered Hebrew myth and legend could I begin to understand its true implications.

Seven

ANGELS IN EXILE

Exactly where did the legends of the Watchers originate? Had they been carried into the Essene communities of the Dead Sea by wandering *zaddiks*, the wild rainmakers who claimed direct descent from Noah and preached the teachings of the Kabbalah? If so, then who were these people and where had they obtained such stories? Had they been passed on by word of mouth among the Israelite tribes since time immemorial? Or did they have some more recent point of origin, perhaps in another Middle Eastern country?

Maybe the key lay in the Bible itself, which, despite the late construction of some of its individual books, could often be dated like the rings of a tree. To the trained eye the approximate date at which certain religious themes, passages or ideas first entered mainstream Jewish thought could be calculated with some degree of accuracy. Therefore, if the term *'îr*, 'watcher', appeared in the Bible itself, then I had every chance of predicting when and how the term first filtered into rabbinical teachings.

Reaching once again for *Hitchcock's New and Complete Analysis of the Holy Bible*, I turned to *Cruden's Concordance* and thumbed through until I found the entries for 'watcher'. There turned out to be just four. The first, in the Book of Jeremiah, speaks of 'watchers' who 'come from a far country, and give out their voice against the cities of Judah', foreigners being implied here, and not angels.[1] The other three references, however, all appeared in the Book of Daniel, one of the very last works of the Old Testament.

Before checking out these entries in Daniel, I again played with *Cruden's Concordance*, this time with respect to named angels, like those frequently mentioned in the Book of Enoch. I quickly discovered that just two are recorded in the whole of the Old Testament – Gabriel and Michael – and both appear *only* in the Book of Daniel. Even more significant was the knowledge that only in the Book of Daniel do there appear clear descriptions of Watcher-like beings that closely resemble those found in both the Book of Enoch and the Dead Sea Scrolls. Why should this be so? What was so special about Daniel?

By the Rivers of Babylon

The Book of Daniel is written partly in Hebrew and partly in Aramaic. Scholars usually date its contents and style to somewhere around 165 BC, the very time-frame attributed to the construction of the Book of Enoch, with which it is so often compared.[2]

From a historical point of view, the book focuses on an era beginning in around 606 or 605 BC, when the Babylonian king Nebuchadnezzar invades Judah and enters Jerusalem. There he sacks the Temple of Solomon and carries away many of its treasures, and on his return to Babylon takes with him some of the city's leading craftsmen. He also takes into his service three or four noble youths, one of whom is Daniel, who is thought to have been around seventeen years of age at the time. According to the bible story, the youths are taken into the care of the royal court and possibly even live in the king's palace. Daniel quickly rises in popularity to become a remarkable figure of great renown, noted for his strict adherence to the Torah, the Holy Law established by Moses, and for his 'wisdom'. He also possesses other more highly prized qualities, including the ability to interpret dreams. In time Daniel becomes governor of the province of Babylon as well as chief governor over the city's 'wise men' – its astrologers, Chaldeans (learned men) and soothsayers.

During this period Nebuchadnezzar apparently experiences a very strange dream. None of the 'wise men' can interpret its meaning, so the king summons Daniel. In his presence, Nebuchadnezzar then recites the contents of his vision in which he has seen 'a tree in the midst of the earth', with 'fair' leaves and fruit, that grew and grew until it reached heaven. Beneath its boughs were the beasts of the field sheltering in shadow, while the fowl of the air 'dwelt in its branches'.[3] Nebuchadnezzar then apparently saw 'a watcher and an holy one [*who*] came down from heaven'. This shining being cried out to the king, telling him to cut down the tree and leave only 'the stump of his roots in the earth'.[4]

These verses in the Book of Daniel are then followed with the lines:

The sentence is by the decree of the watchers, and the demand by the word of the holy ones; to the intent that the living may know that the Most High ruleth in the kingdom of men, and giveth it to whomsoever he will, and setteth up over it the lowest of men.[5]

Daniel, having listened to Nebuchadnezzar's recital of his dream, explains that the mighty tree represents the king himself, whose 'greatness is grown, and reacheth to heaven, and thy dominion to the end of the earth'. It foretells, he says, his imminent downfall, unless, that is, he breaks free of his bonds and accepts the Most High as the only true God.[6] Then finally, for the third and last time, the term *'îr*, 'watcher', appears in the text: 'And whereas the king saw a watcher and an holy one coming down from heaven.'[7]

Nowhere else in the Bible does the term *'îr* appear in connection with the appearance of angels. This placed its usage firmly in the time-frame of the Book of Daniel, written at around the same period as the Book of Enoch. Even further supporting this link is the way in which Nebuchadnezzar's downfall is prophesied by tree-felling imagery, exactly as the destruction of the Watchers is described in some of the Enochian material found among the Dead Sea Scrolls.[8]

The Jews in Exile

The prophet lived long, and was still present at Nebuchadnezzar's palace when events took a turn for the worse for the Jews back in his native Jerusalem. The city had been left alone by the Babylonian army for some years when a new uprising forced Nebuchadnezzar to return to Judah and again besiege the capital. It fell in the year 598 BC, and on his return to Babylon the king is said to have taken into captivity an estimated 10,000 Jews. Another uprising in 586 BC apparently forced him to return once more to Jerusalem, and this time he not only sacked the Temple, he also razed it to the ground. He is also said to have returned to Babylon with almost the entire population of Jerusalem. This must have amounted to a figure upward of 100,000. Henceforth the people of Judah join those already in bondage and enter what is referred to in Jewish history as the period of captivity, or exile.

Nebuchadnezzar eventually dies in 562 BC and is followed by a succession of rulers, the last of whom, Belshazzar, also features in the prophet's story. Daniel apparently continues as governor and dream-interpreter, eventually rising to the position of 'third ruler' of Babylon, after the 'second ruler' Belshazzar, and the 'first ruler' Nabonidus (or Nabû-na'id) – Belshazzar's father, who has left the affairs of the kingdom in the hands of his son while he himself is off fighting a war in Arabia.

It is in the first year of Belshazzar's reign that Daniel is himself troubled by an apocalyptic 'night vision' in which he sees many strange things that act as portents of future events. In this the prophet witnesses a Watcher-like being, with an appearance that could have been lifted straight from the pages of the Book of Enoch, for he says:

I beheld till thrones were placed, and one that was ancient of days did sit: his raiment was white as snow, and the hair of his head like pure wool'.[9]

Comparisons with the description of the infant Noah as given in the Book of Enoch are obvious.[10] Had one account influenced the other? Which came first – the Book of Daniel or the Book of Enoch?

The now elderly prophet is also called upon by Belshazzar to interpret strange handwriting that appears on a wall during a great banquet. The prophet predicts imminent doom, and soon afterwards Belshazzar is killed as Babylon falls to the Persians under the command of Cyrus the Great; the date being 539 BC. One of Cyrus' kinsmen, Darius, is set up on the throne of Babylon, and it is after this date that Daniel is cast into the lions' den because of his fidelity to God. According to the story, the prophet is saved from certain death by divine intervention, and afterwards Darius is said to have issued a decree enjoining 'reverence for the God of Daniel'.[11]

Daniel himself continues to experience dream-visions. For instance, during the third year of Cyrus' reign, presumably over Babylon, the prophet is said to have fasted for three weeks and while standing on the banks of the great river Hiddekel – the ancient Akkadian name for the Tigris – beheld:

a man clothed in linen, whose loins were girded with pure gold of Uphaz: his body also was like the beryl, and his face as the appearance of lightning, and his eyes as lamps of fire, and his arms and his feet like in colour burnished brass, and the voice of his words like the voice of a multitude.[12]

The similarity between the divine being in this account and the 'very tall' men with 'faces' that 'shone like the sun' and eyes 'like burning lamps', who appear before Enoch as he rests in his bed, is undeniable.[13] Only the colour of their skin has changed – from 'as white as snow' in the Enochian text to 'burnished brass' in the Book of Daniel.

The Watcher-like being before Daniel can be seen only by him; however, as the prophet stands trembling at the awesome sight, the apparition announces that he has been negotiating with the Persians, yet, in the words of the angel:

the prince of the kingdom of Persia withstood me one and twenty days; but, lo, Michael, one of the chief princes, came to help me: and I remained there with the kings of Persia.[14]

The identity of the radiant being is never made clear, though its purpose in the waking vision is to inform Daniel of the fate about to befall the exiled Jews now that the Persians have taken Babylon. Yet here, too, is the first reference in the Old Testament to the archangel Michael, who is said to have come to the aid of the apparition during his negotiations with the Persians, a seemingly human action surely outside the domain of angels. Exactly what is going on here is unclear, though it is worth noting that in Hebrew tradition Michael is the archangel who presides over the heavenly affairs of the Israelite nation.[15]

After taking Babylon, Cyrus the Great continues westwards until, just one year later, in 538 BC, he takes Jerusalem. It is only then that the Jews of Babylon are finally given their freedom. An estimated 50,000 apparently return, leaving six times this amount in the land to which they had been taken in bond.[16] Many thousands more journey two hundred miles eastwards to the city of Susa, the old Elamite capital in south-west Persia, where Darius had established a summer palace. Why there should have been this reluctance among the Jews to return to their native country is open to speculation. Perhaps they did not wish to make the long journey back to Jerusalem on foot, or had elderly relatives who would never have survived the return. It is also possible that many of the Babylonian Jews saw new opportunities opening for them, not just in the land that had become their only home, but in Persia itself. Furthermore, both Cyrus and Darius had extended a religious tolerance to those Jews who remained in Babylon and Persia, enabling them to practise their faith relatively unhindered.

According to the Book of Daniel, the now elderly prophet is among those who move on to the Persian court at Susa. Earlier, however, during the third year of Belshazzar's reign, Daniel experienced another dream in which he was taken in mind to the city of Susa. Here he witnessed a symbolic struggle between a ram and a he-goat (representing the overthrow of the Persian Empire by the Greeks, which does not occur until 330 BC). He also heard 'a man's voice between the banks of Ulai (a river named the Choasper, or *Kerkhan*, laying some twenty miles north of Susa), which called, and said, Gabriel, make this man to understand the vision.'[17]

Following these lines, Gabriel then makes his one and only cameo appearance in the Old Testament to explain to Daniel the meaning of his dream-vision. The archangel does not appear again until he announces the birth of both John the Baptist and the virgin-born child to Mary in the New Testament's Gospel of Luke.[18]

Daniel finally dies in Susa, a very old man indeed; however, the plight of the Jews in exile is not yet over. Large numbers stay on in Babylon and Susa until the new Persian king, Artaxerxes, signs a decree permitting the restoration of the Jewish state in 458 BC; the Temple of Jerusalem having been completed and rededicated in 515 BC. Yet still there is a reluctance among the Jews to return to their homeland. Some 5,000 return in the company of a priestly scribe named Ezra, following Artaxerxes' signing of the decree, while in 445 BC a further batch travel with a Jew named Nehemiah, who, prior to the journey, had been cup-bearer, or vizier, to the king.[19] After thirteen years overseeing the restoration of the revitalized Jewish nation, Nehemiah returns to his royal master in Persia, where he finally ends his days. Any Jews still remaining in either Babylon or Susa after this date are simply lost to the pages of history.

A Man of Many Faces

The works accredited to Daniel contain potent, moralistic stories that won favour among the Jews following their return from exile. This was especially so during the terrible suppression they suffered under Antiochus Epiphanes, the king of Syria, who ruled Judaea at the commencement of the Maccabean revolt of 167 BC. It is almost certainly because of these troubled times that many of the fireside stories remaining from the days of the Babylonian Captivity were put into written form.

In all likelihood Daniel was a composite figure, a man of many faces, who embodied the life and deeds of more than one individual, perhaps even certain aspects of the various kings whom he allegedly served. To the post-exilic Jews, however, Daniel represented the imprisoned spirit of God's chosen people, from the time of the Captivity right down to the commencement of the Christian era. In the light of this, could I now make sense of why it was only in the Book of Daniel that Watchers, Watcher-like individuals and named angels appeared as heavenly beings in the Old Testament?

Chart 1. RELEVANT BIBLICAL CHRONOLOGY.

c. 2000 BC
Abraham leaves the city of Ur; Chedorlaomer, the King of Elam, encounters giant races in Canaan.

c. 1300–1200 BC
Exodus out of Egypt by the Israelites under the command of Moses the Lawgiver. Establishment of Twelve Tribes in Canaan; giant races again encountered here.

c. 1020–970 BC
The future king David fights the Philistines, including the giant Goliath of the tribe of Gath.

970 BC
Following the death of David, Solomon takes the throne of a united Israel.

931–889 BC
Solomon dies and the kingdom gradually splits into two separate kingdoms – Israel in the north and Judah to the south.

722 BC
The northern kingdom of Israel falls to the Assyrians and some 28,000 Israelites are taken into captivity; this signals the end of Israel as a nation. The captives never return from Assyria.

606–605 BC
Nebuchadnezzar succeeds to the Babylonian throne.

598 BC
Jerusalem, the capital of Judah, falls to Nebuchadnezzar. The outgoing king, Jehoiakim, and many leading craftsmen are deported to Babylon; these include the young Daniel. Jehoiakim's son Zedekiah takes the throne.

586 BC
Nebuchadnezzar besieges Jerusalem once more. The city falls and is destroyed; the Jews are taken into captivity in Babylon.

562–553 BC
Nebuchadnezzar dies and is succeeded by three successive kings: Amel-marduk, Neriglissar and, finally, Nabonidus. Afterwards the regent, Belshazzar, takes control of Babylon in the king's absence.

540–539 BC
Nabonidus is defeated by Cyrus, king of Persia. Anarchy breaks out in Babylon; the Bible speaks of writing on the wall appearing in Belshazzar's palace during a banquet. Cyrus' army enters Babylon and achieves easy victory.

538 BC
Cyrus takes Jerusalem; all captive Jews in Babylon are allowed their freedom; many move on to Susa in south-west Persia.

537–515 BC
Restoration of the Temple of Jerusalem under Zerubbabel.

478 BC
The Jews still in Susa; biblical story of Esther marrying Xerxes, the Persian king, and thus saving many Jews from massacre.

458 BC
Ezra is sent to Jerusalem by the Persian king Artaxerxes. He takes with him a large number of the remaining Jewish exiles, as well as valuable gifts for the restored Temple.

445 BC
Nehemiah, the Jewish cup-bearer to Artaxerxes at Susa, returns to Jerusalem as its new governor. Kingdom of Judaea is founded.

165 BC
The Book of Daniel is written.

On the Road with Raphael

For the moment I would need to set aside the Book of Daniel, and the Bible as a whole, for I felt this could tell me little more about the origins of the Watchers. Instead, I turned my attention to the so-called Apocrypha, the collection of seventeen books, or portions of books, that, although originally included in the Christian Bible, were dropped by the early Church Fathers of the fourth century AD. I was looking specifically for one book, the Book of Tobit, for it had emerged that this featured another of the so-called archangels – in this case Raphael, who never appears in the Old Testament, but *does* appear as one of the holy Watchers in the Book of Enoch.

The Book of Tobit focuses on the lives of Israelites belonging to the ten tribes who were apparently carried off to Assyria and 'the cities of the Medes' after the fall of the northern kingdom of Israel to Shalmaneser, the Assyrian king, in 722 BC. Yet, unlike the Jews of the Babylonian Captivity, these tribes never returned from their exile, and are assumed to have lived on in isolated communities for many generations afterwards. Like the Book of Daniel and the Book of Enoch, this apocryphal work was actually constructed only sometime after 200 BC.

The story in question features a righteous man named Tobias, the son of Tobit, who is about to leave Nineveh, the old Assyrian capital, for Ecbatana, one of 'the cities of the Medes', in north-west Iran.[20] Here Tobias is to win the hand in marriage of a fair maiden named Sara, the daughter of Raguel.[21] His companion on the long and wearisome journey is Raphael, whose name means 'healer of God'. As they cross the mountains towards their place of destination, the archangel – who withholds his true identity and instead uses the name Azarius – teaches Tobias many wise things. For example, Tobias catches a huge fish in a river, and Raphael instructs him on how he can use each part of its body by saying:

Take out the entrails of this fish and lay up his heart, and his gall, and his liver for thee; for these are necessary for useful medicines . . . the gall is good for anointing the eyes, in which there is a white speck, and they shall be cured.[22]

Worthy words for a healer of God, but an art surely beyond the normal undertakings of a divine messenger of heaven. The journey resumes, and on reaching Ecbatana the archangel is sent on to Rages, another Median city, to collect bags of money on behalf of Tobias' family.[23] Tobias himself eventually wins the hand of Sara, and on the party's return to Nineveh, Azarius reveals his true identity as 'Raphael, one of the seven holy angels',[24] a reference to the group of seven archangels in Hebrew myth and legend.

There seemed little doubt that the story of Tobias and Raphael's journey on the road to Media was merely a quaint fable, created for an allegorical purpose by Jewish story-tellers. Yet the appearance of the archangel in this story seemed important, for it was beginning to look as though angelic beings with specific descriptions, identities, hierarchies and titles had only been adopted by the Jews after their return from exile in Babylon and Susa. If this were true, then from where exactly had these new influences come?

Babylon under the kings Nebuchadnezzar and Belshazzar in the sixth century BC had been dominated by the cult of Bel, or Bel-Marduk, the state god who was seen as a personification of the sun. His worship was abhorred by the Jews as pagan idolatry, even though Daniel, on entering the Babylonian court, had been given the name Belteshazzar, meaning 'prince of Bel'.[25] Since Bel was the god of their oppressors, his cult would never have found favour among the captive Jews, so is unlikely to have had any major influence on the Jewish concept of angels. On the other hand, Babylon at this time was a cosmopolitan city attracting religious cults from every corner of Mesopotamia, so might one of these have found favour and sympathy among the Jews? It is difficult to say, though there *is* good reason to believe that the Assyrian and Babylonian winged temple guardians and sky genii influenced the development of the multi-winged Cherubim and Seraphim. Yet these were never really classed as *mal'akh*, the angels or messengers of heaven.

Iranian Influence

A more fruitful line of inquiry was the major influence that the Persian priesthoods undoubtedly exerted upon the exiled Jews. Many Jewish scribes, prophets and administrators achieved popularity and wealth not just in the old Elamite capital of Susa, but also much deeper into Persia, especially in the north-western kingdom of Media, modern-day Azerbaijan, the setting for much of the

Book of Tobit. So what religious influences might the Jews have been exposed to here?

Before becoming a kingdom in its own right, Media had been a confederation of fierce, mostly highland tribes who had been vassals of the Assyrian Empire of northern Iraq and Syria, before proclaiming their independence in 820 BC. Thereafter they had been ruled by a dynasty of kings, who were known as 'king of kings', the last of whom was overthrown by Cyrus the Great in 550 BC. Two years later, with the unification of all the Iranian and Asian kingdoms, Cyrus established the Persian Empire, initiating a royal dynasty of kings referred to by historians as the Achaemenids. Cyrus now ruled a territory that stretched as far north as the Russian Caucasus, as far east as India and the Chinese Turkman Empire; as far south as Egypt and Ethiopia, and as far west as eastern Europe.[26]

It is not recorded to what faith Cyrus belonged, though it is likely he followed the religion of the Magi, the Median priestly caste of immense power, who were said to have guarded Cyrus' white marble tomb at his capital city of Pasargadae in southern Persia following his interment in 530 BC.[27] Cyrus himself was descended of the old Median dynasty, so he also owed its powerful Magian priesthood some kind of loyalty.[28] The origin of this priestly line is unknown. The Medians were a mixed race, with indigenous cultural and religious influences from the mountainous regions of north-west Iran. The only real comparison to the Magi was the Brahman priestly caste of India, with whom they shared many aspects of belief, customs and worship (see Chapter 8). The most famous Magi were, of course, the three 'wise men' who, so the Bible informs us, brought the three gifts for the infant Christ at the time of the Nativity.[29]

Had the Jews therefore been influenced by the beliefs of the Magi? It was strongly possible; however, there was another, rival religion beginning to take a hold in Persia at this time and this was Zoroastrianism.

The Fall of the Magi

The Magi received their biggest blow in 522 BC when a Median usurper and Magus named Gaumata posed as the regent of Cambyses II, Cyrus' successor, while the king was on a military campaign in north Africa. In so doing the impostor managed to seize control of the Persian throne and proclaim himself ruler of the empire. Cambyses, on hearing of the *coup*, set about returning to Persia, only to be mortally wounded on the home journey. In spite of this tragic accident, Gaumata and his Magi co-conspirators were eventually ousted and slain by Cambyses' successor, Darius, having controlled the empire for several months.[30] Thereafter the Magian priesthood was outlawed and persecuted throughout Persia. Indeed, according to the Greek writer Herodotus, on the anniversary of Gaumata's downfall a festival known as Magophobia was instituted. On this day people were encouraged to kill any Magi priests they came across, a custom apparently still taking place in the mid fifth century when Herodotus himself visited Media.[31]

The relegation of the Magian priesthood to one that was scorned and hated by the people allowed the sudden rise in popularity of what later became known as Zoroastrianism, a revitalized form of Iranian religion named after its much celebrated founder, Zoroaster. From the reign of Darius onwards, Zoroastrianism grew to become the new state religion with its own holy books, priesthood and temples in every major town and city. It did everything it could to stamp out Magianism, even though Zoroastrianism probably owed almost its entire creed to the Median religion's ancient teachings.

The Tower of Daniel

The Median capital of Ecbatana, the modern city of Hamadan, was held to be a very sacred place by both the Magi and the Zoroastrians. It was therefore quite astounding to find that it had been not only the place of destination of the archangel Raphael in the Book of Tobit, but also the site of a 'tower' – constructed by the

Chart 2. RELEVANT PERSIAN CHRONOLOGY.

2000–1000 BC
Establishment of Iranian tribes in central and western Asia, following migrations from the plains of southern Russia.

c. 2000–550 BC
Assyria, Media, Babylonia and Lydia are the dominant powers in the Near East.

630 BC
Traditional birth-date of Zoroaster, the founder of the Zoroastrian faith.

581 BC
The birth of Cyrus the Great, a direct descendant of the Median dynasty of kings.

559–548 BC
Cyrus assumes throne of Anshan in western Persia and then conquers the rest of the Iranian continent; establishment of the so-called Achaemenid period of Persian history.

539 BC
Babylonia falls to Cyrus.

530–522 BC
Death of Cyrus and reign of his successor Cambyses II.

526–521 BC
Dynastic troubles; a Magian usurper seizes the Persian throne for four months. Cambyses dies on return from Egypt. His successor, Darius I, assumes control.

485 BC
Coronation of Xerxes, son of Darius.

464–330 BC
Reigns of Artaxerxes I to Darius III.

330 BC
Defeat of Persia by Alexander the Great; end of independency and influence; cessation of Achaemenid dynasty of kings.

c. 247 BC
Establishment of Parthian dynasty in Persia.

224–5 AD
Ardashir I defeats Parthians in three decisive battles and establishes second Persian Empire, also known as the Sassanian dynasty of kings.

640 AD
Fall of the Sassanian kings after their final defeat by the invading Arabs; end of Persian Empire.

---

prophet Daniel and sanctioned by his patron, Darius I. According to the Jewish historian Flavius Josephus (AD 37–97), the only writer to have preserved any knowledge of this elegant building's great renown, it was said to have been:

. . . wonderfully made, and it is still remaining, and preserved to this day; and to such as do see it, it appears to have been lately built, and to have been no older than that day when any one looks upon it . . . Now they bury the kings of Media, of Persia, and Parthia, in this tower, to this day; and he who was intrusted with the care of it, was a Jewish priest; which thing is also observed to this day.[32]

If this was correct, then it clearly demonstrated the immense esteem accorded to the Jewish priesthood by the Persian kings, and presumably by the Magi, right down to the first century of the Christian era when Josephus wrote these enigmatic lines. Nothing more was known about Daniel's tower, though classical writers say that Ecbatana was originally surrounded by seven walls, each rising in gradual descent and painted a different colour, reminiscent of the seven-tiered ziggurats of Assyria and Babylonia.[33]

Quite obviously there must have been a trafficking of ideas and philosophies between the Magi of Media, the Zoroastrians of Persia and the Jewish exiles. Yet, if this were so, just how much of it might have influenced the contents of the Book of Enoch and the writing of the Dead Sea Scrolls? More important still – had Iran been the point of origin of the post-exilic concept of angels, both of the heavenly and fallen varieties? From even a cursory glance at the teachings of Zoroastrianism, it seemed the answer was always going to be yes.

The Angels of Zoroaster

Like Judaism, Zoroastrianism is a monotheistic religion. And like Judaism, it also accepts a whole pantheon of angels, or *yazatas*, who act in accordance with the faith's supreme being, Ahura Mazda, the 'wise lord'. Those angels closest to godhead are known as the *Amesha Spentas*, or *Amshashpands*, whose origins are thought to have developed out of much older Indo–Iranian myths of central Asia dating back to the second or third millenium BC.[34] These six 'holy, immortal ones', or 'bounteous immortals', with Ahura Mazda, are equated directly with the Judaic concept of the seven archangels,[35] who are found, not just in the Book of Tobit, but also in the Book of Enoch[36] and the Dead Sea literature.[37]

Two notable scholars of Hebrew, W. O. E. Oesterley and T. H. Robinson, recognized the influence of Zoroastrianism on Judaism in connection with everything from its concept of angelology to its understanding of demonology, dualism, eschatology, world-epochs and the resurrection of the soul, *especially in the case of the Book of Enoch*. Furthermore, they concluded that these adoptions from the Persian religion undoubtedly occurred when the Jews were in exile at Susa.[38] These very same opinions have been shared by scholars of Persian antiquity, such as Richard N. Frye, a former Aga Khan Professor of Iranian Studies at Harvard University, who outlined the powerful cross-fertilization between Zoroastrianism and post-exilic Judaism in his 1963 book *The Heritage of Persia*.[39]

There seemed little doubt that I was on the right track in my conclusion concerning the Persian influence on the Book of Enoch, so what about the story of the Watchers – had this come from Iran as well? Canon R. H. Charles, the Hebrew scholar whose English translation of the Ethiopic Book of Enoch still stands among the finest to be produced, appeared to think so. He concluded that the myths concerning the Sons of God coming unto the Daughters of Men, as presented in Genesis 6, belonged 'to a very early myth,

Map 2. The Near East in the first millennium BC.

possibly of Persian origin, to the effect that demons had corrupted the earth before the coming of Zoroaster and had allied themselves with women'.[40]

This same opinion was voiced by Professor Philip Alexander, probably one of the foremost authorities on the Book of Enoch. In an important paper entitled 'The Targumim and Early Exegesis of "Sons of God" in Genesis 6', published in the *Journal of Jewish Studies* in 1972, he had this to say about the origin of the Sons of God:

Angelology flourished in Judaism after the Exile under the influence of Iranian religion. It is very likely that the interpretation of the Sons of God, בני אלהים*, as angels was one of the ways in which these rather alien ideas were grafted into the stock of pre-exilic religion and naturalized.*[41]

In other words, there seemed every possibility that the legends concerning the Sons of God had first been introduced to Genesis, or certainly revised and restored, at the time when the priestly scribes were busy re-editing the Old Testament, following the Jews' final return from Persia around 445 BC. Since the 'Sons of God' was simply another name for the Watchers, it implied that the traditions concerning their fall, as presented in the Book of Enoch, had stemmed originally from Iran.

Truth and the Lie

Persia would also appear to have had a major influence on the Dead Sea literature. For example, in the Testament of Amram it features the two Watchers who appear to Amram, the father of Moses, as he rests in bed. They ask him 'which one of us do you choose to rule you?', following which they identify themselves as 'Belial ... [Prince of Darkness] and King of Evil' and 'Michael ... Prince of Light and King of Righteousness'.[42] Elsewhere in the Dead Sea Scrolls, Belial, the Evil One, is equated with adjectives such as 'Darkness' and 'Lying', and 'the Liar', while his equal and opposite number, Michael, or Melchizedek, is tied with terms such as 'Light', 'Righteousness' and 'Truth'.[43]

The concept of the beholder of the vision being made to choose between light and darkness, truth and lie, righteousness and falsehood, is matched exactly in the Zoroastrian holy books, where an individual is asked to choose between *asha*, 'righteousness' or 'truth', and *druj*, 'falsehood' or 'the Lie'. These dualistic principles are represented on the one hand by Ahura Mazda, the 'wise lord', and on the other by Angra Mainyu (often abbreviated to 'Ahriman' in Persian texts), the 'wicked spirit' or 'prince of evil', who is the Iranian equivalent of Belial, Satan or the Devil.[44] The idea of a choice is also strangely reminiscent of the way in which a Jew must choose between either the path of good or the path of evil during the annual festival of Yom Kippur, the Day of Atonement.

Further confirmation of this link between Zoroastrianism and Dead Sea literature comes from the fact that the followers of the truth among the Essenes were known as 'the Sons of Zadok', i.e. 'Righteousness', or 'the Sons of Truth', while the followers of Belial were known as 'the Sons of Darkness' and 'the Sons of Lying'.[45] Now we may compare this with Zoroastrian literature, where it speaks of the *ashavans*, the 'followers of Righteousness' or the 'followers of Truth', and the *drvants* – the 'followers of the Lie'.[46]

These were important realizations, for they overwhelmingly confirmed the clear relationship not just between Zoroastrianism and Judaism, but also between the Iranian faith and the teachings of the Dead Sea communities, which, like Daniel, adhered strictly to the laws of Moses. Since there seemed every likelihood that these same religious communities were also responsible for such apocryphal and pseudepigraphal works as the Book of Enoch and the Testament of Amram, there seemed every possibility that the source material for the legends concerning the fall of the Watchers really had come from the rich mythology of Iran.

Yet before I followed in the footsteps of Daniel and departed Palestine for the land in the east that lay beyond the mountains of Babylonia, I still needed to establish one final fact: had anyone ever actually suggested that the Book of Enoch was composed outside of Palestine?

Laurence's Lucky Hunch

Canon R. H. Charles appeared to confirm the Persian influence on the Book of Enoch, but what about Richard Laurence, Archbishop of Cashel, who translated the first English edition of the Ethiopic text deposited in the Bodleian Library by James Bruce of Kinnaird in 1773? What had he to say about the text's country of origin? I read his lengthy introduction to the Book of Enoch and was astonished by what I found. Once he had decided to consider the latitude in which the text is set, he then made a detailed study of the length of the days referred to in Chapter 71. He found that the author of the Book of Enoch had divided these into eighteen parts, or segments, with the longest day consisting of twelve parts; the equivalent of sixteen hours in our own twenty-four-hour clock. Laurence realized that a longest day of this length does not occur in Palestine, this fact instantly dismissing it as the original setting for the Book of Enoch. In this knowledge, he searched for a northerly latitude that experienced a longest day of the time span indicated in the text. In so doing, he was able to conclude that the author was referring to an indigenous climate:

not lower than forty-five degrees north latitude, where the longest day is fifteen hours and a half, nor higher perhaps than forty-nine degrees, where the longest day is precisely sixteen hours. This will bring the country where he wrote, as high up at least as the northern districts of the Caspian and Euxine (or Black) Seas; probably it was situated somewhere between the upper parts of both these seas.

If the latter conjecture be well founded, the author of the Book of Enoch was perhaps one of the tribes which Shalmaneser carried away, and 'placed in Halah and in Habor by the river Goshan, and in the cities of the Medes'; and who never returned from captivity.[47]

Laurence knew he was in the right area. To his mind, the Book of Enoch could *not* have been written in Palestine, but had been composed much further north in the region of Russian Armenia, Georgia or the Caucasus, some 5° north of Iran. Although I had doubts concerning the precise region implied here, I had surmised similar conclusions myself after studying the descriptions of the Watcher-like entities referred to in the Enochian texts. These in no way resembled the olive-skinned Jews of Palestine, but instead conjured the image of tall, fair-skinned individuals with white hair and dark feather coats, surviving in a much cooler climate, like that experienced in more mountainous terrains.

Despite these almost wild assertions he had made, the archbishop could not help but continue to believe that the Book of Enoch *must* have been written by a Jew, but one obviously living in the region under question. As a consequence, he put forward the theory that the text's author had perhaps belonged to one of the ten tribes supposedly deported to Assyria and Media following the fall of Israel in 722 BC.

Such a hypothesis made little sense, although the proposed link between the author of the Book of Enoch and the ancient kingdom of Media did strike some sort of a chord. In the archbishop's day, scholars had no clear understanding of Zoroastrianism, nor could they have conceived of its heavy influence on Jewish religious thought, this fact making Laurence's detailed observations all the more pertinent to my own study. Clearly, then, here was yet further proof that I should look towards Iran, and in particular to the Magi priesthood of Media and the Zoroastrian faith of Persia, for the next set of keys to unlocking the mysteries of the fallen race.

Eight

TERRIBLE LIE

I needed to know everything there was to know about the beliefs, customs and devotional worship of the Zoroastrians. I needed to know whether it had been their teachings, or those of the Magi priesthood of Media, that provided the knowledge for the Judaic understanding of angelology, and in particular the story concerning the fall of the Watchers.

Books could provide me only with background information, and I realized I needed much more. I also needed direct contact with this living religion, which still existed as a faith in certain parts of India, mostly around Bombay. It was to here that tens of thousands of Zoroastrians migrated from Persia during the ninth century AD in the hope of escaping the increasing persecutions of the Arab invaders. In India the Zoroastrians were called Parsees – the people of *pars*, or Persia – and it is by this name that they are still known to the outside world.

I also discovered that at the beginning of the twentieth century a community of Zoroastrians established themselves in London, and here erected a temple of worship which remains in use today. I had obtained their address from a friend, and, after various letters and telephone calls in which I put forward my interest in the subject, was rather reluctantly invited to attend one of their seasonal services at the London address. The Zoroastrians' cloak of secrecy was totally understandable. The ignorant had always seen their beliefs, customs and worship as, at best, non-Christian, pagan and archaic in the extreme, while over the centuries the Muslims of both Iran and India had systematically attempted to eradicate their faith completely. Since the fall of the Shah's Pahlavi regime in 1979, those Zoroastrians still remaining in Iran had been forced either to flee the country or to worship in seclusion away from the eyes of the Islamic authorities. This was why Zoroastrian House in London was surrounded by so much secrecy.

There was much I had already learnt about both the Zoroastrians of Persia and the Magi of Media, but the relevance of this historical information still needed to be assessed in my own mind. Any queries could be put to the elders of the temple, who had agreed to speak to me once the service was over.

The journey to the quiet London suburb was by tube. With me was my research assistant Richard Ward, and a female colleague named Debbie Benstead. Once out of the underground, we quickly found the address I had scribbled hastily on a piece of paper the previous week, and looking up saw a large stone building, with an appearance not unlike a late Victorian church and hall combined. Ascending the front steps we entered a stone-floored lobby, already bubbling with activity. Groups of Asians chatted together in their native Persian and Indian tongues – the men dressed in working suits with white skullcaps on their heads, the women in colourful saris and bright headscarves.

Our white appearance and foreign presence easily revealed us as outsiders, prompting a few nervous glances. In response, we smiled politely and attempted not to contravene any temple etiquette. Dressed as formally as our tastes would allow, we waited for someone to approach, until finally, after one or two almost suspicious looks, a well-to-do Asian broke away from his conversation and moved towards us. He introduced himself as the secretary of the society and, having welcomed us to the temple, checked to make sure that Richard and I had brought skullcaps to wear, and that Debbie had a scarf to cover her hair. Cleanliness and purity was of the utmost importance to their faith, for which reason the head must always be suitably veiled to prevent loose hairs from contaminating the sanctity of the temple.

With our headcovers firmly in place, I engaged the secretary in conversation and foolishly referred to Zoroastrians as 'fire-worshippers'. The man looked sternly towards me and replied curtly: 'We are *not* "fire-worshippers". Many people make this mistake. We *venerate* fire as a symbol of our father, Ahura Mazda.'

I felt like sinking into the ground, and apologized profusely. I should have been more careful with my words. Fire in all its aspects had been sacred to Iranians, before even the birth of Zoroaster, its great prophet whose history was shrouded in mystery and imagination. According to classical sources, Zoroaster lived '258 years before Alexander' – that is 258 years before Alexander the Great destroyed the almighty Persian Empire and sacked its famed white-stone city of Persepolis in 330 BC.[1] This gave a date of 588 BC, although there seemed no real indication whether this was when the great teacher was born; when he received his first visionary revelation at the age of thirty; when he converted his mentor, a central Asian king named Vishtaspa, to his new faith at the age of forty; or when he died at the age of seventy-seven.[2] Nor was there any good reason to suppose that this date meant anything at all, for the creed of Zoroaster, or Zarathustra as he was known to the Iranians, was purely a revitalization of a much older Indo-Iranian religion of immense antiquity, preserved in its fullest extent by the Magian priesthood of Media.

Direct comparisons could be drawn between the material in the *Zend-Avesta*, the sacred writings of Zoroaster (Zend being an ancient Persian language), and the mythology and teachings found in India's oldest work of literature, the *Rig Veda*, which dates to *c.* 1750 BC – a time-frame often ascribed to Zoroaster himself.[3] Other sources have suggested that there were not one but two, three, four or even more prophets of history who each bore the title 'Zarathustra', which struck me as the most sensible solution to the problem.

The Latin writer Justin wrote that Zoroaster was the inventor of magic and that he had made a study of the doctrine of the Magi, who, like their counterparts, the Brahmans of India, venerated fire as the sacred symbol of godhead.[4] According to a Byzantine historian, Gregorius Cedrenus, the Magi were founded by the Hellenic hero Perseus as a cult to guard and protect the sacred immortal fire that burned perpetually in an unknown temple, for he recorded:

Perseus, they say, brought to Persia initiation and magic, which by his secrets made the fire of the sky descend; with the aid of this art, he brought the celestial fire to the earth, and he had it preserved in a temple under the name of the sacred immortal fire; he chose virtuous men as ministers of a new cult, and established the Magi as the depositors and guardians of this fire which they were charged to protect.[5]

Zoroaster was said to have immersed himself in the Magi's strange philosophies and teachings, which included the origin of the universe and the study of astrology and astronomy. Other traditions even claim that Zoroaster was himself a native of Media, and that he had been the *restorer* of the religion of the Magi,[6] in much the same way that Martin Luther 'reformed' the corrupt practices of the Catholic Church.

Very little was known about the true history and religion of the Magi. Once their political power had been suitably curtailed by Darius I, they were confined to more menial duties, such as conducting religious rituals, performing animal sacrifices, interpreting dreams and omens, casting spells and communicating with the spirit world – the actions of *magi*cians in every sense of the word, and it is from this usage that we gain terms such as magic, magician and magus. The Magi are known to have worshipped the very oldest Indo-Iranian deities, such as Ahura, an early form of Ahura Mazda, his son Mithra, and Ardvi Sura Anahita, goddess of the waters; the last two being much later incorporated into the religious festivals of Zoroastrianism, like the one we were about to witness.

As the celebrants began filing their way through to the temple, we followed up behind, smiling politely at those leading the way. Beyond the entrance door was a large auditorium with rows of chairs in two huge aisles, many already occupied by men and women idly chatting between themselves or moving around, as if waiting for the beginning of a theatrical production. Beyond the first row was a raised stage supporting a huge, polished brazier, heaped high with small pieces of dry sandalwood in readiness for the *yasna* festival, as it was known. Around its base were offerings of harvest fruits, milk, wine, water, as well as markers to indicate the four directions. On a beam above the front of the stage was a winged disc in which the Assyrian-style representation of Ahura Mazda stood within a dove-tail plume of feathers.

Before Debbie was able to take a seat, an Asian woman approached her and placed a hand on her shoulder. With a somewhat concerned expression on her face, the woman spoke first in her own language. Then, using broken English and careful hand gestures, she conveyed her message. Debbie quickly realized that she was inquiring whether or not she was menstruating. Like all forms of impurity, menstrual blood is considered offensive to the divine presence of Ahura Mazda. Luckily for Debbie, it was *not* the wrong time of the month, and once she had conveyed this fact to the woman, the exchange of smiles indicated she could take a seat.

As we waited patiently, and somewhat expectantly, for the harvest ceremony to begin, I watched in disbelief as people in the auditorium continued to socialize – walking about and exchanging places as if in a public place. Surely some kind of mental stillness and contemplation ought to precede such an important religious service?

A middle-aged woman sitting in the next row smiled in our direction, as if she wished to engage us in conversation. Not quite knowing what to do or say, I asked about the significance of the festival. Understanding my question, she went and fetched a typewritten sheet containing an itinerary of the evening's proceedings. Presiding over this harvest festival was, it said, *Tir*, the *yazata*, or 'archangel', who in the Zoroastrian calendar governs the month of June, as well as the thirteenth day of each month and the influence of the planet Mercury.[7]

The Persian angel *Tir* is a prime example of how Zoroastrianism has influenced the Judaic understanding of angelology, for in Hebrew mysticism he becomes *Tiriel*, who, like his Persian counterpart, presides over all activities appertaining to the planet Mercury.[8] Similarly to the Essene communities of the Dead Sea, Zoroastrians believe there to be an angel watching over every day, every month, every season and every planet. Indeed, these 'watches' made by the angelic intelligences in respect of terrestrial and celestial cycles of time might well explain the usage of the term *'îr*, 'watcher', in both the Enochian and Dead Sea literature. The Zoroastrian understanding of angels almost certainly stemmed from the Magi, from whom Zoroaster established his own teachings.

The more that I learnt about Iranian mythology and religion, the more I began to realize that it was not so much Zoroastrianism that was going to provide me with any real answers but Magianism, the faith of the Magi. Unfortunately, however, since so little had been preserved of their actual myths and rituals, I could only determine this priestly caste's true significance by studying the religion it had created – Zoroastrianism.

It *was* known, however, that the Magi had recognized two opposing types of supernatural beings – the *ahuras* and the *daevas*. The *ahuras* were seen as shining gods living in a state of heavenly glory, while the *daevas* were looked upon as 'false gods', or 'dark and malignant genii',[9] intimately associated with the affairs of humanity. Indeed, the *daevas* were seen as *ahuras* who had fallen from grace to become earth-bound devils (*dev* or *div* in Persian, from which we get the word *dev*il), 'begotten' of Angra Mainyu, or Ahriman, the 'wicked spirit'.[10] Despite the dark nature of the *daevas*, their name actually derives from the word *devata*, meaning, as in the case of the *ahuras*, the 'Shining Ones'.[11]

Once the Arabs had cut their way across Persia in the seventh century AD, Angra Mainyu became transformed into a character named Eblis, or Iblis – an angel 'born of fire', who was said to have refused to bow down before Adam at the command of God, and as a result had been cast out of heaven. Before his fall through pride, however, Eblis had been known by the name Azazel,[12] the name given to one of the leaders of the Watchers in the Book of Enoch; a strange connection not explained in Islamic myth. In Arabic folklore Eblis was seen as the father of the *divs*, or djinn, and from him sprang the evil Peri (*pari* in Persian, *Pairika* in the *Zend-Avesta*), beautiful angels who disguised 'their malevolence under their charming appearance'.[13]

Tales concerning *divs* proliferate in ancient Iranian mythology, where they are portrayed as essentially human-like, yet of great height with horns, large ears and tails. They were often sorcerers or magicians who possessed 'superior power and intelligence' beyond that of mortal beings. In spite of the fact that they could vanish at will, their clear physical nature was displayed on the battlefield, where they were frequently dispatched by sword or battleaxe.[14]

If one takes away the horns, long ears and tails, which were undoubtedly added at a later stage in the development of these legends to demean the character of the *divs*, then you are left with very human-like individuals. Indeed, a *div* is described as 'a god, or personage of a higher class in the scale of earthly beings'.[15] Although the word here is 'earthly', rather than 'mortal', in my opinion the *divs*' great stature, their superior intelligence and their alleged supernatural capabilities made them prime candidates for the role of progeny of the *daevic* race, comparable with the Nephilim of Judaic tradition.

Belief in the physical reality of *divs* and Peri persisted in Iran right through to the early twentieth century. For instance, in the remote border region between Iran and Afghanistan, close to the Amu Darya (Oxus) river, the Tajik tribesmen spoke of the *divs*, or *divy*, as coming 'down from their mountain lairs during winter to remain near settlements, returning only in spring'.[16] Of equal mystery was the belief among the Tajik tribesmen of the lowlands that beautiful Peri could tempt mortal beings into sin and 'take the form of snakes, turtles and frogs', all creatures under the dominion of Angra Mainyu.[17]

More importantly, there appeared to be some indication from early Zoroastrian sources that a kind of fall of the *ahuras*, or 'shining ones', had preceded the appearance of Zoroaster on earth, for according to one commentator the prophet 'dashed to pieces the bodies of the angels, because they had made an evil use of them for wandering on the earth, and especially for amatory dealings with earthly women'.[18] These were the words of nineteenth-century biblical scholar Franz Delitzsch, who fully recognized the extraordinary similarity between this account and the improprieties committed by the Watchers in the Book of Enoch.

The *Ameshâ Spentas* of Iranian lore are undoubtedly to be equated, not just with the seven archangels, but also with the seven *adityas*, or *suryas*, found in the Hindu *Rig Veda*; one of whom, the sun god, is named as Surya. Ancient Indian myth and legend records that the *suryas*' evil enemies were the *ahuras* (spelt *asuras*), who were giants, skilled in the magical arts. Like the Watchers of the Book of Enoch, the Vedic *ahuras* were condemned for having misused the secret wisdom of the gods – casting them in the role of malevolent spirits comparable with the fallen angels of Judaeo-Christian tradition.[19] By coincidence,

Surya also happened to be one of the names of Metatron, the angelic form adopted by Enoch after his translation to heaven.[20] Moreover, some Ethiopian manuscripts of the Book of Enoch give the archangels prefixes such as *'Asarya*, *'Asurye* and *Suryân*,[21] clearly confirming the powerful relationship between Judaism and the Indo-Iranian myths found in both the *Zend-Avesta* and the *Rig Veda*.[22]

I was getting closer, but I still needed further evidence of the relationship between the concept of Watchers and the ancient Iranian belief in the fallen *ahuras*, or *daevas*, corrupting humanity. Perhaps the answers I was looking for could be found within the sacred books of the Zoroastrians.

Suddenly my thoughts were distracted. The constant, low babble permeating the busy auditorium had been broken by the sound of tinkling bells, played in specific sequences. The strange cacophony came from a closed room positioned behind the seated audience. Soon afterwards five priests entered into view, all dressed in long, white linen robes, with white waist cords, white skullcaps and long white muslin masks across their noses and mouths. They walked briskly in single file towards the stage, continually chanting prayers as they went. Having ascended to the level of the fire brazier, a huge overhead extractor fan was switched on by unseen hands. One priest immediately began to kindle a low fire in the enormous brass container, as further pieces of sandalwood and spoonfuls of frankincense were added to the flickering flames. The thick, wafting incense charged the air with a sharp, overbearing aroma that was both unique and vibrant.

Having sat in a circle on the floor around the blazing fire, the fire priests joined hands and began saying prayers and hymns taken from the *Zend-Avesta*. Each one chanted over the voices of his fellow supplicants, without co-ordination or harmony, to produce an enchanting yet discordant babel I had never before experienced in a religious ceremony.

Every so often the priests would pass a small white flower between themselves. It was offered with both hands, which were then grasped by a neighbour's hands. The first priest would then remove his hands to leave behind the flower, before completing the gesture by briefly cupping the second priest's hands with his own.

On other occasions all five supplicants would join hands and link with the flame of truth by means of a ritual poker placed in the fire by one of the priests; a connection that seemed essential to the success of the ceremony.

Once in a while members of the audience would reach for their own battered copies of the *Zend-Avesta* and begin half-heartedly reciting certain *gathas*, before giving up and talking with their neighbours.

The *Zend-Avesta* is the Zoroastrians' most sacred text, but there are other books of equal importance. One of these is the *Bundahishn*, a sacred text written in the late Persian language of Pahlavi. Among its many themes is a unique creation myth, in which the stalk of the sacred rhubarb plant grows and grows until it divides to form two separate human beings – *Masya* and *Masyanag*, the father and mother of the mortal race.[23] The couple exist in a state of purity, but are then seduced by Angra Mainyu[24] (the *daevas* in one account[25]). As a consequence of this seduction, the first couple give worship to him (or them) and not Ahura Mazda, named in the text as 'Ormuzd'. In so doing these first mortals are deprived of their original purity, which neither they, nor any of their descendants, are able to recover unless through the aid of Mithra, the deity who presides over the salvation of the soul.

The Zoroastrians believe that since the first couple committed the carnal sin in thought, word and deed, both they and their descendants became tainted for ever. In spite of the fact that the *Bundahishn* dates only to a time when their forebears first migrated from Iran to India in the ninth century, the text is thought to be based on a now lost Zend original of great antiquity.[26]

In many ways the creation story presented in the *Bundahishn* might be compared directly with the story of the Fall of Man found in the Book of Genesis. Yet even more remarkable is the knowledge that, in some Persian teachings, Angra Mainyu is known as 'the old serpent having two feet',[27] words that immediately conjured an image of Belial, the Watcher with a 'visage like a viper' found in the Testament of Amram.

I would not be the first person to spot the obvious comparisons between the Persian and Hebrew accounts of the Fall of Man. As early as 1888 C. Staniland Wake, in his ground-breaking work,

Serpent-Worship and Other Essays, admitted, after discussing the similarities between the two quite separate myths, that:

The Persian account of the fall and its consequences agrees so closely with the Hebrew story when stripped of its figurative language that we cannot doubt that they refer to the same legend, and the use of figurative language in the latter may well lead us to believe that it was of later date than the former [*i.e. the* Bundahishn].[28]

There is every reason to believe that the Judaic concept of the Fall of Man, the Serpent of Temptation and the fall of the angels derive either directly or indirectly from Zoroastrian or pre-Zoroastrian sources. The serpent of the *Bundahishn is* Angra Mainyu, who *is* therefore the figurative form of the *daevas* (or fallen *ahuras*) who seduce humanity at the time of the Fall, just as the Serpent of Temptation *is* the personification of Belial, Shemyaza or Azazel, the names given to the leader of the Watchers in Enochian and Dead Sea religious literature.

The Law of the Daevas

It was intriguing to think of the prophet Mani rediscovering the Book of Enoch, as well as other lesser-known Enochian literature, during the third century of the Christian era and then reintroducing it back into the newly resurrected Persian Empire both in translation and within his own heretical teachings. These he had carried as far east as central Asia, one of the traditional homes of his predecessor, the prophet Zoroaster. If the legends of the Watchers had originated in ancient Iran, then Mani was taking them back to their own heartland some seven hundred years after they were originally carried into Judaea by the returning Jewish exiles. Could Mani have been aware of the Persian origin of these traditions? Might this have been why he recognized in them the doctrine of truth? If so, then why were Mani and his Manichaean followers so horrendously persecuted by fanatical Zoroastrians, who publicly humiliated his body following the prophet's inevitable death at Jund-i-Shapur, near Susa in south-west Persia, during the year AD 277?

The answer almost certainly lay in the fact that during his ministry on earth Zoroaster is said to have preached out fervently against the *daevo-data*, 'the law according to the *daevas*'.[29] This was the 'law' accepted and promoted by those individuals who, instead of choosing the true path of Ahura Mazda, adhered to the deceitful ways of the *karapans* (priests) and the *kavis* (prince-priests). Although these terms were loosely used to refer to any non-Zoroastrian priest; they especially denoted the Magi priests of Media,[30] whose principal philosophies featured the eternal struggles between the *ahuras* and the *daevas*. Although the Magi accepted the supremacy of Ahura, the prototype of Ahura Mazda, they also made sacrifices to Angra Mainyu, showing their spiritual allegiance to the Prince of Darkness as well.[31]

Such blasphemies made the Magi and their followers the children of Angra Mainyu, supporters of the *druj* – 'falsehood' or 'the Lie'. In effect, they were accused of being liars for accepting and preaching such unholy matters. So vehemently did Zoroaster, and presumably all orthodox Zoroastrians, hate followers of the Lie, that in one ancient text the prophet had this to say about those who accepted the law of the *daevas*:

Whether a man dispose of much or little wealth, he should show kindness to the follower of Truth, but should be evil to the follower of the Lie . . .[32] *(for the man) who is most good to the follower of the Lie is himself a follower of the Lie.*[33]

In other words, those who dared even to listen to the Lie taught by the Magian priests would themselves become followers of the Lie. It was almost as if the Zoroastrians wanted to make sure that no one should even *want* to listen to the terrible Lie being told by the Magi, for fear that it might corrupt their opinions, and in so doing make them followers of the Lie themselves. Such an extreme, fundamental attitude towards the teachings of a rival faith is quite bizarre. It almost conjures up the image of a Magi priest approaching a Zoroastrian who, in fear that he might be told the terrible Lie, covers his ears and says: 'No, I don't want to hear it – it's a lie. I know it's a lie.'

Exactly what sort of 'Lie' could have made a great prophet like Zoroaster so want to prevent his followers from even hearing it?

Was it something he had heard the Magi say when he himself had studied their religion, before embarking on his own career as a teacher of righteousness?

What was it that Zoroaster had tried to hide?

What was the terrible Lie?

Surely it cannot have concerned the Magi's religious practices, or their knowledge of astrology and astronomy. These would not have caused the type of consternation implied by Zoroaster's fanatical attitude towards their teachings. It seems more likely that he was directing these accusations at their belief in the *daevo-data*, 'the law according to the *daevas*'. The fact that the Magi had sacrificed animals in the name of Angra Mainyu must have meant that they never denounced his progeny, the *daevas*, as evil. Far from it, for it would appear that they saw them as equal in power to the *ahuras*, with a role to play in both the religion of Iran and the affairs of humanity.

Even if this solution is correct, then surely such dualistic principles should never have posed such a terrible threat to the teachings of Zoroaster and his followers. There must have been more to it than this – something that made them want to persecute anyone who even contemplated listening to such 'falsehood'. Might the Lie have been more shocking than history has implied?

Was it possible that the Magi believed the material world to be the domain of Angra Mainyu, because the *daevas* had planted their seeds of evil among humanity by revealing the secret wisdom of the *ahuras*? The story in the *Bundahishn* of the corruption of the first couple confirms the existence of such a view in Zoroastrian thought. Even further supporting this supposition is the knowledge that the mark of the Magi is to be found in many parts of the *Bundahishn*, showing their influence on its final construction, either in its lost Zend original or in the surviving Pahlavi version.[34]

The fanatical persecution of Mani and his followers seems to be a revealing example of how fundamental Zoroastrians reacted to someone *resurrecting* the terrible Lie once told by the Magi priests, the followers of *daevo-data*.

I wondered just how many Zoroastrians participating in this seasonal festival were aware of the transgressions of the *daevas*, or of the persecution of those who had once taught about their corruption of humanity? As in the case of Jews, Christians and Muslims, such matters did not feature in their day-to-day worship, and so are unlikely to have been known to them.

The *yasna* festival we attended continued for over an hour and a half, with no real change in the proceedings. Occasionally men and women would approach the stage, pick up a small piece of cut sandalwood from a low pile supplied for this purpose, then hand it to the fire-priest. He would acknowledge their presence before placing their offering among the lapping flames. It appeared to be a means of ensuring good fortune, in much the same way as a Catholic or Orthodox Christian might light a small candle and leave it burning in a church.

At other times, members of the audience would walk around, talking to each other and doing their own thing, seemingly oblivious to what was taking place on the stage before them. This apparent irreverence was most disconcerting, especially as we ourselves could do little more than sit in silent awe for the duration of the service. Yet simply being here instilled in us an overwhelming sense of privilege and humility. Here was a fire ritual that probably dated beyond the origins of the Magi to the mists of antiquity, perhaps even to a time when the fallen *ahuras*, the Shining Ones of Indo-Iranian myth, once walked the earth.

With the festival over, Richard, Debbie and myself were taken into the society's library room and asked to put our questions to the secretary and an Iranian scholar, who was a member of the respected Royal Asiatic Society. They listened carefully to my queries concerning Zoroastrian angelology and directed me to various rare out-of-print books on the subject. Unfortunately, they themselves were unable to help me with my research, though they did speak of traditions connecting the prophet Enoch with the region of Cappadocia in eastern Anatolia, the details of which they promised to send me by return post (they never arrived).

Afterwards the three of us were invited to join a communal meal in a canteen area on the same floor as the temple. We were provided with a welcome vegetarian curry and listened to stories of clandestine Zoroastrian services currently taking place within underground temples in Iran. At one point an over-zealous woman approached our table and began sprinkling holy water in our direction – a sign, it would seem, that we had been accepted into their fold, for one night at least.

We left Zoroastrian House, our heads buzzing with the rich imagery surrounding the strange religious festival we had been allowed to witness. We were not invited back, and in many ways there has never been any need for a second visit.

Somehow I felt I was correct to compare the dualistic elements of the Magian faith with the story of the Watchers. Yet to investigate the matter more fully I needed further evidence of the apparent trafficking between the semi-divine *daevas* and mortal kind, like that so vividly described in Hebrew myth and legend. If this could be found, then it would strengthen the case in favour of an Iranian origin for the Judaic legends of the fall of the angels, and help to explain why the Zoroastrians had become so terrified of the sheer potency of the Lie. This I was to eventually discover; not, however, in the holy books of the Zoroastrians, or among the lost teachings of the Magi, but in a place that I would have considered to be a most unlikely source indeed – in the *Shahnameh*, the legendary history of the Iranian kings.

Nine

BORN OF THE DEMON RACE

Firdowsi was an Arab poet who lived in the eleventh century. He was born in the Islamic province of Tus, or Khurasan, in eastern Persia and came from a family of established landowners. He is best remembered for a book he finished in 1010 AD entitled the *Shahnameh*, or the Book of Kings, which records the legendary history of his country. This he had gained not just from earlier versions of the same stories now lost, but from other similarly lost histories of the Persian race recorded during the Sassanian, or second, empire period, between the third and seventh centuries AD.

These stories include the legendary foundation of the Iranian royal dynasties and the deeds of the earliest kings and their families, as they battled with demons, rival kingdoms, domestic conflicts and political struggles. There is romance, heartbreak, courage, valour and heroics within the pages of the *Shahnameh*, as well as much of interest to my understanding of the fallen race. No one knew exactly when or where the scenarios described in this ancient work might have taken place, if at all. Even though historians have attempted to place specific dates on the succession of divine kings it portrays, it is quite clear that the book's assortment of stories must be assigned either to a distant age or to a world of pure myth and fantasy.

The *Shahnameh* begins with an account of the legendary Kiyumars, the first of the Pishdadian line of kings, who is known by the name Gayomartan or Gayomard in the Avestan literature of the Zoroastrians. He rules from his seat in the mountains as a king of Iran and all the world during a Golden Age of high spiritual and religious values. Yet, like so many of the stories told by Firdowsi, his reign ends in tragedy, in this case with the death of his son, Siyamak, who is killed by a *div*, or 'black demon'.[1]

Siyamak's own son, Husheng (the Haoshanha of Avestan literature), then becomes 'king of the seven climes' or regions of the world. He is the founder of civilization and the discoverer of fire, which he uses to separate iron from rock to become the primordial blacksmith, able to fashion tools and weapons. He is also accredited with the introduction of land irrigation and the sowing of seeds.[2]

In the hundreds of years that follow, kings rise and fall and the exploits of each are outlined in graphic detail. Then the *Shahnameh* enters a long phase of prehistory in which constant wars are waged between Iran and the kingdom of Turan in central Asia. It is during this troubled period of humanity that many great battles are fought and various heroic deeds enacted.[3] It is also during this same phase of pseudo-history that some of the most baffling material begins to surface within its pages – material that appears to echo exactly the stories found in both the Book of Enoch and the Dead Sea Scrolls.

The Miraculous Birth of Zal

The reader of the *Shahnameh* is introduced to a new sub-dynasty of kings, said to have ruled in a region named Sistan, thought to have been in eastern Iran – although geographical connections with the real world are of little value here (see Chapter 11). The first story of importance concerns a king named Sam, the son of Nariman. He marries a beautiful woman who becomes pregnant and gives birth to a boy. Yet, on the child's exposure to the outside world, her husband's cries of joy change to sheer horror and revulsion as he realizes the infant's unearthly appearance: his body is said to have been 'as clean as silver';[4] his hair is described as being 'as white as an old man's', and 'like snow';[5] his face is 'like paradise' and as 'beautiful as the sun';[6] his eyes are black; his cheeks are 'ruddy and beautiful'[7] 'like the rose of spring', while his form is as 'straight as (a) cypress tree'.[8]

Fearful of this ill-omen, the child's mother decides on the spot to name him Zal, meaning 'the aged'.[9] Sam, on the other hand, is persuaded that this infant is not his own but the 'son of some deev (*daeva*) or magician (i.e. a Magi)'.[10] People soon gather to witness the strange sight for themselves, saying to Sam, 'This is an ominous event, and will be to thee productive of nothing but calamity – it would be better if thou couldst remove him out of sight,' for as the text continues:

> *No human being of this earth*
> *Could give to such a monster birth;*
> *He must be of the Demon race,*
> *Though human still in form and face,*
> *If not a Demon, he, at least,*
> *Appears a party-coloured beast.*[11]

Sam makes a passionate plea to Ahura Mazda, asking for what reason he has been given 'a demon-child' that 'resembles a child of Ahriman' and who is 'an entire Peri' of 'the religion of Ahriman'.[12] One can almost sense the sheer distress experienced by Sam and his family at the birth of this strange infant with such pronounced physiological features. To them this birth is seen as a punishment for some unknown crime they have committed. No one can understand what is going on or why this child should so closely resemble one of the *daevic* race.

For Sam and his family the sight they beheld that fateful day was quite abhorrent, but to me a sense of *déjà vu* crept quickly through my veins, for the account of the birth of Zal was almost identical to the miraculous birth of Noah presented in the Book of Enoch. The similarities were too striking to ignore:

Zal is described as having a body 'as clean as silver' with 'ruddy' cheeks 'like the rose of spring'. Noah is described as having a body as 'white as snow and red as a rose'.[13]

Zal is described as having hair 'as white as an old man's', and 'like snow', while Noah is described as having hair 'as white as wool'.[14]

Zal is described as having a face 'like paradise' and 'as beautiful as the sun', while Noah's eyes are said to have 'glowed like the sun'.[15]

Zal is described as 'a demon-child', 'an entire Peri' and the 'son' or 'child of Ahriman' or 'some deev (*daeva*) or magician', while

Noah is described as looking like 'the children of the (fallen) angels of heaven', whose 'conception was (due) to the Watchers . . . and to the Nephilim'.[16]

The only additional information not contained in the Hebrew account of Noah's birth is Zal's black eyes and his appearance as a 'party-coloured beast', or a 'two-coloured leopard' in other accounts – metaphors probably linked to the belief among the Persians that leopards' skins worn by the earliest Pishdadian kings signified 'courage and manhood'.[17]

Somehow there had to be a direct link between the account of the ominous birth of Zal recorded in the *Shahnameh* and the strange birth of Noah recorded in the Book of Enoch. One appeared to have been based on the other, but which had influenced which? Since I had already established that Iranian mythology and religion had helped form post-exilic Judaism, including the Enochian and Dead Sea literature, there seemed every reason to suppose it was the Persian story that had influenced the Judaic variation, and not the other way round. The only other possibility was to suggest that a much older primary source was responsible for *both* stories. If so, then where was this primary source?

All of this was revealing information indeed. Here in the *Shahnameh* was a legend which implied that in ancient Iran, perhaps the place of origin of the Book of Enoch, a new-born child bearing specific physiological characteristics was looked upon as the result of an unholy union between a fallen angel, or demon, and a mortal woman, even though on this occasion there were no accusations of infidelity made against Sam's wife and consort.

Yet why should an infant bearing such seemingly mundane physical characteristics have appeared so abhorrent to the ruling dynasty of Iran? Were new-born infants the world over cast as demon-spawn, or the result of supernatural cohabitation, simply because of their distinctive physical features, or had this belief been confined to Iran alone? The antediluvian patriarchs of the Old Testament would seem to have had a very similar aversion to infants born with what appear to have been extreme white Caucasian features, while the concept of angel children bearing similar traits is known to have persisted in Western culture right down to the twentieth century.

The birth of Zal was perfect confirmation of the clear relationship between the Iranian belief in the corruption of mankind by the *daevas* and the fall of the Watchers in Judaic tradition. There was, however, much more of direct relevance to this debate in the eventful life of Zal, the son of Sam, than simply his birth . . .

Compassion of the Simurgh

In the knowledge that the infant Zal resembles the appearance of the *daevas*, Sam makes the immediate decision to rid himself of this demon-child by depositing him on the slopes of a mountain named Elburz, where he will be devoured by the beasts of prey and the birds of the air. Mount Elburz also happened to be the abode ('kingdom' in one account) of a fabulous bird, 'a noble vulture',[18] known as the Simurgh, whose gender varies from one account to another. In search of food for its young, the hungry Simurgh espies the young child lying among the rocks, crying and sucking on its fingers. Yet, instead of devouring the infant, the bird shows overwhelming compassion and carries it to its nest, high on the mountain, where the Simurgh's own children eagerly await their mother's return. They, too, are kind and affectionate to the mortal child, which is nourished and protected by the Simurgh until it grows to become a fine youth. Some accounts suggest that the bird intended feeding Zal to its young, but that after depositing it on the ground the voice of Ahura Mazda asked the Simurgh to take care of the child, for one day he would bring forth 'from his loins . . . the champion of the world'.[19]

The years go by, and in time Sam mourns the loss of his ill-formed child, whom he assumes to be dead. Then, after a dream-vision that suggests his son is still alive, the king embarks on an unsuccessful journey to find him. A second dream follows, and with renewed vigour Sam makes another journey to Elburz. Having ascended to the top of the mountain, he prays before the throne of Ahura Mazda, saying:

'If that forsaken child be truly mine,
And not the progeny of Demon fell,

('not from the sperm of the ill-descended Ahriman'[20]*)*
O pity me! forgive the wicked deed,
And to my eyes, my injured son restore.'[21]

The Simurgh, having heard the lamentations of Sam, knows it must now return the youth it has protected 'like a nurse' and 'like a father', and to whom it has given the name Dustan. Zal, on learning of his imminent departure, weeps in the knowledge that he is to be separated from the Simurgh and its family, for not only had the mysterious bird protected him, it had also taught him many knowledgeable things, including the language and wisdom of his own country. The Simurgh consoles the youth by saying that it will not abandon him completely. As proof of this affection, the bird plucks a feather from a wing and proclaims: 'Whenever thou are involved in difficulty or danger, put this feather (or "feathers"[22]) on the fire, and I will instantly appear to thee to ensure thy safety. Never cease to remember me.'[23]

Then, in a touching scene, the Simurgh returns Zal to Sam, who blesses both the youth and the 'wonderful bird'. He also admits his shame at having abandoned the child in the first place, and says he will endeavour to redeem himself by treating the boy with the utmost respect and honour he deserves.

Zal grows to become a handsome prince and in time falls in love with a foreign princess, named Rudabeh, the daughter of Mehrab, the 'king of Kabul', and a descendant of the serpent king Zahhak (Azhi Dahâka in Avestan literature), who was said to have ruled Iran for a thousand years (see Chapter 14).

In one account, Mehrab's daughter is described, in the words of one of her slave-girls to one of Zal's own slaves, as 'a handsome beauty who outtops your king by a head. In figure she resembles the teak-tree, though she is like ivory for whiteness, and her face is crowned with a diadem of musk . . . It would be proper, and very suitable, for Rudaba to become the wife of Zal.'[24] In another description of the princess, it is said of her that from 'head to foot she is white as ivory; her face is a very paradise and for stature she is as a plane-tree'.[25]

These special qualities were obviously seen as unique, and for Rudabeh to have out-topped Zal – who was himself of 'cypress-stature'[26] – by 'a head', would presumably have made her an extremely tall woman. Indeed, there seems every indication that Zal and Rudabeh were purposely brought together because they each bore very specific qualities that were deemed necessary to perpetuate the existing line of divine kings.

Inevitably, Zal takes Rudabeh's hand in marriage, and in time she falls pregnant. But prior to the birth of her child, the foreign beauty begins experiencing 'unbearable pains of childbirth',[27] for as Firdowsi explains:

The cypress leaf was withering; pale she lay,
Unsoothed by rest or sleep, death seemed approaching.[28]

In desperation Zal recalls the feather given to him by the Simurgh, and so burns it on a fire. 'In a moment darkness surrounded them, which was, however, immediately dispersed by the sudden appearance of the Simurgh.'[29] The 'kind nurse'[30] consoles Zal by saying that he is soon to become the father of a son 'with the height of a cypress tree and the strength of an elephant'.[31] Furthermore, the great bird proclaims that:

'*. . . the child will not come into existence by the ordinary way of birth. Bring me a poniard of tempered steel and a man of percipient heart versed in incantation. Let the girl be given* [an intoxicating] *drug* [prescribed by the Simurgh[32]] *to stupefy her and to dull any fear or anxiety in her mind: then keep guard while the clairvoyant* [i.e. hypnotist] *recites his incantations and so watch until the lion-boy leaves the vessel which contains him. The wizard will pierce the frame of the young woman without her awareness of any pain and will draw the lionchild out of her, covering her flank with blood, and will sew together the part he has cut . . . There is a herb which I will describe to you. Pound it together with milk and musk and place it in a dry shady place. Afterwards spread it over the wound and you will perceive at once how she has been delivered from peril. Over it all then pass one of my feathers and the shadow of my royal potency will have achieved a happy result.*'[33]

Zal does as the bird directs and as a result 'the giant child was cut from the side of his mother, who immediately she had given birth, exclaimed, "Ba-Rastam" – I am relieved.' From this sudden outburst, the infant was given the name Rustam, meaning 'strong growth'.[34] Afterwards Rudabeh quickly regains her health, thanks to the special healing herb prescribed by the Simurgh, leaving the child to become indisputably Iran's greatest legendary hero.

This is the story of the birth of Rustam as presented in the *Shahnameh.*

There can be little doubt that the infant's unnatural birth harbours extraordinary insights into not only the legendary history of Iran but also the Enochian religious literature of Judaic tradition.

One is immediately reminded of the Ethiopian *Kebra Nagast*, where the Daughters of Cain give birth to gigantic Nephilim babies through the process of Caesarian section. Can it be coincidence that a child of Iranian myth and legend is born into the world in exactly the same manner as the mighty Nephilim? Caesarian section takes its name from Julius Caesar, alleged to have been the first child delivered in this way.[35] Yet here were two quite separate examples of this medical practice being employed in unknown epochs of human history, perhaps thousands of years before the coming of the Romans.

From the tales presented in the *Shahnameh* there appeared to be compelling evidence to suggest that the ancient Iranians really did believe that the *daevas* could not only possess physical form, but that they could also lie with mortal women to produce offspring with physical characteristics that matched, almost exactly, the progeny of the Watchers in Hebraic tradition. To me it was a remarkable discovery, and one that made it all the more likely that the *daevo-data*, 'the law according to the *daevas*', as taught by the Magi priests, did indeed involve knowledge of the carnal trafficking between supernatural beings and mortal kind. It also strengthened my view that the Magi's dualistic doctrine included the belief that the world around us was the creation not of Ahura Mazda but of Angra Mainyu, the 'wicked spirit' – the very tenet of faith preached by Mani and the various gnostic cults many hundreds of years after the *daeva*-worshipping Magi disappeared from the pages of history.

The Glorious House of Sam and Nariman

The mention of Mani with respect to these traditions is also of extreme relevance, for he appears to be able to provide us with even further clues concerning the clear overlap between Iranian myth and Enochian literature. The Manichaeans are known to have translated into various different Asian languages one particular Enochian text concerning the plight of the Nephilim. As this was done, the original Aramaic names of key characters were replaced by those of specific Iranian figures who feature in the *Shahnameh*. For example, in Persian tradition Zal's father is Sam, while Sam's own father is Nariman; the descendants of these mythical kings being referred to as the 'glorious house of Sam and Nariman'.[36] This patrilineal relationship between the two royal figures is matched in Mani's translations of the Enochian literature where the two visionary sons of the fallen angel Shemyaza are given as Sam and Nariman in place of their original Aramaic names of 'Ohyâ and 'Ahyâ.

The usage of these two quite specific names from the *Shahnameh* seems to imply that Mani saw the Iranian royal dynasty of Sam and Nariman as direct descendants of Shemyaza, the leader of the Watchers. Since this kingly line included both Zal and Rustam, who both possessed the physiological features of the fallen race, this supposition was not to be taken lightly.

What might Mani have known about the relationship between Iranian myth and the stories concerning the fall of the Watchers, as well as the birth of Nephilim children and their final destruction in the cataclysms of fire and water? He cannot have been unaware of the clear parallels between the stories surrounding the miraculous birth of Noah and the strange birth of Zal, the son of Sam. How much did this influence him to name the sons of Shemyaza as Sam and Nariman, after the great Iranian heroes who bore these selfsame names? Perhaps Mani had been aware of independent, now lost traditions linking the house of Nariman and Sam with the fall of the *ahuras*.

Scholars have thrown no obvious light on the matter, though W. B. Henning, the linguistic expert who collated the various fragments of Enochian text translated by Mani and his followers, did have this to say: 'the translation of Ohya as Sam had in its train the introduction of myths appertaining to that Iranian hero (of this name)'.[37] In other words, Mani chose these names so that he could *deliberately* introduce these characters to Enochian literature. Why?

Henning also pointed out that in some Manichaean fragments of Enochian material the name Sam is rendered *S'hm*,[38] an interesting observation since in Hebrew *shm* means 'name', 'pillar' or 'high'. It is also the name of one of Noah's sons, as well as the root behind the first part of the name *Shem*yaza. Furthermore, the suffix *yaza* is so closely linked to the Zend word *yazd* or *yazata*, meaning 'angel', or divine being, that there seemed every possibility that the name Shemyaza stemmed originally from Iranian sources.

The Divine Glory

Yet the biggest mystery seemed to be why giant babies, with demon-like characteristics, should at first be abhorred by their immediate family, but then go on to become the greatest heroes or teachers of their age; the cases of Zal and Noah being prime examples. A clue appeared to lie in the metaphors and synonyms used to describe the otherworldly features of these chosen ones. Zal, for instance, is said to have been as 'straight as (a) cypress tree', while Rustam is described as having 'the height of a cypress tree'. This usage of the cypress tree – an evergreen with tall, dark plumes that once grew abundantly on mountain-sides in the Near East – to denote immense stature also appears earlier on in the *Shahnameh*. For instance, Kiyumars, the first king of Iran and 'ruler over the whole world', was said to have reigned from his palace in the mountains like 'a two weeks old moon shining over a slender cypress',[39] while Feridun, the king who finally vanquished the serpent king Zahhak, is said to have been 'as tall' and 'as beautiful as a slender cypress'.[40] The similarity between this metaphor and the reference to Watchers as 'trees' in the Enochian literature was surely no coincidence.

Zal's face is described as 'like paradise' and 'beautiful as the sun', while his queen, Rudabeh, is said to have had a face that was 'a very paradise', references, it would seem, to their shining countenances – matching the Hebrew metaphor in which the faces of both the Watchers and their offspring are said to have glowed 'like the sun'. This same expression is also used in the *Shahnameh* to describe the brilliance that shone from the face of Kiyumars, as well as another king named Jemshid.[41] Here, however, the strange supernatural effect is explained, for according to Firdowsi it was created by the presence of the so-called *khvarnah*, or Kingly Fortune, also known as the *farr-i izadi* (or *farr-i yazdan*), the Glory of God. This is a concept based on the firm belief that some kind of divine essence, or manifestation, could be transmitted through the rightful family chosen by Ahura Mazda.[42] With this holy essence Jemshid was said to have been able to 'mould iron into such equipment as helmets, chain-mail, laminated armour as well as missile-proof vests, to swords and horse-armour',[43] while at the same time it provided him with intimate knowledge of God. Most peculiar of all, 'with the aid of the royal *farr* he fashioned a marvellous throne', which henceforth became his seat of sovereignty.[44]

Nobody knows what the royal *farr* might actually have been, for in one sentence it is a magical power able to forge metal, in the next it is the manifestation of God himself, and finally it is a means of carving hard substances without the use of conventional tools. One thing is for certain, though: without the Divine Glory a king could not reign. Jemshid, for example, eventually loses his *farr* because he 'ceases to believe in a higher power and regards himself as the only and ultimate ruler'.[45] Everybody abandons him – his priests, his army and the people, while the world outside is thrown into utter confusion and discord, ushering in an age of human history when evil, in the form of the 'wicked spirit', Angra Mainyu, is able to control the destiny of humanity.

In the *Zend-Avesta*, Jemshid is equated with an important figure named Yima, a 'king of Paradise', who ruled over the entire world (see Chapter Twenty). He, too, loses the Divine Glory, this time because he finds 'delight in the words of falsehood and untruth'. As a result of this sin, 'the Glory was seen to flee away from him in the shape of a bird' named Varaghna.[46]

Jemshid, or Yima, never regains the Divine Glory, ending his seven-hundred-year reign. The next Iranian hero to possess its magical power is Feridun, the 'slender cypress', of whom it was said the 'royal *farr* radiated from him'.[47]

So what did all this mean? What did the Divine Glory actually represent?

It would appear that, to become a rightful king or hero in Iranian legend, the successful candidate needed to possess certain specific qualities, including great height and a divine countenance, seen as the royal *farr*; indeed, Zoroaster himself was said to have been born with a shining radiance and is depicted with such in at least one stone relief.[48] Was it not curious that both these physiological features were originally associated with the *ahuras*, the Iranian equivalent of the Watchers, who in Indo-Iranian myth were said to have been 'shining' gods of great stature?

In Persian art of all periods, the Divine Glory was generally depicted as a large ring or diadem held by Ahura Mazda, who is shown offering it to one of the kings of Persia, as if to confirm their divine right to rule. Because the diadem finally became the sole representation of the Divine Glory, it seems probable that this concept heavily influenced the rise in importance of the crown in Eurasian beliefs and customs concerning sovereignty and kingship. In other words, the usage of a crown to symbolize the right of a king to rule may well have developed from the shining countenances once associated with the faces of the fallen race.

If these wild assertions were in any way correct, then it implied that, just occasionally, certain infants may have been born with pronounced physiological features that bore *too* close a resemblance to the original 'shining' race, and so were cast out as *direct* progeny of the fallen *ahuras*. In time, however, these traits would have been genetically watered down and misunderstood to such a degree that, in Iran at least, they simply became the necessary qualities of a true divine king, descended of Kiyumars, the first Iranian monarch. Even later these physical traits would have become purely symbolic, with legendary figures such as Zoroaster being posthumously accredited them, simply because it was deemed necessary for a rightful prophet, king or hero of Persia to have possessed such virtues during their own life-time.

The accounts in the Book of Daniel of Watcher-like figures

with shining faces are prime examples of how strongly these concepts must have been adopted by the exiled Jews in Persia, for they do not appear in Judaic tradition until after the period of exile in Susa. To the Hebrews, the presence of such holy qualities would appear to have been viewed a little differently. In their opinion, only a true patriarch or teacher of righteousness, descended of the line of Seth, would have possessed a shining countenance; probably the reason why biblical figures such as Abraham, Elijah, Enoch and Noah were all accredited with having both a facial radiance[49] and great stature[50] in post-exilic apocrypha and folklore.

In much later Christian and Islamic iconography, the divine countenance would have been seen in terms of the halo or nimbus depicted around the heads of angels, saints and holy men; its original meaning having long since been lost. The best example of this style of art is provided by Christ himself, who is often portrayed in Nativity scenes welcoming the three Magi with a shining radiance 'as brilliantly as if covered with phosphuretted oil', or so wrote the nineteenth-century Hebrew scholar Thomas Inman.[51] Little could he have known how these inspired words might turn out to be closer to the mark than he ever thought possible.

Yet somehow the belief in a shining countenance associated with infants born of the angels would appear to have lingered right down to twentieth-century London. The account told to Margaret Norman by her mother of the 'angel child', whose face 'just shone', is a perfect example of this survival. So if such beautiful countenances were once a sign of the 'shining' angelic race, then did this imply that the royal *farr* bestowed upon the legendary kings of Iran had some basis in reality? If so, then how on earth was it able to fashion metal, carve ivory without the use of conventional tools and know God? Might the *farr* have involved some kind of secret knowledge passed down from generation to generation, like that provided to the Daughters of Men by the Watchers? Were the royal dynasties of ancient Iran really blood-line descendants of the *ahuras* and *daevas*, the Shining Ones who fell from grace in Indo-Iranian myth?

Even if a quite obviously unique race of shining appearance and tall stature had once walked the earth, then to try and find them so many thousands of years after their assumed demise seemed an almost impossible task.

There was, however, one vital clue . . .

In the *Shahnameh*, the Simurgh bird features in both the story of the strange birth of Zal and the delivery of his huge son Rustam. This extraordinary creature could act as a nurse and teacher to mortal children. It could be a physician to rightful kings. It could prescribe intoxicating drugs and herbs that anaesthetized pregnant women and healed open wounds. It could also advise on the delivery of giant babies through the process known today as Caesarian section.

How many birds do you know that possess such diverse capabilities?

Clearly, such a 'wonderful' creature was worthy of further investigation.

I felt that somehow this 'noble vulture' would bring me closer to unravelling the mysteries surrounding the origins of the fallen race – but only if I was to accept that the Simurgh may have been not a bird at all but a human being adorned in feathers.

Ten

ON THE EDGE OF DEATH

Evidence to suggest that the 'fabulous bird' Simurgh – nurse, physician and personal adviser to the legendary kings of Iran – had been a human being in disguise was not difficult to find. In one edition of the *Shahnameh*, the footnotes accompanying the story in which the great bird tends the needs of the infant Zal on Mount Elburz explained that 'the fable simply meant a holy recluse of the mountains, who nourished and educated the poor child which had been abandoned by its father'.[1] A holy recluse who impersonates 'a noble vulture' and dresses as a great bird? Who, then, was this 'holy recluse' and what might his or her relationship have been to the royal house of Sam and Nariman?

Other stories that feature the Simurgh also seem to point strongly to the bird's human origin. In one folktale preserved by the Mandaeans – the strange cult of great antiquity existing among both the Marsh Arabs of southern Iraq and the isolated communities of western Iran – the Simurgh is greeted at the court of a shah named Hirmiz like a foreign envoy of great renown. He prepares a throne for the bird, who possesses a female gender, and entertains her with a meal of 'fruits of the mountain-country', since the Simurgh 'does not eat meat'.[2] He also provides a breathtaking display of song and dance by the finest troupe of maidens in the land. Even the birds reared by the dancing maidens are brought in to perform before the enthroned Simurgh, an indication perhaps of some kind of ritual dance in which individuals would adorn themselves with bird feathers. In the many conversations she has with the king, the Simurgh shows a profound knowledge of the secret wisdom and displays powerful visionary abilities.

The wondrous bird entertained by Hirmiz bears all the

hallmarks of having been a woman, a shaman perhaps, dressed as a bird. I could see no alternative explanation, other than to suggest that the whole story was purely allegorical in content.

The Divine Physician

In another story found in the *Shahnameh* of Firdowsi, the Simurgh cures Rustam and his magical horse Rakhsh of mortal wounds inflicted on them by the hero Isfendiyar. Earlier in the text, Isfendiyar had himself managed to slaughter a Simurgh by cutting it in two with his sword, having travelled a great journey 'over desert, plain, mountain, and wilderness until he (had) reached the neighbourhood of the Simurgh'.[3]

As on previous occasions, Rustam's father, Zal, burns one of the Simurgh's feathers on a high place and the fabulous bird appears as if out of nowhere. She tells the elderly king to have no fear as she can cure both Rustam and his beloved horse. Beginning with the animal, the Simurgh uses her beak to remove six arrows and then heals the wounds by passing one of her feathers over Rakhsh's body. Turning to Rustam, she then deals with him in a similar manner – first removing eight arrows, before sucking out the poisonous blood and finally healing him completely by passing feathers over his wounds.[4]

After Rustam has recovered, he solicits the aid of the Simurgh to tell him how he might defeat his rival, Isfendiyar. The 'noble vulture' severely advises against this act of revenge, since Isfendiyar is a hero of Rustam's own race, adding that if she does provide him with the means by which he can defeat his enemy, then this deed will inevitably bring about his own death. Rustam accepts his fate and the Simurgh at once falls into 'deep thought . . . and remained some time silent',[5] perhaps a trance state not unlike those achieved by shamans in tribal cultures.

After regaining consciousness, the Simurgh informs Rustam that he must mount his treasured horse Rakhsh and follow behind her. They travel far and eventually arrive at a place of reeds where grows the magical Kazu-tree, almost as if this had been the sight seen in vision by the bird. The Simurgh then instructs Rustam on how he might make a deadly arrow from one of the tree's branches, which he then uses to kill Isfendiyar, himself dying in the process.

The Drug of Immortality

Before his death, however, Rustam encounters Isfendiyar's brother, Bashutan. He inquires as to how the king has made such a speedy recovery from the mortal wounds inflicted on him only the previous day. In reply Rustam says:

'I am now wholly free from wounds, and so is my horse, for I possess an elixir which heals the most cruel lacerations of the flesh the moment it is applied; but no such wounds were inflicted upon me, the arrows of Isfendiyar being only like needles sticking in my body.'[6]

Rustam was obviously attempting to pass off his wounds as insignificant to Bashutan, since he did not wish to reveal just how close to death he had come before the arrival of the Simurgh. Yet here once again was an example of the highly advanced knowledge of drugs and medicine apparently possessed by this 'noble vulture'. What was this 'elixir which heals the most cruel lacerations of the flesh'? Was it the same 'herb' that, when mixed with milk and musk, healed the wounds inflicted on Rudabeh during the delivery of her child by Caesarian section? In past ages the 'elixir' was looked upon as a much-sought-after divine liquor believed by the ancient alchemists to be able to transform base matter into a state of purity. It was also seen as a fabled super-drug believed to be able to rejuvenate the body and prolong life.

Although the nature or reality of the elixir has always remained a matter of speculation, it has strongly been linked with a sacred drug referred to in Iranian myth as *haoma*, a substance produced from a plant or fungus of uncertain origin. Most Iranian scholars believe *haoma* to be linked with a species of *ephedra*, the genus of a trailing shrub belonging to the family *Gnetaceae*, or sea-grape, while other Persian stories say that it grew either 'on mountain-tops or in river valleys'.[7] When mixed with milk or water, the resulting juice could not only create intoxicating effects, but it could also heal the body and induce alleged supernatural powers.[8] More recent research has suggested that the active ingredient of *haoma* may actually have been the mushroom Fly-Agaric, a major hallucinogen now thought to have been used by shamanistic cultures for anything up to 10,000 years.[9]

Because of its enormous spiritual significance to the Iranian religion, *haoma* became a healing god in its own right, which, because of the plant's apparent curative properties, could bestow health and strength on its worshippers. In some accounts the Simurgh is perceived as the guardian of the *haoma* plant, for as the *Encyclopaedia of Religion and Ethics* explains:

> *. . . in the traditions of the Indo-Iranians,* [the drug is] *closely connected with a mystical bird which took the . . .* haoma *from the place where it lay hidden and brought it to gods and men. The Avesta speaks of the bird* Saena, *which is the Simurgh of the Persians who make him play the same part.*[10]

So the Simurgh revealed the secrets of *haoma* to both the gods and mortal kind. This role is played in early Hindu mythology by the half giant, half eagle known as Garuda. It steals the moon goblet containing the Ambrosia, Amrita, nectar or *soma*, which provides the *asura* gods with supernatural power and renders them immortal. In response, an *asura* named Indra the Thunderer flings his deadly bolt in a vain attempt to prevent this theft. He fails to wound Garuda, but does dislodge one of the bird's feathers, which falls to the ground. The Amrita is delivered by Garuda to 'the serpents' in exchange for the freedom of its mother, who has been held by them in bondage. Afterwards the giant became known as 'the golden sun bird, deadly foe of all serpents', linking it with the two basic totemic forms of the Watchers – the bird-man and serpent.[11]

Garuda was undoubtedly the Indian equivalent of the Simurgh, while the *soma* is, of course, the same as the Iranian *haoma*, which could also prolong life and create supernatural powers. In some legends, *haoma* was said to have grown upon a special tree situated in the proximity of Mount Elburz, known only to the 'immortals', those, assumedly, who could prolong life by taking this superdrug.[12]

The existence and alleged properties of *haoma*, particularly its ability to prolong life, made me recall the passage in Genesis 3 in which Adam and Eve are cast out of Eden for fear that they would eat of the Tree of Life and 'live for ever', in other words become immortal like gods themselves.[13] Might the 'fruit' of the Tree of Life have been *haoma*? All the indications are that such a drug could have originated from a much earlier shamanistic culture, who may well have used it as part of their death-inducing rites, perhaps utilizing the vulture as a symbol of the soul's transformation. Might these have been linked with the enigmatic bird-men of the Book of Enoch? Had such a super-drug been known to the fallen race, and could it provide an answer as to why Mount Elburz was purportedly the realm of the immortals? Had *haoma*, or *soma*, really been given to the mortal world by a fabulous bird?

In addition to the Simurgh's superior knowledge of drugs and medicine, the story of Rustam's killing of Isfendiyar shows the bird to have been skilful in the art of manufacturing deadly accurate weapons, such as the arrow made from the branch of the Kazu-tree. As with the apparent medical knowledge understood by the Simurgh, this is not the sort of knowledge usually equated with the bird kingdom.

Isfendiyar's slaughter of a Simurgh earlier in the same story also demonstrates that the Iranians must have believed there to have been not just one such creature of this description, but *a whole host of them* living in the mountainous region of Elburz. In my opinion, it seemed certain that the term 'Simurgh' was simply a figurative title masquerading the actions and deeds of many people, not just one 'holy recluse' leading a solitary existence among the mountains of Iran. Furthermore, the idea of birds possessing clear human characteristics and traits appeared to be a familiar one in Iranian myth, for it resurfaces again in the writings of Persian Islamic mystics, or sufis, during the Middle Ages.[14]

Had the story-tellers of ancient Iran unwittingly used myth and legend to preserve the former existence of a prehistoric culture which appeared to have been associated with ornithomorphic rites, especially in connection with the eagle and the vulture? If the answer was yes, then why had they chosen these particular birds as their shamanistic devices? Had they held some special place in their ritualistic lives, in the same way as, say, Siberian shamans led symbiotic lifestyles alongside the reindeer and the bushmen of

South Africa saw the reebok as a personification of their own higher states of consciousness?

The Noble Vulture

The key appeared to be the source of inspiration for the Simurgh. In one account it is described as 'a noble vulture', in others as a composite beast with elements borrowed from 'the peacock, the lion, the griffin and the dog'.[15] In still others it is distinctly described as a kind of gryphon – a mythological creature of classical origin, part lion and part eagle. The lion was an animal of Angra Mainyu in Zoroastrian tradition,[16] while the gryphon's association with the eagle derives in the main from a basic misconception. Very often the eagle, as a totemic symbol in mythology, only appears as a substitute for the much uglier and far more disliked vulture, and this has particularly been so in the Old Testament.[17] The connection between the gryphon and the vulture, as opposed to the eagle, is exemplified in the knowledge that one of the principal species extant in the mountains of Iran and Iraq in ancient times was the griffon vulture (*Gyps fulvus*). Although modern ornithologists believe that the griffon vulture gained its name from the gryphon of classical fable, the word 'gryphon' actually means hook-nosed, which is a very apt description of the vulture's bill, implying that the connection between them is the other way around.[18]

So the Simurgh was predominantly a kind of fabulous vulture, and little else, which begged the immediate question: why should the 'noble vulture' have risen to the rank of 'king of birds' in Iranian myth? I looked towards the religious texts of the Zoroastrian faith for answers, and answers I found. Vultures, I quickly realized, have *always* played an integral role in the religion's myths and rituals, especially in respect of its grisly funerary customs.

Excarnation

In the middle of the fifth century BC the noted Greek historian Herodotus visited different parts of the Persian empire on his famous travels. On these journeys he would make a point of observing and recording local customs and ritual practices, which he subsequently entered into his nine-volume work entitled, simply, *History*, and it is Book I of this series that contains reference to strange death-rites he witnessed in Media involving Magi priests, for as he reveals:

Is is said that the body of a male Persian is never buried, until it has been torn either by a dog or a bird of prey. That the Magi have this custom is beyond a doubt, for they practise it without any concealment. The dead bodies are covered with wax, and then buried in the ground.[19]

Other classical writers, including Agathias and Strabo, also mention these so-called rites of 'excarnation', as they are known today, in which the body of the deceased is exposed to the ravages of wild beasts and carrion birds, such as black crows and vultures. According to Herodotus, these practices were confined to male priests and were quite basic in content. They would also appear to have been specific to the Magi, a reference to the priests of Media, and *not* to the rival Zoroastrian priesthood. Herodotus undoubtedly knew the difference between the two, for it was he who reported that the rites of Magophobia – the festival in which people were encouraged to kill any Magi they chanced upon in remembrance of the Magian-led usurpation of the throne during the reign of Cambyses – was still being upheld in his day. So there can be little doubt about his words.

Exposure of the dead continued to be practised in Iran through to the time of the Parthian confederacy of kings – who ruled Persia for a span of nearly five hundred years from the third century BC onwards. It also continued to take place under the Sassanian kings of Persia, who ousted the Parthians during the third century AD. It was during this final phase in the empire's long history that excarnation would appear to have become more widely accepted and practised among all walks of society. Whether they be ecclesiastical or secular, male or female, rich or poor, the bodies of Magians and Zoroastrians were now exposed to the wild beasts and carrion birds. Scholars accept that this great shift in funerary customs and practices among the Persians was almost certainly a result of the heavy influence exerted on both the ruling Sassanian monarchs and the state-run religion by the Magi priests, who had somehow managed to wheedle their way back into some of the most important places of power during this period.[20]

After the bulk of the Zoroastrians of Iran had fled the Arab persecutions and settled in India during the ninth century, excarnation took on a whole new significance. For no obvious reason, it suddenly became more structured, more organized and more widespread; in fact, from this time onwards it would appear that all Zoroastrians, or Parsees as they were now known, became subject to exposure after death. Moreover, instead of excarnation taking place on high open ground, the bodies were now placed in huge stone mortuary buildings, known as *dakhmas*, or Towers of Silence, situated well away from habitation.

Inside each of these great, open-topped amphitheatres was a huge radial platform with three concentric rows of stone slabs called *pavis*, set out like the spokes of an enormous stone wheel. On these the dead bodies would be placed in position by corpse-bearers, and then left to the ravages of vultures, who would take as little as thirty minutes to denude the flesh. Running along the edges of each *pavi* were deep channels for carrying away bodily fluids and rain water. This liquid matter would flow into a central stone-lined pit known as the *bhandar*, and from here it would be conveyed to the outside walls by four equally spaced channels containing a filtering system of charcoal and sandstones. Once the hot sun had dried the clean skeletons, they would be collected up and thrown down into the *bhandar*, where they would eventually turn to dust and be washed away by the rain.

Exposure of the dead actually makes good sense, even if such practices may seem barbaric to the Western world. It is nature's way of disposing of flesh and blood, and what is more it complied with a Zoroastrian tenet which decreed that 'the mother earth shall not be defiled' by impure substances.[21] Yet what prompted the

Fig. 4. Line illustration of one of the *dakhmas*, or Towers of Silence, used by Indian Parsees to expose human corpses to vultures. This process, known today as excarnation, is very possibly the last remnant of a shamanistic practice that pre-dates the rise of Western civilization.

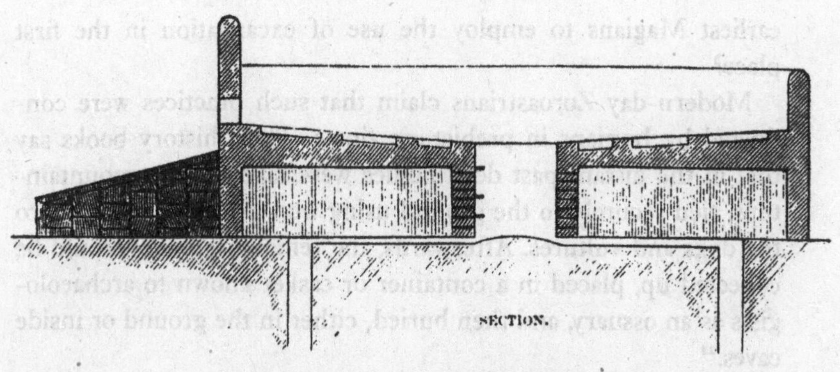

SECTION.

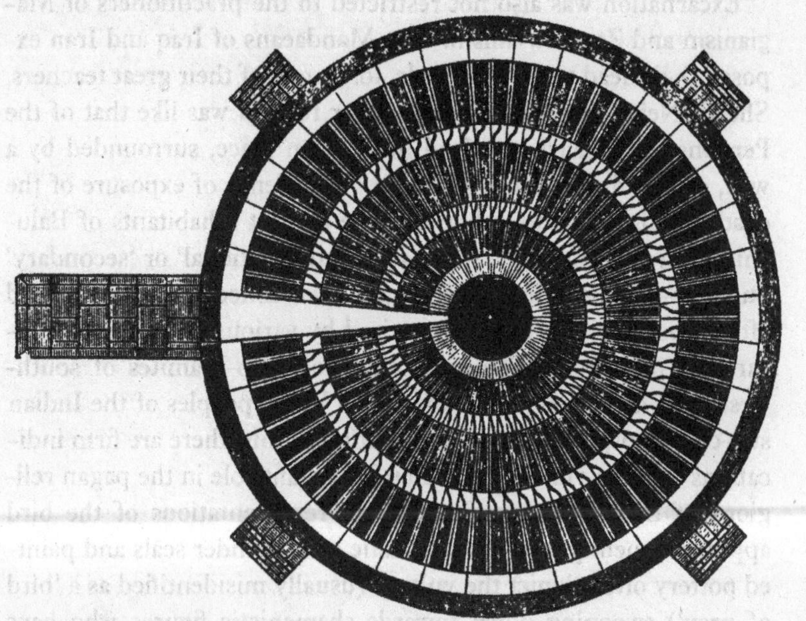

VIEW OF THE INTERIOR.

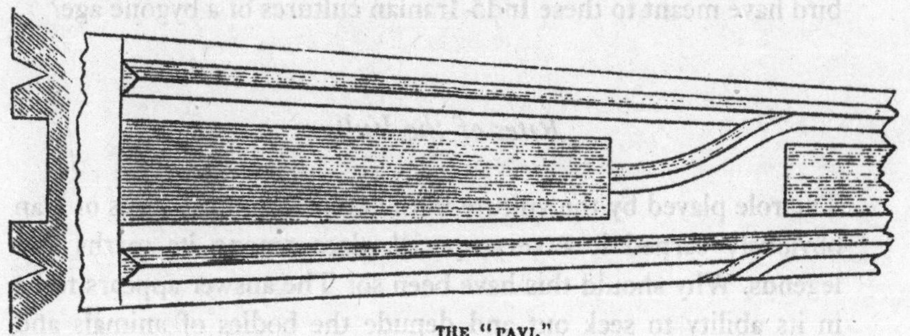

THE "PAVI."

earliest Magians to employ the use of excarnation in the first place?

Modern-day Zoroastrians claim that such practices were conducted by Iranians in prehistoric times. Their history books say that in the distant past dead bodies were taken out to mountaintops, tied securely to the ground using iron pegs, and then left to the dogs and vultures. Afterwards, the remaining bones would be collected up, placed in a container or casket known to archaeologists as an ossuary, and then buried, either in the ground or inside caves.[22]

Excarnation was also not restricted to the practitioners of Magianism and Zoroastrianism. The Mandaeans of Iraq and Iran exposed their dead to carrion birds, for as one of their great teachers, Sheikh Nejm, commented: 'Once our funeral was like that of the Persians. We placed our dead in an open place, surrounded by a wall, and birds came and ate them.'[23] Evidence of exposure of the dead has also been found among the earliest inhabitants of Baluchistan in central Asia,[24] while so-called 'fractional' or 'secondary' burials' – that is, bones which have been collected up and buried after exposure – were once practised by various Indo-Iranian cultures of prehistory. These include the proto-Elamites of south-west Iran, *c.* 3500 BC,[25] and the Indus Valley peoples of the Indian sub-continent, *c.* 2500 BC.[26] In addition to this, there are firm indications that the vulture played an important role in the pagan religions of these cultures, for abstract representations of the bird appear frequently on their ritualistic art. Cylinder seals and painted pottery often depict the vulture (usually misidentified as a 'bird of prey') swooping down towards shamanistic figures who have their arms raised in a devotional manner.[27] So what might this great bird have meant to these Indo-Iranian cultures of a bygone age?

Rites of the Vulture

The role played by the vulture in the excarnation practices of Iran obviously earned it a very special place among its myths and legends. Why should this have been so? The answer appears to lie in its ability to seek out and denude the bodies of animals and human beings in a matter of minutes, making it an obvious symbol of mortality as well as a carrier of the soul into the next world. Furthermore, because it was seen as a bird of flight that often lived in high, mountainous regions, many early cultures believed that it guided the spirit to the starry realms of heaven, reached via the lofty heights of some sacred mountain peak, which constituted the connecting point between heaven, earth and underworld.[28] To the earliest neolithic cultures (i.e. the first, settled farming communities of Eurasia, as opposed to the earlier palaeolithic and mesolithic hunter-gatherers) the vulture symbolized the spirit of death.

Evidence of this powerful belief is to be found in the funerary customs practised until comparatively recent times by the Parsees of India. Once a person had died, it was deemed that his or her soul would remain close to the body for three days, during which time constant prayers and hymns would be recited over the deceased. After the body had lain in the house for this statutory period, the departure of the soul would be ascertained by a process of divination known as *sag-did*. In one variation of this theme – which usually involved observing the reactions of a chosen dog brought into contact with the corpse[29] – the mourning relatives would watch for the shadow of a black crow or vulture to pass over the dead body. When this happened, it was seen as a sign that the soul had departed the house and that the body could now be exposed.[30] Might this custom be linked to the way in which the shadow cast by the feather of the Simurgh was able to aid the healing of Rudabeh's wounds in the *Shahnameh* story concerning the birth of Rustam?

To the ancient Iranians the vulture would appear to have been linked not just with physical mortality, but also with the gradual process of illumination and transmigration of the soul achieved after death, something that was understood by prehistoric cultures through the mental process we know today as near-death experience (NDE). Parapsychological studies into this fascinating subject have conclusively shown that individuals who are classed as clinically dead, before being resuscitated, often experience so-called out-of-the-body sensations, as well as visionary glimpses of the next world and encounters with either deceased relatives or shining beings.[31]

Although we perceive such strange experiences as a modern and purely psychological phenomenon, shamanistic cultures worldwide have always accepted that death-like states can be induced through artificial processes.[32] These have included the use of intoxicating drugs, sensory deprivation, or the actual creation of near-death situations, during which time the brain is tricked into believing that the body is on the edge of death. Trials by fire or water, the introduction of deadly poisons into the body (with the necessary antidote at hand) or death-defying physical feats, such as jumping off cliffs with a rope tied to one leg, and many more similar such feats of endurance, can *all* induce traumatic mental states similar in style to the near-death experience. During such times, astral flight, spirit communication and visionary glimpses of ethereal realms will hopefully take place.

Since the vulture was the ultimate symbol of death, then it seems likely that the ancient Indo-Iranian cultures invoked the spirits of these giant birds to guide them on their other-worldly journeys in search of universal knowledge, inspired truth and divine illumination. This close relationship with the vulture in their religious practices would have involved shamans adorning themselves with coats of feathers and conducting the necessary tribal rites in the belief that this would aid them in achieving astral flight. Lastly, when physical death did overcome any prominent member of the community, they would have continued this symbiosis with the spirit of the vulture by using excarnation in the hope that their souls would be successfully guided into the next world.

Çatal Hüyük

From the archaeological evidence of secondary burials and exposure among the Indo-Iranian cultures, there is every reason to suggest that the cult of the vulture was once widespread. Despite this knowledge, there was not enough evidence in Iran itself for me fully to understand the extent or nature of this strange cult of the dead, or how it might be linked with the traditions concerning the fallen race of Judaic religious literature. For this I had to journey across the rugged mountain ranges of Iran, Iraq and Syria to the vast plains of Anatolia, close to the old town of Konya, in southern Turkey.

Here, one chilly November day in 1958, a British archaeological team led by an expert in Anatolian studies, named James Mellaart, arrived to survey a great double-mound of earth known locally as Çatal Hüyük. Turf and ruin-weed covered everywhere, but here and there the harsh south-westerly winds had peeled away the top soil to reveal tell-tale signs of human occupation – scattered mud-bricks, discarded hand-tools, broken potsherds and patches of grey ash. At the time those present had no idea of the immense importance of this discovery, for when the excavations began in 1961, Mellaart and his team started to uncover a vast metropolis – a network of shrines and dwellings belonging to a protoneolithic community that had lived between 8,500 and 7,700 years ago.[33] From the extraordinary level of detail and decoration of the sub-surface buildings, as well as the jewellery, the tools, the weapons and the murals found within the double-mound, it soon became clear that the Çatal Hüyük culture had been extremely advanced in its beliefs, lifestyle and artistic capabilities. Nothing like this had ever been found before, either in Turkey or anywhere else in the world. It was so unique that many scholars now believe that Çatal Hüyük may provide important clues concerning the rise of civilization in the Old World.

Walking among the many religious shrines while the excavations were in progress between 1961 and 1964, the visitor would have seen life-size bulls' heads with horns protruding from the decorated plaster, as well as high-relief leopards either stamped with ringed trefoil designs or spread-eagled in the birth position. He or she would also have seen wall after wall of abstract geometric or polychromic patterns such as double-axe designs, hand-imprints, lozenges, zig-zags and huge, circular eyes, all painted either in ochre red or black. These have now either faded or been removed by the Turkish authorities to a museum at Ankara, where they may still be seen today.

It was, however, the vulture shrines that were by far the most perplexing enigma of Çatal Hüyük, for they raised poignant questions about the strange ritual practices conducted beneath the plains of Anatolia during the seventh millennium BC. Shrine VII, for instance, left the visitor awestruck. Covering two complete walls was a gigantic mural depicting seven enormous vultures, some up to five feet in wing-span. They were frozen in mid-flight and appeared to be swooping down to devour six headless, matchstick men, four of whom were crouched up with their legs bent towards their chests. The birds' characteristic bald heads, their short legs and distinctive crests identified them as *Gyps fulvus*, the griffon vulture, the source behind the Simurgh of Iranian myth and legend.[34] Walk into another shrine and you would have seen a mural depicting human figures trying to beat off vultures that seemed to be attacking a corpse.

Walk into Shrine VI and you would have found probably the most important scene of all – a detailed fresco showing vultures in association with erect, wooden-framed towers, their open-topped roofs linked to the ground by angled stairways.[35] In one case two huge birds could be seen perched on top of the tall structure, poised to envelop a sole human head with their curled wings. Next to this image was another similar tower with a headless, matchstick man hanging upside down and a vulture on each side, ready to attack. At the base of the stepped ramp were two figures, perhaps priests, walking away from the towers. Each wore a knee-length kilt and an upper garment with triangular-shaped shoulder-pads.

There seems little doubt that this last mural had been executed as an abstract representation of excarnation – the inverted matchstick man symbolizing a lifeless body about to be denuded by carrion birds. The high wooden towers with their open roofs and stairs could be compared with the *dakhmas*, or Towers of Silence, of Parsee tradition. The solitary head, in one instance, signified the soul being released from the body to begin its journey to the otherworld under the protection, *or wing*, of the *genius* of the vulture, which is believed by many present-day prehistorians to have possessed a female gender.[36] And the feminine attributes of the vulture cannot be denied, for on one wall of a shrine were found modelled human breasts in plaster, inside which were actual skulls of vultures, their bills protruding to form nipples. Another mural showed a recurring design featuring a vulture and a plump mother goddess clutching a new-born baby;[37] indeed, there was so much

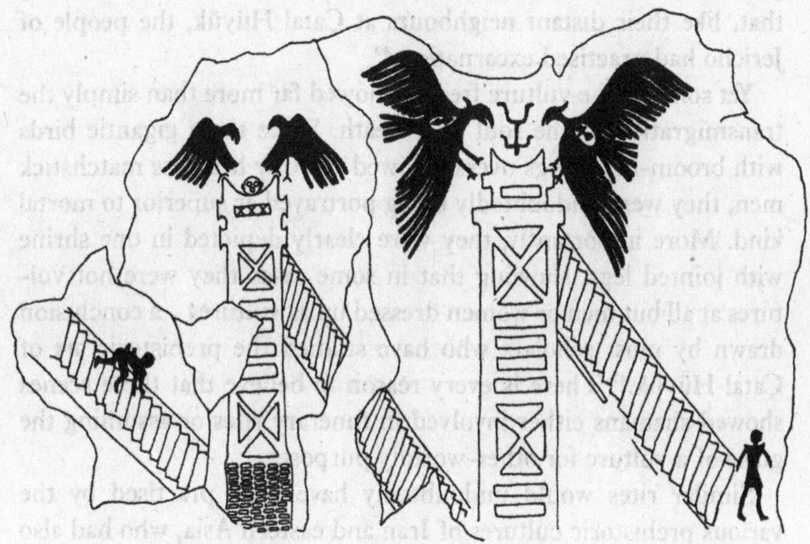

Fig. 5. Wall mural from one of the 8,000-year-old shrines at Çatal Hüyük in Turkey showing vultures devouring human corpses exposed on wooden towers. The process of excarnation, or exposure of the dead, was a major feature of vulture shamanism in early neolithic times and is almost certainly behind its survival among the Zoroastrians of Iran and India.

female symbolism in the shrines that it seems certain that the primary function of the Çatal Hüyük culture had been the celebration of life, death and rebirth into the next world.

Confirmation that excarnation had been integrally linked with the rites performed in the vulture shrines at Çatal Hüyük was the overwhelming evidence of secondary burial found in many graves, some located beneath the floors of houses. Within the shrines themselves archaeologists also uncovered several skulls, one with sliced cowrie shells as eyes.[38] These had almost certainly been used for oracular purposes in the belief that the seat of the soul was in the head, even after the point of physical death. Plastered skulls, probably used for similar ritual purposes, were also found in some of the lowest occupational levels at Jericho in Palestine, where an important protoneolithic township had thrived from the ninth millennium BC onwards (see Chapter Twenty-One).[39] Evidence of partial or secondary burials was uncovered here too, indicating that, like their distant neighbours at Çatal Hüyük, the people of Jericho had practised excarnation.[40]

Yet some of the vulture frescos showed far more than simply the transmigration of the soul after death. Since these gigantic birds with broom-like wings overshadowed the tiny headless matchstick men, they were undoubtedly being portrayed as superior to mortal kind. More importantly, they were clearly depicted in one shrine with jointed legs, showing that in some cases they were not vultures at all but men or women dressed up as vultures – a conclusion drawn by most scholars who have studied the prehistoric art of Çatal Hüyük.[41] There is every reason to believe that these scenes showed shamans either involved in funerary rites or assuming the guise of a vulture for other-worldly purposes.

Similar rites would undoubtedly have been practised by the various prehistoric cultures of Iran and eastern Asia, who had also employed the use of excarnation in their funerary practices. The last surviving fragments of this shamanistic tradition were, it appeared, the religious beliefs and customs of the Zoroastrians, who, through the intervention of the Magi priests during Sassanian times, had inherited an archaic tradition already many thousands of years old.

The Çatal Hüyük culture came to a sudden demise around 5600 BC, having left behind no less than thirteen different levels of occupation. What happened to these people is still unknown. Some founded a new site beyond a local river, which thrived for around seven hundred years, while others would have taken up residence at the nearby settlement of Hacılar, near the town of Burdur. Here James Mellaart had previously uncovered extensive evidence of a later, though more basic neolithic community which had occupied the site between 5700 and 5000 BC.[42]

No one could deny the importance of the culture at Çatal Hüyük, with its unique preservation of what was quite clearly a vulture cult paralleling that practised in Iran during prehistoric times. I had, however, been wondering what possible relevance it might have to my knowledge of the fallen race when I chanced upon certain almost throwaway remarks James Mellaart made about this protoneolithic community in his essential book *Çatal*

Hüyük: A Neolithic Town in Anatolia, first published in 1967. Not only did the culture practice one of the earliest recorded forms of primitive agriculture and metal-working, but it also appeared to have possessed advanced technical skills totally inexplicable to archaeologists. These perplexed Mellaart to such a degree that he had been forced to ask:

How, for example, did they polish a mirror of obsidian, a hard volcanic glass, without scratching it and how did they drill holes through stone beads (including obsidian), holes so small that no fine modern steel needle can penetrate. When and where did they learn to smelt copper and lead, metals attested at Çatal Hüyük since Level IX, c. 6400 bc?[43]

With respect to this highly advanced stone industry of Çatal Hüyük, Mellaart admitted that it marked the climax of an 'immensely long ancestry'[44] that reached back into palaeolithic times, well before the end of the last Ice Age, which had been over in Europe and Asia for around two thousand years. So where might this superior knowledge have come from? Had it been the fallen race of Enochian and Dead Sea tradition, who would also appear to have utilized a form of bird shamanism to obtain astral flight and dream-visions, and were said to have revealed to humanity the arts and sciences of heaven?

An abstract clue suggested that the answer would indeed be yes.

The artist Alan Sorrell was commissioned by the archaeological writer Edward Bacon to draw an impression of how the interior of one of the vulture shrines at Çatal Hüyük might have looked at the height of its devotional usage in the mid-seventh millennium BC. Using whatever knowledge had been gained from the years of research and excavation at the site, Sorrell produced a detailed picture of remarkable relevance to my work. It depicts three vulture shamans, adorned in beaked headdresses and garments of feathers, who kneel before a huge bull's head protruding from a wall before them. One tends a human skull placed in a wicker basket as sunlight pours in through openings cut into the uppermost sections of the timber-framed roof of the building, illuminating vulture frescos and still more bulls' heads on the far wall. A fourth figure in a hooded robe sits in meditation, while on the floor are further skulls and a square hearth in which burns a small fire.

Looking at Alan Sorrell's compelling picture for the first time sent a tingle down my spine; it also put a wry smile on my face. Here was a conceptual representation of vulture shamans who had lived on the Anatolian plateau 8,500 years ago. Yet there was something strangely familiar about their appearance – something which made me recall the Enochian legends where the Nephilim are described as 'bird-men' and the Watchers are said to wear garments 'very dark' or with 'the appearance of feathers'. The similarity between Alan Sorrell's artist's impression of vulture shamans at Çatal Hüyük and Billie Walker-John's line drawing of the feather-coated Watchers was too close for comfort.

Was it possible that the Watchers really were distorted memories of a shamanistic culture who had once inhabited a mountainous region, perhaps in Iran, and possessed a knowledge of science and technology well beyond that of other less evolved races of the Near East? If so, then were they also behind the legends of the Simurgh's contact with the earliest kings of Iran, who would appear to have possessed distinct physiological features resembling those of the fallen race? And what about the stories concerning the fall of the shining *ahuras* and the rise of the *daevic* race – the traditions best preserved in the dualistic teachings of the Magi priesthoods of Media, modern-day Azerbaijan. Could the apparent transgressions of this tall race of bird-men, with white Caucasian features and long viper-like faces of east Asian appearance, account for these Iranian legends as well?

My hunches told me I was still on the right track. What was more, left in my mind was the tantalizing possibility that, prior to my own interest in the subject, Alan Sorrell's imaginative interpretation of Çatal Hüyük's vulture shamans was perhaps the closest anyone had ever come to accurately depicting a real-life angel.

Eleven

IN THE REALM OF THE IMMORTALS

Tales of the wondrous feats and skills possessed by the Simurgh must have been recounted by story-tellers around the camp-fires of isolated communities for thousands of years. The most memorable occasion of its appearance, they would have said, was the time when Zal called the great bird to his presence so that it could provide him with a means to deliver his son Rustam from the belly of his mother. And if at any time Zal needed the Simurgh's assistance, all he needed to do was burn one of its feathers.

By anyone's standards, such strange, unnatural fables were comparable with the European folktales in which the Fairy Queen appears to the lucky beholder to grant three wishes. Indeed, somewhere within these children's stories are marked similarities to the deeds of the Simurgh and the fallen race as a whole – too far removed, however, to be of any real relevance to the present study. Even so, the legends of the Simurgh might well encode invaluable information concerning a lost prehistoric culture that recognized the spirit of the vulture as the patron of death and as the guardian of the soul during its other-worldly journeys.

Yet did the memory of this forgotten race also leave behind other, more abstract legacies among the peoples of the Old World? Did it, for instance, influence the belief adhered to among Greek women until fairly recent times that, if they held the feather of a griffon vulture while giving birth, it would guarantee a swift delivery of their child?[1] Was this a distant echo of the way in which the Simurgh was said to have aided the delivery of the infant Rustam? Did these superstitious women believe that, by not clutching a vulture feather, they might give birth to babies of such size that it could kill them?

I think the probable answer is yes; however, such archaic customs were also probably linked to the close association in prehistoric times between the vulture and the Great Mother, the earliest form of goddess worshipped in Europe and Asia. In ancient Egypt, for example, the hieroglyph used to denote 'vulture' was also synonymous with the word 'mother'.[2] And in addition to easing childbirth, feathers of the griffon vulture, the great swooping bird depicted on the walls of the subterranean shrines of Çatal Hüyük, were held to be able to cure blindness and protect the holder against the bites of snakes and scorpions, creatures associated with Angra Mainyu, and his offspring the *daevas*, in Iranian tradition.[3] Might this close association between vultures and serpents have stemmed from the presence of these two quite specific totems among the proposed shamanistic practices of the fallen race?

In Hindu mythology the ability to be able to destroy snakes was accredited to Garuda, the fabulous bird who was seen as the 'deadly foe of all serpents'. Even though this fabulous creature was often equated with the eagle, the description of its movements makes it more likely to have been a vulture, a view proposed by at least one authority on vulture lore.[4]

Further connecting the potency of magical feathers with the vulture is the knowledge that, as late as the thirteenth century, at least one actual Simurgh feather was still thought to exist. In the medieval sufi classic entitled *The Conference of the Birds* by the Persian poet Farid ud-Din Attar, it says that one was 'still . . . on view' in China.[5] The author goes on to say that: 'If this same feather had not floated down, the world would not be filled with his [*the Simurgh's*] renown.'[6] Apparently, 'rumours of its fame spread everywhere',[7] implying that it had become the focus of pilgrimages from afar. Whether this feather had been plucked from the wing of a vulture or some other large bird shall never be known, yet the very existence of such holy relics shows the great significance accredited to the vulture's mythical counterpart.

Among the Avestan writings of Zoroaster there is an example of talismanic qualities being attributed to the feathers and bones of angels. In one legend the prophet asks Ahura Mazda what he might do if struck by 'the curse of the enemy'. The Wise Lord tells him that he should rub his body with the feather of Verethragna, an angel of victory who takes on ten different incarnations, including that of a great bird and a man.

With that feather thou shalt curse back the enemies. If a man holds a bone of that strong bird, no one can smite or turn to flight that fortunate man. The feather of that bird brings him help.[8]

The name of this ornithomorphic incarnation of Verethragna is Varaghna – the bird that transmits the royal *farr* from one person to another in Avestan tradition. This therefore linked the shining countenances of the divine kings of ancient Iran with the feather and bone of an angel who was said to have adopted the form of a bird.

Did such relics of angels really exist in past ages? It is impossible now to say; however, what we do know is that *representations* of angel relics were once revered as the genuine item in Christian tradition. One such example from Britain is a cluster of white goose feathers preserved in the parish church at Pewsey, in the county of Wiltshire, which were said to have been dropped 'in the Temple' by the archangel Gabriel. Little is known about these particular feathers, which were found inside a stone pillar during restoration work in 1800. It *is* known, however, that several churches in Europe once possessed similar feathers which were probably acquired in the Holy Land at the time of the Crusades.[9]

Even though the angelic feathers of Pewsey belonged to a goose and not a vulture, there *were* firm connections between angels, vultures and Zoroastrianism. For instance, in Islamic religious lore the angel Sa'adiya'il is said to have been the leader of a group of angels who took the guise of vultures.[10] Even though this angel is of Islamic origin, he is also found in a slightly different form in earlier Judaic tradition. Here he is the 'archangel' Sadayel, whose name, along with those of Raphael and Tiriel, was found inscribed within a pentagram on a ring amulet used for divine protection.[11] In Zoroastrian tradition, Sa'adiya'il becomes the *yazata* Sadwes, or Satavaesa, one of the three companions of Tir, while in Manichaean lore he is equated with a rain-making divinity of the same name.[12]

Vulture feathers. Simurgh feathers. Angel feathers.

Did they all stem from the same original source?

Was it possible that the Watchers had really been a prehistoric culture who practised vulture and perhaps snake shamanism, and lived in some remote mountainous region of Iran many thousands of years ago? How might I go about tracing its roots? The most immediate solution appeared to be finding the true whereabouts of Mount Elburz, the mythological home of the Simurgh and the source of the sacred plant *haoma*.

My mind kept returning to the *Shahnameh* story in which Sam had left his 'demon' son Zal to the mercy of wild animals and vultures. In my opinion, there had to be a connection between the rites of excarnation carried out in high open spaces during prehistoric times and the lofty heights of Mount Elburz where the Simurgh bird had made its home.

Only the piles of open books on Zoroastrianism scattered across my work-top could provide me with an answer, so I carefully reread the sections on funerary rites and customs and eventually chanced upon something of immense significance.

The Iranian Expanse

Zoroastrians believe that once the soul departs the physical body at the commencement of the fourth day after death – the same day as it is exposed to vultures in a Tower of Silence – it makes a hazardous journey to a mythical location known as Cinvat Bridge, where it is judged by the god Mithra and the angels Sraosha and Rashnu. If the soul is allowed to cross this perilous causeway, which stretches between this world and the next, it enters an ethereal domain known as *Airyana Vaejah (Eranvej* in the *Bundahishn* of the Parsees), inhabited by immortals, or those that are beyond death. The name *Airyana Vaejah* means, literally, the Iranian, or 'Aryan', Expanse, and in mythological tradition this paradisical world was situated at the centre of Khvaniratha, the earth's great land-mass.[13]

From *Airyana Vaejah* had come the first humans, as well as the dynasty of Pishdadian kings, the heroic race that began with Kiyumars, the first king, and ended with the dynasty of Nariman and Sam. Here, too, could be found Mount Elburz – the abode of the

Simurgh, Iran's most holy mountain, which is referred to in Zoroastrian tradition as Mount Hara, or Mount Harburz.

Although these legends quite obviously related to mythological realms of fanciful construction, there was good reason to suggest that the concept of *Airyana Vaejah* had been based on actual geographical locations that certainly played a significant role in the development of Iran's most ancient cultures, perhaps even the genesis of the Iranian race.

So where, then, was *Airyana Vaejah*?

Let's look at the possible clues.

To the south of Mount Elburz, or Hara, was the so-called Vourukasha Sea, a huge expanse of water that supposedly covered one third of the world and was the gathering-point of all water.[14] In the centre of this inland sea, presumably on an island, were said to have been two divine trees – the first being the Tree of All Remedies, which was also known as the Tree of All Seeds, or the Saena (Senmurv in Pahlavi, Simurgh in later Persian) Tree. On the branches of this wondrous tree the 'king of birds' perched, even though this tradition obviously contradicted Firdowsi's *Shahnameh* account, which placed the Simurgh actually on Mount Elburz. Near by this tree was the 'mighty Gaokerena' tree, which possessed healing properties and bore fruit that provided immortality to those souls that achieved salvation, a reference once again to the *haoma* plant. Together these two sacred trees equated respectively with the Tree of Knowledge of Good and Evil and the Tree of Life in the Book of Genesis.

Airyana Vaejah is referred to in the texts as 'the first, the best of dwelling-places and lands', that once experienced a winter of ten months' duration and a summer of two months, a point which has led some scholars to locate it in the region of Khwarezmia, an ancient Iranian province in central Asia.[15] Others have suggested that the Vourukasha Sea was either the Black or Caspian Sea, despite the fact that neither can be said to have ever covered one third of the known world. This would have placed Mount Elburz, and therefore *Airyana Vaejah*, in central Russia, since this holy mountain was said to have been located on the *north* side of the Vourukasha Sea.

Clearly there were many elements to this mythical domain which were either highly distorted or else related to an ancestral homeland outside of Iran altogether, perhaps even on a different continent.[16] Mount Elburz, on the other hand, is traditionally associated by the Persians with the summit of Mount Demavand, which lies in the aptly named Elburz mountain range. This forms an unbroken chain around the southern coast of the Caspian Sea, north of the capital Tehran. So, was this the domain of *Airyana Vaejah*?

Before any real conclusions could be drawn, it was important to remember that even the most orthodox Persian scholars accept that Iranian mythological locations were determined purely by the myth-makers themselves, and were often changed to suit the landscape in which the nomadic story-teller was reciting his or her fable.[17] Equating the mythical Mount Elburz with the snowy peaks of Mount Demavand, and the Elburz range as a whole, was almost certainly a misnomer. The Persians favoured these mountains over and above any others for the simple reason that they signified the most distant northerly horizon, implying that the name of the actual mountain range had probably derived from this association alone, and *not* because it was the site of the *original* 'Mount Elburz' of myth and fable. Furthermore, if the mythical Mount Elburz *was* to be linked with the snowy heights of Mount Demavand, then the Vourukasha Sea could never have been either the Black or Caspian Seas, since both lay to the *north* of the Elburz range, not to its south, as in the traditions of *Airyana Vaejah*. Even so, it was silly to make such precise statements, for myth and legend have a habit of becoming grossly distorted over a period of many millennia.

So if not Mount Demavand, where might I place the geographical Mount Elburz? I felt a clue lay in the fact that many of the legends regarding Mount Elburz, or Hara, had actually stemmed from Magi tradition. They had unquestionably influenced the development of many of Iran's ancient myths, which were already hoary with age when Zoroaster adopted them into his own faith. Since the domain of the Magi had been the remote mountainous regions of north-west Iran, then perhaps I would have to look towards this direction for a possible solution to this perplexing enigma.

And simply by studying the Magi-influenced texts of Zoroastrianism, it became abundantly clear that they had placed Iran's most sacred locations in or around Media, modern-day Azerbaijan. Indeed, it had undoubtedly been down to their influence that in the *Bundahishn* the realm of *Eranvej* – the *Airyana Vaejah* of the older texts – is clearly located 'in the region of Azerbaijan'.[18]

This was all very well, but what credence could be placed on the word of the Magi? Why should I have reason to believe their word over and above any other Iranian tribe or kingdom's claim to know the true whereabouts of its holiest of places? Remember, in the opinion of Zoroaster the Magi were 'followers of the Lie', who preached only falsehood and untruths. The answer seemed to be in the fact that it was not just the Magi who favoured Azerbaijan as their spiritual homeland.

Mountain of the Madai

The Mandaeans of Iraq and Iran, for instance, had their own ideas about the mythical realm of the gods. We know that they, too, attached great importance to the Simurgh bird,[19] and once performed rites of excarnation. I had therefore been intrigued to discover that they placed their ancestral homeland in the vicinity of somewhere they referred to as the Tura d Madai, the Mountain of the Madai.[20] This, so the Mandaeans hinted, was situated in a mythical domain known as *Mshunia Kushta*, 'the ideal world',[21] which appeared to have striking similarities to the Iranian concept of *Airyana Vaejah*, or *Eranvej*.

The name Madai, as opposed to Mandai, is thought, with very good reason, to mean Media, since the Median peoples had originally been known as the *Mad* or *Mada*.[22] To the Mandaeans, the Mountain of the Madai lay somewhere 'in the north', which, if taken literally, would have placed it directly in line with the mountainous regions of northern Iraq, north-western Iran, on the western edge of the kingdom of Media. This was a solution generally accepted by Mandaeans themselves; for one priest, pressed on where exactly the Mountain of the Madai could be found, had responded to the British author E. S. Drower when she was making an in-depth study of this culture in the 1930s: 'It is, I think, in Iran, for Madia (Media) is in Iran.'[23]

Adding further confirmation to this view is the knowledge that European scholars have long backed the idea that the Mandai were originally a Median tribe, and that their priesthood, the Nasurai, were themselves descended from the Magi priesthoods.[24] If correct, it seemed fairly certain that not only did the Mountain of the Madai correspond with the mythical Mount Elburz, or Hara, but that it had also been located somewhere in the vicinity of the Magian homeland of Azerbaijan.

Among the Angels

Mandaean mythology is a confusing mixture of Babylonian, Persian, Judaic and gnostic Christian traditions, meaning that the origin of specific stories is often impossible to place in a definite time-frame or geographical context. Despite these difficulties, I had been intrigued to find that it was from the Mountain of the Madai that their 'first priest', Anush, or Enoch, had originated.

And, yes, this Enoch was indeed the same antediluvian patriarch found in Judaic tradition.[25] The fact that Enoch had been revered by the Mandaeans should not have come as any surprise, for he was venerated in Iraq more than he ever was in Palestine. Yet, to the Arabs, he was known by the name of Edris, or Idris – a great prophet and teacher who had once lived in Iraq. Indeed, until fairly recent times thousands of Arabs are known to have made regular pilgrimages to Edris' supposed tomb in a village just outside Baghdad.[26] This connection with Enoch was very important, for in Azerbaijani tradition Enoch was said to have been the teacher of Kiyumars, the first legendary king of Iran and all the world, who had ruled from his seat of power in the mountains of *Airyana Vaejah*.[27]

There was, however, further tantalizing evidence to link Enoch with Azerbaijan. In the surviving fragments of the Dead Sea text known as the Genesis Apocryphon, Methuselah goes in search of his father Enoch for advice on the birth of the infant Noah. To this end he journeys to a place named 'Parwain',[28] where the patriarch is said to live 'among the angels'.[29] In most translations, the original Aramaic word is rendered as Paradise, although Parwain is the actual name given. I was therefore quite stunned to find that in Mandaean tradition the Mountain of the Madai was linked not just with Anush, or Enoch, but with a 'white mountain' named 'Parwan' or 'Mount Parwan'.[30] Although it is not specified whether this was simply an alternative name for the Mountain of the Madai, or another holy mountain altogether, the name 'Parwan' was very interesting indeed. It would appear to have been derived from the old Median word 'Parswana', meaning 'rib, side, frontier', used to describe the peoples and territories *beyond* the borders of Media itself. These would have included the region of Parsa to its south and, more significantly, the mountainous region known as Parsua to its west.[31] Was Enoch therefore believed to have lived 'among the angels' in the harsh mountainous territories *beyond* the limits of the ancient kingdom of Media? In the remote region of Parsua, to the west of Media, perhaps? Is this where the Watchers had come from? Was it also the true whereabouts of the *Airyana Vaejah*, the abode of the immortals and the seat of the prehistoric god-kings of Iran, who had borne clear physical characteristics of the fallen race and could well have been their direct descendants?

Suddenly, the mountainous region of Azerbaijan was beginning to take on a whole new meaning in my search to find the roots of the fallen race. Unfortunately, however, all roads appeared to lead back to the Magi priesthood, who obviously had vested interests in ensuring that the kingdom of Media contained the most sacred locations of Iranian mythology. Could I therefore believe their word? The answer lay, not so much with the Magi themselves, as in the fact that cultures and religions throughout the Middle East had always recognized the isolated regions beyond the plateaux of Media, not only as the cradle of civilization, but also as the place where the preserver of the seed of humanity had alighted from his ark following a universal deluge.

Azerbaijan forms the easternmost flanks of a vast snow-capped expanse of mountains that stretch west to the Taurus range of eastern Anatolia and northern Syria; north to the remote mountainous regions of Russian Armenia; and south-east along the length of the Zagros mountains, as they gradually descend towards the Persian Gulf and act as a virtually impenetrable barrier between Iraq and Iran. This enormous, mostly desolate part of the earth, home for the most part to wandering nomads, bands of warring rebels, isolated religious communities and the occasional village, town or city, is known to the world as Kurdistan – the cultural and political homeland of the much troubled Kurdish peoples. And yet, according to biblical and apocryphal tradition, it was here, too, that the Garden of Eden, the Cave of Treasures, the resting place of Noah's Ark and the stamping ground of the great patriarchs could be found, and I realized that it was to here I would need to look in my search for the realm of the immortals.

Twelve

EASTWARD, IN EDEN

And the Lord God planted a garden eastward, in Eden; and there he put the man whom he had formed. And out of the ground made the Lord God to grow every tree that is pleasant to the sight, and good for food; the tree of life also in the midst of the garden, and the tree of the knowledge of good and evil. And a river went out of Eden to water the garden; and from thence it was parted, and became four heads.[1]

These are the words of the Book of Genesis. They tell of the existence of a terrestrial garden created by God in a place called Eden. It is beyond the eastern gate of this idyllic realm that Adam and Eve are cast, once God has realized that they have tasted of the Tree of Knowledge of Good and Evil.

So what exactly *is* the Garden of Eden? And what did it mean to the early Jews? And if it was connected with the story of the fall of the Watchers, then how did it link to the concept of heaven and paradise?

The word 'Eden' is considered by Hebrew scholars to mean 'pleasure' or 'delight',[2] a reference to the fact that God had created the garden for the pleasure of humanity. This is not, however, its true origin. The word 'Eden' is in fact Akkadian – the proto-Hebrew, or Semitic, language introduced to Mesopotamia by the people of Agade, or Akkad, a race that seized control of the ancient kingdom of Sumer, in what is today Iraq, during the second half of the third millennium BC. In their language the word 'Eden', or *edin*, meant a 'steppe' or 'terrace',[3] as in a raised agricultural terrace.

Turning to the word 'paradise', I found that this simply inferred a 'walled enclosure', after the Persian root *pairi*, 'around', and *daeza*, 'wall'. It is a late-comer to Judaeo-Christian religious literature and was only really used after the year AD 1175.[4] The English word 'heaven', on the other hand, is taken from the Hebrew *ha'shemim*, a plural form of a word interpreted as meaning 'the skies'. It can also be used to refer to 'high places', such as lofty settlements.[5] Moreover, the Hebrew word-root *shm* can also mean 'heights', as well as 'plant' or 'vegetation', implying, perhaps, that the word 'heaven' might more accurately be interpreted as 'planted highlands'.[6]

This quick round of etymological translation, in my opinion at least, conjured the image of a walled, agricultural settlement with stepped terraces placed in a highlands region. Was I doing the fabled Garden of Eden an injustice by thinking of it in such a mundane manner? And was I right to suggest that Eden, heaven and paradise had been one and the same place? Surely heaven is a utopian realm created by our psychological necessities, or at best the ethereal domain where the souls of the departed will rejoice with God and his angels on the Day of Judgement.

The Journey to Heaven

Hebrew myth records that the first mortal to enter the Garden of Eden after the expulsion of Adam and Eve was the patriarch Enoch.[7] Scholars would suggest that this rather naïve assumption stemmed originally from a literal translation of the lines in the Book of Genesis which imply that Enoch had been translated to heaven and did not die in the usual manner. It is a theme dealt with in extraordinary detail within Enochian literature, where Enoch is not simply taken to heaven, he is actually given a guided tour of its seven individual 'heavens' before being returned to the physical world.

This quite extraordinary tale begins with the unexpected arrival of the two 'very tall' men, with radiant faces and raiments that have 'the appearance of feathers', who enter Enoch's home and demand that he go with them. Having made his departure, the righteous patriarch is then taken up on to the wings of these two 'men' who carry him off to heaven. On approaching the paradisical realm,

Enoch is allowed to rest temporarily on a moving cloud, and here he gazes out over 'the treasures of the snow and ice' and espies 'the angels who guard their terrible store-places'.[8] Also set out before him is 'a very great sea, greater than the earthly sea'.[9] Turning to the first of the seven heavens, Enoch is then escorted through its gates, beyond which he finds two hundred astronomer angels and their elders who 'rule the stars and their heavenly service'.[10] If, for one moment, I could consider that the patriarch might actually have visited some kind of terrestrial, as opposed to ethereal, domain, then might these words suggest an elevated observatory dedicated to the study of astronomy and the measurement of time?

Moving on to the Second Heaven, Enoch is abhorred to find angelic prisoners 'suspended', awaiting some form of eternal punishment.[11] This made me recall the inhumane manner in which Shemyaza, the leader of the two hundred rebel Watchers, had been suspended upside down for his crimes against humanity. Those angels who guarded these poor, wretched souls are themselves 'gloomy in appearance, more than the darkness of the earth'.[12] Seeing the mortal, the shackled prisoners cry out for the patriarch to pray for them, to which he responds: 'Who am I, a mortal man, that I should pray for angels?'[13]

Wise words from a man confronted with a scene he could never have thought possible – angels in prison. To incarcerate immortals hardly seemed like the righteous actions of incorporeal messengers of God.

Passing swiftly on to the Third Heaven, Enoch eventually finds himself in the Garden of Eden, which he describes as:

> *a place such as has never been known for the goodliness of its appearance. And I saw all the trees of beautiful colours and their fruits ripe and fragrant, and all kinds of food which they produced, springing up with delightful fragrance. And in the midst (there is) the tree of life, in that place, on which God rests, when He comes into Paradise. And this tree cannot be described for its excellence and sweet odour. And it is beautiful more than any created thing.*[14]

From the roots of this tree come four streams – one of pure honey, one of milk, one of oil and the last of wine. These separate into four directions and 'go down to the Paradise of Eden' before 'they go along the earth, and have a revolution in their circle like also the other elements'.[15] There is also:

another tree, an olive tree always distilling oil. And there is no tree there without fruit, and every tree is blessed. And there are three hundred angels very glorious, who keep the garden, and with never ceasing voices and blessed singing, they serve the Lord every day.[16]

The Garden of Eden appears to have more in common with an Israeli kibbutz, or with the gardens of a Christian monastery, than with an ethereal kingdom peopled by angelic hosts. Moreover, the reference to the Tree of Life on which God 'rests, when He comes into paradise' is strangely reminiscent of the Tree of All Remedies, or the Tree of All Seeds, on which the Simurgh bird rests in Persian tradition. This heavenly tree is said to have been placed in the centre of the Vourukasha Sea, which is itself located in the *Airyana Vaejah*, the Iranian domain of the immortals. Curiously enough, like the Garden of Eden, the Vourukasha Sea is seen as the gathering point of all water, fed by a mighty river named Harahvaiti. From this waterway come two separate rivers that flow out towards the east and west and spread throughout the whole of the land. They then return to the sea, their waters cleansed of any impurities.[17]

The two men then show Enoch 'a very terrible place' where crazed prisoners are held captive by ruthless angels who carry savage weapons and commit unmerciful torture. It is a place of darkness, with only a gloomy fire that burns constantly. The text relates that this dreadful prison is reserved for all those who do not honour the word of God and commit any one of a whole list of heinous crimes that were undoubtedly added to by each different story-teller or translator who retold this tale.[18]

In the Fourth Heaven Enoch enters what appears to have been another observatory, where he is able to study the 'comings and goings forth and all the rays of the light of the sun and moon'.[19] Here he is able to measure the descent of the celestial bodies and compute their light, for he says that the sun 'has a light seven times greater than the moon'.[20] He also realizes that there are 'four great stars' with another 8,000 stars in their charge.[21] Here, once again, the angels' apparent interest in astronomy is reaffirmed. The study of the stars is, of course, listed among the forbidden sciences revealed to mortal kind by the rebel Watchers.

And so to the Fifth Heaven, where Enoch finds the two hundred Watchers who have transgressed the laws of heaven by revealing the forbidden arts and taking wives from among the Daughters of Men. For their misconduct, they have been incarcerated like lowly prisoners. As the mortal passes by they, too, call out for him to help their claim of innocence. These fallen angels are described as *grigori* – the Greek for Watchers. They are said to have looked 'like men', and to have borne a height 'greater than that of the giants (i.e. their Nephilim offspring)'.[22] Enoch also recalls how 'their countenances were withered',[23] bringing to mind the way in which the mythical Iranian kings would lose the royal *farr* if they turned their backs on the path of truth.

In the Sixth Heaven Enoch encounters seven bands of angels whose faces, he says, were 'shining more than the rays of the sun. They were resplendent, and there is no difference in their countenance, or their manner, or the style of their clothing'.[24] Like the angels in the First Heaven, these shining beings watch 'the revolution of the stars, and the changes of the moon, and the revolutions of the sun', even further evidence that the term 'Watchers' relates not to their observation of mortal kind, but to their observation of the movement of stars and their study of the cycles of time. Here the angels 'superintend the good or evil condition of the world', a reference perhaps to the study of climatology and seismology, and the way in which it affects the earth. These Watchers also 'arrange teachings, and instructions, and sweet speaking, and singing, and all kinds of glorious praise', for 'these are the archangels who are appointed over the angels'.[25]

In the seventh and final heaven Enoch witnesses whole hosts of great archangels, Cherubim, Seraphim, and all sorts of incorporeal powers that attend the throne of God.[26] In a separate rendition of this story, the patriarch finds himself alongside a wall built of 'crystals' that is surrounded by mysterious 'tongues of fire'.[27] Its 'groundwork' appears to be made of the same crystal-like stone, while of the building's interior, he recalls: 'Its ceiling was like the path of the stars and the lightnings . . . A flaming fire surrounded the walls, and its portals blazed with fire.'[28] The temperature here also seemed contradictory, for it appeared to him 'as hot as fire and [*as*] cold as ice', all at the same time. There were apparently 'no delights of life therein', in other words he found no furniture or decoration, showing the apparent spareness and emptiness of this 'house'. Yet then fear overcame Enoch, who suddenly found himself trembling and quaking at the awesomeness of the strange sights around him. I recall feeling exactly the same when I visited St Paul's Cathedral as a boy – the vastness of its interior seemed so overbearing that it made me cry.

Moving quickly on to a second 'house' with a similar appearance, which 'excelled in splendour and magnificence and extent', Enoch now perceived a 'lofty throne' of crystal. Upon this were moving wheels as bright as the 'shining sun', and from beneath it appeared to come 'streams of flaming fire', so bright that he could not look upon them. And 'sat thereon' the throne was the Great Glory, whose 'raiment shone more brightly than the sun and was whiter than any snow'.[29] I will give you Enoch's own recollection of how he felt at that moment:

None of the angels could enter and could behold His face by reason of the magnificence and glory, and no flesh could behold Him. The flaming fire was round about Him, and a great fire stood before Him, and none around could draw nigh Him.[30]

Following Enoch's brief encounter with the Great Glory of God, he is led away and, still in the company of the two feather-clad 'men', departs the seven realms of heaven. The Watcher-like figures take him as far as the 'extremity of heaven' and here they leave him to return to his own world.

Like anyone who has just witnessed some of the most awesome sights a mortal can ever expect to see, Enoch is mind-blown and afraid. In what must have been virtual madness, he falls on his face and screams out to himself, 'Woe is me! what has come upon me!'[31]

Here the story of Enoch's visit to paradise is concluded.

Clearly then, Eden was not some delightful garden created by God for the pleasures of Adam and Eve! Admittedly the Enochian text does resume its narrative, making the archangel Gabriel go back and fetch the half-crazed Enoch in an attempt to get him to re-enter heaven. There is even mention of the patriarch visiting an eighth, ninth and tenth heaven, yet this section has the look of a late interpolation hoping to emphasize to the reader that Enoch ends his life in paradise, in accord with the statements in the Book of Genesis concerning his translation to heaven.

Heaven – Fact or Fantasy?

No one would deny that the account of Enoch's visit to heaven is fanciful in the extreme; indeed, much of its phantasmagorical narrative is difficult to take seriously. In spite of this admission, I honestly believe that it contains a kernel of truth – first-hand, second-hand or probably even third-hand accounts of an actual settlement of an extraordinary nature that once existed in this world. Perhaps it was somewhere visited by someone who had no real understanding of the nature and purpose of what he or she was witnessing first-hand.

Enoch's words are virtually meaningless, but they hint at the very real possibility that, not only was the Garden of Eden equated with the location named heaven, but that it was also home to the Watchers. If these bold assertions were correct, then it suggested the existence of a remarkable highland settlement that included astronomical observatories, schools of learning, productive orchards containing fruit-bearing trees, well-attended cultivated terraces and seemingly even dark prisons and places of torture for those of the race who transgressed its heavenly laws.

Might the memory of this settlement have been preserved among the earliest Semitic or Iranian peoples living in the foothills and plains below this other-worldly domain? Did these lowland cultures preserve the memory of those who belonged to this settlement – a race which, through its extreme physiological features and shamanistic qualities, had become the viper-faced bird-men and shining angels of Hebraic tradition?

Might the descent of the Watchers 'on' Mount Hermon, as recorded in the Book of Enoch, refer not to their flight from heaven to earth, but to their actual descent down a hilly mountainside to the foothills and plains, where they were able to walk among the less evolved pastoral communities, like gods walking among men, like immortals walking among mortals, like the dead walking among the living?

Might the sight of these tall, feather-coated individuals with long radiant faces, snow-white hair, pale ivory-like skin and ruddy cheeks have instilled utter fear in these people, to such a degree that their appearances made them into the demons, devils and evil spirits of much later cultures?

Might the trafficking between these walking serpents of the highlands and the developing cultures of the lowlands have been the basis behind the idea of the Sons of God coming unto the Daughters of Men?

Turning to the Iranian traditions concerning the *ahuras* and *daevas*, I wondered whether knowledge of the angelic paradise visited by Enoch might lie behind the concept of the *Airyana Vaejah*, the Iranian Expanse, which had been the ancestral home of Iran's mythical kings.

All these things were certainly possible. More important, however, was to establish whether Eden existed in our minds alone, or whether it was out there somewhere, waiting to be rediscovered.

The Rivers of Paradise

If Eden *had* once existed as an actual geographical location, where might I start looking for it? Rivers appeared to be the answer, for the Bible records that in Eden one major water-course divided to become four 'heads', each of which grew into a river. The names of these are given as the Pishon, Gihon, Hiddekel and Euphrates.[32] Of these four, only the last can properly be identified by name. The Euphrates flows through Turkish Kurdistan, Syria and Iraq before emptying into the Persian Gulf. The other three rivers were identified by early theologians with, respectively, the Indus of Asia (although occasionally the Ganges of India), the Nile of Africa and the Tigris of western Asia, which, like its sister river the Euphrates, flows through Iraq and empties into the Persian Gulf. The other two were chosen as suitable substitutes simply because they were looked upon by scholars as the mightiest rivers of the classical world. In no way could it be said that all four of these rivers rose in the same geographical region, a problem that was conveniently overlooked by theologians before the rediscovery of cartography in the sixteenth century AD.

Since that time the blatant discrepancy of the four chosen rivers of paradise has been used as evidence by religious critics to demonstrate that the Garden of Eden was merely a conceptual realm without any geographical reality. Yet, to the Israelites at the time of Moses, Eden was unquestionably an actual location, for as the Book of Genesis clearly states: 'And the Lord God planted a garden eastward, in Eden.'[33]

Eastward? Eastward of where? Eastward of Israel? Eastward of Jerusalem? As Jerusalem has been the holiest place in Palestine since the establishment of the Israelite kingdom at the beginning of the first millennium BC, then presumably the Genesis statement meant eastwards of this ancient city. So, if I was to take an easterly bearing from Jerusalem, where would it take me? Reaching for a large-scale map of western Asia, I laid it open and took up a ruler. The line followed a course just below the 32nd parallel through the modern Arab republics of Jordan and Saudi Arabia, and finally into Iraq. So, had the ancient city-state of Babylon been implied by the compilers of Genesis? It seemed unlikely, since Babylon was seen by Jews as a place of gross iniquity, especially after their oppression at the time of the Captivity. Continuing eastwards, the line reached the southern extremes of the Lower Zagros mountain range. East of here were the Iranian plains, hardly the most obvious candidate for the birth-place of the Jewish race. Perhaps, then, the Zagros was being implied by the expression 'eastward, in Eden', for I was hardly likely to find the Mountain of God, on which Eden was said to have been situated,[34] in the middle of the Iraqi desert.

That the Jews believed the Garden of Eden to be somewhere in the vicinity of Iraq is pretty clear, for all the earliest events in the Book of Genesis focus around this region, known within its pages as 'the land of Shinar'.[35] This was a reference to the land once known as Sumer, or Sumeria, where from 3000 BC down to around 1900 BC there existed a series of city-states which controlled the plains between the foothills of Iraqi Kurdistan and the Persian Gulf in southern Iraq. Here the descendants of Noah flourished in the generations after the Great Flood, until, the Bible tells us, a mighty tyrant named Nimrod constructed a tower that reached towards heaven itself – an act that prompted God to strike down this abomination and punish the world. Henceforth its population would be made to speak in many tongues instead of the one single language used until that time.[36] One classical writer named Eupolemus records that the tower owed its foundation to 'the Giants', who included Nimrod himself. Apparently, after the structure was destroyed by divine wrath, these giants ('Titans' in Greek) had been 'scattered over all the earth'.[37] Quite obviously the tower is seen to have been located at Babylon – which is erroneously said by Judaeo-Christians to have derived its name from the word 'babel', or confusion. Despite some sterling research by various scholars and archaeologists of the Victorian age, no hard evidence has ever been found to verify the actual existence of either Nimrod or his fabled tower.[38]

There were, however, other more sound reasons for locating the land of Eden in the highlands above the 'fertile crescent' of ancient Sumer. Some bible commentators have long considered that, since two out of four of the rivers of paradise rise in the mountains of Turkish Kurdistan, the other two must also be major rivers that have their headwaters in this same region. They have therefore seen fit to link these – the Pishon and Gihon – with the Greater Zab and Araxes, both of which do rise in northern Kurdistan.[39] So strong had this link become by the time of the Babylonian Captivity that many Jews erroneously started to identify Eden with a place called *Bit Adini*, or Beth Eden, a town on the Lower Euphrates seized by the Assyrian army.[40]

Since there has never been any suitable alternative to this solution, Jews and Christians alike now accept that the Garden of Eden must have been located in this region of the world, firmly connecting the abode of the angels with the highlands of Kurdistan. Yet was this right? Could this region really have played such an important role in the development of Judaeo-Christian myth and legend? Certainly all the indications from Iranian and Mandaean sources appeared to suggest that their mountain of origin was situated somewhere in the vicinity of ancient Media, which once stretched westwards to encompass the whole of Iranian Kurdistan. But did these traditions refer to the same area where the Jews and Christians believed the Garden of Eden to have been located?

The Place of Descent

Before I made any final judgements, I needed to understand why the early Israelites saw this far-off land as the place of origin of the human race. For this I turned to the Genesis account of the Great Flood with its hero Noah, who, as I already knew, had been born with clear Watcher traits.

As any Jew or Christian will know, Noah is warned by God of an impending deluge, and so gathers together his wife, his three sons, and his sons' wives, and together they construct an enormous sea-going vessel, made of gopher wood and pitched inside and out with bitumen. On this they assemble two of every kind of beast of the earth and bird of the air. The company wait on their 'Ark', and finally the rains come and the earth is covered with water to a depth of 15 cubits. For 40 days it rains unabated, and after a further 150 days the waters begin to subside. A raven is then unsuccessfully sent out by Noah to find land. Later a dove is dispatched for the same reason, and this time it returns with an olive leaf in its beak.

Soon afterwards the Ark comes to rest at a place referred to in the Bible as 'the mountains of Ararat', a mythical location known in Armenian tradition as *Nachidsheuan*, the Place of Descent. The use of the rather vague term 'mountains of Ararat' has long caused heated debate among theologians. 'Ararat' is the Akkadian rendition of 'Urartu', the name given by the Assyrians of Upper Iraq to a powerful Indo-Iranian kingdom, first referred to in texts dating back to 1275 BC. The Urartu culture grew to become a major influence in the Near East until its final demise around 590 BC.[41] Initially the people of Urartu inhabited only the area around Lake Van – an enormous inland sea some sixty miles across and around thirty-five miles wide – situated on the border between Turkish Kurdistan and the Russian Republic of Armenia. Their kingdom gradually expanded, however, to encompass a wide geographical area that reached as far east as the shores of Lake Urmia in ancient

Media, as far north as the Caucasus mountains and as far west as northern Syria.

The 'mountains of Ararat' could therefore be a reference to any one of a whole range of prominent mountains in what is today the desolate border area between the countries of Russian Armenia, Iran, Iraq and Turkey. Despite this vagueness on the part of the Bible, Christians have seen fit to associate the 'mountains of Ararat' with the twin-peaks of Greater Ararat – the highest mountain (16,946 feet) in Turkish Kurdistan.

Over the years fundamentalist Christians, and more open-minded explorers, have attempted, with varying degrees of success, to locate the remains of Noah's Ark on Mount Ararat. Sightings of alleged 'arks' in the vicinity of its bleak summits make extraordinary reading, and should not be dismissed out of hand;[42] however, the Christians are alone in identifying Greater Ararat with the Place of Descent.

In the Koran, the holy book of Islam, the story of Noah's Ark and the Great Flood is repeated. Yet in this version the vessel comes to rest 'on the mountain of Judi' – Judi being an Arabic word meaning 'the heights'. A strong Kurdish tradition links this mythical location with Al Judi, or Cudi Dağ a mountain that rises to the height of 6,436 feet and is located some sixty-five miles south of Lake Van in Turkish Kurdistan.

In the early years of the twentieth century, two Englishmen, the Rev. W. A. Wigram and Edgar T. A. Wigram, spent some years studying the cultural history of Kurdistan. They discovered that the Kurds were in no doubt as to the authentic Place of Descent, for in their 1914 book *The Cradle of Mankind*, the Wigrams spoke of animal sacrifices being annually offered up by all faiths on Al Judi to commemorate Noah's landing here, for, as they reported at the time:

Christians of all nations and confessions, Mussulmans [i.e. Muslims] *of both* Shiah *and* Sunni *type, Sabaeans (Mandaeans), Jews, and even the furtive timid Yezidis are there, each group bringing a sheep or kid for sacrifice; and for one day there is a 'truce of God' even in turbulent Kurdistan, and the smoke of a hundred offerings goes up once more on the ancient altar.*[43]

This archaic festival would take place on 14 September – the generally accepted date on which the Ark came to rest on dry land. At the base of the mountain there is apparently a village named Hasana, where, according to the Wigrams, men 'still point out Noah's tomb and Noah's vineyard, though this last, strange to say, produces no wine now'.[44]

Such traditions are in themselves hollow, especially as the foothills around Greater Ararat proclaim similar such associations.[45] Despite this confusion, the first-century AD Jewish writer Flavius Josephus also spoke specifically of 'Mount Judi near Lake Van' as the resting-place of the Ark.[46]

Whatever the exact location of the so-called Place of Descent, the importance placed on central and northern Kurdistan by the compilers of the Pentateuch was difficult to ignore. It had been standard practice for bards and story-tellers of all ancient cultures to use sites of national and/or local importance when reciting tales of a spiritual or cultural significance, especially in the company of kings and nobles. No one wanted to venerate holy places in far-off lands that might once have been occupied by their culture, but were now in the hands of their sworn enemies. Unless, that is, they held such a significance that they could *never* be forgotten or replaced. This could only mean that the Israelite tribes at the time of Moses believed that the highlands of Kurdistan held some deep spiritual significance to their race, for here they located not just their place of genesis, but also the point at which the world had renewed itself after a universal deluge.

Furthermore, according to the Jewish Talmud, the patriarch Abraham was said to have spent ten years in prison – three in Kutha, near Babylon, and seven in Kardu, the old Semitic name for Kurdistan,[47] showing his own integral link with the region.

The Cradle of Mankind

If the highlands of Kurdistan really had played such an important role in the development of Hebrew myth and legend, then perhaps I was to take seriously the idea that the earthly paradise, and, by virtue of this, the abode of the Watchers, had actually been located in this country. Since the local Kurdish peoples were so sure about the whereabouts of the Place of Descent in the Noah story, then surely they would hold similar convictions concerning the location of the Garden of Eden. If an advanced culture like the Watchers really had existed in this geographical region, then its memory would surely not be forgotten. Indigenous cultures, such as the Kurds, who had led isolated and often nomadic lifestyles until comparatively recent times, must have retained the knowledge of such human activity in their midst.

The two Wigrams spent many years in Kurdistan recording previously unknown customs and legends. Indeed, so thorough was their study of the Kurdish race that modern scholars still use their much-sought-after book, *The Cradle of Mankind*, as a valuable reference work. So what had they learnt concerning the alleged existence of the Garden of Eden among the Kurdish highlands?

First, there seemed little doubt that the Kurds saw the four rivers of paradise as being the Euphrates, Tigris, Greater Zab and Araxes, the last of which empties into the Caspian Sea to the east. Indeed, so strongly did the local Nestorians, or Christians of the Assyrian Church, believe that the Greater Zab was the river Pishon that, according to the Wigrams, its patriarch would often sign-off his official letters 'from my cell on the River of the Garden of Eden'![48]

It was, however, the headwaters of the Euphrates and Tigris that would appear to have most shaped the Kurds' belief in the Garden of Eden's geographical reality. These two rivers curl their way around the solid wall of mountains that act like an impenetrable fortress to encircle Lake Van. The Wigrams speculated that the Garden of Eden had been situated either in the vicinity of the city of Van, the site of the old Urartian capital of Tushpa on its eastern coast, or somewhere around the ancient city of Bitlis beyond its south-western shoreline.[49]

Descendants of Giants

Did the Garden of Eden, the birthplace of the human race, as well as the seven heavens visited by Enoch, once exist in the vicinity of

Lake Van? Very possibly. Armenian legend asserts that the Garden of Eden now lies 'at the bottom of Lake Van', after it was submerged beneath the waves at the time of the Great Flood.[50] What is more, the lake is also connected with the descendants of Noah. On the lake's west bank is the province of Tarawn, where, according to the fifth-century AD Armenian historian Moses of Khorenats'i, Noah's son Sem (Shem) had settled temporarily after the Ark had come to rest on the mountains of Ararat. He had lingered for two months by a river and a mountain, which even today bears the name Sim, or Sem. His son Tarban is also said to have settled in this same area, along with his thirty brothers, fifteen sisters and their husbands. It is for this reason that the location is also known as Ts'rawnk', meaning 'dispersion' – an apparent reference to the dispersion of Tarban's sons and family.[51]

The warm waters of this huge inland salt sea would have provided the area with a mild, temperate climate able to sustain human life and cultivation of the sort spoken of in the Enochian literature, while the wall of mountains surrounding the watery expanse would have acted as a natural shield against the intrusions of the outside world.

Any one of the many mountains that soar into the sky around Lake Van might well have constituted the Mountain of Paradise – the curiously named Mount Nimrod, or Nemrut Dağ, on its south-western shoreline, being a prime candidate. This preserves the name of Nimrod (or Bel), the mighty king of the land of Shinar, who in Armenian tradition not only was a giant, but also enlisted the aid of fellow-giants to help him build the mountain-like Tower of Babel,[52] the story also recorded by the classical writer Eupolemus. One of these giants was, according to Moses of Khorenats'i, a figure named Hayk, the son of T'orgom, who was a direct descendant of Yapheth (Japheth), another of the three sons of Noah.

Hayk was said to have been the founder of the Araradian, or pre-Armenian, race,[53] and it was on the north-west of Lake Van that he had established the province of Hark' – a place-name apparently reflecting the fact that it had been here that the ancestors of his father T'orgom had settled, presumably after the destruction of the Tower of Babel.[54] Nemrut Dağ is likely to have derived its name from an Armenian tradition which asserts that Nimrod was killed by an arrow shot by Hayk during a major battle between two rival armies of giants to the south-east of Lake Van.[55]

I found it more than a little curious that the pre-Armenian race should claim descendency from a race of giants, or Titans, who supposedly settled close to Lake Van and were themselves descendants of Noah, the child born with distinct Watcher traits in Enochian and Dead Sea tradition. Indeed, in the Armenian language, the name Hayk is directly associated with the word 'gigantic', as if to emphasize the great stature of their most distant ancestor.[56] Whatever the actual reality of this tradition, these local legends helped to strengthen the link between this area and the mythical homeland of the Watchers.

Nemrut Dağ, at 9,567 feet, also happens to be the largest inactive volcano in Kurdistan. It possesses an enormous crater six miles across, which is known to have been used in the past as an effective hiding-place for Kurdish rebels.[57] Indeed, vulcanism has played a major role in the shaping of the local terrain, with the lava flow from Nemrut Dağ having provided the dam which allowed the formation of Lake Van in the first place. Among the other great volcanoes of Kurdistan is Greater Ararat, north-east of Van. So active has this region been, even in more recent ages, that the Wigrams were forced to admit that if the Garden of Eden *had* once been placed in this area, then it 'now lies buried beneath the lava of these volcanoes',[58] as opposed to lying at the bottom of the lake.

I mention this vulcanism, for it is clear from the Book of Enoch that when Enoch visited the earthly paradise, the surrounding landscape contained 'a mountain range of fire which burnt day and night',[59] an allusion perhaps to active volcanoes. On one occasion he witnesses 'a river of fire in which the fire flows like water and discharges itself into the great sea towards the west'.[60] If this might be equated with the 'great sea' viewed by him on approaching the First Heaven, then it could imply that he had witnessed lava flowing into an expanse of water. Might the volcano have been Nemrut Dağ and the 'great sea' Lake Van? If so, then this great watery expanse might also provide us with a geographical location for the Vourukasha Sea of Iranian tradition.

I would not be the first to realize the obvious link between the vulcanism of Kurdistan and the fiery realms portrayed in the Book of Enoch. The French writer on ancient mysteries, Robert Charroux, in his 1964 book *Legacy of the Gods* reviewed the Watcher material presented in the Book of Enoch and surmised that the region of Kurdistan had been the setting for the fall of the angels. He added that: 'The guilty angels are hurled into the Valleys of Fire, which may refer to the Land of Fire (Azerbaijan) near which Noah's Ark landed.'[61]

Charroux had looked beyond the snowy heights of Mount Hermon in the Ante-Lebanon range to seek a solution to the mysteries of Enoch, and had come to similar conclusions to myself. This was obviously good news, but it did little to prove the case. As the Wigrams had realized, any obvious remains of the Garden of Eden – and, more importantly, the Watchers' proposed settlement of 'Heaven' – were probably now buried beneath tens of feet of hardened lava flow. So there was little point in mounting an archaeological expedition to the area just yet. For the moment I would concentrate on the Kurds themselves, in an attempt to establish whether any of their religions, indigenous or otherwise, had preserved knowledge of the Watchers' presence, starting with the strange, devil-worshipping sect known as the Yezidi.

Thirteen

THE PEACOCK ANGEL

October 1846. Upper Iraq. Austen Layard, the British explorer, diplomat, titan of archaeology and lover of oriental customs ascended the foothills, north of Mosul, on a sturdy horse. For the trip into Iraqi Kurdistan he was accompanied by Hodja Toma, the dragoman of the vice-consulate, and a priest, or *kawal*, sent to act as their mountain escort by Sheikh Nasr, the chief priest of the Yezidis, a Kurdish religious sect known to Europeans as the 'devil-worshippers'.[1]

After a night spent in a small hamlet near Khorsabad, the party continued across open plains to the village of Baadri, the home of the sect's chief, Sheikh Hussein Bey. As the village came into view, the Yezidi leader appeared in person on the horizon. Following behind him on foot was an entourage of priests and villagers adorned in flowing robes and wearing thick headgear in either black, brown or white. As they approached, Layard realized that Hussein Bey was 'one of the handsomest men' he had ever seen. At around eighteen years of age, he had regular and delicate features, lustrous eyes, and long dark ringlets that fell from beneath his thick black turban.

Layard endeavoured to dismount so as to greet the Bey courteously, but before he had a chance to do so, the fellow attempted to kiss his hand, a ritual he promptly refused to oblige. Instead the two men embraced, while still on their horses, as was the manner of this country. The Bey insisted that the two of them should dismount and walk together. This done, they strolled side-by-side, exchanging pleasantries as they entered the village.

Inside the chief's *salamlik*, or reception room, filled with carpets and cushions, a stream of fresh water passed by them, fed from a neighbouring spring. All running water was of immense sanctity to the Yezidi, as it was to both the Magians and the Mandaeans of Iraq and Iran. Once the Englishman and the 'devil-worshipper' had begun engaging in conversation, an audience of curious villagers started to gather at the other end of the room. They simply listened in respectful silence, seemingly with the Bey's full permission.

How different were the two cultures represented by these two great men. Sir Austen Henry Layard (1817–94) had been responsible for the recent excavations on behalf of his patrons Sir Stratford Canning and the British Museum at the ancient ruins of Nimrud, the Assyrian ruins situated at the confluence of the Tigris and Upper Zab rivers, near the city of Mosul.

As a traveller, Layard respected the native religions of the region, and this included the secretive Yezidis of the Kurdish foothills. He had heartily accepted an invitation from the Bey to be the first European to witness the sect's strange rites during its yearly *Jam*, or religious festival. This was to take place over a several-day period in the village of Lalish. Being a good Christian, Layard naturally had reservations about attending such a devil-worshipping festival, but these fears were fast being alleviated in the company of the religion's tribal leader.

The isolated Yezidi tribes were probably the most obscure of the three quite separate yet interrelated cults of the *yazata*, *yazd* or *yezad*, the Persian for 'angel' or 'angels', which still thrived in certain parts of Kurdistan. Each paid lip-service to the Islamic faith, whether of the Shi'ite or Sunni persuasion, and yet each also held true to its own unique cosmogony, mythology and ritual practices, which had more in common with Magian or gnostic dualism than with the Muslim or Judaeo-Christian faiths.

The Angelicans

The appellation of 'devil-worshippers' had been given to the Yezidis by the earliest European travellers, yet their creed ventured far beyond such an ignorant description. The name Yezidi derived from the nature of their beliefs, which focused primarily around an indigenous breed of angelic beings. In many ways their name can be translated as the 'angelicans', and originally this would appear to have been the name by which all the Kurdish angel cults were known. Yet chief among the Yezidi angels was a unique and very important figure indeed. His name was, and still is (for the Yezidis still exist), *Melek Taus*, the Peacock Angel. He corresponds with the Judaeo-Christian concept of the Evil One – Satan or Lucifer – but this association hardly does him justice, for Melek Taus is seen as a supreme being, with authority over worldly affairs. To these people he was the creator of the material world, which he made from the scattered pieces of an original cosmic egg, or pearl, inside which his spirit had previously resided.

According to one Yezidi text known as the *Mes'haf i Resh*, or 'the Black Book' – the contents of which were entirely unknown to Europeans in Layard's time – it reveals that:

In the beginning God (Kurdish Khuda*) created the White Pearl out of his most precious Essence; and He created a bird named* Anfar. *And He placed the pearl upon its back, and dwelt thereon forty thousand years. On the first day* [*of Creation*], *Sunday, He created an angel called 'Azâzil, which is* Melek Tâwus, *the chief of all* [*angels*].[2]

The beliefs of the Yezidi tribes of Kurdistan are littered with ornithomorphic themes. The *Anfar* is almost certainly a cosmic form of the Persian and Zoroastrian Simurgh bird. More importantly, the Yezidi holy book, which is thought to date in its present form to the thirteenth century AD, states that the first name of the Peacock Angel had been '*Azâzil*, an Arabic rendering of Azazel, one of the leaders of the Watchers in Judaeo-Christian apocrypha.

Yezidis have attempted to contain their own limited, and often contradictory, knowledge and understanding of the Peacock Angel within the Islamic account of the fall of Azazel, or Eblis. According to the Koran, the Fallen Angel was outcast by God for having refused to bow down before Adam, the creature made of clay, since he himself had been born of fire. In the traditional rendition of the story, Azazel is doomed to walk the earth eternally, but according to the Yezidi version, God *forgave* Azazel, who was then reinstated in Heaven.

The Peacock Angel is undoubtedly seen by the Yezidi tribes as a form of Satan, or *Shaitân* as he is known in Arabic, since every effort is made *not* to mention this name out aloud. Fail to do so and the culprit would be struck blind. This fanatical attitude goes so far as banning the use of words that even sound like *Shaitân*. Furthermore, no one is allowed to make a curse in the name of *Shaitân*, unless it is out of earshot of neighbours and is directed at those not of the faith.[3]

Like the Zoroastrians and the Dead Sea communities of post-exilic Judaea, the angelicans of Kurdistan have always revered whole pantheons of *yazatas*, or angels. And in similar with these other angel worshippers, the Yezidi hold that a group of seven, sometimes six, head the angelic hierarchy – these, of course, can be equated with both the Iranian concept of the *Amesha Spentas* and the Judaeo-Christian belief in seven archangels. The leader of the main Yezidi group of angels is *Lasifarûs*, a cosmic incarnation of *Melek Taus*, who is specifically said to speak Kurdish, as if to demonstrate his indigenous nature.[4] Scholars have attempted to connect his name with Lucifer, the Christian form of Satan, which seems highly probable indeed. The rest of the seven angels are given standard Christian-Islamic names such as *Jebra'il* (Gabriel), *Mika'il* (Michael), *Ezra'il* (Azrael) and *Esrafil* (Raphael). Another angelic hierarchy of the Yezidi are the *Chehelmir*, or *Chelmir*, who number forty.

All this was, of course, quite unknown to Layard as he sat with the current Yezidi leader Hussein Bey in his *salamlik*. He was the son of one of the greatest sheikhs of their tribes, Ali Bey, who had defended their people against countless attacks from Kurdish Muslims, the Ottoman Turks, as well as the Islamic armies of both Iraq and Iran. Quite obviously they saw the Yezidis as not just infidel, but as heretics *par excellence*, fit only to be wiped out completely unless they renounced their faith and became Muslims themselves.

In past centuries the Yezidis had been very powerful, covering extensive areas all over Kurdistan, but slowly their tribes had been persecuted and destroyed until there were now only isolated groups left in the Iraqi and Turkish foothills of Kurdistan, as well as further south in the vicinity of Jebel Sinjar, a solitary mountain in the Iraqi desert, whose name translates as the mountain of the 'bird'.[5] Yezidis have also survived in small pockets across central Kurdistan, as well as in the Russian Caucasus and in various

Fig. 6. Entering the village of Lalish in the foothills of Iraqi Kurdistan. Here Yezidis come each year for the annual *Jam* festival in honour of their principal avatar, or saint, Sheikh Adi. The conical towers, or *mazârs*, mark Yezidi shrines and tombs.

satellite communities in northern Syria, Lebanon, Anatolia and Iran. Today their tribes represent some 5 per cent of the Kurdish population,[6] yet as each year passes their numbers diminish even further.

Layard spent the evening pleasantly chatting with Hussein Bey, and in the morning the two men travelled by horse to Lalish. Hussein himself was dressed in bright robes, and accompanying them was a large contingent of horsemen, who constantly discharged guns into the air and sang Yezidi war songs. Also with them were musicians, who played pipes and tambourines, and a whole procession of Yezidi villagers, who followed behind on foot. The journey was long and arduous, seemingly ever upwards. Occasionally the party would be forced to dismount from their horses and ascend precarious mountain paths in single file.

Having reached the summit of one final pass, the party looked down into a wooded valley to see a large cluster of buildings, interspersed here and there with brilliant white conical spires, each one vertically ribbed into many ridged sections. Known as *mazârs*, these towers marked the position of Yezidi shrines and tombs. All at once the tribesmen discharged their guns into the air in celebration of their arrival at Lalish. Almost immediately this indiscriminate use of firearms was answered by another volley of shots from the village itself.

As the procession descended down into thick oak woodland, it began to pass many other pilgrims making their way to the tomb of Sheikh Adi, the cult's main avatar (the living incarnation of a divine being), in whose honour the annual *Jam* festival is held. He is supposed to have lived during the twelfth or thirteenth century AD, and is believed to have been an incarnation of *Melek Taus* himself. Even though Sheikh Adi is recognized as the founder of the Yezidi faith, both the religion and the tribes are ascribed a much earlier date of origin. Interestingly enough, the Yezidi sacred work entitled the *Mes'haf i Resh* is written in a very ancient Kurdish language known as *Kermânji*, which, at the time of its composition in the medieval period, was confined to the rugged Hakkâri mountains south of Lake Van, close to the suggested location of the Garden of Eden. Indeed, this very area was the traditional stronghold of Sheikh Adi, who, despite a belief among modern Yezidis that he was born in the Bekaa Valley of Lebanon, was once known as Adi al-Hakkâri, or Adi of Hakkâri.[7]

Roots of the Yezidi

Sheikh Adi had obviously revitalized an existing set of beliefs already adhered to among the Kurdish tribesmen, yet where exactly these people had obtained their quite unique religious views is not known. Yezidi cosmogony and mythology were unquestionably non-Christian and non-Islamic in origin, although they did appear to bear some striking similarities to the teachings of the Persians, in particular the religion of the Magi. The Yezidis believe in a form of dualism, where they give equal respect to both the 'good' and 'evil' principles of their religion. This therefore paralleled the Magi's belief in the eternal struggle between the *ahuras* and *daevas*, the root of virtually all later dualism in the Near

East. So were the Yezidis descendants of the Median Magi? The answer has to be yes, for the angelicans believe that the next incarnation of *Melek Taus* will come in the form of a personage named Sheikh Mêdî, or Mahdî – an avatar who will bear the blood and power of the ancient spiritual leaders of Media.[8] That the Yezidi are among the last survivors of the faith of the Magi is not disputed. Scholars are in no doubt that it was the Magi, and not the Zoroastrians, who had influenced the development of Yezidism.[9]

Clinching the connection was the belief among the Yezidi that Sheikh Adi had himself been a Magian. According to the Wigrams in *The Cradle of Mankind*: 'there seems some historical evidence that he (Sheikh Adi) lived in the tenth century (a disputed date), and that he was originally a Magian who had fled from Aleppo (in Syria) when the Magian cult was suppressed'.[10] It was he who had established the Yezidi creed and sacred books, and it will be his spirit that is going to come again in the final days; hence the prophecy about the incarnation of Melek Taus as Sheikh Mêdî, or Mahdî.

The Shrine of Sheikh Adi

As Hussein Bey and Layard journeyed through the oak wood, they watched as women broke away from their chores to rest for a few minutes and as the men busily reloaded their rifles in readiness for the next party of pilgrims to appear over the mountain pass. Soon the European and the sheikh were greeted by the chief Yezidi priest Sheikh Nasr. He approached with the principal members of the priesthood, who were all dressed in white. Nasr appeared to be about forty years of age, and the warmth with which he and his priests greeted Layard was commendable. They all insisted on kissing his hand as he remained on his horse, despite his clear dislike of this custom. Hussein and Layard then dismounted and began the last part of the journey on foot.

The tomb of Sheikh Adi contained an outer and inner courtyard which led into a darkened room within which was the saint's tomb. This ancient building had almost certainly once been a Nestorian church, before these local Christians had departed the area.[11]

Layard quickly realized that entry into the inner courtyard was by barefoot only, so he removed his shoes before venturing further. Once inside the open enclosure, he sat down alongside Hussein Bey and Sheikh Nasr on the carpets provided. Only the sheikhs and *kawals*, the two principal orders of priesthood, were allowed to join them in this sacred area. Each took seats around the walls of the precinct, some of which was shaded by enormous trees that grew within the courtyard. Beyond them on all sides was a rocky valley that seemed to act as a natural amphitheatre overlooking the events taking place below, for pilgrims were already gathering beneath the shades of trees or on roof-tops in readiness for the evening's proceedings. At one end of the sanctuary was running water said to issue from a spring that had been miraculously diverted to this place from the more famous spring of Zemzem at Mecca by Sheikh Adi himself.

The Black Serpent

Around the east and west doorways into the darkened tomb was an assortment of devotional images carved in high relief. Many of these were obscure, their symbolism uncertain. They included items such as combs, assorted birds (probably peacocks), crescents, hatchets, stars, as well as various animals, including a lion. Most striking of all was a long, black snake carved to the right of the eastern entrance, close to where tiny red flowers had been attached to the wall using black pitch.[12] Layard tried in vain to find out the meaning of this serpentine form from Sheikh Nasr, who merely stated that it had been carved for decoration by a Christian mason some years beforehand. This explanation, Layard quickly realized, was a little short of the truth, for the carving was paid the highest respect by all Yezidis who daily coated it in charcoal to preserve its stark black lustre.[13] Each person, on entering the tomb, would stop to kiss the black snake, as if it held some special place in their personal beliefs.[14]

And Layard was right, for the serpent did hold a special significance in the Yezidi religion. Not only was it venerated on feast days,[15] but it was also a symbol of totemic magic. Descendants

Fig. 7. The exterior wall of Sheikh Adi's tomb within the Yezidi village of Lalish in Iraqi Kurdistan. To the right of the door is the much-venerated black snake, a symbol of Azazel, the Greatest Angel in Yezidi beliefs.

of certain Yezidi sheikhs, in particular Sheikhs Mand and Ruhsit,[16] the latter being found in the villages of Baibân and Nasarî in the Mosul Vilâyet, believed they had power over serpents and were immune from the effects of snake poison. European travellers referred to these people as snake-charmers, for they would go from village to village displaying their magical talents to any household willing to pay them.[17]

The British author E. S. Drower, whose book *Peacock Angel* is one of the only documented studies of the Yezidis, encountered a snake-charmer and his 'ugly little' daughter Jahera, or 'Snake-Poison', during a visit to the village of Baashika in 1940. Mrs Drower described how she watched the sheikh, a descendant of Sheikh Mand, and his daughter enter a courtyard with huge patterned snakes coiled around their shoulders. The father then proceeded to remove the serpent from his daughter's neck before dropping it to the ground. It slithered 'along in the sparse grass looking very evil indeed. It was five or six feet in length and its body two inches or more in thickness.'[18] The sheikh then caught the snake and placed it back on the child's shoulders. Mrs Drower having given the odd couple 'an offering', the sheikh and his daughter posed for photographs, holding the snakes' flat heads close to their lips, before moving on to the next household.[19] Mrs Drower asked her Yezidi host whether the claims regarding the magical powers attributed to the snake-charmers were real, only to be told that they had seen Jahera handle a poisonous snake fresh from the fields, and that the snakes do not have their fangs removed.[20]

Snake-charming is a form of showmanship. It is also the outer manifestation of snake shamanism, which appears to have been extremely important to the angel-worshipping Yezidis since time immemorial. The fact that these magical talents were said to have been passed down from generation to generation implied a hereditary lineage of immense antiquity. It is unclear exactly what the serpent represented to the Yezidi, although its veneration would suggest that it played a similar role to that of the Peacock Angel, in other words it was a symbol of Azazel, or Shaitân. It must also have represented the spiritual energy and magical potency of the snake shamans themselves.

So where had this symbol of magical potency come from? Did it signify, not only the hereditary shamanism among the Yezidi, but also its original source? Snake shamanism and viper-like features would appear to have been characteristics associated with the Watchers. So if they really *had* existed as an actual culture living in this same region during prehistoric times, then it was possible that the Yezidis' veneration of the serpent was a memory of their presence and influence.

Power of the Evil Eye

Layard noticed that in the centre of the inner courtyard in front of Sheikh Adi's tomb stood a square plaster case, inside which was a small recess filled with what seemed to be small balls of clay. These were eagerly purchased by the pilgrims as if they had some special purpose to play. On inquiring as to what was going on, Layard was informed that these balls had been made from mud collected from the actual tomb of Sheikh Adi, which is placed next to a muddy spring. Yezidis regard them as sacred relics able to ward off evil spirits, including the evil eye, which is paid unparalleled attention among all the Kurdish faiths. For instance, at a Yezidi sacred place named Dair Asî in the Sinjar region, there is a secret rock cleft where 'those afflicted with the influence of the "evil eye" deposit their gifts in order to alleviate their misfortune'.[21] Yet even more fearful of the evil eye are the Muslims and Christians, for as Mrs Drower recorded, few mothers 'would dare to take their babies abroad without sewing their clothes over with blue buttons, cowries, and scraps of Holy writ, either Qur'an or Bible'.[22] Blue is the Yezidis' most sacred colour and is never worn by them for this reason, yet to all the other Kurdish faiths it is used to ward off the evil eye. Why was there this great fear of the evil eye in Kurdistan? And why did the colour blue play such a contradictory role among the Kurdish faiths? The matter of the evil eye is discussed in a subsequent chapter, but the colour blue I shall deal with now.

In the Persian *Shahnameh* turquoise blue is the colour of sovereignty and kingship. The Pishdadian kings wore blue crowns and garments, a tradition also echoed in ancient Sumer and Akkad, where the monarchs were adorned in items fashioned from blue lapis lazuli stone. Since the mythical kings of Iran were said to have borne strong physiological features of the *daevas*, then perhaps this colour was deemed to possess divine characteristics appertaining to the fallen race. If so, it might explain why later generations of humanity came to either revere or fear this colour, depending on the nature of their faith. Evil has always been used to ward off evil, which is why church gargoyles and grotesques are said to keep away demons, and why eye charms are used to repel the evil eye, so blue must have been used by Kurdish Muslims and Christians in a similar capacity.

The Jam Begins

At midday, Sheikh Nasr, the chief priest, stood up, signalling that everyone else should do likewise. Layard followed suit, walking with the party as it moved from the inner to the outer court, which by now was a hive of frenzied activity. Some peddlers sold handkerchiefs and cotton items from Europe while others sat before bowls of dried figs, raisins, dates or walnuts collected from different parts of Iraqi Kurdistan. Men and women, boys and girls, appeared to be involved in feverish conversation, the din rising at the sight of Hussein Bey and Sheikh Nasr, whom they now respectfully saluted. The party continued through the outer court and moved into the open air, where an avenue of tall trees offered a welcome shade. A constant sound of pipes and tambourines pervaded the air as Layard joined the various sheikhs and *kawal* priests, who proceeded to sit down in a circle around a sacred spring. All watched as women approached to take water from the little reservoir below the fountain.

As this was in progress, lines of pilgrims continued to approach along the avenue of trees. Layard could not help noticing among them 'a swarthy inhabitant of the Sinjar' with long black ringlets and piercing black eyes. Over his shoulder was slung a matchlock gun, while his long white robe rustled about in the warm breeze. Behind him came the rich and the poor – men in colourful turbans with ornate daggers in their belts, women wearing long, flowing gowns with their long hair in neat tresses, and poverty-stricken families dressed in ragged white clothes. They all approached the fountain, as if it was the penultimate station along the pilgrim route to the tomb of their saint. The men would lay down their arms before kissing the hands of Hussein Bey, Sheikh Nasr and the white-skinned European, who was treated with equal respect by everyone. They then made their way towards a small stream where each person washed both themselves and their dirty garments in readiness to enter the outer courtyard. As this was happening, firearms were still being discharged in response to those who announced their own entry into the valley in a likewise manner.

Perpetual music, song and dance filled the afternoon, and eventually Layard decided to retire to the roof of a nearby building. Here he was supplied with food by black-turbaned *fakir* priests and a wife of Sheikh Nasr. Down below in the inner court other *fakir* priests had appeared carrying lamps and cotton-wool wicks that were placed in niches on the outer walls of the tomb as well as in the surrounding valley. Layard saw that Yezidis would run their right hand through the flame and then rub the opposite eyebrow with the resulting black soot. Women would do likewise for young children, or for those less fortunate than themselves. As in the Magian and Zoroastrian faiths, fire is sacred to the Yezidi.

As nightfall came, the valley looked star-spangled with a myriad of tiny flames flickering in the cool evening breeze. But something else now stirred. Literally thousands of people – Layard estimated up to 5,000 – moved about the slopes like a great moving sea of orderly activity. Many carried lighted torches and lamps, further illuminating the trees dotted all around the valley.

Layard watched as large numbers of sheikhs, dressed immaculately in white; *kawals*, adorned in black and white; *fakirs*, wearing brown robes and black turbans; as well as numerous women priests attired in white, began to assemble in the inner court for what appeared to be the climax of the *Jam* festival. The *kawals* played sweet melodies on flutes and tambourines, which grew steadily in pitch and intensity. Accompanying the pleasant sounds was a slow choral chant that radiated from the men on the surrounding slopes. This continued unabated for over an hour, the pitch hardly varying at all. Occasionally contrasting harmonies would emanate from the priests positioned in the inner court. Gradually the whole bizarre cacophony quickened its pace and volume, until finally it blended to become an eerie wall of harmonic sound that seemed to hang motionless in the air.

The tambourines were then banged louder and louder as the flutes were played with ever more ferocity. Voices were raised to their highest pitch, while women warbled a strange low shrill that seemed to make even the rocks reverberate with constant sound. Overcome by the ecstasy of the highly charged atmosphere, the *kawals* began to discard their instruments as they started flinging themselves around in wild trances, induced by the almighty crescendo of noise. Each fell to the ground when their body could take no more.

And then the focus of their ritual was made apparent to the chosen few for the first and only time that day. In the inner court, out of view of the masses, a sheikh delicately clasped an item in a red cloth coverlet, something that appeared to be of immense spiritual significance to these people.

Slowly the priest removed the red covering, and immediately held aloft what lay beneath it. In his hand was a strange statue of a bird, made either of brass or copper. It was perched upon a tall stand, like a weighty candlestick, that appeared to be made of a similar metal. The image itself seemed crude with a bulbous body and a long hooked beak, like that of a predatory bird. Its name was *Anzal*, the Ancient One,[23] the embodiment of *Melek el Kout*, the Greatest Angel, whose presence had now been summoned.[24]

This strange bird icon of immense antiquity was the Yezidis' chief subject of veneration. So who was the Greatest Angel? And what possible significance did this archaic worship have to my knowledge of the fallen race?

The Greatest Angel

Aside from the sculptured bird icon kept at the tomb of Sheikh Adi at Lalish, there were apparently six more of these so-called *sanjaqs*, a word meaning either 'standard' or 'dioceses'.[25] Each of these examples was made to be carried in a dismantled state by travelling *kawals*, who would move from village to village looking for a suitable venue to conduct a very strange ceremony in which the priest would invoke the spirit of *Melek Taus* into the bird icon, using a form of trance communication.

The *sanjaq* icons are greatly revered by the Yezidis, and until 1892 it was claimed that none had ever fallen into the hands of enemies.[26] Who exactly *Anzal*, the Ancient One, might have been is sadly not recorded. It was probably another form of Azazel, the Peacock Angel. A possible clue as to its identity may, however, come from the candlestick-like stand on which the images perch. This almost certainly symbolized the divine tree on which the *Saena*, or Simurgh bird, sat in Persian tradition, suggesting that these stands represented the seat of all knowledge and wisdom, passed on to Yezidis through the presence of the Ancient One.

That these metal images became identified with the peacock bird is a complete mystery since peacocks are not indigenous to Kurdistan. Some were introduced to Baghdad during the Middle Ages. They were also to be found in Persia, which is probably why

Figs. 8 and *9.* Two examples of *sanjaqs*, the metal bird icons venerated by the angel-worshipping Yezidi of Kurdistan. On the left is one seen by Sir Austen Henry Layard in 1849, and on the right is another sketched by a Mrs Badger in 1850. Are these strange icons abstract memories of Kurdistan's protoneolithic vulture shamans?

Aristotle referred to them as 'the Persian bird'.[27] Yet it is in the Indian state of Rajasthan that the peacock is most revered. Hindus here see it as sacred to Indra, the god – or *asura* – of thunder, rains and war. Much folklore and superstition also surrounds this bird in India. For instance, in similar with its mythical counterpart Garuda, it is said to be able to attack and kill snakes.[28] It is also believed to hypnotize its intended female partner into submission,[29] while its distinctive call and dance is said to announce the arrival of the monsoon rains.[30]

Only the last accredited ability of the peacock is based on any truth, for the bird senses the oncoming rains and attempts to have one last fling before its feathers get so wet that it is forced to shed them! Yet the other two legends are significant in themselves, since they have both contributed to the bird's veneration among the Yezidi. Like the peacock, the Yezidi relish a power over serpents, as witnessed by the snake-charming descendants of Sheikhs Mand and Ruhsit. The hypnotic gaze of the peacock is integrally linked with the power of the evil eye, and it is interesting to note that peacock feathers have long been considered effective deterrents against this baleful influence.[31]

The striking blue, black and green eyes on a peacock's feather must also have played a major role in establishing the bird's sanctity among the Yezidi, especially since the colour blue is given such respect by their faith. Another curious superstition concerning the peacock feather is its believed ability to prevent the decay of any item placed with it, perhaps a distant echo of the connection between the Simurgh and the drug of immortality.[32]

Descendants of Noah

It was, however, the link between peacocks and rain-making that seemed of greatest importance, for as with the wild *zaddik*-priests of the Dead Sea, the Yezidis claim direct descent from Noah – in their case through an unknown son named Na'umi.[33] They say that from Noah's other son, Shem, who was reviled by his father, came all the other races of the world. This therefore implied that the Yezidi tribes were not only unique, but that their ancestors had a special relationship with the hero of the Great Flood.

The Yezidis in fact believe there to have been two floods,[34] not one – the last of which, the Flood of Noah, took place 'seven thousand years ago'.[35] On what information they base this chronology is unknown. In their own rendition of the traditional story, the Ark had drifted on the open sea until it accidentally struck the tip of Mount Sinjar. A major disaster was averted, however, when the quick-thinking snake promptly slithered across to the gaping hole and corked the leak using its curled-up body. (The Armenian Church claims that this same incident occurred at Sipan Dağ, a mountain on the northern shores of Lake Van.)[36] The vessel was then able to continue its journey, which ended, as in the case of Judaic, Islamic and Kurdish tradition, at Judi Dağ, not Mount Ararat.[37] Yezidis attend the annual sacrifices that take place each year on Al Judi to commemorate the offerings given up to God by Noah after the Ark had come to rest on dry land.[38]

Nomadic Rainmakers

The Yezidis seem to possess a great affinity for the Noahic tradition, almost as if they believe themselves to be the inheritors of his succession, as well as the antediluvian cosmogony he brought with him into post-diluvian times. They see him, along with Seth and Enoch, as one of the 'first fathers' of their tribes, who they say were conceived by Adam alone.[39] This intimate connection with Noah is highly significant, for as with the Dead Sea communities, the Yezidi recognize a certain type of wild, nomadic priest known as the *kochek*. These individuals are regarded as seers, visionaries, mediums and miracle workers – gifts which they apparently receive from hereditary sources. Moreover, like the *zaddik*-priests of the Dead Sea, the *kochek* have the power to bring rain. One folk-story recorded by the Yezidi scholar R. H. W. Empson tells how a *kochek* named *Bêrû* was asked by the sheikhs of various communities to bring rain during a particularly dry season. Having agreed to do this within seven days, the *kochek* ascended to heaven, where he managed to secure the assistance of Sheikh Adi himself. Together they took the matter to a heavenly priest named Isaac (*Is'hâq*), who informed *Bêrû* that his request would be granted. After seven days no rain had fallen, so the *kochek* was called before the Yezidi chiefs to explain himself. He pointed out that heaven received so many requests for rain that they would have to wait their turn like everyone else. Shortly afterwards the rains did come, vindicating the supernatural powers of the *kochek*.[40]

Could it be that the *kocheks'* apparent ability to influence the weather was one of the feats originally accredited to the fallen race, for rain-making activities have always played a prominent role in shamanistic practices around the world. The fact that the Yezidi saw themselves as inheritors of ancient ancestral traditions going back to Noah would appear to hint at this possibility. If so, then there seemed little doubt that the geographical focus of this tradition has always been the area around Judi Dağ in Turkish Kurdistan.

The Secret Cavern

Yezidi myth and legend must contain many elements inherited from older indigenous cultures of the Kurdish highlands. Who these people were, and what their relationship might have been to the Watchers, is unknown, yet one tentative clue comes from a series of strange carvings greatly venerated by the Yezidi. They are situated in a cavern at a place named Ras al-'Ain, on the Syria-Turkish frontier, and were seen, and described to the Baghdad authorities, by E. S. Drower in 1940.

To reach this secluded site, Mrs Drower had followed an elderly Yezidi woman named Sitt Gulé up a precarious rock-face. The two had climbed higher and higher, using available crevices as foot-holds, until the woman took them around a right-hand bend where they suddenly encountered deeply worn steps. These entered a lofty cavern in which a gushing spring issued from behind a rock-face. On inquiring as to who was worshipped here, the woman had replied 'Kaf', or more correctly *kahaf*, a Kurdish word meaning 'cavern'. Yet Sitt Gulé clearly believed this to be the name of the *genius loci*, or guardian spirit, of the place, for she went on to point out his image to the Englishwoman.

Looking around, Mrs Drower noticed that the walls contained niches, blackened with the smoke of a thousand lamps, as well as various shelves for offerings and lights. There were also three large panels in which were carved extraordinary images of human forms. One was unfortunately defaced beyond all recognition. The second contained 'a single seated figure facing the worshipper, almost Buddha-like in its dignity and repose'.[41] Although the figure was not cross-legged, he was seated in a 'concave frame', shaped like the lotus thrones of Buddhist art. He also wore 'a conical cap', like those worn by Tibetan holy figures. In the third panel was a 'seated and bearded personage also wearing a conical cap', and advancing towards him were a procession of people 'on a wave of movement and worship'.[42]

On the other side of the chamber, beyond the stream of running water and over the spring-head itself, was a human face in low relief. Although somewhat damaged, it was similar in style to the other two figures, with a beard and conical hat. Yet it was what she saw cut into the polished floor that most baffled Mrs Drower, for she could trace 'an oblong with twelve small round depressions, placed six a side'.[43] She surmised that this design represented some kind of 'gaming board', which seems unlikely bearing in mind the immense sanctity of the place.

To what ancient culture did this secret cavern once belong? And what did these strange carvings of holy figures, with beards and conical hats, seated on lotus thrones, actually represent? No one knows. The only thing that can be said with any certainty is that the carvings were extremely old, and did not belong to the faith of either the Yezidi or the Magi. The clear Buddhist appearance of these serene carvings cannot be overlooked, although they are unlikely to have had any direct connection with the teachings of Buddha, the Indian prophet, who is said to have died in 543 BC. The conical hats are variations of what became known in Greek classical art as the Phrygian cap, which usually denoted a person of Anatolian or Persian origin. The earliest wearer of the Phrygian cap, or cap of Hades, was the mythical hero Perseus, who was said to have brought 'initiation and magic' to Persia and to have founded the cult of the Magi to guard over the 'sacred immortal fire'.[44] There is clearly a great mystery in these ancient carvings, and unravelling this could identify the origins behind both the Magi priesthoods of Media and the angel-worshipping cults of Kurdistan.

The great antiquity of the Yezidis is spelt out by themselves, for they employ enormously long periods of time to calculate the age of the world. They say there have been seventy-two different Adams, each living a total of 10,000 years, each one more perfect than the last.[45] In between each Adam has been a period of 10,000 years, during which no one inhabited the world. The Yezidis believe that the current world race is the product of the last of the seventy-two Adams, making the earth a maximum of 1,440,000 years old. Such precise calculations are in themselves nonsensical; however, these figures (as I shall explain in Chapter Twenty-three) were not simply plucked out of thin air. Far from it, for they relate to astronomical time-cycles of extreme antiquity and represent a knowledge of universal numbers present in myths and legends world-wide.

I felt strongly that the ever-diminishing Yezidi cult held important clues in respect to the supposed presence of the fallen race in Kurdistan. Yet it was among another of the Kurdish angel cults, the mysterious and secretive Yaresan, as well as in the myths and legends of other local cultures, that their dark secrets are revealed in even greater detail.

Fourteen

CHILDREN OF THE DJINN

The Yaresan are a proud, fierce tribal culture, recognized by their distinctive red costumes. Somehow they have managed to remain even more elusive than the Yezidis, their religion being known only to a few scholars even today. Any member of their faith who was approached by early European travellers, and asked about their beliefs, would simply answer with the words *ahl-i haqq*, meaning, 'We are worshippers of the truth.' Although not wrong, such a response was a little misleading, since the word *haqq*, 'truth', was a pun on their real inner beliefs, revolving around the word *haq* (spelt with one q) – the name they give to the Universal Spirit, the creator of the universe.

Like the Yezidis, the Yaresan are organized into isolated communities, which currently make up around 10 to 15 per cent of the modern Kurdish population. They are to be found mostly in the region of Kermanshah in the Lower Zagros, although they have also survived in scattered pockets in the Elburz mountain range of Iran, in the highlands of Azerbaijan and in northern Iraq.[1] The earliest Yaresan religious texts are written in a sacred language known as Gurâni, which takes its name from one of the oldest tribes of Kurdistan. Many surviving Gurâns are Yaresan, although the religion itself encompasses other tribes as well. The origin of Yaresan beliefs is even more obscure than those of the Yezidi. Nobody knows for sure how old the faith might be, although it is known to have taken its final form during the late medieval period. Despite this, scholars consider that their beliefs, customs and rituals are among the oldest still surviving in Kurdistan, and are seen as dating back to the very earliest phases in the development of the Iranian religion.[2]

The truth worshippers possess a complex cosmogony that has distinct parallels with their Yezidi neighbours. They believe that the Universal Spirit, *Haq*, once resided in what they see as a 'pre-eternity', symbolized by a pearl and manifested through their supreme avatar, the Lord God *Khâwandagâr*. This manifestation began the first of Seven Epochs, after which the world was created. The *Haq* then formed a group of seven holy angels, known as the *Haftan*, who bear striking similarities to those revered by the Yezidi. In a subsequent epoch the creation of the physical world was followed by the genesis of humanity, helped, of course, by the angelic hierarchy. Subsequent epochs have seen the emergence of sequences of seven avatars, incarnate angels in bodily form, the last of whom have manifested for the seventh and final time in this present age.[3] The Yaresan's chief avatar of the Fourth Epoch was a character named Sultan Sahâk, whose immense veneration goes far beyond preserving the memory of one mortal being.

In the Shadow of Sultan Sahâk

Sultan Sahâk is accredited with a life on earth sometime between the eleventh and thirteenth centuries, and it is after him that the Yaresan say they gained their name – *yâr-i sân*, 'the people of the Sultan'.[4] Yet it is also apparent that this great saint has been seen – as Kurdish scholar Mehrdad Izady rightly expresses it – as a kind of 'superhuman, a supreme avatar of the Universal Spirit, who lived many centuries, possessed mysterious powers, and lives on as a protective mountain spirit in caves on the high peaks'.[5] Clearly, then, he was no ordinary figure of history. He seemed to be someone more like the fabled King Arthur of British tradition, whose memory embodies the lives of many kings and warriors, and whose story has enveloped much earlier Indo-European myth and legend.

So who was this super-hero of the Yaresan, and how might he be linked with the traditions of the fallen race?

Contradictory as it may at first seem, Sultan Sahâk can be directly equated with a dark, mythical tyrant named Zahhak, the demon or serpent king who appears in Firdowsi's Persian epic, the *Shahnameh* of the eleventh century AD.[6] This anti-hero is said to have ruled the world during an age of chaos and disorder after Jemshid (or Yima) had lost the royal *farr*, or Divine Glory, through greed, following a reign of three hundred years. According to Firdowsi, Zahhak had been a true hero of the Iranian mythical dynasty before he succumbed to the trickery of Angra Mainyu, with whom he entered into an evil pact. In exchange for ruling the world, the wicked spirit was allowed to enter into Zahhak. As this took place, black snakes grew from each of the king's shoulders, and thereafter these had to be satisfied each day with the brains of young men kidnapped from villages far and wide. Even though Zahhak tried to cut away the snakes from his shoulders, they simply grew back again and demanded more sacrifices.

Having reigned for a thousand years the demon king is eventually tricked and captured by Feridun. He is interred inside Mount Demavand, where he is chained and tortured, and left to die a slow painful death. It is said that he still remains there today, blood seeping from his heart. Feridun's victory over the wicked tyrant allows him to take up the vacant position of king of Iran and all the world, which he reigns in peace and prosperity for a full five hundred years.[7]

This is the traditional account of Zahhak's long reign as portrayed in Firdowsi's *Shahnameh*. The Zoroastrian literature gives a very similar account, yet cites Azhi Dahâka as the name of the king. Here he is said to have been among the greatest of the *daevas*.[8] In addition to this, it is claimed that he contrived to pair a mortal woman with a male *daeva* and a mortal man with a female Peri, and in so doing created the Negro race, quite obviously a deliberate racial slur on black Africans.[9]

Such was Azhi Dahâka's legendary story. The reality is that this demon king owes at least part of his existence to an actual historical personage named Astyages (584–550 BC), the last Median ruler, who was overthrown by his grandson Cyrus the Great, the first king of the Persian Empire. Astyages, the name given to this monarch by the Greek historian Herodotus, is said to have borne the royal title of *Rshti-vegâ Azhi Dahâka*,[10] and it was the degenerate memory of his alleged wickedness that supposedly created the demonic tyrant featured in both Persian and Avestan literature.

This explanation is, however, only partially correct, for Azhi Dahâka's character and symbolism undoubtedly derived from several quite diverse sources. For instance, the Median kings were known to their Iranian neighbours by the title *Mâr*, which in Persian signified a 'snake', giving rise to traditions among the Armenians of 'the dragon (*vishap*) dynasty of Media',[11] or the 'descendants of the dragon', i.e. the mythical descendants of Azhi Dahâka himself.[12] Strangely enough, the word *Azhdahâ*, an abbreviation of Azhi Dahâka, is now the only Persian word denoting a 'snake'.[13] Indeed, it would appear that Azhi Dahâka came to symbolize not only the serpentine form of *Angra Mainyu*, but also his incarnation on earth.

In addition to this, the idea of snakes growing from the shoulders of Azhi Dahâka appears to have been a direct borrowing from the mythology of neighbouring Mesopotamia. Here a serpent god named Ningišzida, who bore the title 'Lord of the Good Tree', was depicted in art with snakes rising out of his shoulders in exactly the same manner as the demon tyrant had been portrayed in Armenian and Iranian mythology.[14] Ningišzida's role varied – in some accounts he is a guardian of underworld demons, while in others he guards the gate of Anu (or An), the Sumerian concept of heaven.[15] In all these capacities he was undoubtedly linked to the Hebraic concept of the Serpent of Eden – the good tree being either the Tree of Knowledge of Good and Evil or the Tree of Life. Confirmation of this connection is in the fact that the Armenian scholar Moses of Khorenats'i records that an ancient folk-song speaks of the descendants of Azhi Dahâka as being venerated in at least one 'temple of the dragons'.[16] Also in Armenia are a number of prehistoric megaliths, or standing stones, that take the form of serpents which are known as *vishaps*, or dragons, showing the immense antiquity of this cult. More importantly, at least one Armenian scholar has associated this archaic worship of the *vishap* with the Sumero-Babylonian cult of the snake.[17]

The connection between Azhi Dahâka and the Median kings is also significant, for it was through their downfall that Zoroastrianism was able to climb so rapidly to the position of state religion in Persia. At the same time, many of Media's Magian priests had jumped ship, so to speak, and embraced this revitalized form of the

Iranian religion, and it was probably at around this very period that Azhi Dahâka gained his exclusively demonic character among the Persian peoples. As a consequence, the final Median king somehow became the personification of the terrible Lie preached by the serpent-worshipping Magi priesthoods, as well as a national anti-hero in Persian myth and legend.

Descendants of the Dragon King

In complete contrast, however, was the way in which Azhi Dahâka had been viewed by many of the Kurdish tribes who were previously subject to the Median dynasty of kings. To them the demon king was the hero and Feridun the villain! So much had they revered the memory of Azhi Dahâka that they came to believe that their entire race was descended of him. The story-tellers even readapted his legendary history to suit their needs. They claimed that a plot had been hatched by two of the king's stewards to substitute one of the human brains fed each day to the king's twin snakes. Instead of two human brains, they would feed them one sheep's brain and just one human brain in the hope that it would fool the serpents. Their plan worked, enabling them to daily liberate one of the two young men imprisoned for this sacrificial purpose. Each freed prisoner was given goats and sheep and allowed to escape into the mountains, and this was the supposed origin of the Kurdish peoples.[18]

The exact interpretation of this quaint myth is open to speculation, although it implied that the Kurdish race owed its entire existence to the two smart-thinking stewards of Azhi Dahâka, and by virtue of this to the king himself. Yet because this great tyrant was also seen as a *daeva*, or demon, he could never have been accepted as an anti-hero by the devout, angel-worshipping Yaresan. In their religion, the serpent is a symbol of lust and carnal delights. It is also a device of the Fallen Angel – Azazel or *Shaitân*. They therefore transformed Azhi Dahâka into an avatar named Sultan Sahâk.

The Yaresan today seem blind to Sultan Sahâk's true origins, and would vehemently deny any connection with his dark half,

Azhi Dahâka. This strange dichotomy in Yaresan beliefs is not speculative, but is accepted by Kurdish scholars such as Izady.[19] Yet the influence of Sultan Sahâk goes far beyond the Yaresan, and is apparently found in various guises throughout the Upper Zagros region. He is also known by the name Sultan Is'hâq, or Isaac, the divine priest who features in the story about the Yezidi *kochek* named *Bêrû*, who visits heaven in order to request rain on behalf of the Kurdish peoples.

So what was the true origin of Azhi Dahâka? Why was this dragon king accredited with being the progenitor of the Kurdish race? And why has his memory lingered so long? The answer appeared to lie in the fact that, before his fall, the tyrant was seen as one of the mythical kings of Iran. Since these monarchs would seem to have borne distinctive Watcher traits, could it be that Azhi Dahâka represented a faint echo of the presence and blood lineage of the fallen race – remembered in Armenia as the *vishaps* or dragon descendants – who lived during some distant age of humanity? It is to be recalled that, according to Firdowsi, one of Azhi Dahâka's, or Zahhak's, descendants had been the beautiful Rudabeh – the ivory-skinned princess whose face was 'a very paradise', whose skin from head to toe was as 'white as ivory' and whose height out-topped her future husband Zal, himself a giant of a man, 'by a head'.[20] All these features were clear Watcher traits, like those presented in Enochian and Dead Sea material.

Remember, too, that the Armenians actually claim descent from a race of giants under the leadership of Hayk, whose name is equated with the Armenian word for 'gigantic'. Bringing together these two quite separate traditions is the fact that in a sub-text entitled 'From the Fables of the Persians', included by Moses of Khorenats'i in his *History of the Armenians*, the author says that Azhi Dahâka '[lived] in the time of Nimrod'[21] and that he was one of the chieftains who seized local territories after the giants, or Titans, had divided the races following the destruction, or fall, of the mythical Tower of Babel.[22] Could this 'fall' simply preserve yet another distorted memory of the 'fall' of the Watchers, and their gradual dispersion on to the plains surrounding the highlands of Kurdistan?

The Utopian City of Tigranakert

Moses of Khorenats'i's *History* tells of the deeds and virtues of a much celebrated Armenian king named Tigran the Great, who ruled between 95 and 55 BC. He recounts the monarch's many great achievements, before going on to record that Tigran's ancestors came originally from Kurdistan and that they also claimed descendency from the dragon king Azhi Dahâka. Apparently the family fled their homeland because of the tyrant's continued oppression and settled in Armenia, out of which the mighty Tigran had arisen.[23]

At first this information might not seem to be of any special interest to my research into the fallen race, for many Kurds believed in a descendancy from Azhi Dahâka. Then I discovered something about Tigran which seemed to strike a nerve and was not to be overlooked.

Tigran the Great was a great warrior king who gained the crown of Armenia after winning back large tracts of land previously overrun by the mighty Parthian rulers of neighbouring Persia. He had then gone on to conquer Phoenicia, Syria, Upper Mesopotamia (northern Iraq) and Kurdistan. In 88 BC, King Mithridates IV of Pontus, a small kingdom in north-eastern Asia Minor (modern-day Turkey), enlisted Tigran's support in defeating the Roman army in neighbouring Cappadocia and Phrygia – both also in Asia Minor. Five years later, in 83 BC, Tigran was invited to become sovereign of Syria, following the collapse of the Seleucid dynasty. He reigned here for a full eighteen years, during which time Tigran was seen as the most powerful pontentate in the whole of western Asia.[24]

At the height of his success, Tigran decided to build a royal capital as his new seat of power in an area now occupied by the modern-day city of Siirt, in the heartland of Kurdistan.[25] Around this new city Tigran established a kingdom named Tigranuan, or Tigranavand. Not only did this appear to have been the very region ruled by his Kurdish ancestors before their departure for Armenia, but it also happened to be close to where Eden would seem to have been geographically placed.

Admittedly this principality had been strategically important in controlling and defending the Persian Royal Road that cut through the Kurdish highlands; however, as Kurdish scholar Mehrdad Izady admits, Tigran's decision to build his citadel outside of Armenia 'can be interpreted as a sign that he felt his Kurdish past more than has been thought'.[26] Tigranakert, as this royal city was called, quickly grew to become a great centre of learning in the style of the Greeks, with scholars invited to come there from all over the old Hellenic world. The Greek biographer Plutarch (AD 50–120) described Tigranakert as 'a rich and beautiful city where every common man and every man of rank studied to adorn it'.[27]

Within its huge defensive walls, Tigran quickly established a cosmopolitan population that included Assyrians, Cappadocians, Medians and Greeks from Cilicia on the Mediterranean coast, many, according to Plutarch, transported there after Tigran's army had razed their own cities in battle.[28] This great cultural mixture of peoples ensured that Tigranakert became the focus of different religious cults and philosophical ideals, something Tigran seems to have wanted to foster.

Unfortunately, however, Tigranakert was finally sacked and despoiled by the Roman general Lucullus in 69 BC, after which its multinational population and Greek scholars were returned to their own countries. Despite its downfall, the city remained a great wonder right down to Islamic times, when it is recorded that one Muslim general prayed that he might take it without bloodshed, upon which its eastern gates were said to have been flung open by invisible hands.[29]

What then was the significance of Tigran's great city?

The writings of Moses of Khorenats'i would appear to suggest that, not only had Tigran and his descendants believed themselves to be descendants of Azhi Dahâka, but that they had also worshipped him in the form of an anthropomorphic serpent, similar in aspect to the Sumerian snake god Ningišzida.[30] If this was the case, then there seemed every reason to believe that the Armenian tyrant located Tigranakert in central Kurdistan because he wished to recreate Azhi Dahâka's own seat of power. Since the Kurds traced their ancestry back to this serpent king, it would imply that the place of genesis of the Kurdish race – in other words, Azhi Dahâka's kingdom – corresponded very well with the site of Eden, the place of genesis of the human race according to Hebrew tradition. If the descendants of the Watchers really had instigated the serpent dynasty of Iranian kings, then it seemed likely that Azhi Dahâka had come to symbolize the legacy of the Watchers in the minds of the Kurdish peoples. Had Tigran therefore tried to create some kind of utopian city in full awareness of the region's past associations with the Serpent of Eden, the Lord of the Good Tree?

Yaresan Creation Myths

The Yaresan creation myths are quite unique in that they give two sets of names for the first couple. Not only are they referred to as Adam and Eve, but they are also known as *Masya* and *Masyanag*, their counterparts in the ninth-century *Bundahishn* text.

One Yaresan account tells how Azazel secured the services of the Serpent and the Peacock before entering paradise to tempt Adam and Eve into sin. Once inside the terrestrial garden, Azazel transformed himself into a handsome angel and encouraged Eve and then Adam to partake, not of the forbidden fruit, but of the forbidden *wheat* – an apparent symbol of material wealth among the Yaresan. As a result of his intervention, the first couple were expelled from paradise along with Azazel, the Serpent and the Peacock.[31] This myth clearly demonstrates how the Kurds linked the fall of humanity with both the Serpent and the Peacock Angel, who are both seen as animal forms of the Fallen Angel. Once again, these are the most important totemic symbols of the Watchers.

The Kurdish Jews – who inhabited the area around the city of Arbela in Iraqi Kurdistan from the first century BC onwards until their final migration to Israel in the 1950s – also possessed a variation of the creation myth involving Adam and Eve. In their story, the Serpent of Eden appears, like Azazel in the Yaresan account, as a 'young, good-looking man'.[32] Curiously enough, in this account the Serpent tries to seduce *Adam*, and *not* Eve. In fact, it says that he often used to hang around the Garden *before* even the creation of Eve![33]

Both these stories show the belief among the Kurdish peoples that the Serpent of Eden was looked upon as a handsome angel who used the power of seduction to lure humanity to fall through disobedience. They were even more like an allegorical representation of the fall of the Watchers than their Judaeo-Christian counterpart. Why, then, had the Kurds placed a slightly different slant on the story of the Fall of Man? Did they have reason to update the story-line based on indigenous traditions concerning the fall of the angels?

Birds of the Angels

The Yaresan believe intensely in angels, many of whom appear to have distinct human qualities. One angel, named Mohammad Beg, claimed that in a previous incarnation he had been the fabulous bird *Anqa*, as well as the ancestor of *Masya* and *Masyanag*, the first *human* beings.[34] The *Anqa* was an Arab form of the Simurgh, and since this bird's mythical homeland in the *Airyana Vaejah* (the *Eranvej* in the *Bundahishn*) was most probably Kurdistan, this revelation was extremely important. It implied that the human race had been born of an angel equated with a fabulous bird somewhere in the highlands of Kurdistan.

I had also been intrigued to discover that, in Yaresan tradition, Sultan Sahâk is accredited with a miraculous birth connected with a great bird. It is said that a divine being known as the Royal White Falcon had alighted on a stick perch. On its departure the Virgin Lady Dayerak unwound her skirt, 'on which the Falcon [*had*] settled'. Afterwards, she refolded her skirt, before unwinding it again to find a child there.[35] This is all the legend says, although the clear connotation is that some kind of sexual union took place in which the virgin was inseminated by the seed of the Royal White Falcon, who signifies the carrier of divinity. Its role is identical to that of the Varaghna – the bird that transmits the royal *farr* from one king to the next in Avestan tradition.[36] The perch itself is very likely a variation of the divine tree on which the Simurgh rests in Iranian myth.

Sultan Sahâk's strange birth attempts to demonstrate that the avatar was born of a divine parentage and that he was inspired by the Glory of God, bestowed on him by the seed of the Royal White

Falcon.[37] Once again this brought home the overwhelming link between serpents, predatory birds, divine wisdom and kingly glory among the indigenous tribes of Kurdistan. Why had these particular symbols gained such a prominent place among the angel-worshipping tribes? Had they inherited them from tribal ancestors who had preserved the memory of the Watchers' presence in this region? Certain very strange legends found among the native Yaresan and Jewish communities of Kurdistan, concerning the race of beings known as the djinn, would seem to suggest the answer might well be yes.

Born of the Djinn

The djinn, so the thirteenth-century Yaresan work entitled '*Ajayeb ol-makhluqat* tells us, are 'a kind of animal' that have the ability to change their shape and appearance. They can appear as snakes. They can appear as scorpions, and they can even appear as human beings. In Muslim theology, the djinn were said to have been created two thousand years before Adam. They ranked alongside the angels and the chief among them was Eblis. For refusing to bow down before Adam, the djinn, along with Eblis, were cast out of heaven forever to roam the earth as demons.

In Yaresan lore, the story of the fall of the djinn runs a little differently. They say that once this ancient race had lived on earth without any kings or prophets among them. Then they began to revolt against the human prophets, and the world quickly degenerated into lawlessness. On seeing what was happening on earth, God sent an army of angels to deal with the rebellious djinn. The warriors of heaven prevented the evil ones from penetrating too deeply into the land by pushing them towards the sea.[38] The angels finally took many djinn captive – among them the young Azazel, who was subsequently brought up in heaven.

This connection between the warring djinn and Kurdish folklore does not end here, for I found that among the legends of the Kurdish Jews there existed a most revealing tale. It featured that celebrated Israelite king Solomon, said to have been the wisest man in the world. The story tells how one day the monarch had ordered five hundred djinn to find him five hundred of the most beautiful virgins in the world. They were not to return until every last one was in their possession. The djinn had set about their immense task, going to Europe to seek out these maidens. Finally, after gathering together the correct number of virgins, the djinn were about to return to Jerusalem when they learnt that Solomon had passed away. In a dilemma, the djinn had to decide on what to do. Should they return the girls to their rightful homes in Europe, or should they keep them with them? Because the young virgins had 'found favor in the eyes of the jinn, the jinn took them unto themselves as their wives. And they begot many beautiful children, and those children bore more children . . . And that is the way the nation of the Kurds came into being.'[39]

In another rendition of the same story, a hundred genies are dispatched by Solomon to search out a hundred of the world's most beautiful maidens for his personal harem. Having achieved this quota, Solomon then dies and the hundred genies decide to settle down with the maidens amid the inaccessible mountains of Kurdistan. The offspring of these marriages result in the foundation of the Kurdish race, 'who in their elusiveness resemble their genie forefathers and in their handsomeness their foremothers'.[40] 'It is because of this story that the title "children of the djinn (i.e. genies)" is occasionally applied to the Kurds by their ethnic neighbours.'[41]

Why should the Jews of Kurdistan have possessed such stories about their gentile neighbours? Why should they see them as descendants of the djinn, who were never considered to have possessed corporeal bodies? And why should they have suggested that the Kurds bore physical resemblances to these djinn? They believed the djinn had settled in this mountainous region, and so they must have felt that the ancestors of the Kurds migrated to the region at some early stage in the history of the world.

For some reason, the Kurdish Jews assumed the djinn to have come from Jerusalem and the virgins, or maidens, from Europe. Why was this? And what constituted these alleged physiological similarities with the race of djinn? Did this suggest that the 'children of the djinn' bore both Watcher traits *and* white 'European' features? Certainly, there are two distinct races in Kurdistan – one olive skinned and of medium height and build with dark eyes, and the other much taller, with fair skin and, very often, blue eyes. E. S. Drower noticed this on her visit to the Yezidi village of Baashika in the Iraqi Kurdish foothills during 1940. She reported that 'many we saw in the village' were 'tall, well-built' men with 'fairish' faces of 'an almost Scandinavian type', adding that: 'Amongst the children of the village some were as flaxen-fair and blue-eyed as Saxons.'[42] The ethnological origin of these individuals with clear white Caucasian features is not known, although it is easy to see how they could have been accused by the Kurdish Jews of having European ancestry.

I was beginning seriously to believe that the Kurds really were *different* in some way, and that their origins held important clues regarding the presence and ultimate fate of the Watchers. Furthermore, this was not the only evidence that Kurds were often born with physiological features resembling those of the fallen race.

Fear of Changelings

One terrible fear among the Yezidi is that, during the first seven days after birth, an infant can be invisibly substituted for a demon child belonging to a race of 'evil fairy' known as Rashé Shebbé, or Shevvé.[43] For this very reason, the mother has to remain in bed during this initial period of vulnerability. The idea of 'fairy' children being exchanged for mortal babies is well known in European folklore, where the substitute infant is referred to as a changeling. The reality of such strange fears lies quite obviously in the fact that certain babies have been born with physiological features that are identified as traits of the 'demon' or 'fairy' race, and are therefore assumed to have been exchanged at birth. In the Near East, however, these legends refer not to small impish individuals, as in the European concept of 'fairies', but to the djinn and Peri – the progeny of Eblis, who before his fall was the angel Azazel. This therefore implied that the 'changeling' children of Yezidi tradition seemingly bore Watcher traits, bringing the debate back to the strange births of infants such as Noah, Rustam and Zal.

With this knowledge it becomes clear that the Yezidi women feared that their own children would develop features akin to those of the djinn, or the fallen race, and that in an attempt to prevent such ill-fated births precautionary measures would be taken.

Why should this fear of changelings exist so strongly among the Yezidi? The answer can only be that such 'demon' babies were once commonplace among Kurdish families, hinting at the rather disconcerting possibility that they could have been genetic throwbacks to a time when two quite separate racial types intermarried to produce offspring bearing the features of either parent, perhaps explaining why the offspring of the djinn and the maidens 'in their elusiveness resemble their genie forefathers and in their handsomeness their foremothers'. In time the chances of such inherited genes producing extreme traits obviously diminished, but every so often a giant child bearing the features of a 'demon' would be born into a community. As a consequence, it would be identified as a changeling that had been exchanged at birth by evil spirits.

These then were the 'children of the djinn'.

This knowledge of the Kurdish changelings could well represent further evidence in support of the idea that forbidden trafficking had taken place between the proposed Watcher culture and the earliest indigenous peoples of Kurdistan. But could such evidence be trusted? How old were these superstitious practices? So much of the Kurdish folklore, myths and legends seemed highly distorted, naïve and somewhat confused, making these accounts very difficult to decipher with any degree of certainty. Despite such shortcomings, hidden among them were several recurring symbols that seemed to crop up again and again – angels, demons, djinn, immortality, serpents, anthropomorphic birds, sovereignty, kingship and great cycles of time.

Missing, however, from the Yezidi and Yaresan literature was any real tradition that placed the biblical Eden in the highlands of Kurdistan.

Perhaps the Yezidi and the Yaresan were too close to the source of this mystery to have realized the immense importance once placed on this region by foreign religions. Only the Nestorian Church of Assyria (Upper Iraq) and the Church of Armenia embraced and promoted the idea that the Garden of Eden lay at the headwaters of the four rivers of paradise.[44]

Perhaps this was the point to begin looking much further back in time. The native religions of Kurdistan would seem to have preserved fragmented accounts of the Watchers' assumed presence in these parts; however, the most ancient cultures of Mesopotamia would appear to have recorded not only the existence of the fallen race, but also the *precise history* of their highland settlement among the mountains of Kurdistan.

Fifteen

WHERE HEAVEN AND EARTH MEET

The last years of the nineteenth century, Nippur, southern Iraq. Beyond the call of the distant muezzin the constant sound of pickaxes hitting the hard, stony ground filled the burning, dust-clogged air. Arab labourers, their heads wrapped in coloured headgear, worked furiously in the bright sunshine to clear away dirt and rubble from the rectangular trenches, cut deep into the ancient earth. Every hour some new find revitalized their enthusiasm to dig deeper.

News spread that fresh artefacts had been uncovered – close to the foundations of the E-kur, or Mountain House. This was the great temple of Enlil, the supreme god of the Sumerian pantheon and the legendary founder of this powerful city-state more than five thousand years earlier.[1]

On learning of this discovery, Professor J. H. Haynes of the Babylonian Expedition of the University of Pennsylvania, navigated the labyrinthine pathways between the trenches and ditches that seemed alive with frenzied activity. Finally he reached the remains of the E-kur temple, which stood beside the crumbling mud-brick ziggurat known to the Sumerians as Dur-an-ki, or the 'Bond of heaven and earth'.[2]

Guided by the voices of those who had made the find, Haynes quickly examined the newly dug pit. What he saw were eight fragments of a broken clay cylinder which, although partially defaced, clearly bore inscriptions in the wedge-like cuneiform alphabet. Its positioning, here among the ruins of the E-kur, strongly suggested that it was a foundation cylinder deposited following repairs on the temple during the reigns either of Narâm-Sin (2254–2218 BC) or his successor Shar-Kali-Sharri (2217–2193 BC), the last two kings of Agade, or Akkad, the royal dynasty of Semitic origin, who had ruled supreme in Sumer for a total of 141 years during the second half of the third millennium BC.[3]

Dr Haynes was never to know the immense significance of this foundation cylinder, or of the extraordinary inscriptions on some of the other clay tablets found during this period by his team in the vicinity of the E-kur building and dating to a similar age. Along with many other more highly prized treasures from Nippur and other Mesopotamian city-states, the broken cylinder and inscribed tablets were taken back to the University Museum of Philadelphia by the Babylonian Expedition's chief archaeologist, Professor H. V. Hilprecht. They were never removed from their packing cases, but instead were dumped in the museum's basement until their eventual rediscovery by George Aaron Barton, Professor of the Bryn Mawr College, Philadelphia, during the second decade of the twentieth century.[4] Aware of Haynes's and Hilprecht's earlier work, Barton decided to translate the E-kur foundation cylinder, which he found scattered about in three different transit boxes.[5]

After many painstaking hours of dedicated work, Barton became more and more excited about the contents of the cylinder's inscription, which was written in unilingual Sumerian. Arranged in nineteen columns on the eight fragments were, he believed, 'the oldest known text' from Sumeria, and 'perhaps the oldest in the world'.[6] It featured many of the ancient gods, including Enlil, Enki, the god of the watery abyss, as well as a little-known snake goddess named Ṣir. She seemed to be synonymous with Enlil's spouse, Ninlil or Ninkharsag, leading Barton to conclude that Nippur had once been a cult centre for this ancient snake goddess.[7] By contrast, the contents of some of the other tablets he translated were seen by Barton as a trifle mundane; there was a version of the Sumerian creation myth and what seemed to be hymns and eulogies to deified kings or localized deities, but little else.

Despite his initial excitement in respect of the clay cylinder, Barton could only conclude that the Nippur tablets he translated exhibited 'the neighborly admixture of religion and magic so characteristic of Babylonian thought . . . If not the religious expression of a democracy.'[8] So, having completed his work, Barton left behind the Nippur texts, which were published in 1918 by Yale

University Press under the rather dull title of *Miscellaneous Babylonian Inscriptions*, and there the matter rested for the next sixty years.

Then, during the 1970s, a copy of Barton's by now extremely rare book came into the possession of a former exploration geologist named Christian O'Brien. He had studied natural sciences at Christ's College, Cambridge, and had worked for many years in Iran with the Anglo-Iranian Oil Company, now British Petroleum (BP). He was also a reader of cuneiform script and could see, even at a cursory glance, that Barton had misinterpreted much of what the E-kur foundation cylinder and some eight of the ten published Nippur tablets actually recorded, prompting him to retranslate each in turn. What he found shocked him completely.

As each new tablet was completed, more and more pieces of a slowly emerging jigsaw began to fit into place. Much of the texts appeared to tell the story of a race of divine beings known as the Anannage (*a-nun-na(ge)*), or the Anunnaki (*a-nun-na-ki*), the great, or princely offspring, or sons, of heaven and earth,[9] who arrive in a mountainous region and set up camp in a fertile valley. They call the settlement *edin*,[10] the Akkadian for 'plateau' or 'steppe' (see Chapter Twelve), as well as *'gar-sag*, or Kharsag, a term meaning, according to O'Brien, either the 'principal, fenced enclosure' or the 'lofty, fenced enclosure'.[11]

The Anannage gradually develop an agricultural community that includes land cultivation, field systems, plant domestication, and the creation of water-irrigation ditches and channels. Sheep and cattle are placed in covered pens, and cedar-wood houses are constructed as dwellings.[12] Among the larger building projects undertaken by the Anannage is the construction of a reservoir to provide Kharsag with a more advanced form of land irrigation, as well as the erection of larger edifices, such as the Great House of the Lord Enlil, which stood on a rocky eminence above the Settlement.[13] The texts also speak of a 'granary', the 'building [of] roads', 'a maternity building for mothers', and a place known as 'the Building of Life in the High Place'.[14] In the valley surrounding the settlement are apparently 'loftily-built tree plantations', 'lofty cedar-tree enclosures' and orchards planted with trees that have a 'three-fold bearing of fruit'.[15]

The Kharsag tablets, as O'Brien began to refer to them, apparently detailed how the community had thrived for an immensely long period of time. Harvests were usually plentiful, with some excess grain being produced. It would even seem that they allowed outsiders into the community as both partners and helpers to 'share the bounty'.[16]

The principal founders of the settlement were fifty in number, the main leaders being Enlil, the Lord of Cultivation, and his wife Ninkharsag, the Lady of Kharsag, also known as Ninlil. Repeatedly she is referred to as 'the Shining Lady' and, more significantly, as 'the Serpent (*Sịr*) Lady'[17] – the title that had led Barton to assume she was some kind of snake goddess worshipped at Nippur. Also included in the group were Enki, Lord of the Land, and Utu, or Ugmash, a sun god. The Anannage possessed a democratic leadership, although a chosen council of seven would apparently come together when major decisions were made concerning the future of Kharsag.[18] Just occasionally the supreme being, Anu, whose name means 'heaven', or 'highlands', would join the council to advise on their deliberations.

Different situations and events that arose in the settlement are outlined in some detail. For instance, one text speaks of a major epidemic that appears to have swept through Kharsag, for it explains:

The stone jars were pressed down with grain [i.e. there had been a good harvest]. *The Serpent Lady hurried to the Great Sanctuary. At his home, her man – the Lord Enlil – was stricken with sickness. The bright dwelling, the home of the Lady Ninlil, was stricken with sickness.*

Sickness . . . sickness – it spreads all over [the settlement] . . . Our splendid Mother – let her be protected – let her not succumb . . . Give her life – let her be protected from the distress of sickness . . . There is no rest for this Serpent; from sickness to fever . . .[19]

Even Enlil and Ninlil's own son, Ninurta, is struck down by the mystery illness. His mother calls for all light to be shut out, both day and night until the child regains its health. Those affected do finally get better, although strict new laws are introduced in an attempt to ensure that there is no repeat of this mystery sickness, for as the text explains:

In Eden, thy cooked food must be better cooked. In Eden, thy cleaned food must be much cleaner. Father, eating meat is the great enemy – thy food at the House of Enlil.[20]

Having finished retranslating this particular tablet, O'Brien began to realize that he had hit on a prehistoric jackpot, for as he excitedly recorded at the time:

The parallels between this epic account and the Hebraic record at the Garden of Eden are highly convincing. Not only is 'Eden' twice mentioned [in this tablet alone], *but the reference to the 'Serpent Lady', as an epithet for Ninkharsag . . .* [is] *clear confirmation of the scientific nature of the work carried out by the equivalent Serpents in the Hebraic account.*[21]

The 'Serpents in the Hebraic account' was a reference to the Watchers and Nephilim of the Book of Enoch.

Even further confirming this link between Watchers and Anannage was the reference on two occasions to Ninlil's husband Enlil as the 'Splendid Serpent of the shining eyes'.[22] This recalled the vivid descriptions of the Watchers given in the Enochian and Dead Sea literature, particularly in the case of the Testament of Amram.

Had O'Brien really uncovered an account of the Watchers of Eden?

The Fall of Kharsag

Later tablets spoke of a 'winter of bitter cold', unlike anything Kharsag had ever seen before. For a time the Anannage managed to hold out in the bleak arctic-like conditions, but more cataclysms were to follow. First there came a 'great storm'. Then there was further destruction from flooding, presumably after the snow and ice melted. A storm-water course was quickly constructed that stretched from the heights of the mountains to the edge of the plantations, and for a time this worked, keeping out the rising flood waters. Yet then an even harsher winter came upon them, and this would appear to have been the final straw, for as the tablet records:

The demon cold filled the land; the Storm darkened it; in the small households of the Lord Enlil, there were unhappy people. The House of Destiny was covered over; the House of the Lord Enlil disappeared [under snow] . . . The four walls protected the Lord from the raging cold. The fate of the Granary rested on its thick walls – it was preserved from disaster, from the power of the storm-water . . . The flood did not destroy the cattle.[23]

Warm clothes, communal gatherings and good cheer kept the remaining Anannage alive. Fires raged in enormous fireplaces, and it seemed they might survive the long winter, but then another disaster struck. The vineyard workers apparently made the decision to open the reservoir's sluice-gates in an attempt to 'irrigate morning and night'.[24] Yet the 'firm, deep watercourse was destructive; its noise was great; the power of its flowing was frightening . . . in the night, many strong houses which the Lord had established, were flooded . . .'[25]

What happened next shall perhaps never be known, for the remainder of this particular tablet was too damaged for translation. The penultimate tablet speaks of even greater devastation, essentially by storms, but there is reference also to lightning destroying the shining house of Lord Enlil, and of the repeated presence of darkness ('darkness hung over the hostile mountains'[26] and 'the goats and sheep bleated in the darkened land'[27]).

The final tablet speaks of mass disaster and lamentation. In the wake of the continual darkness, broken only by frequent thunderstorms, there came perpetual rain. The reservoir filled up and overflowed, quickly flooding the irrigated fields and then, finally, the low-lying parts of the settlement. Those buildings on higher ground were again said to have been struck by lightning, prompting Enlil and Ninlil, and presumably other Anannage, to try and contain the damage being inflicted on what remained of Kharsag.

Yet the end was at hand. The Anannage knew they were fighting a losing battle, forcing Enlil to admit:

'My Settlement is shattered; overflowing water has crushed it – by water alone – sadly, it has been destroyed.'[28]

The mass devastation caused during this period of climatic turmoil had brought to a close the idyllic settlement of Kharsag. O'Brien came to believe that this break-up of the Anannage had led to an important dispersal of individuals who inadvertently paved the way for the foundation of the city-states of Mesopotamia, some time around 5500 BC.[29]

From these god-men of a previous age had come the first Near Eastern civilization, controlled by a number of city-states. Each of these had been peopled by indigenous races, but administered by the direct descendants of the Anannage, the serpents with shining eyes. They had preserved the memory of the Kharsag settlement until its story was finally set down on clay tablets and deposited in the E-kur by Akkadian priests during the reign of either Narâm-Sin or Shar-Kali-Sharri.

Such was the mind-blowing story presented in *The Genius of the Few*, a book written by Christian O'Brien, with his wife Barbara Joy O'Brien, and published in 1985. Unfortunately, because O'Brien's book fell between the devil and the deep blue sea – in that it was shunned by both the academic community and the ancient mysteries audience – it did not receive the popular success it undoubtedly deserved. All copies quickly disappeared, but one luckily found its way into a second-hand bookshop in Maldon, Essex, where in 1992 my colleague Richard Ward noticed it among the shelves of books on archaeology.

Had O'Brien Been Correct?

The explosive nature of Christian O'Brien's theory presented in *The Genius of the Few* was recognized immediately by Richard and myself. If O'Brien had been correct in his translation of the Kharsag tablets, then this was the most convincing evidence yet for not only the reality of Eden but also the independent existence of a highly advanced culture living in a mountainous region of the Near East during prehistoric times. O'Brien had identified the texts' 'serpents' with 'shining eyes' as the Watchers of the Book of Enoch, while in his opinion Kharsag was to be equated with the seven heavens visited by the patriarch Enoch.[30]

Even more significant was the reference to the council of seven

Anannage who apparently came together to make major decisions on behalf of the Kharsag settlement. These so-called Seven Counsellors, or Seven Sages, were much celebrated in Sumerian myth and legend; furthermore, in Assyrian scripts belonging to the reign of King Ashurbanipal (668–627 BC), the seven Anannage, or Anunnaki, are mentioned in the same breath as the 'foreign gods' of Assaramazash, clearly a reference to the Iranian god Ahura Mazda and the six *Amesha Spentas*, thus inferring that the two sets of divine beings were perhaps one and the same.[31] If this was indeed the case, then it meant that the council of seven Anannage were almost certainly the root source behind not only the *Amesha Spentas* but also the seven archangels of Judaeo-Christian tradition. These, it must be remembered, are cited in the Book of Enoch as the chief among the Watchers who remained loyal to heaven at the time of the fall.

There was, however, no indication among the Kharsag tablets of a 'fall' of the Anannage, although there is no reason to suppose that the texts were in any way complete. Moreover, references to the Anannage exist in other Sumerian texts, and these throw much greater light on the subject. It seems the Anannage were originally only gods of the 'heaven of Anu'. Only later had they been separated into two quite separate camps – the gods of heaven and the gods of *ki*, 'earth'. Amounts are even given – there were three hundred Anannage under the command of the god Anu in heaven and six hundred under the command of the underworld god Nergal, who lived 'in the earth'.[32]

Did this information constitute evidence, as O'Brien believed, of some kind of fragmentation of the original Kharsag settlement, whereby a large group of rebel Anannage had decided that instead of remaining in isolation among the mountains, they would descend on to the plains of ancient Iraq and live among humanity? Was this the same story as presented in the Book of Enoch concerning the 'fall' of the two hundred rebel Watchers? Certainly, there are various strange stories preserved in Sumerian mythology which relate how the Anannage had once walked among mortal kind. For instance, they were said to have designed and laid the foundations of the ancient Sumerian city of Kish.[33] They were also 'put to work to help build the temple (in the city) of Girsu',[34] while in another myth they were given a 'city as a place in which they might dwell'.[35] This 'place' is likely to have been Eridu, Sumeria's oldest city-state, which is said to have had no less than fifty Anannage attached to it,[36] the same number that appears in the Kharsag texts. Excavations have revealed that Eridu was founded as early as *c.* 5500 BC,[37] the very date suggested by O'Brien for the break-up of Kharsag.

Yet had O'Brien been correct in his translation of the texts?

Academics who have followed in the footsteps of Professor George Barton would utterly dismiss O'Brien's rather 'colourful' interpretation of the Kharsag texts. They would support Barton's translation and reconfirm the orthodox view that they were simply miscellaneous religious texts of the late Akkadian period, *c.* 2200 BC. Furthermore, they would point out that the 'creation myths' contained on the tablets are conceptual and that any reference to Enlil and his Mountain House related to his temple at Nippur and *not* to some 'highland' settlement of the gods existing in prehistoric times. What O'Brien was therefore saying was utter nonsense and should be ranked alongside books on ancient astronauts and the lost land of Atlantis.

There the matter would rest.

One part of me wanted to believe this was correct. I struggle to support the more academic, down-to-earth views of our past history, as I know that straying too far off the beaten track can only mean ridicule and scorn, whether you are wrong or whether you are *right*. Yet O'Brien was no ancient astronaut theorist. His arguments against the orthodox interpretation of individual texts appeared convincing indeed.[38] Admittedly, O'Brien appeared to be over-enthusiastically convinced that the Kharsag tablets represented something more than simply ancient Sumerian religious texts. Yet his translations made far more sense than those originally produced by Barton, and on this basis I would continue my own review of the subject.

In Search of Kharsag

All the indications were that Kharsag had been situated in a high mountainous region,[39] so high in fact that 'some Anean trees could not be cultivated'.[40] This does not appear to refer to the rugged plains around Nippur.

Where then had this highland settlement been located?

In an attempt to answer this question I studied various other early Mesopotamian texts and began to find tantalizing evidence for the existence of just such a mountain retreat of the gods. For example, the Akkadians of the third millennium BC would appear to have believed that Kharsag, or Kharsag Kurra (*'gar-sag kurkurra*) as it was also known, was a sacred mountain located to the north, 'immediately above'[41] the northern limits of their country.[42] To them it symbolized the cradle of their race, and was located in a kind of primordial version of Akkad itself.[43] Here, too, were 'the four rivers',[44] paralleling exactly the Hebraic concept of the four rivers of paradise. Beyond Kharsag Kurra 'extended the land of Aralli, which was very rich in gold, and was inhabited by the gods and blessed spirits'.[45]

Akkadian myth therefore blended together both the Hebraic account of paradise and the contents of the Kharsag tablets, lending immediate weight to O'Brien's retranslation of these ancient texts. So where had this mythical domain of the gods been located? There was no question on the matter. It lay immediately north of Akkad, in other words in the mountains of Kurdistan. The later Assyrians of the first millennium BC, who adopted many of the Akkadian myths and legends, had spoken of 'the heavenly courts' of Kharsag Kurra in connection with the 'silver mountain' – a reference to the Taurus mountain range of Turkish Kurdistan, west of Lake Van, which was known to the Akkadians as the Silver Mountain.[46]

A similar domain of the gods is featured in what must rank as Mesopotamia's most celebrated literary work – the Epic of Gilgamesh.

The Hero Gilgamesh

The Sumerian hero of this name had probably been a historical figure – seemingly a king of the city-state of Uruk in central Iraq, sometime during the first half of the third millennium BC. The texts say that he had been a *lillu*, 'a man with demonic qualities',[47] and that he had been worshipped as a god at various shrines. At Uruk, for example, he is recorded as having been adopted as the personal deity of a king named Utu-heğal, *c.* 2120 BC, as well as by his immediate successors, who ruled from Ur, a city-state in Lower Iraq between *c.* 2112–2004 BC.

It was probably during this same age that a series of poems featuring the deeds of Gilgamesh were set down for the first time, for there exist several variations of his epic which date to the first half of the second millennium BC. Among these poems is one entitled 'Gilgamesh and Huwawa' or 'Gilgamesh and the Cedar Forest'.[48] The story begins with the beguiling of Enkidu, a wildman who lives in the mountains, but who is finally tamed and persuaded to begin a new life among mortal kind.

Enkidu grows to enjoy his new lifestyle, but in so doing he loses his courage and strength, so Gilgamesh suggests that they go into the mountains where they must find and kill a 'monster' named Huwawa (or Humbaba). This strange being has been made guardian of a great cedar forest by the god Enlil. At first Enkidu is reluctant to embark on this fearsome quest, as he himself has come across Huwawa on his own journeys across the mountains; however, he finally agrees to the proposal on the insistence of Gilgamesh.

Huwawa is described as 'a giant protected by seven layers of terrifying radiance',[49] who also possesses a hideous face, long hair, whiskers, and lion's claws for hands. Eventually the two heroes track down the giant, but at first spare his life. Then, in a fit of rage, Enkidu finally dispatches Huwawa.

The significant aspect of this poem is the section entitled 'The Forest Journey', where Gilgamesh and Enkidu approach the cedar forest for the first time. It is said to have stretched before them 'for ten thousand leagues in every direction', and as the text reveals:

Together they went down into the forest and they came to the green mountain. There they stood still, they were struck dumb; they stood still and gazed at the forest, at the mountain of cedars, the dwelling place of the gods [author's emphasis]. *The hugeness of the cedar rose in front of the mountain, its shade was beautiful, full of comfort; mountain and glade were green with brushwood'.*[50]

What was this 'dwelling place of the gods'? The text suggests it is the 'green' mountain that stood within the vast forest. In front of this mountain is a huge cedar that seems to have its own significance in the story. Such lone trees, usually of immense height and size, are found in mythologies throughout the world and represent the point where heaven and earth meet. In mythological studies, such trees are known as the *axis mundi*, or the cosmic axis, and almost invariably they are linked with certain recurring themes, such as a holy mountain and a spring or wellhead that supplies the whole world with water. Kharsag itself is described in the opening lines of one of the tablets as the place 'where Heaven and Earth met',[51] confirming its role as a cosmic axis. It was undoubtedly also 'the dwelling place of the gods', for Enlil, Enki, Ninlil, Ninurta and Utu were five of the most important deities of the Sumerian pantheon.

So where exactly had this great cedar forest of the gods been located?

In the oldest forms of the Epic of Gilgamesh written in Sumerian, the text is quite clear: it is in the Zagros mountains of Kurdistan.[52] Later forms of the epic written in Assyrian times speak of the forest as being in Lebanon, although this is almost certainly incorrect. Palaeo-climatological research has shown that such forests replaced the cold tundra and sparse grasslands that had covered the lower valley regions of the Kurdish highlands after the final retreat of the last Ice Age, somewhere around 8500 BC. The appearance of powerful Asian monsoons in northern Mesopotamia and north-western Iran around this time had brought about dramatic changes in the climatic conditions of the Kurdish highlands, creating vast inland lakes as well as the proliferation of lush vegetation during the spring and summer months. Thick forests of deciduous trees, including cedars, began to grow in the valleys and on the mountain slopes, while the higher elevations turned into lush grasslands, ideal for cultivation. Indeed, these severe climatic changes corresponded almost exactly with the first appearance of the earliest neolithic communities in Kurdistan (see Chapter Seventeen).[53] Yet then, sometime between 3000 and 2000 BC, these Asian monsoons slowly retreated, leaving the region devoid of its essential spring and summer rains. As a consequence, the lower valleys suffered most, with a reduction in the variety of vegetation, and a slow desiccation of the neighbouring lowland regions, a process that continues to this day.[54]

It was also during this last period of prehistory that the Sumerians began wholesale felling of these vast mountain forests, both for building construction and as charcoal for brick furnaces and domestic fires. As a consequence, by the start of the first millennium BC the cedar forests of the Zagros no longer existed. Not only did this bring about huge ecological damage to the region, it also paved the way for gross geographical inaccuracies both in later versions of the Epic of Gilgamesh, and in many other myths and legends of this period. Since the editors of these texts lived in an age when not even their distant ancestors could remember such a 'cedar forest' having ever existed in the Zagros, their presence in the texts was inadvertently associated with the more obviously well-known cedar forests of the Ante-Lebanon range. Indeed, as the Kurdish expert Mehrdad Izady points out: 'some modern scholars, noting the geographical discrepancy but perplexed by the long absence of any large cedar stands in the Zagros, have come to interpret the ancient words of the (Gilgamesh) epic as "Pine Forest" rather than "Cedar Forest"'.[55]

The Argument for Mount Hermon

Knowledge of the existence of these cedar forests in the Zagros mountain range of Kurdistan was a major blow to O'Brien's interpretation of the Kharsag tablets. Having assessed their contents, he had used almost identical palaeo-climatological evidence to establish that the cedar forests of the Lebanon dated back to the same post-glacial period, *c.* 8000 BC in his reckoning. With this knowledge, O'Brien concluded that the Kharsag settlement must have been located in the Ante-Lebanon range during this very same age. Indeed, he actually put forward a foundation date of 8197 BC for the settlement, based on these studies.[56] O'Brien then went on to demonstrate that this information proved that Kharsag was synonymous with the Eden/heaven settlement of the Book of Enoch, because it had been geographically located in the vicinity of Mount

Hermon, which is itself in the Ante-Lebanon range. Curiously enough, the Akkadian word for 'cedar' is *erenu*, or *erin*, which is phonetically the same as *'îrin*, the Hebrew word for Watchers. As the term 'trees' is used as a synonym for the Watchers in Enochian literature, while the mythical kings of the *Shahnameh* are likened to cypress trees, I feel this etymological link between the Watchers and cedars must be more than simply coincidence.

Since there is clear evidence for the former presence of cedar forests in the Zagros, it seems much more likely that Kharsag was located either in this region, or in the eastern Taurus range, and *not* in far-off Lebanon. The most bizarre confirmation of this supposition comes from O'Brien himself, for after summing up the geographical evidence presented in the Kharsag tablets, he admits:

It is strongly reminiscent of the Zagros Mountains of Luristan and Kurdistan, to the north of Sumer, on the north-eastern flank of the Fertile Crescent. But these mountains are now oak-tree bearing, and have no history of cedar forests . . . We are left with only the far north-western part of the Fertile Crescent covered by Lebanon.[57]

This is simply not true, and even further damaging O'Brien's belief that Eden/heaven/Kharsag had been located in the Ante-Lebanon range was the reference in Genesis 2:8 to God planting a garden 'eastward, in Eden'. Mount Hermon cannot be seen as eastward of anything, other than the old city of Sidon on the Mediterranean coast. Despite these errors of judgement on O'Brien's part, the importance of his retranslation of the Kharsag tablets cannot be overstated, for he returned to the world what might well represent the oldest surviving account of heaven on earth.

Yet did this tradition have a separate existence outside of the Kharsag tablets? And did these also lead back to the mountains of Kurdistan?

The Search for Dilmun

Eden and Kharsag are not the only names by which the dwelling-place of the gods was known to the Sumerian and Akkadian cultures. There are also legends regarding an alleged mythical paradise known as Dilmun, or Tilmun. Here the god Enki and his wife were placed to institute 'a sinless age of complete happiness', where animals lived in peace and harmony, man had no rival and the god Enlil 'in one tongue gave praise'.[58] It is also described as a pure, clean and 'bright' 'abode of the immortals', where death, disease and sorrow are unknown[59] and some mortals have been given 'life like a god'[60] – words reminiscent of the *Airyana Vaejah*, the realm of the immortals in Iranian myth and legend, and the Eden of Hebraic tradition.

Although there is good evidence to show that the name Dilmun was directly connected with an island state established at Bahrain in the Persian Gulf by the Akkadian king Sargon of Agade (2334–2279 BC),[61] there is also clear evidence to suggest that it was a mythical realm in its own right. For example, there are references to 'the mountain of Dilmun, the place where the sun rises'.[62] Since there is no obvious candidate for this 'mountain' in Bahrain, and in no way can this island be described as lying in the direction of the rising sun with respect to Iraq, then it seems certain that there were two Dilmuns.

So where had this mythological Dilmun been located?

A chance, unexpected discovery gave me an answer. Glancing through Mehrdad Izady's authoritative book *The Kurds – A Concise Handbook*, published in 1992, I happened to see references to a Kurdish tribal dynasty known as the Daylamites, who had established a number of powerful Middle Eastern kingdoms during the medieval period, the most famous being the Buwâyhids (or Buyids) who reigned between AD 932 and 1062. Having succeeded in taking the important 'Abbâsid caliphate of Baghdad, the Daylamites had pushed forward to establish a Kurdish empire that stretched from Asia Minor to the shores of the Indian Ocean.[63]

Yet as Izady points out in his book: 'Confusion surrounds the origin of the Daylamites.'[64] The main centre of their tribal dynasty had been the Elburz mountains, north of Tehran, where many scholars assume they rose to prominence. Yet if the tribe were to be traced back to pre-Islamic times, and in particular during the rule of the Parthian kings of Persia, between the third century BC and the third century AD, a different picture emerges. Their true ancestral homeland had been a region in north-western Kurdistan named Dilamân, or Daylamân, where their modern descendants, the Dimila (Zâzâ) Kurds still live.[65]

Dilamân? This sounded a lot like Dilmun.

Could they possibly be one and the same?

The ancient church archives of Christian Arbela (the modern Arbil) in Iraqi Kurdistan, confirm this same geographical location by recording that *Beth Dailômâye*, the 'land of the Daylamites', was located 'north of Sanjâr', around the headwaters of the Tigris.[66] Furthermore, as Izady reveals: 'The Zoroastrian holy book, *Bundahishn*, (also) places Dilamân . . . *at the headwaters of the Tigris*, and not in the Caspian Sea coastal mountain regions [*author's italics*].'[67]

I could hardy contain myself on reading these words – the *Bundahishn*, as well as at least one other major Kurdish source, placed Dilamân, the ancestral homeland of the Dimila Kurds, 'at the headwaters of the Tigris'! Quickly I checked the accompanying map and confirmed the worst: 'Dilamân' had been located south-west of Lake Van, close to Bitlis, in exactly the same area that I had placed the Garden of Eden! Quite obviously, these words belonged to different languages and were separated by thousands of years of cultural development in the Near East. This I accepted; however, place-names are one of the few things that can be preserved and reused by successive cultures without major alteration. It was feasible therefore that the indigenous peoples of north-west Kurdistan had not only preserved the original Mesopotamian place-name of Dilmun, but had also adopted it as a tribal title.

Source of the Waters

The links between Dilmun and the headwaters of the Tigris and Euphrates rivers did not end there. The god Enki, who along with his wife was said to have been the first inhabitant of Dilmun, was seen as god of the Abzu – a vast watery domain beneath the earth from which all springs, streams and rivers have their source. In this capacity he was guardian protector of Sumer's two greatest rivers, the mighty Euphrates and Tigris, which were usually depicted as arched streams of water, either pouring out of his

Map 3. Eastern Kurdistan, showing the traditional locations associated with both the Garden of Eden and the Ark of Noah.

shoulders or emerging from a vase held in his hand. Fish are depicted swimming up these streams, like salmon attempting to reach the source of a river.[68]

As sacred guardian of these two rivers, Enki would have been seen as the protector of the river's sources. In this way, he would undoubtedly have been associated with the headwaters of these rivers, where both the Christian records of Arbela and the *Bundahishn* text appear to place the mythical realm of Dilmun, and Hebraic tradition places the Garden of Eden.

The Red-headed Tribesmen

The principal religion of the Dimili Kurds is Alevism, the third, and perhaps the most enigmatic, of the Kurdistani angel-worshipping cults. Most of its adherents now live around the foothills of Turkish Kurdistan in eastern Anatolia. There is, however, one last bastion of Alevi tribesmen still surviving amid a sea of Sunni Islam in northern Kurdistan, and this just happens to be on the south-western shores of Lake Van.[69]

So who were these mysterious Alevi tribesmen who worshipped the angels?

The Alevis take their name from the word *alev*, meaning 'fire', an allusion to its great reverence among their faith. Although in its present form Alevism dates only to the fifteenth century AD, its roots stretch back into the mists of time and encompass many diverse influences, mostly Iranian in origin. They are not Muslims, although they do recognize a series of avatars, or divine incarnations, the most important of which is Ali, the first Shi'ite imam or saint. In contrast, Azhi Dahâka is not forgotten by these people, for he features in an important Alevi ceremonial gathering known as the *Ayini Jam*.[70] Among the more obscure ritual customs of the Alevis is an archaic practice in which they insert a sword into the ground in order to communicate with the universal spirit.[71] Women are also allowed to participate in all ritual gatherings, particularly the *Ayini Jam*, something that has laid the Alevis open to accusations of sexual improprieties taking place at such events, which are not open to outsiders.

The Dimili Alevis are also known as the Qizilbâsh, 'the red heads', in reference to their distinctive deep-red headgear, which they adopted in honour of Ali, the son-in-law of Muhammed, who had apparently said: 'Tie red upon your heads, so that ye slay not your own comrades in the thick of the battle.'[72]

Closing the book, I could hardly believe what I had read. To say I was overawed by these discoveries is an understatement. Had the Daylamite, or Dimili, tribes of Turkish Kurdistan managed to preserve the name of Dilmun, or Dilamân, from the prehistoric age right down to medieval times? More importantly, did the red-headed Alevi tribesmen guard age-old secrets concerning the Watchers' apparent presence in this region? And what of their home territory, south-west of Lake Van – had this really been the location of Dilmun, the Mesopotamian domain of the immortals, as well as Kharsag, the settlement of the Anannage, and Eden, the homeland of the Watchers?

It was a thought-provoking idea, and the circumstantial evidence for Dilmun's placement in northern Kurdistan looked good. Yet, before I moved on, I needed to find out whether any further clues concerning the alleged existence of the fallen race could be traced within the myths and legends left by the ancient city-states of Mesopotamia. I was soon to discover that in ancient Iraq, more than anywhere else, the memory of the god-men who had once walked among mortal kind had lingered far longer than I could ever have imagined.

Sixteen

SLEEPING WITH GODS

Long ago, when gods still walked among mortal kind, there was an eagle who lived peacefully alongside a serpent inside a great tree. Never did the two have any quarrel with the other. Both reared their young in separate parts of the tree, until one day, while the serpent was out hunting for food, the eagle decided to gobble up its neighbour's children. On returning to its nest, the serpent was horrified to find its babies gone and so lay down and cried. The god Shamash saw the snake's plight, and suggested to it a plan of action. It was to hide inside the carcass of an ox, and there wait until the eagle came to feed.

This the serpent did, and on the arrival of the great bird it wrought a most terrible revenge. First it caught the eagle. Then it broke its 'heel'. Then it plucked out its feathers and finally it threw the bird into a deep pit.

Meanwhile, down on the plains Etana, the king of Kish, was sad. His queen had borne him no child, and he did not wish to die without an heir. There seemed but one answer to this problem. He had heard that there existed among the mountains 'the plant of birth', which could make barren women fertile. If only he could find a way of asking the gods of heaven where he might obtain this great drug. In desperation, he cried, and the god Shamash heard his calls and provided an answer. Etana must befriend and rescue the eagle from the pit, and then enlist its help in finding 'the plant of birth'. This Etana duly did, and once the bird had been given its freedom, it flew over the mountains in search of 'the plant of birth'. Unfortunately it was unsuccessful in its quest, and so suggested that they visit Ishtar, the Mistress of Birth, who would provide an answer.

The eagle then said to Etana: 'Be glad, my friend. Let me bear thee to the highest heaven. Lay thy breast on mine and thine arms on my wings, and let my body be as thy body.'[1] *Etana agreed to this plan, and the couple climbed together towards the heaven of Anu. They soared higher and higher into the sky, as the earth gradually grew smaller and smaller. Finally they reached the gate of heaven and, after bowing down together, entered inside.*[2]

Here the story preserved on the last of three ancient stone tablets ends, and as no further tablets have been found, we can only speculate on how it might conclude. Presumably Etana attained a solution from Ishtar, and as a result died in the knowledge that his heir would succeed him. According to the Sumerian king-list, Etana ruled a healthy 1,560 years, and left as a successor his son Balih, so the visit to heaven must have been successful!

The tale of Etana would appear to have been a popular one in ancient Mesopotamia, especially during the rule of the Akkadian kings in the late third millennium BC, as cylinder seals bearing the image of a figure riding on the back of an eagle have been unearthed at several locations.[3]

Yet this tale of Etana and his flight to heaven was more than simply a bedtime story told to small children, for it contained various abstract images already associated with the fallen race. There is the battle between the serpent and the eagle who live inside a great tree, which undoubtedly symbolized the cosmic axis joining together heaven and earth. Might this struggle between these two animal forms, both so strongly associated with the Watchers, represent some kind of conflict between the two separate factions of Anannage – those of heaven and those of the earth? Etana believes that the gods of the 'heaven of Anu' possess knowledge regarding a wonder-working drug known as 'the plant of birth', which an obliging eagle unsuccessfully helps him to search for. This brought to mind the medical knowledge of the Persian Simurgh and the healing properties of the sacred *haoma* plant – the secret of which was known only to the immortals. Could the two separate traditions be linked in some way?

Riddle of the Sacred Marriage

Stories surrounding the mythical life of the hero Gilgamesh also contain many quite extraordinary features that are never suitably explained by scholars. In a little-known classical work entitled *On the Nature of Animals*, written by the Roman naturalist and writer Claudius Aelianus (*fl.* 140), it records the strange birth of Gilgamesh. The story begins with a 'Babylonian' king named 'Seuechoros' being warned by his temple 'magicians' that his daughter, the princess, is soon to give birth to a son, who will one day usurp the throne. He therefore orders that she be kept under watch and guard within the 'acropolis'. Despite these precautions, the daughter becomes pregnant and inevitably gives birth to a son. Fearful of the king's wrath, the guards take the child to 'the summit' and cast it to the winds. At that very moment an eagle flies by and, having caught hold of the infant, carries it to a lofty orchard where the youth is tended until adulthood. He is given the name 'Gilgamos', and when the time is right he returns to the city and, predictably, seizes the throne from his grandfather.[4]

What kind of symbolism did this simple tale mask? How did the daughter get pregnant? Why was the child cast to the winds? Who, or what, was the eagle, and where was the orchard? No answers are provided by Claudius Aelianus, who is the only writer to have preserved this story of Gilgamesh's early life. Turning, however, to Sumerian myth, the hero's epic provides a few missing pieces of the jigsaw. His father is given as a king of Uruk named Lugalbanda, while his mother is said to have been 'the wise wild cow' Ninsûn, a 'lofty' goddess.[5] Not only is Gilgamesh described as *lillu*, a demon, but because of his mother's divinity he is said to have been 'two-thirds' divine and 'one-third mortal'.[6]

Who was Ninsûn? Why is she described as a goddess? How did her status allow Gilgamesh to be part god, part human and part demon?

Repeatedly in ancient Sumerian and later Babylonian texts we find references to the so-called 'sacred marriage'. Here the king, or a chosen substitute, would become an *en*-priest and join in sacred union with the 'goddess', originally Inanna (Akkadian Ishtar), the

Lady of Heaven. Alternatively, a chaste *entu*-priestess, often the king's daughter, would join in 'marriage' with the god, usually Nanna-Suen, or Sin, the lunar deity. This event would take place yearly in a specially prepared room in a temple building, with its purpose being to ensure 'the productivity of the land and fruitfulness of the womb of man and beast'.[7] Evidence suggests that the 'sacred marriage' ceremony goes back to the earliest dynastic period of Sumer, *c.* 2500 BC, and that it was performed in many of the city-states right down to late Babylonian times during the first millennium BC.[8] Quite obviously, scholars have always seen this 'sacred marriage' as a purely symbolic event – humans taking the role of gods and the deity in question 'entering' the sacred room in metaphorical terms only.

But is this all it was – kings playing gods and priestesses playing goddesses? Perhaps. There are, however, records of a consummated 'sacred marriage' between an *entu*-priestess and a local 'storm god' in the Syrian town of Emar in the fourteenth century BC,[9] while Herodotus speaks of a similar ritual that supposedly took place in the 'topmost tower' of the ziggurat of Babylon. Here on 'a couch of unusual size, richly adorned . . . a native woman . . . chosen for himself by the deity out of all the women of the land' would spend her nights.[10] And as Herodotus adds: 'They [*the priests of Marduk*] also declare – but I for my part do not credit it – that the god comes down in person into this chamber, and sleeps upon the couch . . .'[11]

Although these accounts must be treated with extreme caution, they might well preserve more ancient traditions in which both male and female Anannage, or Watchers, were able to combine in sexual union with mortals in a co-ordinated manner to produce semi-divine progeny that were classed either as part divine, part demon and/or part human, depending on how they were perceived by the royal family. If so, then it might help explain why certain kings appended their name with a star-shaped ideogram signifying that they were a 'god' – *dingir* in Sumerian and *ilu* in Akkadian – or why individuals such as Gilgamesh were said to have been *lillu*, 'a man with demon-like qualities'.

Narâm-Sin, the Akkadian king in whose reign the Nippur cylinder was most likely deposited, had adopted the epithet *ilu*, 'god',[12] while his grandfather, Sargon of Agade, the first Akkadian king to rule Sumer, was said to have been born of a mother who was herself a *lillu* 'changeling'.[13] The Akkadian epithet *ilu* was much later transformed into the Hebrew suffix *el* (or *il* in Arabic), which is used in connection with so many angelic names, both fallen and otherwise, and is interpreted by Jewish scholars as meaning 'of God'. In actuality, the word-root *el* means 'shining', 'bright' or 'light',[14] bringing to mind the heavenly *farr* of the mythical Pishdadian kings of Iran.

This knowledge also makes some sense of the 'miraculous' conception and subsequent birth of Gilgamesh, and why the child had to be spirited away to an orchard by an obliging 'eagle'. Had the child been taken away at birth by one of the Anannage, the 'eagle', and reared in Kharsag, the 'orchard', before being returned to Uruk where he eventually succeeded his grandfather? Might it also be possible that the 'lofty' goddess Ninsûn – the mother of Gilgamesh in the alternative version of his parentage – preserves the memory of a 'sacred marriage' between a tall, female Watcher and a mortal king, in this case Lugalbanda?

These were incredible thoughts, I knew, but they had to be postulated. Furthermore, an understanding of the 'sacred marriage' ceremony now makes more sense of the Etana story. After the eagle has been unsuccessful in finding 'the plant of birth', Etana experiences three dreams concerning his heirless situation. In the last of these, he and the eagle have already reached 'the heaven of Anu'. After bowing down together, they enter inside. Etana explains what happens next:

> '*. . . I saw a house with a window that was not sealed.*
> *I pushed it open and went inside.*
> *Sitting in there was a girl*
> *Adorned with a crown, fair of face.*
> *A throne was set in place, and [ ]*
> *Beneath the throne crouched snarling lions.*
> *I came up and the lions sprang at me.*
> *I woke up terrified.*'[15]

In response to hearing the contents of Etana's dreams, the eagle responds: 'My friend, [the significance of the dreams] is quite clear! Come let me carry you up to the heaven of Anu.' Obviously we do not know what happened when Etana and the eagle really did reach heaven, but it was usual in ancient texts for the prophecies of dreams to come true, right down to the last word. This therefore implies that Etana did enter a house and find a girl 'fair of face' seated on a throne. Her crown obviously signified that she was of a divine or royal line. The snarling lions were guardian forms that Etana would have to appease before he could approach her properly. But what happened next? In my opinion, there is every reason to suggest that some kind of 'marriage' took place, and that as a result of this bonding Etana gained his heir. The presence in the text of Ishtar, the Mistress of Heaven, who featured in the annual 'sacred marriage' during historical times, seems to imply that this was indeed what took place. Etana had gone to heaven to achieve an heir through some kind of ritual 'marriage' with a suitable 'goddess'. Might this 'goddess' have been a female Watcher?

It was a tantalizing thought, but one without anything more than circumstantial evidence to support its argument. Yet it opened the door to the possibility that not only were the earliest Sumerian and Akkadian kings in open contact with the Watchers of Eden, but that they had also been mating with individuals of this angelic culture during 'sacred marriage' ceremonies, either in their own city-states or in the Eden/Kharsag settlement. Just how many Sumerian and Akkadian kings actually believed they were the product of these divine unions?

Crime of the Imdugud

Fabulous birds, like the eagles in the Etana and Gilgamesh accounts, feature again and again in Sumerian, Akkadian and much later Assyrian and Babylonian myths of the first millennium BC. Most important among the legends are those concerning the monstrous thunderbird known as the Imdugud (Anzu in Akkadian). This mythical creature was seen as a lion-headed eagle of immense size that possessed a beak like a saw, and which, when it flapped its wings, could bring about sandstorms and whirlwinds. The Imdugud's principal story revolves around its theft of the so-called Tablets of Destiny from the god Enlil (Ellil in Akkadian), which, when in its possession, gave 'him power over the Universe as controller of the fates of all'[16] enough to endanger 'the stability of civilization'.[17] At first no god would volunteer to retrieve the stolen tablets. Then the god Ninurta stepped forward and offered his services to his father Enlil. These being accepted, the god goes in search of the Imdugud's nest 'on its mountain top in Arabia'.[18] Eventually he finds the thunderbird, which he then attacks with lightning bolts. The monstrous bird is eventually killed and the tablets are returned to Enlil.

The Imdugud is clearly the Simurgh in its Mesopotamian guise, since both birds are seen as half lion, half eagle. Furthermore, the thunderbird can be compared with the Simurgh's Indian counterpart, Garuda the half giant, half eagle of Hindu mythology. The similarities between the Imdugud's theft of the Tablets of Destiny and Garuda's theft of the Amrita, Ambrosia or *soma* of the gods are self-apparent, and have long been realized by students of mythology.[19] Might Imdugud's 'theft' of the tablets relate not so much to destiny as to the revealing of forbidden knowledge – including the use of the *haoma/soma* plant of immortality – to mortal kind by rebel Watchers dressed in feather coats?

It was the Zagros range, however, that was the true home of the Imdugud, for in another work, entitled the Epic of Lugalbanda, Gilgamesh's father comes across an Imdugud fledgling in its nest within this mountain range. He tends the young bird until the adult Imdugud 'and its wife' return.[20] Furthermore, Lugalbanda was himself seen as a manifestation of the thunderbird. In this guise he was said to have stolen 'the sacred fire from heaven for the service and mental illumination of man',[21] a role played by Prometheus in Greek tradition. For his theft and trickery, Prometheus was chained to Mount Caucasus in Transcaucasia, and for thirty years an eagle would come each day and pluck out his liver, which would then grow anew.

Although it is not my intention to cite Greek legends in support of the possible associations between the ancient Iraqi civilizations and the Watchers of the highlands of Kurdistan, it seems clear that the story of the theft of the divine fire, by both Lugalbanda and Prometheus, must originate from the same source material as the Garuda/Imdugud legends.

Fig. 10. The monstrous half-lion, half-eagle named Imdugud, or Anzu, being attacked by the god Ninurta. From a stone relief found at Nimrud in northern Iraq and belonging to the reign of the Assyrian king Ashurnasirpal II (883–859 BC). Does this mythical creature's theft of the Tablets of Destiny in Sumero-Akkadian tradition preserve abstract astronomical data over 10,000 years old?

Stela of the Vultures

The mighty thunderbird also appears alongside the god Ningirsu, a localized form of Ninurta, on a famous stone frieze known as the 'Stela of the Vultures', which dates to the Early Dynastic Period, *c.* 2470 BC. It commemorates a victory at war by a Sumerian king named Eannatum and shows the Imdugud, with its wings out-stretched, above a flock of vultures that carry away the heads and arms of slain warriors. Ningirsu is shown with a vulture in his left hand, from which comes a huge net filled with naked prisoners.[22]

Fig. 11. An eagle-headed deity from a stone relief found at Nimrud in Upper Iraq. Could such mythical creatures have been based on the contact between the earliest Mesopotamian races and the proposed Watcher culture of the Kurdish highlands?

This victory stela appears to draw together the basic associations between the Imdugud, the vulture and the god Ningirsu/Ninurta, a legacy which was inherited by the Assyrian nation of northern Iraq, who rose to power in the eighteenth century BC. Carved stone reliefs found at the palace of Nimrud on the Upper Tigris show a lion-headed winged beast, almost certainly the Imdugud, about to strike Ninurta, who holds lightning bolts in each hand. It also seems certain that the feathered tail of the Imdugud influenced the development of the Assyrian winged disk, which portrayed the god named Ashur, who was possibly a form of Ninurta, standing upon a plume of feathers.[23] Curiously enough, it is this very symbol that was much later adopted as the sole pictorial representation of the Zoroastrian god Ahura Mazda.

Strange how certain themes appear to go around in circles.

Was I really stretching the imagination by suggesting that Mesopotamian winged monsters, such as the thunderbird, were not simply the personification of atmospheric forces, as the scholars have always believed, but abstract symbols of the fallen race? Sometimes I felt I was, but then a new piece of evidence would come along and strengthen my convictions even further, and one such piece of evidence was the so-called Kutha tablet.

Bodies of Birds

During excavations at the palace of the Assyrian king Sennacherib (704–681 BC) in Nineveh by Austen Layard in 1849, two large chambers were revealed 'piled a foot or more deep in tablets' bearing cuneiform inscriptions.[24] Three years later, in the nearby palace of Sennacherib's grandson Ashurbanipal (668–627 BC), another huge horde of similar tablets was uncovered. They constituted a library collection that totalled around 25,000 tablets, or parts of tablets, which were each duly catalogued and dispatched to the British Museum.

On translation of these tablets, it was realized that the Assyrian kings of this period, in particular Ashurbanipal, had scoured the length and breadth of the empire searching for old inscriptions, ancient legends and variations on known myths for inclusion in this massive personal library, comparable only with its more famous counterpart in Alexandria.

Many of the thousands of tablets acquired by Ashurbanipal had been copied by the Assyrian scribes into Akkadian, the written language of the day, while others had been left in their original script. Why exactly the Assyrian king had amassed this unprecedented library is unknown. It is obvious, however, that he had a keen interest in preserving the rich mythology surrounding his culture's ancestral heritage, for as he stated in one tablet:

The god of scribes [i.e. Nabû, the guardian spirit of the library] *has bestowed on me the gift of the knowledge of his art.*
I have been initiated into the secrets of writing,
I can even read the intricate tablets in Shumerian;
I understand the enigmatic words in the stone carvings from the days before the Flood.[25]

In 'the days before the flood'? Clearly Ashurbanipal must have been a very learned figure, and if the Watchers really had survived as a culture in the mountains of Kurdistan, then surely the tablets amassed by Ashurbanipal would record their existence.

Sadly many thousands of these texts are unavailable to study. Yet one seemed to record the existence of bird-men in Sumer's distant past. Entitled the Kutha tablet, or the 'Legend of Creation from Cutha (Kutha)', its original author recorded that it had been written 'in the (Babylonian) city of Cutha, in the temple of Sitlam, in the sanctuary of Nergal'.[26] Unfortunately, the text – like so many others – is incomplete and fragmentary, making it that much more difficult to read, but its significance is plain enough. It concerns the incursions into Mesopotamia of an unknown race of demons, fostered by the gods in some nether region, who waged war on an unnamed king for three consecutive years. The invaders are said to have been:

> *Men with the bodies of birds of the desert, human beings*
> *with the faces of ravens,*
> *these the great gods created,*
> *and in the earth the gods created for them a dwelling.*
> *Tamat (Tiamat) gave unto them strength,*
> *their life the mistress of the gods raised,*
> *in the midst of the earth they grew up and became great,*
> *and increased in number,*
> *Seven kings, brothers of the same family,*
> *six thousand in number were their people.*[27]

Who exactly were these 'men with the bodies of birds'? There is no academic answer. All we know is that when they appeared a storm cloud would come over the land (storm clouds are symbols of demons). They would slaughter those whom they took captive, before returning to some inaccessible region for another year.

Although merely a taster of what this fragmentary text actually contains (much of which is unintelligible), there seemed to be just enough evidence to lend weight to the possibility that this was a very ancient, garbled account of confrontations between an unknown king and a bird-like race comparable with the degenerate Nephilim of the Book of Enoch. Was it possible therefore that, long after the fragmentation of Kharsag, the offspring of certain rebel Watchers engaged the earliest Sumerian and Akkadian kings in military combat? Is this what the Kutha tablet records – military conflicts between Nephilim and mortal kind? It was a disturbing prospect, and one that raised fundamental questions, such as how widespread did this culture become? And when did it die out? If evidence such as the Kutha tablet can be shown to be an account of very real events, then it could mean that the descendants of the original Watchers and Nephilim were still a force to be reckoned with right down to the third millennium BC. It was in this epoch that the Anakim and Rephaim, the giant descendants of the Nephilim, are alleged to have controlled vast areas of neighbouring Canaan (see Chapter Six).

The Descent of Ishtar

Bird-men like those of the Kutha tablet feature again in the following account of the descent of the goddess Ishtar into the underworld, for as she explains herself:

I descend, I descend to the house of darkness, to the dwelling of the god Irkalla:
To the house entering which there is no exit,
to the road the course of which never returns:
To the house in which the dwellers long for light,
the place where dust is their nourishment and their food mud.
Its chiefs also are like birds covered with feathers

and light is never seen, in darkness they dwell.
In the house my friend which I will enter,
for me is treasured up a crown;
with those wearing crowns who from days of old ruled the earth,
to whom the gods Anu and Bel have given terrible names.
The food is made carrion, they drink stagnant water.[28]

These dwellers of an infernal region appear to be exactly the same as the bird-men in the Kutha tablet, although whether this underground realm is the same as the 'dwelling . . . in the midst of the earth' in which they lived is unknown. That their 'food is made carrion' implies vultures or ravens, and the fact that they have worn crowns and ruled the earth 'from the days of old' suggests that they were primeval beings of immense antiquity, who had obviously impressed their memory on the minds of much later story-tellers and narrators of religious epics.

What happened to these people? What was their ultimate fate?

The Search for Ut-napishtim

Returning to the Epic of Gilgamesh, I found many more symbols of the fallen race on closer scrutiny, particularly within the sequence of events that follow the death of the wildman Enkidu, who was finally killed by the gods for murdering the giant Huwawa.

On hearing of this tragic event, Gilgamesh embarks on a quest across the mountains in an attempt to discover the secret of immortality. He has been told that a forebear, who knows the ways of the gods, can give him some answers. His name is Ut-napishtim, and the hero finds this ancient one on an island across the waters. On sight of the old man, Gilgamesh realizes something is terribly wrong. He expects to meet an immortal, a god in his own right, but instead he finds a human being just like himself.

Ut-napishtim then recites the story of how he alone of humanity had been warned by the god Ea (Sumerian Enki) of an impending flood that was about to consume the world. With this knowledge he had constructed a huge vessel covered inside and out with bitumen. On to this he had placed his family and relations, along with the best craftsmen, and all the beasts of the field.

A dark cloud had then gathered overhead, turning light into perpetual darkness, and bringing fear even to the Anannage, who withdrew to the 'heaven of Anu', where they cowered and crouched like dogs 'by an outside wall'.

For six days and seven nights the almighty winds and terrible floods had raged, but then eventually the tempests had abated and the rains slowly ceased. The light returned and the waters receded. As the vessel rocked back and forth on the waves, Ut-napishtim looked for dry land, which began 'emerging everywhere'. Soon the ship had come to rest on 'Mount Nimush'. For six days the mountain held the boat fast and would not let it budge. Then on the seventh day, Ut-napishtim sent forth a dove, which had flown around and then returned to the ship 'for no perching place was visible to it'. He had then sent forth a swallow, which likewise returned. Then finally, he had sent forth a raven, which 'ate (carrion), preened, lifted its tail and did not turn round'. Ut-napishtim had then released the animals to the four winds, before going up to the mountain peak and making an offering to the gods of 'reeds, pine and myrtle'. In response they had gathered 'like flies . . . over the sacrifice'.[29]

The Gift of Immortality

As a reward for having saved both the human race and the animal kingdom from extinction, the gods had granted Ut-napishtim and his wife the secret of immortality. It was never, however, to be given to the mortal race, so the Flood hero refuses to let Gilgamesh have it. Instead, he instructs him on how he might find a plant which has the power to rejuvenate youth (probably one and the same thing as the plant of immortality). This he will find at the bottom of the Abzu, the watery abyss beneath the earth, sacred to Ea (Enki). Gilgamesh plunges into the dark waters with stones tied to his feet, and reaches the plant of life, which is as thorny as a rose, and is known as 'The Old Man has Become a Young Man'. Yet later, while out bathing, a snake (a Watcher?) smells the plant and eats it, after which it sloughs its old skin and emerges shiny and young.[30]

Gilgamesh's quest to find the secret of immortality ends here, bringing the epic to a close. Although he was unsuccessful in his attempts to find the plant in either of its forms, the existence of this text shows just how strongly the Sumerians believed that the gods possessed such a wonder-working drug. And when the hero comes face to face with Ut-napishtim, he is surprised to find that he looks like any other human being, even though he possesses the secret of immortality.

Evidence of this sort suggests that there once existed a highly developed culture who knew how to prolong life by taking a drug made from the extracts of a certain plant, or plants. If this is correct, then by how much was this drug able to increase the normal life-span of an individual? Was it fifty years? A hundred years? Two hundred years? Perhaps even more? Longevity of this order would have meant that the Watchers might have been able to outlive 'mortal' humans by many generations, making them seem 'immortal' in the eyes of those who did not possess the knowledge of this wonder-working drug.

Is it really possible that the Watchers could have lived across 'mortal' generations, like the vampires of popular myth? When might the last one have died? And did any survive into modern times? Is this all just too incredible to even contemplate? Humanity has striven unsuccessfully to discover the elixir of life for many thousands of years. It wants to know what the gods once knew, and perhaps one day it will find an answer.

Domain of the Edimmu

The connection with vampires is not as absurd as it might at first seem. In fact, it could hold the key to understanding the ultimate destiny of the Watchers. Assyrians and Babylonians of the first millennium BC believed fervently in vampires – hungry, blood-sucking beings called *Edimmu*, created as a result of the 'intermarriage between human beings and the spirit world'.[31] They lay waiting to seize upon humanity, draining the life-blood from households. The dead could become *Edimmu* simply by being neglected after death. If the body was left unburied, or the deceased's relatives failed to provide good food for the departed soul once the body was in the grave, then it could be taken by a vampiric 'robber-sprite'.[32] Thereafter the dead would return to the earth in order to satisfy their hunger by drinking blood.[33]

Although these *Edimmu* were seen by the Assyrians and Babylonians as 'half-ghostly, half-human',[34] it would appear that they might well have had a more earthly origin, and had perhaps been a physical race who lived underground. It was said that the *Edimmu* lived in an underworld domain identified by scholars with 'the house of darkness', 'the dwelling of the god Irkalla' visited by the goddess Ishtar.[35] Here, remember, 'the dwellers long for light' and the chief among them are 'like birds covered with feathers'.

One incantation speaks of these vampires in the plainest of terms, stating that they are 'spirits that minish the land' who are of 'giant strength and giant tread',[36] in other words giants. These demons are said to have been 'full of violence'. They 'rage against mankind' and 'spill their blood like rain, devouring their flesh (and) sucking their veins'.[37] Most curious is the fact that there were apparently seven of these giant vampires,[38] a direct parody of the council of seven Anannage who governed the 'heaven of Anu'.

Might this cabal of seven *Edimmu* preserve some kind of distorted memory of the Anannage, or Watchers, who descended on to the plains of ancient Iraq? Did these vampires of great stature live out of the light in some kind of underground city of the sort described in the account of Ishtar's descent into the underworld, as well as in the Kutha tablets? Perhaps the distorted memories of this degenerate race really were behind the notion of immortal, blood-sucking vampires of the sort so popularized in Gothic horror from Victorian times through till the present day.

As Old as Methuselah

The profound knowledge of immortality among the 'gods' of both Iraq and Iran also began to make sense of the baffling lines of Genesis 6:3, squeezed in between the verses concerning the coming of the Sons of God unto the Daughters of Men, for they proclaim:

And the Lord said, My spirit shall not strive with man for ever, for that he also is flesh: yet shall his days be an hundred and twenty years.

Up until this time the generations of Adam had possessed much longer life-spans, the longest being Enoch's son, Methuselah, who was said to have been 969 years' old when he departed this world; hence the saying 'as old as Methuselah'. The Sumerian king-lists also speak of individuals living for impossible lengths of time before the age of the Flood. Did the lines of Genesis 6:3 therefore suggest that up until this time mortals may have possessed knowledge of this 'immortality' drug to extend their natural life-spans? Yet because of the part this drug had played in the downfall of the Sons of God, it would no longer be given to humanity, meaning that the maximum age an individual could now expect would be 120 years. If this was true, then it could mean that the accounts of fabulous birds presenting the plant or secret of immortality to humanity are distorted memories of the way in which certain Watchers had transgressed the heavenly laws by giving this forbidden knowledge to the human race.

Hebraic tradition asserts that the consequences of this forbidden trafficking between the two races – immortals and mortals – had been a series of global cataclysms of a climatic and geological nature, including the Great Flood. Somehow the same theme had been bound up in Sumerian and later Assyrian mythology as well.

I felt there was no need to make the obvious comparisons between Ut-napishtim's account of the Flood preserved in the Epic of Gilgamesh, and the story of Noah's Ark found in both the Bible and Koran. Yet where was this 'Mount Nimush', said to have been the place where Ut-napishtim's vessel had come to rest on solid ground? Assyrian scholars have tentatively identified it as the 9,000-foot Mount Pir Omar Gudrun in the Zagros range, south of the Lower Zab river.[39] This, however, is by no means certain, for a Babylonian priest and historian of the third century BC named Berossus also recorded an account of the Flood in a Greek work entitled *Babyloniaka*, based on what appears to have been a Sumerian original. He names the Noah figure as Xisuthros and states that the vessel came to rest on the 'Gordyaean mountains of Armenia'[40] –

Gordyene being the name given to central Kurdistan in classical times.[41] It is generally supposed that Berossus had been referring to Al Judi, which is situated within this range.

This supposition is strongly supported by the immense interest the Assyrian king Sennacherib, Ashurbanipal's grandfather, seems to have had in the ancient flood myth. Jewish Talmudic tradition records that: 'On his return to Assyria, Sennacherib found a plank, which he worshipped as an idol, because it was part of the ark which had saved Noah from the deluge.'[42] If this assertion is correct, and the king *had* visited the Place of Descent of the Ark, then it is extremely unlikely that he would have known of the flood myth through Hebraic sources as is supposed by the Jews. It is much more conceivable that he had studied the Ut-napishtim story contained in the Epic of Gilgamesh – copies of which were found in the library rooms at Nineveh. I had therefore been intrigued to find that, during his military campaigns in Kurdistan, Sennacherib had taken time out to visit Al Judi, where he had carved a mighty image of himself standing before the gods,[43] and where fragments of wood and bitumen from Noah's Ark could apparently be picked up by travellers.[44] Why had he gone to Al Judi, if not to offer sacrifice at the alleged site of the flood hero's stone altar, which remained in the form of four stone pillars at the base of the mountain?[45] There is certainly no record of this great king having carved similar images at the base of Mount Pir Omar Gudrun, the other proposed site of Mount Nimush.

Preserver of the Seed

In the wake of the cuneiform tablets found in Sennacherib and Ashurbanipal's library rooms at Nineveh, much older – but far less complete – copies of the Mesopotamian flood myth were discovered. One found at Nippur, and dated to 1700 BC, was written in Sumerian and seems to have provided the basis for the story told by Berossus some 1,450 years later. Here the saviour of humanity is not Ut-napishtim, but King Ziusudra. The text is fragmentary and short, but ends with the following lines:

The king Ziusudra
Prostrated himself before An (Anu) (and) Enlil
...
(Who) gave him life, like a god.
At that time, the king Ziusudra
Who protected the seed of mankind at the time (?) of the destruction,
They settled in an overseas country, in the orient, in Dilmun
...[46]

Once again, immortality is bestowed upon the saviour of humanity who lives out the remainder of his life at Dilmun, very likely the mythical realm of the gods in the mountains of northern Kurdistan. Ziusudra is said to have 'protected the seed of mankind', a statement paralleled almost exactly in the Book of Enoch. Here the Most High instructs the archangel Uriel to go down and tell Noah that 'he may escape and (that) his seed may be preserved for all the generations of the world'.[47] Hebrew scribes never used phraseology lightly, suggesting that there was a direct link between the Sumerian and biblical accounts of the flood. Both Ziusudra and Noah carry the 'seed' of humanity into the post-diluvian age, and this does not just mean through their lineage, for it would also appear to refer to the preservation of antediluvian knowledge of the sort revealed to mankind by the Watchers.

Evidence of this is found in Berossus' work *Babyloniaka*, in which it is recorded that the god Kronos appeared to Xisuthros in a dream to announce that humanity was about to be destroyed by a flood. The god therefore orders him to 'bury the beginnings, middles, and ends of all writings in Sippur (Sippara), the city of the Sun(-god)'.[48] Once the flood has receded, Xisuthros and his family are told to return to Sippur and dig up these writings, after which they go on to found many cities and shrines, including Babylon.[49]

If they existed, then what did these 'writings' contain? Was it the records that Sennacherib and Ashurbanipal had so eagerly attempted to track down and preserve in the library rooms at Nineveh? Knowing of the strange fascination both kings appear to have held for this important subject, I feel this must be a very real possibility.

As I had already established, knowledge of the forbidden sciences revealed to mortal kind by the rebel Watchers had finally been carried from Mesopotamia into Palestine, where it was recorded in works such as the Book of Noah, which subsequently became the basis for the Book of Enoch. Had these carriers of the 'seed' of Noah and Ziusudra included the nomadic *kochek* rainmakers of Yezidi tradition, as well as the wild *zaddik*-priests of the Dead Sea communities?

If so, had this 'seed' been carried into Canaan by migrating Semitic tribes, who had come out of the 'land of Shinar' at the time of the patriarch Abraham, sometime around 2000 BC? Or had this antediluvian knowledge only reached Judaea in post-exilic times? Either way, it seemed likely that in addition to the enormous influence that the Magian and Zoroastrian faiths of Iran had contributed towards the legends concerning the fall of the Watchers, the rich mythologies of ancient Iraq would appear to have influenced our knowledge of the angels of heaven.

According to the archaeologists and historians, the Mesopotamian city-states formed the earliest known civilization of the Old World. From its first foundations in the sixth millennium BC, it grew over a period of 2,500 years to become what was perhaps the most sophisticated culture on this planet. The Sumerians developed the first coloured pottery, the first medical operations, the first musical instruments, the first veterinary skills and the first written language. They also became highly accomplished engineers, mathematicians, librarians, authors, archivists, judges and priests. Their organized society and political administration was virtually unique, and yet, despite all this abundance of knowledge and capability, a big question mark still looms over the origins of this ancient race.

The Sumerians and Akkadians clearly stated that they had inherited this knowledge from the gods. So who were these 'gods'? Had they really been the Watchers – the tall, viper-faced bird-men whose homeland would appear to have been on the shores of Lake Van in northern Kurdistan? To answer this question, I would have to go beyond the recorded mythologies of Mesopotamia and look towards the evidence left behind by the earliest inhabitants of the Near East, for only this could truly determine whether the gods had once walked among mortal kind.

Seventeen

IN THE FOOTSTEPS OF THE WATCHERS

Every week more and more books on the absorbing subject of the development of race and culture in the Near East were turning up at the local library, having been ordered by me *en masse* at an earlier date. I desperately needed to reduce the existing pile before any more arrived, otherwise the workload would become impossible to handle. Among the thirty or so already in my possession were some extremely rare tomes that had a fixed lending period of three weeks. These I would not be able to reorder for perhaps three to four months.

In response to my cries for help, Richard Ward agreed to spend some time helping me read through as many books as possible. One Sunday morning, we sat down to begin an intense marathon of very serious reading indeed.

The Neolithic Explosion

Several books into the session, and I was beginning to realize that something very significant had gone on in Kurdistan, shortly after the first recession of the last Ice Age, around 9500–9000 BC. From what I could see of the picture, the region appeared to have become the centre of a neolithic explosion unparalleled anywhere else in Eurasia, beginning with a simple transition from food gathering to food cultivation. For instance, at a mound in northern Syria which overlooks the rushing waters of the Upper Euphrates, some of the very oldest evidence of proto-agriculture and animal farming has been unearthed. Radiocarbon dating of organic material found at the site, known locally as Tell Abu Hureya, has shown that the domestication of primitive forms of barley, wheat and rye may have occurred as early as 9500 BC.[1]

Aside from the wild grasses already mentioned, there is evidence to suggest that oats, peas, lentils, alfalfa and grapes had also first been cultivated by the precursors of the Kurdish peoples.[2] The discoveries of grindstones, mortars and pestles have indicated the level of sophistication of this farming activity, even in its earliest phases. The remains of dogs, goats, pigs and sheep found at three important Kurdish archaeological sites, dated to between 8000 BC and 6000 BC, show that animal domestication was also spreading hand in hand with land cultivation.[3]

The transition from hunter-gathering to settled communal living allows time for experimentation, and in Kurdistan this led to the development of the very first metallurgy in the Old World. Two sites have confirmed the use of copper instruments as early as the first half of the fifth millennium BC, while even earlier evidence of copper deposits and a single lead bead have been detected at an important protoneolithic site named Jarmo,[4] situated on the Lesser Zab river in Iraqi Kurdistan. These examples could well date to as early as 6750 BC,[5] some 350 years before copper and lead smelting is known to have been practised at Çatal Hüyük in central Anatolia, *c.* 6400 BC.[6]

That metallurgy should have developed first in Kurdistan was perhaps inevitable, for both the Zagros and Taurus ranges are teeming with ore deposits, so much so that the area surrounding one neolithic site named Çayönü, located some 120 miles east-south-east of Lake Van, has been producing copper and bronze objects non-stop for the past seven thousand years.[7]

The earliest known examples of 'lightly fired clay vessels' also come from Kurdistan. They were found at a site named Mureybet, in northern Syria, and radiocarbon tests have shown that these vessels date to around 8000 BC.[8] At another site, Ganj Dara, near the Iranian town of Kermanshah in eastern Kurdistan, archaeologists have uncovered evidence of fired pottery and small clay figurines that date to the early eighth millennium BC, far in advance of the stone, wood, plaster and basketry work typical of this stage in humanity's gradual evolution. Hard, fired pottery quite obviously helped to revolutionize the social and functional lifestyles of these early peoples. For the first time, bowls, cups, plates and vases became an integral part of their day-to-day world.

It was perhaps in order to deal with the most basic forms of commerce with neighbouring communities that the oldest known form of bartering tokens were developed by the tribal communities of the Kurdish highlands in the eighth millennium BC. These tokens gradually became more complex, until larger clay cases were made in which the smaller tokens could be kept safely without being damaged or defaced. By 3000 BC the token system had been completely replaced by sequences of markings inscribed on to the clay cases, and soon afterwards the first baked-clay tablets bearing ideogram scripts started appearing in the lowlands of Sumeria – their shape reflecting the fat cases originally used to contain the loose tokens. In other words, what was perhaps one of the earliest forms of written language in the Old World had developed initially in the highlands of Kurdistan.[9]

Despite this shift on to the Iraqi plains, Kurdistan did go on to develop its own brand of written script known as 'proto-Elamite', which appears for the first time around 2500 BC at a site named Godin, near the modern town of Kangâwar, in the Lower Zagros. This meant that although it was now way behind its lowland neighbours, Kurdistan could still boast one of the earliest literate communities in the Near East.[10] Yet it had been the earliest neolithic communities of Kurdistan that undoubtedly catalysed the genesis of the first city-states of Mesopotamia, places such as Eridu, Nippur, Ur and Uruk.

Uncertain Forces

Such were the beginnings of civilized life in Kurdistan. From its first foundations between 9500 and 8000 BC, this one region produced some of the first known examples of animal domestication, metallurgy, painted pottery, proto-agriculture, trade, urbanization and written language. No one could deny the extraordinary advances made in this region over a period of some five thousand years, and no Mesopotamian scholar would deny the way in which the Kurds had influenced the development of the Sumerian civilization in the Fertile Crescent of Iraq and Syria. Yet it seemed to have been far more than simply this, for as the Kurdish scholar Mehrdad Izady has pointed out:

The inhabitants of this land went through an unexplained stage of accelerated technological evolution, prompted by yet uncertain forces. They rather quickly pulled ahead of their surrounding communities, the majority of which were also among the most advanced technological societies in the world, to embark on the transformation from a low-density, hunter-gatherer economy to a high-density, food-producing economy.[11]

What inspired this 'accelerated technological evolution' and what were these as yet 'uncertain forces'? Had it simply been the fact that, following the recession of the last Ice Age, there had been great changes in the regional flora and fauna, conducive to the rapid spread of a cultural revolution? Or had there been more to it – an injection, perhaps, from an outside influence bringing with it new ideas, new ways of thinking, new beliefs in spiritual concepts and new myths and legends?

I took a break from our long hours of reading and went to make a much-needed pot of Earl Grey. At the back of my mind was the hope that this injection from outside Kurdistan may have been connected with the sudden appearance in the region of the proposed shamanistic culture, known to us as the Watchers. Kurdistan could not have been perceived by various Near Eastern cultures as the cradle of civilization and the abode of the gods unless this belief had some basis in truth. The evidence from archaeology appeared to support the view that something very special had occurred in Kurdistan, but did we need to invoke outside influences when none were necessary?

The Black Glass of Lake Van

So far Richard and I had uncovered no trace of an indigenous Kurdish culture resembling the characteristics of the Watchers, or of a neolithic community that might constitute the Anannage's highly advanced Kharsag settlement.

The only interesting piece of information I had discovered in this last respect were details concerning the so-called Halaf culture. This had been the name given to the artistic uniformity that spread among the various Kurdish neolithic communities between *c.* 5750 and 5000 BC.[12] The culture takes its name from Tell Halaf, a mound that overlooks the Khabur river near the village of Ras al-'Ain, on the Syrian-Turkish frontier, where evidence of a very distinctive style of community life was first identified by a German archaeologist, Max Freiherr von Oppenheim, just before the First World War.[13] The Halaf lifestyle could be discerned by its circular mud-brick dwellings known as *tholoi*, as well as by its unique glazed pottery.

The presence of the Halaf artistic style has been noted at many sites in Kurdistan, but more significant was the fact that, throughout this early period, they would appear to have been the controllers in the trade of the black volcanic glass known as obsidian. Most importantly, the Halaf's centre of operations would appear to have been around Lake Van, where they obtained the raw obsidian from the foothills below Nemrut Dağ, the extinct volcano on its southwestern shores.[14] This was one of the mountains I had suspected as being behind the account of the flowing rivers of fire emptying into a great sea mentioned in connection with Enoch's visit to the First Heaven.

If the Watchers had opted for a location suitable not just for land cultivation but also for easy access to the surrounding plains of Armenia, Iran, Iraq, Syria and Turkey, then Lake Van would have made a perfect choice. Had the Halaf culture's trade in black obsidian therefore been connected with the presence of the proposed Watcher culture in the very same area? Had they used black obsidian as a means of bartering with local farming communities?

Thought-provoking as this idea seemed, it did little to confirm or deny the existence in the region of a previously unknown culture which fitted the descriptions given of the Watchers as presented in Enochian and Dead Sea literature. Hopefully this would come from a more in-depth study of the anthropology and archaeology of the region.

Cave of the Angels

Back in the other room, Richard sat before a scattered pile of obscure books on all aspects of Kurdish exploration. Picking up another title, I started to read about the work of two American palaeontologists named Ralph and Rose Solecki. In the 1950s they had excavated a huge cave at a place called Shanidar, which overlooks a deep rocky valley containing the Greater Zab river. It was then that I stumbled across something of immense significance to our research.

The Shanidar cave is reached by a steep winding path that leads to a gigantic mouth twenty-six feet high and eighty-two feet in width. Its earthen interior has revealed no less than sixteen occupational levels spanning a period of 100,000 years, including some very important Neanderthal burials.[15] The Soleckis had also uncovered the bones of animals caught by the cave's hunter-gathering communities for food. These finds made interesting reading, but were of no direct concern to me since they related to a very early period indeed. What did interest me was the discovery within the cave of a huge deposit of goat skulls and avian remains, which consisted almost entirely of the wings of large predatory birds. These had been deliberately buried close to the only stone structure present at the site, and were found covered with patches of reddened earth (usually a sign of red ochre, which was often sprinkled over human burials in early neolithic times[16]). Carbon 14 dating of the organic deposits associated with the remains indicated a date of 10,870 years (±300 years), that is 8870 BC.[17]

Rose Solecki had taken charge of making an in-depth study of the bones, and had begun by seeking professional advice from experts in different fields. The animal skulls were examined by Dr Charles Reed of the University of Illinois in 1959, who confirmed that they all belonged to wild goats.[18] The wings of the birds were studied by Dr Alexander Wetmore of the Smithsonian Institution, as well as by Thomas H. McGovern, a graduate student in the Department of Anthropology at Columbia University. They identified four separate species present and as many as seventeen individual birds: four *Gyptaeus barbatus* (the bearded vulture), one

Gyps fulvus (the griffon vulture), seven *Haliaetus albicilla* (the white-tailed sea eagle) and one *Otis tarda* (the great bustard) – only the last of which is still indigenous to the region. There were also the bones of four small eagles of indeterminable species.[19] All except for the great bustard were raptorial birds, while the vultures were quite obviously eaters of carrion, and, as Rose Solecki later observed, were 'thus placed in a special relationship with dead creatures and death'.[20]

Of the 107 bones identified, 96 (i.e. 90 per cent) were wing bones, many of which had been still in articulation when buried – i.e. still held in position by fleshy material. Furthermore, slice marks on the bone ends indicated that the wings had been deliberately hacked off by a sharp instrument, and that attempts had been made to cut away the skin and feathers covering at least some of the bones.[21]

Rose Solecki and her team discounted the possibility that the bird wings had formed part of some kind of communal meal, since there was no evidence to indicate that they had been changed through cooking or burning. What was more, the fact that these mostly articulated wings of at least seventeen birds, including vultures, eagles and a bustard, had been found with fifteen goats' skulls clearly suggested that they had been deposited in connection with some kind of ritualistic event. She also pointed out that catching such enormous raptorial birds would have been no mean feat in itself, and that, as a consequence, there seemed every likelihood of them having first been caught at a young age, then reared to full size specifically for ceremonial purposes.[22]

Yet the discovery of these severed bird wings had posed obvious problems for Rose Solecki. Why had only certain types of birds been selected for this purpose, and what exactly had been the role played by these enormous predatory birds in the minds of those who had placed them within the Shanidar cave?

Wings of Shamans

In an important article entitled 'Predatory Bird Rituals at Zawi Chemi Shanidar', published by the journal *Sumer* in 1977, Rose Solecki outlined the discovery of the goat skulls and raptorial bird remains. She suggested that the wings had almost certainly been utilized as part of some kind of ritualistic costume, worn either for personal decoration or for ceremonial purposes.[23] She linked them with the vulture shamanism of Çatal Hüyük, which had reached its high-point a full two thousand years *after* these birds' wings had been deposited 565 miles away in the Shanidar cave. She obviously recognized the enormous significance of the finds and realized that they constituted firm evidence for the presence of an important religious cult in the Zawi Chemi Shanidar area (to give the archaeological site its full name), for as she concluded in her article:

The Zawi Chemi people must have endowed these great raptorial birds with special powers, and the faunal remains we have described for the site must represent special ritual paraphernalia. Certainly, the remains represent a concerted effort by a goodly number of people just to hunt down and capture such a large number of birds and goats.[24] . . . [Furthermore] *either the wings were saved to pluck out the feathers, or . . . wing fans were made, or . . . they were used as part of a costume for a ritual. One of the murals from a Çatal Hüyük shrine . . . depicts just such a ritual scene; i.e., a human figure dressed in a vulture skin . . .*[25]

Here was extraordinary evidence for the existence of what appeared to be the cult of the vulture among the highlands of Kurdistan, *c.* 8870 BC! All this was happening, moreover, just 140 miles south-east of Bitlis on Lake Van, during a time-frame coincident to the dramatic leap in evolution experienced by the highland peoples of Kurdistan.

Nowhere else in the whole of the Middle East had a discovery of this nature been made. The wing bones of griffon vultures, eagles and falcons were found in the so-called Hayonim cave, located in the Western Galilee area of Israel, at a level comparable with that of the Shanidar cave.[26] These deposits were attributed to the protoneolithic Natufian culture who had inhabited the region during the seventh and eighth millennia BC. Unfortunately, however, these raptorial bird remains were deposited with the bones of various other much smaller birds, so diminishing their possible ritual significance.

My mind began to reel with possibilities. What on earth had been going on in this cave overlooking the Greater Zab, which, of course, was one of the four rivers of paradise? The exhaustive excavation work of Ralph and Rose Solecki ably demonstrated that the Shanidar cave had been a place of winter habitation for nomadic tribesmen for at least 100,000 years, so how were we to explain this sudden intrusion around 10,870 years ago? Who were these local shamans who deposited huge wings alongside some fifteen goats' skulls? Where had they come from, and what might they have been doing in the cave? Sheltering perhaps? Living there? Conducting some kind of animalistic rite? Or following the course of the river from, or towards, its headwaters?

It was very tempting to suggest that the remains found in the Shanidar cave were in some way linked with the proposed Watcher culture and their highland settlement of Eden or Kharsag. Regardless of the pitfalls, I was going to do it anyway. I had predicted that a shamanistic culture utilizing the vulture as a symbol of death and rebirth had existed in the highlands of Kurdistan before the rise of civilization in the fourth millennium BC, and here it was – virtually indisputable evidence to support the theory. Yet if the vulture shamans of northern Kurdistan *had* existed *c.* 8870 BC (±300 years), then it is as well to remember that this theory was put forward to explain the available evidence concerning the origins of angels and fallen angels as presented in Enochian and Dead Sea literature. So if the vulture shamans of Kurdistan had existed, it strengthened the case for angels having been flesh-and-blood beings who had once walked freely among mortal kind.

Furthermore, I quickly realized that I was not the first to connect the discoveries of the raptorial bird remains found in the Shanidar cave with the phenomenon of angels. On the subject of the Yezidis' devotional reverence to *Melek Taus*, the Peacock Angel, the Kurdish scholar Mehrdad Izady had concluded:

> *The artistic combination of wings and non-flying beings like humans* [to form gods] . . . *as well as wing-like adornments to priestly costumes, are common in many cultures, but the representation of the supreme deity as a full-fledged bird is peculiarly Yezidi. The evidence of sacrificial rites practised at ancient Zawi Chami (Shanidar) may substantiate an indigenous precursor to modern Yezidi practice.*[27]

He had also suggested that the great bustard, whose remains were unearthed in the cave, is a more likely bird for the Yezidis to have adopted as its object of veneration, since it is indigenous to the region, unlike the peacock, which is native to India and Persia, and not Kurdistan.[28] In addition to this, the eagle and indeed the vulture are, with their hooked beaks, far more representative of the Yezidi's metal bird icons than the peacock.

This was good confirmation that a shamanistic cult attached to the bird remains found in the Shanidar cave may well have gone on to influence much later religious traditions of Kurdistan, including its indigenous angel-worshipping cults. It was also the evidence I needed to connect together angels, bird-men and the highlands of Kurdistan.

Could it be remotely feasible that these mountainous vulture shamans had descended on to the plains of ancient Iraq, via the Greater Zab, to take wives from among the Daughters of Men? Had it been them, or their tribal associates, who possessed the wonder-working drug of 'immortality' and revealed to mortal kind the forbidden arts and sciences of their elders and forebears? Had their offspring been the hybrid Nephilim who ran riot, drinking blood, and causing pain and suffering in the world? Did these individuals constitute what later became the 'gods' and 'demons' who had apparently done so much to build the civilizations of Sumer and Akkad? The circumstantial evidence in support of such wild contentions was increasing all the time.

Rites of the Goat

Yet I could not forget the fifteen goats' skulls also found with the avian remains at Shanidar. Rose Solecki had suggested that these, too, must have been utilized for ceremonial and ritualistic purposes by the shamans, so how could they fit into the picture? The answer was quite simple – Azazel. He had been one of the leaders of the Watchers, as well as the progenitor of the djinn and the true face behind the Peacock Angel of Yaresan and Yezidi tradition. Moreover, as I had already noted, the Pentateuch records how each year on the Day of Atonement a goat would be cast into the wilderness 'for Azazel', carrying on its back the sins of the Jewish people (see Chapter Six).

Azazel's chosen form was the goat, and in this capacity he had also been the ruler of a monstrous race of demons named the *seirim*, or 'he-goats'. They are mentioned several times in the Bible and were worshipped and adored by some Jews. There is even an indication that women had actually copulated with these goat-demons, for it states in the Book of Leviticus: 'And they shall no more sacrifice their sacrifices unto the he-goats (*seirim*), after whom they go a-whoring',[29] perhaps a distant echo, once again, of the way in which the Watchers had taken wives from among mortal kind. This clear relationship between the Watchers and he-goats was so strong that it led the Hebrew scholar J. T. Milik to conclude that Azazel 'was evidently not a simple he-goat, but a giant who combined goat-like characteristics with those of man'.[30] In other words, he had been a goat-man – a goat shaman.

Azazel had originally been synonymous with Shemyaza, his companion leader of the Watchers, while both may well derive their name from the Hebrew word *azza*, meaning 'the strong', or *uzza*, meaning 'strength'. I had therefore been intrigued to find that the Akkadians had worshipped an anthropomorphic goat-form named Uz. On one stone tablet found at Sippara in Lower Iraq, Uz is shown on a throne clad in a robe of goat skin. He watches 'the revolution of the solar disc, which is placed on a table and made to revolve by means of a rope or string'.[31] Uz was also the word for 'goat' in Akkadian, strongly suggesting that Azazel acquired his name from this earlier 'god' clothed as a goat. Had the god Uz therefore derived his *own* existence from some distant memory of the goat shamanism practised by the Watchers?

So, like the serpent and the vulture, the goat would also appear to have been one of the primary totemic symbols of the Watchers – an appellation that over the millennia degenerated into a stark symbol not only of carnal lust and debauchery but also of ultimate evil. It was strange to think that the animal skulls found in the Shanidar cave might in some strange way have been responsible for the goat's unfathomable revilement in both the Christian and Jewish world.

I could understand how the noble vulture or the cunning serpent could become important symbols to a shamanistic community, but trying to comprehend the apparent interest they might have seen in the mountain goat seemed a little more difficult. I could only assume that, since the goat was among the first animals to be domesticated in Kurdistan, its life cycle must have become intrinsically interwoven with that of its keepers. Its agile climbing abilities, even on the most dangerous slopes; its visual alertness to predators and, very possibly, its sexual prowess (embodied in the phallic appearance of its large curved horns), must have combined to make it an ideal totemic symbol for, on the one hand, ceremonial activity, and on the other astral journeys across the bleak, rugged terrain of the Kurdish highlands.

Goat shamanism in Iraqi Kurdistan might also have left another, quite unexpected mark on local folklore. The Wigrams, in their book *The Cradle of Mankind*, speak of a belief among the inhabitants of the plains below Mosul of 'a fearful type of vampire' known as the *hibla-bashi*, a satyr, half man, half goat, who 'lures travellers from the path, and sucks their blood'.[32] One of them is said to have had a tomb at a place named Aradin, in the lower hills.[33]

Were the stories of the *hibla-bashi* therefore mixed up memories of the more degenerate Watcher, or Nephilim, goat-men, who would descend from the Kurdish foothills to indulge in rather uncouth sanguine practices? As I had already realized, the vampire legends of eastern Europe appeared to have some kind of relationship with the Assyrian and Babylonian stories concerning the supernatural beings known as *Edimmu*, who may well constitute tangible evidence of the Nephilim's presence on the plains of ancient Mesopotamia. It is also worth remembering that the cursed souls of the blood-drinking Nephilim were cast out to become the damned, unable to take food '[but nevertheless hunger] and thirst'.[34] Similar beliefs have surrounded the djinn, the progeny of Azazel and supposed progenitors of the Kurdish race, who likewise drank blood in an attempt to satisfy their constant hunger and thirst.[35]

Among the People of Jarmo

Satisfied by these dramatic discoveries in our quest to find a solution to the fall of the angels in Kurdish archaeology, Richard and I read on, exchanging the odd comment here and there and recording on tape any relevant passage or story. Reaching towards the visually less interesting end of the pile, I frowned just a little when I reached to pick up a large-format book entitled *Prehistoric Archaeology along the Zagros Flanks*, edited by an archaeologist, Professor Robert J. Braidwood, and published in 1983. I knew the book would contain much new research on Braidwood's excavations at the early neolithic site of Jarmo, a twenty-three-foot-high mound positioned on a steep hill, close to a gorge containing the Lesser Zab river, near the village of Chemchemal in Iraqi Kurdistan. Here the American professor had co-ordinated a series of exhaustive excavations between 1948 and 1955. The site was found to consist of sixteen occupational levels which had begun around 6750 BC.

At Jarmo a large farming community, living in square, multi-roomed houses with mud ovens and sunken baked-clay basins, successfully cultivated the land, produced fruit and grain, brought up animals and smelted copper for anything up to two thousand years.[36] These early neolithic peoples led basic but functional lifestyles, using spoons to eat, bone needles to repair clothes, and stone spindle-whorls to make clothes and probably even to weave carpets. They also used knives and tools with blades made of obsidian obtained from the foothills around Nemrut Dağ on Lake Van.[37]

One can almost imagine a happy, contented community living a tranquil existence above the fast-flowing river. The men would spend their time hunting game, while the women would attend the fields, grind cereals for bread and cakes, and control family life. These people's greatest love would have been the land itself, which they would have seen as the living embodiment of the Great Mother, whose baked clay images have been discovered here.

As I read through Braidwood's book, the image of Jarmo's Utopian lifestyle was suddenly shattered when I came across a paper entitled 'Jarmo Figurines and Other Clay Objects', written by

Vivian Broman Morales, who had spent a great amount of time studying and cataloguing the 5,500 or so clay figurines unearthed from the earliest occupational levels onwards.[38] Because of the abundance of these slightly baked clay images, it was possible to conclude that the Jarmo people had paid particular attention to the environment around them, capturing individual aspects and features, perhaps in the same way that we use photography today.

Among them were a variety of animal forms, such as bears, goats, pigs and sheep. Nearly all of the human figurines were heads only, even though Morales surmised that many of them would originally have been attached to bodies made of a perishable material. Most of the heads were of a conventional shape and form, and may well have been representations of individuals in the community. Some, however, seemed infinitely stranger. They portrayed long tapered or diamond-shaped faces, with thin lips and pointed jaws, unlike any human around today. Their eyes, too, were strange. They were made of pinched pellets of clay that gave the impression of closed or slit-like eyes, like those of east Asian racial types.[39] One figurine in particular depicted a seemingly bald-headed individual with extremely long facial features, high cheek-bones, a long jaw and incised, elliptical eyes.[40]

As I studied these illustrations, I felt an eerie sense of recognition. These were extraordinary images for the Jarmo people to have made without good reason. What on earth were they trying to represent by moulding such inhuman forms in clay? Vivian Broman Morales could only conclude that the strange heads demonstrated the 'individuality and originality in producing small, even tiny, objects which have no evident meaning in present-day evaluation, though they obviously meant something very precise to the manufacturers'.[41] She could only add that these images 'resemble markedly the head of the "lizard" goddess figures of the Ubaid period'.[42]

The 'lizard' goddess? There was no way that these heads could represent lizards. In my opinion they were ophidian – in other words, the faces of human-like serpents. This, of course, raised the inevitable question of why an apparently peaceful community of the seventh millennium BC should have felt the need to create such strange images, alongside many other more obvious human heads

Fig. 12. An anthropomorphic head from Jarmo, Upper Iraq, *c.* 6750–5000 BC. The characterized long head and beady eyes suggest a racial type unusual to the region and may well constitute an actual representation of a Watcher-like individual.

with regular facial features. Quite obviously the serpent played a very important role in their lives, but if so, why?

No one can say for sure why the Jarmo people should have produced such distinctive abstract art. Yet my mind kept returning to the vision of the Watcher named Belial who appeared before Amram. His face was said to have been 'like a viper', words echoed in the Kharsag account where the god Enlil is described as the 'serpent with shining eyes'. Was it possible that, if the Watchers had existed as an actual community living around Lake Van, their influence had extended into the protoneolithic community of Jarmo, which lies some 250 miles south-south-east of Bitlis and around 115 miles south-south-east of the Shanidar cave? Certainly there was a direct connection between Jarmo and Lake Van, for it was from there that the black obsidian was obtained for making knives and tools. If this was indeed the case, then it was just possible that the strange serpentine heads captured in abstract form the distinct facial features of the Watchers.

One might almost be tempted to picture the sudden appearance among the Jarmo community of extremely tall ivory-skinned individuals with snow-white hair and dark floor-length feather coats that gently rippled in the mountain breeze. As they drew closer, their long, viper-like faces, high cheek-bones and strange slit-like eyes would be enough to instil fear among any who witnessed their approach.

How the Jarmo people might have viewed these stern-faced strangers – who would perhaps appear as if out of nowhere and then proceed to walk among them for brief periods before returning to the highlands – is difficult to say. There seems every likelihood that, if the Watchers *had* once existed in physical form, then they would have been looked upon either as divine or demonic beings, probably both. Neither good nor bad, but simply amoral.

We can only speculate on what the strangers might have wanted with the people of Jarmo. Had it been supplies? Had they come to barter with raw obsidian from Nemrut Dağ? Had they come to secure individuals for construction projects at Kharsag? Or had they come looking for suitable women whom they could take as wives? In exchange, perhaps they had instructed them in the art of agriculture, land irrigation, metallurgy, plant lore and astronomy.

From the evidence conveyed by these serpentine figurines, it seems plausible that some kind of trafficking may have taken place between the people of Jarmo and the Watchers of Eden. If this was correct, then other early neolithic communities must also have received visits from the viper-faced strangers. Perhaps the appearance among these communities of black obsidian from Nemrut Dağ was a tell-tale sign of the Watchers' presence, especially during the Halaf period, *c.* 5750–5000 BC. What I really needed to know, however, was whether or not there existed any more obvious evidence of the Watchers' supposed contact with the neolithic cultures of the Near East. A clue appeared to lie in the words of the archaeologist Vivian Broman Morales, who had compared the Jarmo figurines with 'the "lizard" goddess figures of the Ubaid period'.

What exactly had she meant by 'lizard goddess figures'? And when or what was the "Ubaid period'? I was about to find out.

Eighteen

SHAMAN-LIKE DEMON

Following the disappearance of the Lake Van obsidian traders sometime around 5000 BC, a new culture began to emerge on the plains of ancient Iraq. These were the al-ʿUbaid people, or just ʿUbaid, after the mound settlement of Tell al-ʿUbaid, some four miles north of the ancient city-state of Ur, where their presence was first discerned by the British archaeologist Sir Leonard Woolley in 1922.

Digging into the low mound amid the shimmering heat waves that filled the desert of central Iraq, Woolley was amazed at the apparent ease with which he was able to find evidence of this previously unknown culture that had once dominated the country. Everything lay close to the surface, beneath the soft dusty earth. Painted potsherds were found at a depth of three feet, and then came flint and obsidian tools as well as fragments of 'reed matting plastered with clay mixed with dung or less often, with a mixture of earth and bitumen'.[1] This lay upon a hard surface of river silt on which the incoming tribes had erected their primitive structures of 'reed plastered with clay',[2] close to the flooded marshlands of the Lower Euphrates. Indeed, there is every reason to suggest that these people were the distant ancestors of the much-troubled Marsh Arabs of modern-day Iraq.[3]

Woolley could never have guessed at the immense importance of these fairly insignificant-looking finds, for in the years to come they would provide the missing link between the neolithic explosion in the Kurdish highlands and the spread of civilization and kingship right across the Fertile Crescent of ancient Mesopotamia.

Around 5000 BC the ʿUbaid people descended from the Upper Zagros mountains to take over various existing sites of occupation throughout Upper Iraq.[4] They then spread gradually southwards to establish new communities, including the one at Tell al-'Ubaid, *c.* 4500 BC. Many of their sites of occupation were inherited from an earlier, more advanced culture known as the Samarra, who had been the first to introduce land irrigation and agriculture to the region. The Samarra had also been behind the establishment of Eridu, the first Mesopotamian city, in around 5500 BC. In one temple complex dated to this early period, evidence of a ritual pool and large quantities of fish remains have been unearthed, leading scholars to suggest that the Samarra's principal deity was a primordial form of Enki, the much later Sumerian god of Abzu, the watery abyss,[5] who subsequently became divine patron of Eridu.

So far there was nothing to suggest the presence of the Watchers among these precursors of the Sumerian civilization. Vivian Broman Morales had, however, spoken of the 'Ubaid culture's strange 'lizard goddess figures', which she compared with the ophidian, or serpentine, clay heads found by Robert Braidwood and his team at Jarmo in Iraqi Kurdistan. These 'lizard goddesses' I had found depicted in various books that featured the art of the 'Ubaid culture. They took the form of strange anthropomorphic figurines, either male or female (although mostly female), with slim, well-proportioned naked bodies, wide shoulders, and strange reptilian heads that scholars generally describe as 'lizard-like' in appearance.[6] These show long, tapered faces like snouts, with wide slit-eyes – usually elliptical pellets of clay pinched to form what are known as 'coffee-bean' eyes – and a thick, dark plume of bitumen on their heads to represent a coil of erect hair (similar coils fashioned in clay appear on some of the heads found at Jarmo[7]). All statuettes display either female pubic hair or male genitalia.

Each 'Ubaid figurine has its own unique pose – some female statuettes stand with their feet together and their hands on their hips. At least one male figurine has its arms horizontally placed across its lower chest area and holds what appears to be a wand or sceptre in its left hand; plausibly a symbol of divinity or kingship. The figurines also appear with several oval-shaped pellets of clay covering their upper chest, shoulders and back. These almost certainly represent beaded chains of office.

By far the strangest and most compelling of the reptilian

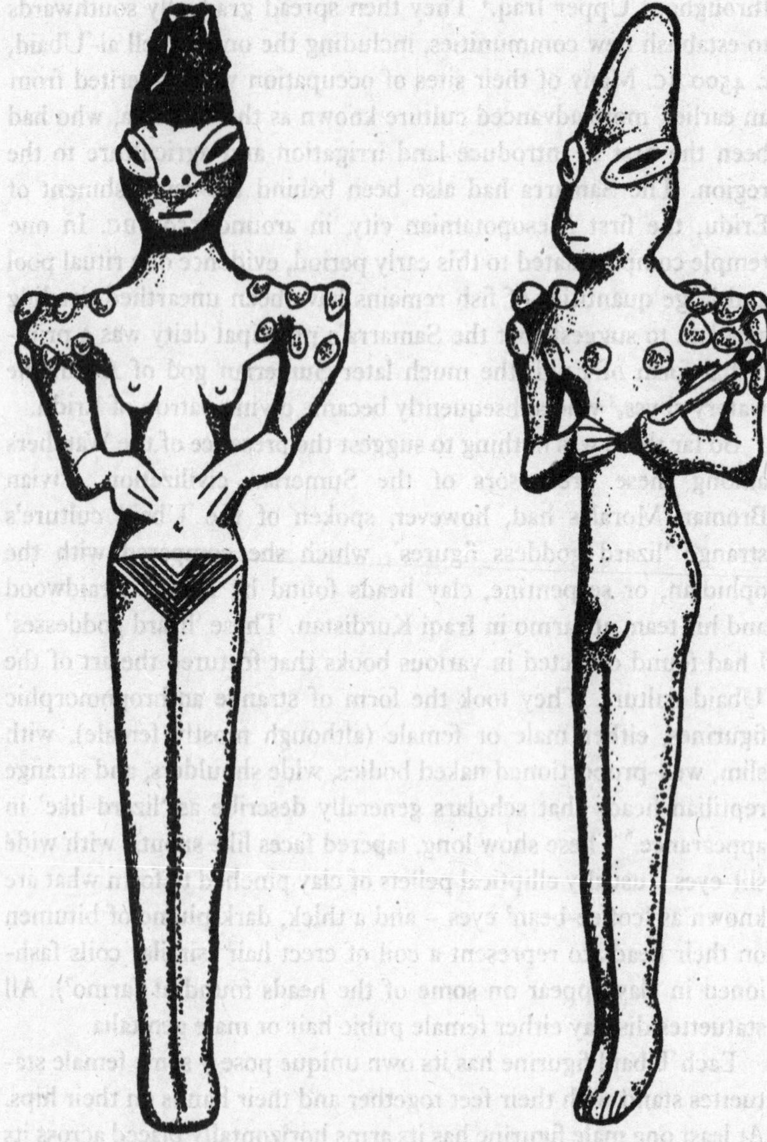

Fig. 13. Two examples of the strange 'lizard'-like figurines found within graves in Iraq and belonging to the ʿUbaid culture, *c.* 5000–4000 BC. Evidence suggests they may be abstract representations of *Edimmu*, the much-feared vampires whose origins are perhaps based on distorted memories of Watcher descendants known as Nephilim.

statuettes is a naked female who holds a baby to her left breast. The infant's left hand clings on to the breast, and there can be little doubt that it is suckling milk. It is a very touching image, although it bears one extremely chilling feature – the child has long slanted eyes and the head of a reptile. This is highly significant, for it suggests that the baby was seen to have been born with these features. In other words, the 'lizard-like' heads of the figures were not masks, or symbolic of some animalistic god-form, but abstract images of an actual race believed to possess reptilian features.

In the past these 'reptilian' figurines have been identified by scholars as representations of the Mother Goddess[8] – a totally erroneous assumption, since some of them are obviously male – while ancient astronaut theorists such as Erich von Däniken have seen fit to identify them as images of alien entities.[9] In my opinion, both explanations were attempting to bracket the clay figurines into popular frameworks that are insufficient to explain their full symbolism. Furthermore, since most of the examples found were retrieved from graves, where they were often the only item of any importance, Sir Leonard Woolley had concluded that they represented 'chthonic deities' – that is, underworld denizens connected in some way with the rites of the dead.[10] In addition to this, it seems highly unlikely that they represent lizard-faced individuals, since lizards are not known to have had any special place in Near Eastern mythology. Much more likely is that the heads are those of snakes, which are known to have been associated with Sumerian underworld deities, such as Ningišzida, Lord of the Good Tree.

So what did these anthropomorphic serpents really signify?

The differences in chronology between the Jarmo heads and the 'Ubaid figurines suggest that this distinctive form of serpentine art had developed in the highlands of Kurdistan as early as 6750 BC before being transferred on to the Iraqi plains around 5000 BC. By this time, however, the art had become somewhat removed from the more basic serpent-like facial features of the much earlier Jarmo heads. The snake had been a major feature among the religious practices of ancient Mesopotamia, where it was identified with divine wisdom, sexual energy and guardianship over otherworldly domains. Furthermore, Armenian folklore, as well as the religions of the Median Magi and the Yezidis of Iraqi Kurdistan, would tend to indicate that worship and veneration of the serpent had remained an important element in the religions of both Iraq and Iran right through till modern times.

This knowledge does not, however, explain why the ʿUbaid culture should have needed to place serpentine figurines in the graves of its dead. Ritual practices are often born out of fear and superstition, so might they have believed that something awful would happen to the deceased if these statuettes were *not* placed in the graves? If so, then what was it they so feared might happen to them? And why use obvious serpent imagery? And what sort of serpents might they have been? Those that slither along the ground, or those that walk into a community, breed fear among the inhabitants and take away men and women for their own purposes – if, that is, we are to believe the Hebraic accounts of the fall of the Watchers and the plight of the Nephilim. Might the use of these serpent figurines have developed as a direct result of the cross-contact between the Watcher culture of the Kurdish highlands and the neolithic communities of the Iraqi-Kurdish foothills, who passed on these superstitious observances to the earliest inhabitants of the Fertile Crescent sometime around 5000 BC?

The ʿUbaid figurines might therefore have been used as good-luck totems against the Watchers' believed influence over the dead. Yet this still did not explain why these people should have needed to protect their deceased in this way. The chances are that the ʿUbaid feared that their dead could become *Edimmu*, or vampires, even after being placed in graves. If so, then why should they have feared this might happen in the first place?

There were no clear answers. Not as yet.

For a better understanding of the Watchers' possible contact with this primitive culture, we would have to return to the foothills of the Zagros mountains where the ʿUbaid had also left their mark on history.

The Goat-men of Susa

Elam is the name given in the Bible to a country situated in the Lower Zagros region of southern Kurdistan, on the borders between Iraq and Iran. It is a territory known today as Khuzistan. In Genesis 10, Elam is cited as one of the 'sons of Shem', who was himself one of the three sons of Noah.[11] Later, during the age of Abraham, it is Chedorlaomer, the king of Elam, who smites the different giant races of Canaan.[12] It was also to Elam's capital, Susa, or 'Shushan', that Daniel and many more of the Babylonian Jews journeyed after they were given their freedom by Cyrus the Great, the king of Persia (see Chapter Six). Indeed, Daniel is said to have died here, and the peculiar honeycomb spire that marks his much-venerated tomb still dominates Susa's sedate skyline.

Yet this important stage of Elam's strange history is young when compared to its most distant past. Evidence from early neolithic sites, such as the mound settlement of Ali Kosh, west of the village of Mussian in the Lower Zagros, has shown that this region was occupied as early as the eighth millennium BC.[13] Tell-tale signs of the Halaf culture have also been found at these early sites. Despite the presence of these outside influences, the land of Elam would seem to have possessed its own unique religious ideals and artistic style, which persisted across the millennia.

It was around 5000 BC, however, for a period of anything up to a thousand years, that the 'Ubaid culture held sway in Elam.[14] Archaeological excavations from the final phase of their influence have revealed a large variety of unique stone stamp seals of a highly shamanistic nature.[15] Each depicts what the scholars have described as an anthropomorphic 'goat-headed demon', with incised marks on its body to signify body hair and its arms raised out and upwards. These totemic figures are intriguing in their own right. It is, however, the imagery that accompanies them that is of special interest, for in one instance the figure appears to be controlling serpents; in another a serpent passes behind the goat-man; and in a third, the figure appears to be controlling two huge 'birds of prey'[16] that rise *up* towards its body.

As I looked at the seals I realized that the 'goat-headed' demons of the archaeologists were very probably goat-men, or goat shamans. The snakes perhaps represented the supernatural potency attached to these shamanistic characters, while the 'birds of prey' seemed almost certain to be vultures. The raised position of the goat-men's arms implied control and manipulation of these

Fig. 14. Three stamp seals from the 'Ubaid or proto-Elamite culture of south-western Iran showing anthropomorphic goats controlling serpents and vultures. Do these goat 'demons' preserve some memory of the advanced shamanistic culture thought to be behind the accounts of angels and Watchers in Judaeo-Christian tradition?

animalistic forces. Once again the link between goats, snakes and vultures in Near Eastern mythology had been demonstrated.

That vultures, and not 'birds of prey' in general, are depicted on the stone stamp seals is dramatically confirmed by the knowledge that the peoples of Susa, *c.* 3500 BC, regularly practised exposure of the dead.[17] Although this form of burial was not usual for the

'Ubaid culture of ancient Iraq and Iran, it is by no means inconceivable that they, too, practised excarnation. The culture's connection with the Marsh Arabs of Lower Iraq is a tantalizing link here, for the indigenous religion of this culture is Mandaean, which also practised exposure of the dead in ancient times.[18] Furthermore, decorated pottery dated to the earliest phases of proto-Elamite history is decorated with clear vulture imagery.[19]

Might these 'Ubaid stamp seals have some bearing on the goat and vulture shamanism thought to have taken place at the Shanidar cave on the Greater Zab, *c.* 8870 BC? I felt the answer was undoubtedly yes, for they appeared to confirm that the 'Ubaid settlers of Elam must have been heavily influenced by the shamanistic activities taking place in the Upper Zagros, and I was not alone in thinking this way. In an important paper entitled 'Seals and Related Objects from Early Mesopotamia and Iran' published in 1993 in a book entitled *Early Mesopotamia and Iran – Contact and Conflict c. 3500–1600* BC, Edith Porada of Columbia University, New York, discusses the Susa stamp seals. She then goes on to outline the discovery by Ralph and Rose Solecki of the goat and bird remains inside the Shanidar cave. After careful assessment of the evidence, she concludes that:

> *. . . the evidence . . . suggests that there was an early concept of a creature or creatures, which combined the features of goat and powerful bird in a manner unknown to us; that the human figure with the horned animal head on stamps of the Ubaid period was a powerful, shaman-like demon capable of warding off serpents.*[20]

What did she mean by 'a powerful, shaman-like demon capable of warding off serpents'? What sort of solution was this?

'Shaman-like demon' does not appear as an entry in standard encyclopaedias. I could only suppose that these shaman-like demons were synonymous with the goat and vulture shamans of Kurdistan, who were themselves synonymous with the bird-men, goat-men and walking serpents of Enochian and Dead Sea tradition. In other words, by 'shaman-like demon' she had in fact been alluding to the proposed Watcher culture.

Cult of the Great Goddess

In prehistoric Susa it was the Watchers' goat-like aspects that would appear to have been best preserved in visual art, but elsewhere in the ancient world it would seem to have been their connection with the vulture that became the mainstay of early religious iconography. In Yezidi and Yaresan tradition they were personified as the Ancient One, the Peacock Angel, and as the black serpent Azhi Dahâka or Sultan Sahâk. In Sumeria they were mythologized as bird-men and serpent gods such as Ningišzida, while elsewhere in the Near East the vulture attributes of the Watchers became the ultimate symbol of the Great Mother, particularly in her aspect as the goddess of death and transformation.[21]

Constantly archaeologists have unearthed stylized goddess figurines from the neolithic age with abstract bird-like qualities, such as long beaks, short wing-like arms and wedge-shaped tails. These have been found in such far-flung places as Crete, Cyprus, Syria, mainland Greece, in the Balkans and Danube basin of eastern Europe, at Mohenjo-Daro in the Indus Valley and as far east as Baluchistan in central Asia.[22] Many also possess strange, slit-like eyes, like those of the serpentine clay heads found by Robert Braidwood and his team at Jarmo in Upper Iraq.

In time the individual components of the vulture shamans would appear to have separated out to become abstract symbols in their own right. For instance, in a burial site at Tel Azor, about four miles from Jaffa, in Israel, around 120 fired clay ossuaries (or bone-boxes) were discovered grouped together in a cave. Many have beaked noses on raised front ends and wedge-shaped backs, and each contained the denuded bones of individuals who had been subject to excarnation after death.[23]

Fear of the Evil Eye

Eventually all traces of the vulture itself were completely lost, leaving only specific abstract symbols to signify the age-old potency of this great bird of death and transformation. Feathers, as I had already established, had been used to ease childbirth, ward off snakes and heal wounds, while its eyes would appear to have suffered a much worse fate. For instance, in a Sumerian tablet from the city-state of Lagash dated to the third millennium BC, it speaks of the 'divine black bird' of the 'terrible eye'.[24] D. O. Cameron in his important work *Symbols of Birth and of Death in the Neolithic Era* was certain that this referred to the large black pupil and contrasting white iris of the vulture, and had concluded that:

> . . . *in the process of time the original meaning of the vulture symbol* [i.e. its eye] *also became obscured. It was replaced by a kind of apotropaic magic, whereby a person could avoid harm by wearing a charm which was protective – in this case another eye which could outstare the eye of death* . . .[25]

So the eye of the vulture eventually became the evil eye. In Kurdistan charms against the evil eye would invariably be cowrie shells,[26] a significant choice since they closely resemble the pinched 'coffee-bean' eyes of the Jarmo heads, which, I feel, went on to influence the development of the neolithic bird goddess figurines found throughout the Middle East. If true, it seems certain that belief in the evil eye may well have begun at places such as Jarmo in the Kurdish highlands because of its community's apparent contact with the proposed Watcher culture.

It was intriguing to think that this power attributed to the evil eye might well have originated, not from the vulture – or, indeed, from the snake – but from a memory of those who had once borne these animalistic features. Was it possible that the Watchers' compelling eyes, said to have been 'like burning lamps', were responsible for the development of this age-old superstition? Perhaps the Watchers, these bird-men with viper-like features, were seen to have possessed hypnotic qualities similar to those accredited to the serpent. One can almost imagine the inhabitants of a primitive farming community, such as Jarmo, averting their eyes from the stern-faced Watchers in the belief that their hypnotic gaze could control a person's free will.

The Nephilim Head

If the Watchers really had walked among mortal kind, then the memory of their existence would appear to have become more and more abstract as the millennia rolled on. By the time these traditions entered Judaea following the Babylonian Captivity of the Jews in the sixth century BC, the memory of this ancient shamanistic culture had become mythologized as angels, fallen angels, Watchers and *bene ha-elohim*, the Sons of God.

Already present in Palestine had been a clear belief in the existence of 'those who had fallen', the Nephilim, as well as a strong cult of the Great Mother, in her aspect as the vulture of death. Abstract bird symbols appear frequently in early Canaanite art, and sometimes these seem to have been combined with strong serpentine imagery as if to bring together these two quite disparate traditions of Nephilim and Great Mother. One perfect example of this strange fusion is a one-and-a-quarter-inch-high copper figurine officially identified as 'a Canaanite god, *c.* 2000 BC'.

This item, now in the author's personal collection, possesses a long serpentine neck, cut with a deeply incised zigzag. Its 'human'

Fig. 15. Canaanite 'god' cast in copper, *c.* 2000 BC. The cobra hood, beaked nose, 'coffee bean' eyes and long neck, inscribed with a serpentine zigzag, are all characteristic symbols of the Nephilim, the name given to the fallen race by the earliest Israelites.

head is shaped like the hood of a cobra – the termination of which is curled over to form a kind of snake headdress. On the inside of the cobra hood is a three-dimensional human face, composed of a bird beak, a tiny mouth and two distinctive 'coffee-bean' eyes, like those found on the Jarmo heads. Blended together here, whether by accident or design, were some of the most important abstract symbols of the fallen race. Furthermore, the zigzag is an indisputable serpentine symbol,[27] while the stalk-like neck is indicative of the long-necked Anakim, the supposed progeny of the Nephilim who inhabited the land of Canaan in prehistoric times.

This small figurine is the closest I have ever come to finding a representation of a Nephilim giant – or at least their abstract memory, which appears to have been preserved in ancient Canaan more strongly than anywhere else in the Middle East. Little could the Babylonian Jews returning from the Captivity have realized just how much of an impact the revitalization of these age-old myths of the fallen race would have upon the face of world religion over the next 2,500 years of human history.

I had put forward the theory that the fall of the angels recorded in Enochian and Dead Sea literature referred to the trafficking between two quite different human cultures – one of a highly evolved nature living in a highland region referred to as Eden or Kharsag, and the other a more primitive culture living in the surrounding foothills and plains. The great wealth of circumstantial evidence suggested that this solution had at least some basis in truth, and that the homeland of these so-called 'angels' or 'Watchers' had been northern Kurdistan, very possibly on the southern shores of Lake Van. The vulture shamanism conducted at the Shanidar cave, *c.* 8870 BC, as well as the serpentine clay heads fashioned at Jarmo, *c.* 6750 BC, and the 'lizard-like' figurines and stone stamp seals of the 'Ubaid culture, *c.* 5000–4000 BC, were all tantalizing evidence to this effect.

There were, of course, many unanswered questions. For example, if the Watchers *had* once existed, then where did they come from? Were they indigenous to Kurdistan, or had they migrated there from some foreign land? What was the nature of the cataclysms that had supposedly destroyed the Nephilim at the time of the Great Flood, and when exactly had these taken place? And, more pressingly, how on earth did the highly advanced and unique Çatal Hüyük culture fit into the picture? I quickly realized that, by answering the final question first, I could begin to unravel the other great mysteries still attached to the origins of the fallen race.

Nineteen

BORN OF FIRE

Below the watchful eye of Erciyas Dağ (12,500 feet), the largest volcano in the old Turkish kingdom of Cappadocia, lies a virtually lunar landscape. Soft volcanic tufa, or hardened lava, has been eroded by the forces of nature to form curious shapes and curves unlike anything else on the planet. More curious still are the rock towers, formed by the wind as it has raced around large boulders of dark andesite and basalt resting on the soft tufa to create different-coloured cones of astounding charm and beauty. From the fourth century AD through till medieval times, Christians of the Early Church tunnelled out troglodyte habitations inside these natural towers. They even established churches and chapels within them, and these, along with the other wonders of Cappadocia, today attract tourists from all around the world.

Realm of the Peri

What seemed of greater significance to me was the fact that these strange towers were known as 'fairy chimneys'. Such a description seemed most appropriate, for those capped with boulders of rock really did look like tall, slim mushrooms of the sort that might make an ideal home for the fairy folk of myth and fable. Yet the naming of these cones had nothing to do with European folktales concerning the elfish denizens of fairyland, for in Turkey the towers are known as *peri bacalari*[1] – the fire chimneys of the Peri, the beautiful fallen angels of Persian lore. Local tradition asserts that Erciyas Dağ, or Mount Argaeus, as it was known in classical times, is the dwelling-place of Eblis, the ancestor of the Peri – a theme exploited in the 1986 film *Born of Fire*,[2] which features the Cappadocian fairy chimneys and, for reasons never made clear, subtle vulture imagery.

Somehow the indigenous peoples of Cappadocia had come to believe that the troglodyte dwellings carved out of the towering rock cones that litter the local landscape were originally created by fallen angels who had used them as fire chimneys.

Why?

What great secrets might these fairy chimneys hold? What had these towers of the Peri signified to the earliest inhabitants of Cappadocia? And how, if at all, might they relate to the Watcher birdmen of Kurdistan and the vulture shamans of nearby Çatal Hüyük? Something told me that this region held important clues concerning the origins of the fallen race – so much so that I decided to pay Cappadocia a visit. On-site investigations might well reveal vital clues not apparent from reading standard reference books on the general history of eastern Turkey.

I was accompanied on the trip[3] by a friend named Ken Smith, who shared my interest in the possibility of an advanced culture having once existed in the Near East during prehistoric times. We left Ankara aboard a coach around first light, and had finally rolled into a small town named Aksaray at 8 a.m. local time. Weary from a lack of sleep over the previous two nights, we climbed aboard a local minibus, or *dolmus*, in a virtual somnambulistic state and headed out towards the heart of Cappadocia.

With nondescript Islamic folk music blasting out of the minibus stereo, I stared blankly at the bleak, rugged landscape, which for some reason reminded me of the setting for the fantasy film *Conan the Barbarian*. The main character, a fierce but noble warrior named Conan, played on screen by Arnold Schwarzenegger, worships an ancestor who had been the first person to forge an iron sword, giving him the power to become a god.

The chances were that very little of this wild rugged terrain had changed over the past 10,000 years; certainly since the time of the Çatal Hüyük culture, which had thrived over 8,000 years beforehand just 165 miles south-west of Kayseri, or Caesarea, Cappadocia's capital city in Roman times. Looking around at the local people in the *dolmus*, many either on their way to work or going to market, I wondered whether any of these might be direct descendants of Çatal Hüyük's highly advanced neolithic community. I very much doubted it, for there had been so many major migrations into the region across the millennia that the local inhabitants must possess a very mixed racial background. For instance, between the fifth to third centuries BC, Cappadocia supported a very large Persian community, which included Magian priests from Media.[4] In the third century BC, it became an asylum for large numbers of Kurdish refugees escaping tribal and national hostilities in the extreme eastern limits of Anatolia.[5] While in medieval times the local population was swollen by many thousands of Armenian Christians escaping persecution in their own country.

Much earlier, however, Akkadian merchants in the reign of Sargon of Agade, who reigned *c.* 2334–2279 BC, had set up a trading colony at Kültepe (ancient Kanesh), some twelve miles from Kayseri.[6] Clay tablets of the period record that they possessed a thriving metal industry which exported silver, gold and semi-precious stones back to ancient Iraq. They would also appear to have imported raw materials such as tin from Azerbaijan and woven fabrics from their native homeland.[7] This town is known to have survived until at least 1600 BC, by which time Cappadocia had been taken over by an Indo-Iranian race known as the Hittites.[8]

Ice Age Anatolia

Over four thousand years before the merchants of Akkad established their trading post in Asia Minor, Çatal Hüyük had displayed advanced forms of agriculture, metallurgy, as well as an inexplicable stone technology that, according to the archaeologist James Mellaart, marked the climax of an 'immensely long ancestry'.[9] Where exactly this 'immensely long ancestry' had come from is not known. Even though Çatal Hüyük would appear to have had trade links with other parts of Anatolia and the Mediterranean coast, there is no real evidence to say whether they originated on the spot, or had migrated to the region from elsewhere. All the archaeologists know for sure is that the Çatal Hüyük culture appeared suddenly on the Konya plain amid a backdrop of very unstable climatic conditions. For example, there is good evidence to suggest that Anatolia was plunged into a mini ice age, *c.* 8850–8300 BC, following a relatively mild period after the recession of the last Ice Age proper, *c.* 9500–9000 BC.[10]

This glacial relapse would have brought with it intensely long periods of snow, ice and freezing conditions, which would have forced indigenous populations to seek refuge in cave shelters in an attempt to survive on a day-to-day basis. This was significant, for the Çatal Hüyük folk's construction of its mostly sub-surface shrines and houses, all huddled together without exterior doors or windows, was clear evidence that they had evolved from a race that had once experienced a subterranean lifestyle, a point noted by archaeological writer Edward Bacon, who in his book *Archaeology – Discoveries in the 1960s* wrote:

> *It is almost as though the remotely ancestral houses of these people* [of Çatal Hüyük] *had been troglodytic holes in the ground . . . and that these dwellings had so to speak gradually emerged into the upper air, but still retaining the logic of undersurface dwellings.*[11]

Recalling that the main religious cult of Çatal Hüyük had involved a form of vulture shamanism, my mind flicked to the account of Ishtar's descent into the underworld. She was said to have descended into 'the house of darkness' where 'the dwellers long for light' – the chief of whom 'are like birds covered with feathers'.[12] Certainly, the priest-shamans of Çatal Hüyük and the Watchers of Kurdistan could be described as 'like birds covered with feathers', but had they ever lived underground?

The First Blacksmiths

There was another curious aspect of the Çatal Hüyük culture that needed attention, and this was their apparent interest in volcanoes. On the north and east walls of shrine VII. 14 of Level VII, dated to 6200 BC, James Mellaart and his team had uncovered a huge mural showing a town of closely grouped terraced houses, thought to represent Çatal Hüyük itself. Beyond this suburban setting was a huge twin-peaked mountain, above which were lines that signified a volcanic eruption. Sequences of dots denoted clouds of ash and the discharge of larger boulders, while other lines emanating from the base of the mountain appeared to depict the flow of lava.

There can be little doubt that this painting portrayed an eruption of the twin-peaked Hasan Dağ, a mountain of 10,673 feet lying at the eastern end of the Konya plain, in sight of Çatal Hüyük. That an artist should have felt moved enough to have captured this experience for posterity is intriguing in itself, for if nothing else it constitutes what is probably the oldest ever 'photograph' of a historical event.

But there seems to have been more to this pictorial record than simply capturing an historical event, for the Çatal Hüyük folk would appear to have taken an interest in other volcanoes of eastern Anatolia as well.[13] From their foothills they collected various raw materials, including the all-important black obsidian glass, from which they made fine jewellery, knife blades and highly polished mirrors of incredible workmanship.[14] Remember, black obsidian was also the earliest trade centred around Nemrut Dağ on the south-west shores of Lake Van, the proposed homeland of the Watchers, at a time when the volcanoes of Kurdistan were probably still very active.

And the connection with volcanoes did not appear to have been purely material, either. The decorations in each of Çatal Hüyük's sub-surface shrines were strictly organized into certain quarters: bulls on the north walls, so that they faced the southerly Taurus mountains; death imagery on east and north walls, so that it faced the setting sun, while the birth-related symbolism on the west wall faced the direction of the rising sun *and* the various volcanoes.[15] This directional system clearly implied that the culture's interest in volcanoes was linked with the idea of spiritual birth, or indeed rebirth. At worst, it showed some kind of veneration of volcanoes, and, presumably, of fire as a whole.

As I had already established, fire had become the highest symbol of divinity in Indo-Iranian myth and ritual, with the oldest known fire altars dating back as early as 2000 BC.[16] Both fire and vulcanism would have been linked by the people of Çatal Hüyük with the emerging art of metalworking, still in its infancy during the seventh millennium BC. Not only would copper and lead smelting have become a sacred occupation in its own right, but blacksmiths would have been classed as fire priests under the dominion of the *genii* of the fiery domains. In the Persian *Shahnameh* of the eleventh century, for instance, the early mythical king named Husheng (Haoshanha in much earlier Avestan literature), is said to have been the founder of civilization and the discoverer of fire, which he used to separate iron from rock for the first time. In this capacity he became the primordial blacksmith with the power to fashion metal objects, just like the ancestral god in *Conan the Barbarian*.[17]

So the significance of fire, and in particular of volcanic fire, becomes clearer – it signifies the magical power by which the blacksmiths could change rock into metal objects such as jewellery, tools and weapons.

The Cabiri of Phrygia

Sometime around 1200 BC the Anatolian plain as far east as Kayseri was overrun by a warlike race known to classical history as the Phrygians, who established the kingdom of Phrygia. According to very ancient classical sources, this kingdom had been the abode of a race of fire-*genii* known as the Cabiri. Indeed, according to the writers Plutarch and Strabo there had even been 'a country of the Cabiri' situated 'on the borders of Phrygia'.[18] Greek mythology asserts that the Cabiri had been the first metalworkers – 'underground smiths' associated with the fire of volcanoes – born of Vulcan (or Hephaestus). He was the divine blacksmith and god of fire, from whom we derive the root for words such as 'volcano' and 'vulcanism'.[19]

The origins of the Cabiri are obscure, for they crop up in legends connected with several places, including the Greek island of Lemnos, Egypt, Thessaly and Phoenicia, and each time the story varies slightly. However, it is generally accepted that the original Cabiri legends came from Phrygia, and that they may well represent abstract memories of Asia Minor's most ancient metalworkers.[20] Since we know these to have been the Çatal Hüyük folk of the Konya plain, then there is no reason not to link this culture with the traditions concerning the Cabiri's metalworking exploits at the dawn of civilization.

The country of the Cabiri never really existed in historical terms, but the fact that it was said to have been beyond the borders of Phrygia is significant, since beyond the eastern borders of this classical kingdom was the heartland of Cappadocia. Might the Cabiri have been the original inhabitants of the fire chimneys of the Peri? The mere thought of 'fire chimneys' conjured the idea of metal-smelting in hot furnaces. Had the Cabiri been the first metalworkers of Cappadocia, as well as the precursors of the Akkadian merchants who returned to this same region many thousands of years later to smelt gold, silver and other metals? If so, then who were the Cabiri?

I glanced across at the driver of the *dolmus* as he began fiddling with the radio tuner in an attempt to find a more suitable station. Each one seemed to be playing modern Turkish folk music, until by chance he hit a station that began blasting out the opening bars of The Bangles' inimitable hit 'Walk Like an Egyptian', much to the confusion and consternation of the other passengers, who were apparently unfamiliar with Western-style rock music. Its presence here, as we passed through this primordial landscape with its sun-scorched plains and jagged hill-lines, seemed surreal in the extreme.

Houses of the Djinn

At the busy bus station of Nevşehir, our final destination point, local taxi drivers awaited the arrival of tourists in the hope of offering their services as tour guides at a competitive price. Having attempted to ignore them all, Ken and I found ourselves bartering with a young Turkish student who was offering to show us local sites of interest, many of which were already on our list. After some discussion, we gave in and agreed that he would act as our driver for the next day or so.

Throwing our hand-luggage into the boot of his bashed-up old car, we found ourselves heading out to the rock castle of Uçhisar, perhaps one of the largest of the volcanic cones in the region. So big was its interior, that it had become home to whole communities of people from the Christian era right down to the present day. It even houses a hotel, with wine on tap! From an opening in the castle's honeycomb network of disused troglodyte rooms, a breathtaking view of the whole region could be obtained. Like a symbol of omnipotent godhead, the snow-capped peak of Erciyas Dağ seemed to dominate the eastern skyline. Stretched out before us in every direction were literally thousands of fairy chimneys in different shades of red, orange, yellow, black and white, many of them between seventy-five and eighty feet high.

Our driver introduced himself as Ahmed, a student of Turkish history and archaeology. He said he liked acting as a guide to tourists because it allowed him to learn English, for he had good intentions of applying for a university place in Britain. I bombarded him with questions relating to the local terrain, but most of these he found near impossible to answer. Everything he needed to know under normal circumstances had been written out in English on hand-held wooden boards, which he could recite parrot fashion at each site.

He did say that the mythical builders of the fairy chimneys were seen by local people not so much as Peri but as djinn, which even today they believe to inhabit the rock towers. Immense superstition surrounds the rock cones and no local will go near them, except for a very good reason indeed. They say that only those who are being punished for some crime, or who have been kidnapped by the djinn, enter such places.[21]

In one lonely volcanic valley at a place named Zelve, every cleft in the rock had been tunnelled out to form countless hundreds of individual troglodyte dwellings that penetrated deep into the soft volcanic rock. Scholars believe they were originally inhabited by communities of Christians under the control of early Church Fathers of Caesarea, such as St Basil the Great (AD 330–79) and St Gregory of Nyssa (AD 335–95). Now they were homes only to huge flocks of pigeons that circled overhead emitting a constant aerial babble which seemed quite eerie in this strange troglodyte realm of the djinn.

Archaic Christianity

During the next twenty-four hours we visited fairy chimneys throughout the area, including those that made up the famous complex of rock churches just outside the village of Göreme. The interiors of these were generally of one basic style, consisting of an eastern apse, adjoined to a domed nave with side-aisles and chapels separated by carved arches and pillars. The decoration, however, was of two distinct sorts – so-called early Christian art, consisting of simple ochre-red drawings, and more accomplished coloured frescos of the early medieval period, which featured images of Christ, the Panagia (Virgin Mary), the angels and the saints, all done in the style of the Byzantine Church of Constantinople (modern Istanbul). It was, however, the much cruder 'Christian' art that drew my attention, for aside from containing more obvious Maltese- and calvary-style crosses, as well as other recognizable symbols of the Early Church, some of the rock churches contained meander patterns and geometric designs that appeared to match exactly the wall-paintings that had decorated the 8,500-year-old shrines at Çatal Hüyük. The comparison of the two quite distinct styles was startling and could not be denied. For instance, on the walls of shrines VI.A and VI.B at Çatal Hüyük there were geometric decorations that matched very closely those to be seen on the upper walls of St Barbara's church at Göreme.[22]

This may at first seem like a quite remarkable discovery, but there was a logical solution to this mystery. As James Mellaart had realized, many of the intricate geometric patterns found among the wall-paintings of Çatal Hüyük appeared to imitate the repetitive designs woven into the thin woollen rugs known as *kilims*, still made today in eastern Turkey.[23] This implied that some of these carpet patterns were several thousand years old and had their roots in the earliest neolithic communities of the region. Indeed, in shrine VII at Çatal Hüyük, Mellaart found two wall-paintings in the *kilim* style that bore what appeared to be stitch-lines around the outside edges, suggesting that the mural had been copied from the design on a rug.[24]

The *kilim* connection showed an indirect continuity of styles and patterns from protoneolithic Çatal Hüyük, right down to the Christian era, a time-frame of at least six thousand years. Yet this theory in no way accounted for a variety of quite obscure imagery to be seen on the walls of some of these rock churches at Göreme, particularly in the church of St Barbara and a small, unnamed chapel next to the so-called 'Dark Church'. On the ceiling of the former were various painted circles containing strange angular lines, zigzags and points that, if not randomly chosen, seemed to represent a primitive form of hieroglyphics. There were also whole sequences of rectangular boxes and round-edged triangles, some containing zigzag lines, others with small circles or lines on their corners, as if signifying appended heads and limbs. These sat upon double-lined 'stilts', some bearing zigzag patterns. What these images represented is unknown, although my first impressions were that the stilt-like lines implied a descent underground.

The most peculiar feature of all to be seen in St Barbara's church was a crude red-ochre line painting of a strange bird with a large wedge-shaped tail, an upturned open beak and a bulbous body covered in cross-hatching to represent feathers. Christian scholars would suggest that it represented a peacock, one of the symbols of the 'resurrection' in Early Church iconography, found not only in the troglodyte churches of Cappadocia but also within the catacombs of Rome. This theory did not, however, explain the bird's hands, arms and articulated legs, which clearly implied that the image portrayed an anthropomorphic figure, plausibly a shaman, dressed in the garb of a bird. There were even indications that the raised beak might actually be a form of totemic headdress.

What on earth was a clear depiction of a bird shaman doing inside the fourth- or fifth-century church of St Barbara at Göreme? There was no logical solution to this curious enigma, other than to suggest that the earliest Christians of Cappadocia must have been the inheritors of much older shamanistic traditions that dated back as far as the early neolithic period. This was a tantalizing possibility; however, another was to suggest that this was not Christian imagery at all, but the artistic expression of a culture that had previously used these rock-cut dwellings for their own ritualistic purposes before they were seconded for Christian usage.

We left behind the rock churches of Göreme convinced that

there were genuine mysteries still to be unravelled here: mysteries which predated the Christian era by a very long time indeed.

Subterranean Worlds

As we found the car, Ahmed asked Ken and I what we would like to visit next. 'Do you want to see the underground cities?' he had suggested helpfully. 'They attract many, many tourists every year.'

Contemplating his words for a long moment, I asked him: 'What underground cities?'

'There are many of them around here,' he casually responded. 'They were made by the Christians escaping the Arab persecutions. They went underground to hide from them. Many thousands of people they could hold, perhaps even 20,000 in Derinkuyu.'

To say I was dumb-struck would be an understatement. Underground cities holding up to 20,000 people; constructed deep underground just so that the Christians could hide from the Arab Islamic onslaught of 642 AD? Something did not quite add up. Surely the logical course of action for any community or culture fearing the crushing might of an invading army would be to retreat to safer regions. Indeed, this is exactly what a great number of the secular and monastic Christians of Cappadocia had done, establishing new settlements in Eastern Europe, particularly in Greece. It sounded like madness to dig a hole in the ground and hide away in the hope that your persecutors would eventually withdraw from the region.

Once we decided we must visit at least one of these underground cities, Ahmed drove us out to a village named Kaymakli. Its particular subterranean kingdom had been discovered only in 1964, and it had still not been explored thoroughly. No one knew exactly how many levels it possessed, although the upper four storeys had now been made safe for visitors.

Entering the underground city, we descended flights of stone steps and found ourselves in corridor after corridor hewn out perfectly from the volcanic rock, which hardens on exposure to the air. Each passageway seemed enormous, with a width of anything up to ten or so feet across and headroom of well over six and a half feet. Into each passage opened other connecting tunnels, leading to still more sections of the complex. On each side of the corridors were maze-like complexes of rooms and halls that had once formed bedrooms, food warehouses, water stores, wine cellars, temples and, yes, even a Christian church. Each room had been cut with such accuracy from the bedrock that it was clear that only thin walls divided it from its neighbours. Ventilation was provided by a whole system of shafts that connected all levels with the surface, while huge wheel-like doors made of hard dark stone and known locally as *tirhiz*, or *tarkoz*, could be used to seal off each individual section or level as and when required.[25]

There was no real indication of exactly who had constructed this subterranean citadel, although the presence of the church certainly confirmed that early Christians had occupied at least some of its levels. Rock-cut tomb hollows had been found on the sloping rocks above the city, and these may also have been of Christian origin. Yet, apart from this evidence, there was no obvious reason to suggest that the Christians of Cappadocia had actually constructed this city complex.

On the way out I stopped at the ticket office to purchase two books on local history. Both contained sections on the underground cities, but one of them, *Cappadocia – Cradle of History* by Ömer Demir, seemed infinitely more important. Since 1968 Demir had investigated the underground cities in his capacity as historian and archaeologist, and therefore he probably knew them better than anyone else. He had worked on-site with foreign archaeological teams and had felt sufficiently knowledgeable on Cappadocia's long history to write a book about the subject.

Ahmed returned us to Nevşehir, and as soon as we had settled into a second-floor hotel room overlooking the main street, I decided to read Demir's book from cover to cover, despite somewhat weary eyes after so little sleep during the previous few days. I was glad I did, for I quickly realized that this local archaeologist had stumbled across something of immense significance with respect to Cappadocia's subterranean world.

There were not just a few underground cities, as I had imagined, but an incredible thirty-six of them scattered about the

Cappadocian landscape. Most had never properly been explored, although the largest one known so far was located in the nearby town of Derinkuyu. Curiously enough, its existence had remained unknown until 1963, when one of its entrances was accidentally discovered by local people. Two years later it was opened to the public. Demir quite aptly described this vast underworld, covering an estimated two and a half square miles, as 'the eighth wonder of the world'.[26]

So far eight different levels had been explored at Derinkuyu, though between eighteen and twenty are known to exist. The first three storeys alone contained approximately 2,000 households, providing accommodation for an estimated 10,000 people.[27] Scholars have estimated that anything up to 20,000 people could have lived comfortably in the Derinkuyu complex at any one time, and if this figure is considered in the knowledge that at least another thirty-five similar cities exist in the region, then it paints an awesome picture of what appears to have been going on here in ancient times. Anything between 100,000 and 200,000 people would have been able to live comfortably in these citadels for any conceivable length of time. More incredible still is the fact that long tunnels are known to have linked several of these cities. One such tunnel, situated on the third storey at Derinkuyu, is thought to connect with the underground complex of Kaymakli five miles away.[28] Moreover, the passageway in question contains ventilation ducts to the surface and is large enough to enable between three to four people to walk upright, side by side, along its entire course.

Does this description sound like the handiwork of pious Christians trying to avoid the capture of Arab invaders?

Not in my opinion.

Deep below Derinkuyu

It seems quite amazing that the people of Derinkuyu never stumbled on the existence of its lost citadel long before. The name of the town means 'deep well', a reference to the many wells that acted as ventilation shafts from all levels of the complex to the surface and supplied the inhabitants with constant supplies of water. These wells, often marked on the surface by a pair of upright monoliths, had been the town's main source of water until 1962, yet never had they twigged that each one was connected to a vast underground city directly below their feet.

The Derinkuyu complex has no less than fifty-two of these ventilation shafts, which descend to depths of between sixty-five and seventy-seven yards. Temperatures within the city complex remain a constant 7–8°C, meaning that it would have been an ideal place of refuge during either extremely hot or extremely cold weather conditions. As at Kaymakli, huge wheel-like stone doors were able to seal off each section, while no less than 15,000 air ducts connected the first subterranean level with the surface, a distance of between eight and ten feet. The strange thing is that these shafts have diameters as small as four inches, a near-impossible achievement without the use of metal-tipped drills.[29] The early Christians are not known to have had such sophisticated tools.

Another mystery that has baffled the experts is what happened to the rubble displaced by the construction of the Derinkuyu complex? Some have supposed that a local hill called Söğdele to the west of the town might provide an answer, while Ömer Demir has suggested that the loose rock and ballast was poured into local streams and carried down towards Kaymakli.[30] Both these theories have their shortcomings, although the most important conclusion that can be drawn from this unsolved mystery is that the city must be immensely old, for it would have taken an extremely long time for all trace of these excavations to have disappeared so effectively.

So who did construct the subterranean kingdom of Derinkuyu, not to mention the other thirty-five cities scattered about the region?

Ömer Demir is convinced that parts of Derinkuyu are extremely ancient. Even though no datable artefacts or remains have been uncovered from periods earlier than the Christian era, there are major differences in the architectural and building styles of the different levels. He is convinced, for instance, that although the Christians may have *lived* in different sections of Derinkuyu, they only constructed, or redesigned, some of its storeys.

So how old did he believe these citadels to be?

According to Demir, parts of the underground complex could

well have been constructed during the late palaeolithic age, the epoch in human history marked by the cessation of the last Ice Age, *c.* 9500–9000 BC.[31]

On what evidence did he base this theory?

In 1910 an English archaeologist named R. Campbell-Thompson discovered hand-axes, rock chips and other upper palaeolithic artefacts in the Söğanli stream, some sixteen miles from Derinkuyu.[32] These were of a sort that could conceivably have been used to carve out the soft tufa rock ejected in molten form by Erciyas Dağ during a remote geological age. In itself this knowledge was insufficient to date the Derinkuyu citadel; however, Ömer Demir had become convinced that it must have been present during the Hittite age, since the foundations of their buildings were situated around the well-shafts belonging to the subterranean city.[33] Furthermore, unlike the various other Hittite towns that were razed to the ground when the Phrygians overran Cappadocia around 1200 BC, the buildings of Derinkuyu were left untouched. Demir supposes that this may well indicate that the Hittites escaped the Phrygian onslaught by taking refuge in the first level of the underground city.[34]

These were his views. Clearly we needed to visit Derinkuyu and speak with Ömer Demir to see if he could add anything further to his extraordinary theory.

The House of Darkness

Following a second day of sightseeing in the Göreme area, Ken and I took a *dolmus* out to Derinkuyu in the sweltering summer heat. From the outside of the underground city nothing is visible to the eye, except a slightly raised bank with an opening that appeared to be disgorging brightly attired tourists. Inside, however, we found a vast cyclopean domain unlike anything I could imagine anyone *wanting* to build.

In theory, there was simply no need to construct complete towns underground, unless you were attempting to escape from the world outside. Once again I recalled Ishtar's account of her descent into 'the house of darkness' where 'there is no exit' and 'the dwellers long for light'. I remembered too the words of Edward Bacon commenting on the sub-surface dwellings and shrines at Çatal Hüyük: 'It is almost as though the remotely ancestral houses of these people had been troglodytic holes in the ground.'

Strangely enough, on the levels considered by Demir to be among the oldest, the headroom in the corridors was much higher than other sections or levels, giving a maximum height of around seven feet. In the 'later' storeys, the headroom was so low that we had to stoop to navigate the tunnels, which were also much narrower in these areas. Why build some sections with extremely high ceilings when common sense deems that they need only be as high as is necessary?

Who then was this tall race that had inhabited the earliest phases of Derinkuyu? Might they have been the troglodytic ancestors of the Çatal Hüyük culture, who had established their own sub-surface city just 115 miles to the south-west? The epoch surrounding the climatic and geological upheavals that accompanied the last Ice Age is the only time when humanity has spent long periods of time hiding away from the outside world. In archaeological terms, this epoch is known as the upper palaeolithic, and it was during this same age that the stone implements found near Derinkuyu, and cited by Demir as evidence of the underground city's immense age, had been fashioned and used.

Perhaps inevitably, Ken and I managed to get lost within the labyrinthine network of roads, tunnels, stairways and rooms that filled all eight storeys. Once we had found our way back into the bright sunlight, we tracked down Ömer Demir to the ticket office, for he is now curator and guardian of the citadel. He was a tall, slight figure, mature of age, with dark, greying features and a bushy moustache, like those sported by so many men in Turkey.

The archaeologist welcomed us politely, and after finding common ground I asked him whether he had discovered any further clues to suggest that the oldest phases of the city dated to the late palaeolithic era. Using what little English he knew, he went over the same story concerning the stone tools found in the local stream. He said he was also now convinced that the oldest parts of the complex had been hewn out, not by metal tools, but by stone implements – a conclusion drawn after studying the different building styles in the various levels. Like Ken and me, he had also realized that the oldest parts appeared to have much higher ceilings, as if they had been designed to suit a tall race of people.

Other than this, he could offer no further proof of his theory, but did then proceed to give us quite a shock. It seemed that other ancient mysteries researchers had also taken a keen interest in the underground cities of Cappadocia. David Zink, author of such new age archaeology books as *The Stones Speak* and *The Stones of Atlantis*, had placed a special significance not only in Derinkuyu but also in the strange 'Christian' wall-paintings found in St Barbara's church. He and his team of experts had even been given permission by the local authorities to 'restore' this imagery. In addition to this, it seemed that the ancient-astronaut theorist, Erich von Däniken, had also visited Derinkuyu. He, however, had concluded that the citadels were constructed by a now lost civilization to escape the threat of aerial attacks from extraterrestrials who said they would return to punish the human race if it disobeyed the universal laws![35]

For me, the answer was perhaps a little more down to earth, even though I did accept the possibility that the Derinkuyu complex may well have been constructed towards the end of the last Ice Age. Von Däniken had, however, drawn attention to some pertinent points about Derinkuyu and the other underground cities, including the perhaps obvious fact that their inhabitants would still have been dependent on the outside world for food, since plant produce cannot be grown without sunlight. This therefore made nonsense of the suggestion that the citadels had been built as refuges against attack. The exterior land cultivation necessary to sustain a community of between 10,000 and 20,000 for any length of time would have betrayed the presence of any such subterranean population. All the attackers would have needed to do was wait by the blocked entrances and simply starve them out.

No, the earliest inhabitants of these underworld domains were hiding not from people, but from the forces of nature. Only with an aggressor like nature could a community still exploit the environment outside for hunting and land cultivation without the threat of a potentially disastrous siege.

But who were these unknown people who had lived in the underworld?

Derinkuyu sits in a huge geological basin between two great volcanoes – Hasan Dağ around thirty-five miles to the south-west and Erciyas Dağ, some forty miles to the east-north-east. Why site an underground city so near to volcanoes that were very possibly still active during the last Ice Age? The obvious answer was the presence of the soft tufa lava, ideal for hollowing out by human hands. Yet was there more to this reasoning than simply that?

It seems plausible that the Çatal Hüyük folk revered the volcanoes of eastern Anatolia as the source of life. Did they therefore believe that their ancestors had been born of fire, like the djinn and Peri of much later Arabic tradition? Were the inhabitants of the underground cities also behind the Phrygian legends of the Cabiri, the 'underground smiths' associated with the fire of volcanoes? Had the descendants of this unknown culture gone on not only to inhabit the fairy chimneys of Cappadocia but also to found the Çatal Hüyük culture of central Anatolia? Perhaps the remnants of this advanced civilization had supplied the people of Çatal Hüyük with its superior knowledge of how to polish obsidian mirrors without scratching their surface, and how to drill holes so fine that a modern steel needle cannot penetrate them. If so, then who exactly was this advanced civilization and what might its connection have been to the proposed Watcher culture of Kurdistan?

Twenty

HELL-FIRE AND FLOOD

Once animals, gods and mortals lived together in peace and harmony within the Airyana Vaejah, *the great Iranian Expanse. Here, in a tranquil garden of flowing streams, abundant crops and verdant landscapes as far as the eye could see, there were golden summers for seven months, and mild winters during the rest of the year.*

Then something terrible happened. Everything changed. The heavenly garden became an inhospitable wasteland of ten months' winter and just two months' summer. This onslaught of the land was blamed on Angra Mainyu, the Wicked Spirit, who wanted to bring death and destruction to the earth. Animals and humans died amid the freezing temperatures of the 'fatal winter'. Great plagues raged among those who survived the freezing cold, which seemed to penetrate everything and everywhere. The air was as cold as the waters, which were as cold as the earth, which was as cold as the trees. And all the time snow fell constantly.

The earth became a horrible place.

Fortunately, Ahura Mazda, the Good Spirit, had been able to warn the fair-faced Yima, the good shepherd of high renown, of the approach of this time of darkness when the 'vehement destroying frost' would engulf the land.[1] *He had also warned him that 'all three sorts of beasts shall perish, those that live in the wilderness, and those that live on the tops of the mountains, and those that live in the depths of the valleys under the shelter of stables.'*[2]

In order that Yima should be able to save the animal kingdom and the righteous among mortal kind, Ahura Mazda had informed him to: 'make thee a var *the length of a riding ground to all four corners. Thither bring thou the representatives of every kind of beast, great and small, of the cattle, of the beasts of burden, and of men, of dogs, of birds, and of the red burning fires'.*[3]

Inside this var *Yima was told to 'make water flow' so that he could place 'birds in the trees along the water's edge, in verdure which is everlasting'. Here, too, he was also to plant examples of all greenery and fruits. So long as all these things remained firmly inside the* var *the good shepherd was told that they 'shall not perish'.*[4]

Finally, after a great many generations, the 'vehement destroying frost' passed away, and Yima was able to lead the Iranian people and the animal kingdom out of the var *and back into the world outside. The plants and fruits were also returned to the light and these grew again with renewed vigour. So the world was saved through the instigation of fair Yima, the son of Tahmuras, who was the greatest ever king of Iran and all the world.*

This is the story of Yima as told in the Avestan literature of Zoroastrian tradition, which perhaps dates back as early as the sixth century BC (see Chapters Seven and Eight). Yima may be compared with the righteous Noah, the flood hero of Hebraic tradition, although the Iranian account bears many contrasting differences to its biblical counterpart. To start with, there is no flood, and secondly, instead of Yima constructing a huge sea-going vessel in which he houses the animal kingdom and his immediate family, he is instructed by Ahura Mazda to make a *var*, a word meaning a subterranean fortress or city. Strangely enough, in Persia the term *ark*, the word used to describe Noah's vessel, actually means 'citadel' or 'fortress'.[5]

Yima constructed the *var* in order that the Iranian race could survive the 'vehement frost', the freezing conditions and the perpetual snow that was said to have accompanied the 'fatal winter' that raged in the world during this mythical age. So what was going on here, and when might these events have taken place in recorded history?

There seems little doubt that the so-called 'fatal winter' preserved in Iranian literature refers to the final onslaught of the last Ice Age, which began around 15,000 BC and ended in the Near East perhaps as late as 8500–8300 BC.[6] That the Iranian race might have preserved some primordial memory of the last Ice Age was difficult enough to handle, but the idea that their most distant ancestors had constructed a vast underground fortress to escape the climatic attack seemed even more extraordinary.

The description of Yima's *var* bore so many similarities to the subterranean world beneath the plains of Cappadocia that some kind of relationship between the two seemed apparent. For instance, in the *var*'s 'upper part', Ahura Mazda instructed the fair-faced king to 'lay out nine avenues; in the middle, six; in the lower part, three',[7] giving a total of eighteen main streets. The Wise Lord further added that: 'In the streets of the upper part thou shalt place one thousand couples, men and women; six hundred in the streets of the middle part; three hundred in the streets of the lower part.'[8] This gave a total of 1,900 couples, or 3,800 adults; the text says nothing of children or relatives. This count makes a slight difference to the eight people saved by Noah on the Ark!

Ahura Mazda also says that 'over the *var* thou shalt open a window for the light',[9] words that made me recall the openings and air-shafts of the underground citadels of Cappadocia.

So where had Yima's *var* been placed? Do the texts say?

Sadly not. Yet since the *var* was said to have been located in the *Airyana Vaejah*, the domain of the immortals and the place of origin of the Iranian race, then it had almost certainly been situated somewhere in the vicinity of Kurdistan.

Might the *var* have been located in the mountains?

I felt it unlikely. There has always been a transmigrational relationship between the peoples of the Kurdish and Armenian highlands and those who live on the plains of eastern Anatolia, and vice versa. In fact, Cappadocia was actually considered to have been a satellite region of Kurdistan right down until the sixteenth century, when it was finally lost to the Turkish empire.[10] This meant there was every likelihood that if the Cappadocian underground cities really did date back to late palaeolithic times, then they could easily have become the subject of myths and legends that filtered into Iranian mythology via the oral traditions of eastern Kurdistan.

Leaving specific locations aside for one moment, it might well be the case that Yima's *var* was never intended to be seen as an actual underground citadel, merely a symbol of how the Iranian people had survived the onslaught of the geological upheavals and climatic changes that had apparently heralded the end of the last Ice Age. In this way there could have been any number of underground fortresses that would all have constituted the *var* spoken of in Iranian literature, whether they had been placed in Cappadocia, Kurdistan or Iran itself.

Beneath the Ice

Was it *really* possible that certain cultures had gone underground during the final stages of the last Ice Age? The evidence from Çatal Hüyük would certainly suggest that the earliest ancestors of this culture had once lived in this manner. If so, then what might life have been like for the late palaeolithic inhabitants of eastern Anatolia? For painfully long periods, fierce snow blizzards would have swept across the plains, bringing arctic-like conditions. This would have meant that only the toughest animals, or the most resilient of humans, could have survived in the open air for any length of time. Those with any forethought of these coming climatic changes could quite conceivably have constructed vast underground citadels in the softest volcanic rock, even though this would have meant living in constant fear of the active volcanoes.

Underground temperatures would have remained relatively constant, probably around 7–8°C. This would have meant that anyone could have lived quite comfortably without the use of open fires for any length of time, provided, of course, they wore plenty of clothing. The storage of food during milder periods would have enabled the population to suitably nourish itself on a regular basis, although these provisions would have needed to be supplemented by hunting expeditions across the snow and ice. In this manner underground life could have continued *ad infinitum*. The only signs to suggest that the complex was even there would probably have been a ring of defensive spikes, possibly topped with banners and animal skulls, and, of course, the monolith-marked ventilation shafts.

Fantasy? Perhaps. Yet there is compelling evidence from around the globe to suggest that during the final phases of the last Ice Age something immensely catastrophic really did force its inhabitants either to take cover or to climb to the top of the highest mountain. Moreover, these cataclysmic events had not been confined to the

Near East. They would appear to have occurred in one form or another in almost every country of the world, and to have been preserved in the myths and legends of literally hundreds of different cultures. Yet before I go on to describe what appears to have taken place, we need a few words on the history of the last Ice Age.

According to geologists, enormous ice sheets and glaciers enveloped most of North America and Europe for a period of anything between 30,000 and 50,000 years. Yet then, for some unapparent reason, they started to recede during the eleventh millennium BC. In a matter of just two to three thousand years the ice sheets vanished completely, bringing to a close not only the Ice Age, but also the geological era known as the Pleistocene epoch. This great thaw coincided with a gradual rise in the surface temperature over much of the western hemisphere, which, although accounting for the melt-down of the ice sheets, in no way explains exactly why the Ice Age came to a close. Indeed, geologists and palaeo-climatologists have very little idea how ice ages form, why they occur *only* in certain regions and why they suddenly go away.

Catastrophic Death

Elsewhere in the world during this same period there are clear indications of dramatic changes going on in regions which were not affected by the ice sheets. For instance, sometime during the eleventh millennium BC in the northern parts of Siberia literally thousands of animals, mammoths in particular, simply froze to death.[11] Many were found still standing upright with grass in their mouths and stomachs, indicating that they had been eating at the moment when their fate was sealed. Some of those studied revealed that their frozen skin still contained red blood corpuscles, hinting strongly at the fact that death had been caused through suffocation, either by water or by gases. It is to be remembered that, contrary to popular belief, woolly mammoths did not live in arctic conditions. They inhabited more temperate zones where grasslands and wet boggy forests prevailed.

In the 'mud' pits of Alaska, Professor Frank C. Hibben, a

renowned palaeontologist, discovered extensive evidence to show that tens of thousands of animals had suddenly met with a most hideous fate, for as he remarks in his 1946 work, *The Lost Americans*:

In the dark gray frozen stuff is preserved, quite commonly, fragments of ligaments, skin, hair, and even flesh . . . The evidences of violence there are as obvious as in the horror camps of Germany. Such piles of bodies of animals or men simply do not occur by any ordinary natural means.[12] *. . . Mammoth and bison alike were torn and twisted as though by a cosmic hand in Godly rage. In one place, we can find the foreleg and shoulder of a mammoth with portions of the flesh and the toenails and the hair still clinging to the blackened bones. Close by is the neck and skull of a bison with the vertebrae clinging together with tendons and ligaments and the chitinous covering of the horns intact . . . The animals were simply torn apart and scattered over the landscape like things of straw and string, even though some of them weighed several tons. Mixed with the piles of bones are trees, also twisted and torn and piled in tangled groups; and the whole is covered with fine sifting muck, then frozen solid.*[13]

Violent volcanic upheavals have been blamed for the tremendous ferocity behind the mass destruction of the Pleistocene animals, particularly in Alaska. Evidence of this theory has come from blackened layers of volcanic ash in both the Alaskan and Siberian regions.[14] Yet there seems to have been far more to it than simply this. Hibben estimated that over 40 million animals had died in the continent of America alone, while many species – such as giant beaver and sloths, mammoths, mastodons, sabre-tooth cats and woolly rhinoceroses – had become extinct almost overnight.[15] For him:

The Pleistocene period ended in death. This is no ordinary extinction of a vague geological period which fizzled to an uncertain end. This death was catastrophic and all-inclusive . . . The large animals that had given their name to the period became extinct. Their death marked the end of an era.[16]

All around the world there is also overwhelming evidence to show that, while the old ice-caps were melting, new ones were taking their place. The continent of Antarctica, for instance, began its gradual glaciation towards the end of the last Ice Age and was still relatively free of ice in certain regions right down until 4000 BC. Other evidence indicates that a short relapse, a kind of mini-ice age, where the ice sheets began advancing once more, occurred in Europe and Asia Minor sometime between 11,000 to 10,000 years ago.[17] More curious is evidence from locations as far apart as northern Armenia[18] and the Andean Altiplano of Bolivia and Peru, not only of the extinction of animals during the eleventh and tenth millennia BC, but also of dramatic elevations in the terrain's altitude above sea level.[19]

Receding ice-caps, mass animal extinction, geological upheavals, climatic changes and the raising of the earth – what had happened to the planet to cause such global catastrophes? Geologists have no real theories and palaeo-climatologists simply rub their chins and try to ignore the evidence staring them in the face. So what *is* the answer?

Hapgood's Answer

The most sober theory that fits the majority of the evidence was first put forward in 1955 by the late Charles Hapgood, Professor of Geology at Keene State College, Keene, New Hampshire, and endorsed at the time by no less a personage than Albert Einstein. Hapgood noted that studies of rocks recording the magnetic poles at the moment of their solidification showed how, since the beginning of geological history, the geographical poles have shifted their position as many as two hundred times – sixteen shifts occurring during the Quaternary or Pleistocene epoch alone.[20]

The phenomenon of poles shifting or reversing is no big deal to geologists. They, however, attempt to explain away these changes in terms of a theory known as continental drift, something most of us will have learnt about in geography class. This is where vast continents are seen to slide around on the soft layers of magma which exist some thirty to forty miles below the earth's outer shell, its so-called Crystal Lithosphere. Using the continental drift theory to explain shifts and/or reversals in the poles' axis did not, in

Hapgood's opinion, explain many of the global upheavals believed to have accompanied such changes. As a consequence, he concluded that although continental drift must be involved in the process of pole shifting, at the point when this occurs the *whole* outer shell of the earth buckles and slides in unison. If you can imagine the whole outer peel of an orange turning as the inner core of juicy segments remains immobile, this will give some idea of what earth crust displacement apparently looks like.

This all-encompassing turning motion would lead to a slow shift of the earth's axis relative to its surface, as well as the disappearance of the old polar ice-caps and the appearance of new ones in areas that had previously experienced more temperate climates. Hapgood concluded that crustal displacement had almost certainly taken place on at least three occasions during the past 100,000 years, this explaining the various periods of glaciation in corresponding regions of the globe at different times. Each slip would have caused a series of tremendous upheavals, followed by a period of relative calm, then another series of upheavals, followed by another period of calm, and so on and so forth, for anything up to several thousand years until the shift was complete.

More importantly, Hapgood also felt that crustal displacement caused dramatic changes in land elevation relative to sea level.[21] Such changes in altitude and/or climate must have taken place in many parts of the world, each bringing with them not only the extinction of many animals but also, presumably, catastrophic geological upheavals such as volcanic eruptions, major earthquakes and, quite inevitably, tidal waves and mass flooding on an unimaginable scale. Moreover, as a secondary effect, volcanic dust would have been cast into the air, causing sudden drops in air temperature. This in turn would have created increased rainfalls, drowning many more animals; while violent gales and tornadoes would have wreaked even further devastation.

Hapgood concluded from the available evidence on the Pleistocene epoch that, from around 50,000 to around 17,000 years ago, the northern polar cap had been located somewhere in the area of Hudson Bay in Canada, while the southern polar cap had been placed in the Australian Antarctic Territory, somewhere off Wilkes Coast in the Pacific Ocean. Since little sunlight reaches polar re-

Fig. 16. Photograph taken at an unknown Mayan site in the Yucatan by explorer Teobert Maler (1842–1917) of a stone frieze showing a Noah-like figure escaping a deluge, as a volcano erupts and a cyclopean structure collapses. Does this relief show the cataclysms that accompanied the cessation of the last Ice Age, *c.* 10,500–9000 BC?

gions, and that which does is too weak to have any noticeable effect on the climate, large areas of North America had experienced ice sheets up to two miles thick. Then, at a date he placed at around 15,000 BC, a great shift took place in the earth's crust. Why, exactly, this should have happened Hapgood could not say; but the consequence was that North America 'slid' southwards, taking with it the whole western hemisphere, while on the other side of the globe the eastern hemisphere was equally tilted northwards.

This global shift resulted in the northern pole moving a full 30 degrees, or 2,000 miles (3,200 km), to its current position in the Arctic Circle – which was then relatively free of ice. At the same time the southern pole shifted 2,000 miles on to the continent of

Antarctica. Because of the severe lack of sunlight, polar regions act like vast refrigerators, creating cold icy wastes that eventually allow the formation of new ice-caps.[22]

Meanwhile, the upper parts of the eastern hemisphere, such as Siberia and Alaska, which had unexpectedly found themselves much closer to the northern pole, would have begun experiencing unprecedented geological upheavals and harsh arctic conditions of the sort that led to the mass extinction of the animals already noted.

Hapgood believed that the earth's last crustal displacement would have taken a period of approximately five thousand years to complete, giving an end-date around 10,000 BC – a time-frame fitting very well with the climate changes known to have occurred in the Near East during this epoch.

An outline of the crustal displacement theory subsequently appeared in two essential books penned by Hapgood – *Earth's Shifting Crust*, published in 1958 (later revised and republished in 1970 as *The Path of the Pole*), and *Maps of the Ancient Sea Kings*, first published in 1966. Each book suitably explained much of what occurred towards the end of the last Ice Age, and this I wholly accepted. Yet could the effects of crustal displacement also explain why the population of Asia Minor would appear to have gone underground? Was it simply because of the arctic conditions outside, or could there have been other, more pressing reasons for them to have hidden themselves away?

Fire from Heaven

Stories of what would appear to have been a fiery conflagration, followed, or preceded, by a universal flood, abound in myths and legends found throughout the world. For instance, in the Popol-Vuh, the sacred text of the Quiché Indians of Guatemala, there is a graphic account of violent catastrophes on a grand scale, for it tells us that:

The waters were agitated by the will of Hurakan, the Heart of Heaven, and a great inundation came . . . Masses of a sticky material [pitch] *fell . . . The face of the Earth was obscured, and a heavy darken-*

ing rain began. It rained by day, and it rained by night . . . There was heard a great noise above, as if by fire. Now men were seen running, pushing each other, filled with despair. They wished to climb upon their houses, but the houses, tumbling down, fell to the ground. They wished to hide in caves, but the caves caved in before them . . . Water and fire contributed to the universal ruin at the time of the last great cataclysm which preceded the Fourth Creation.[23]

The Quiché also record that: 'Terrific rains and hailstorms and a fall of burning pitch . . . made life so hard that the survivors, four men and four women, decided to take refuge somewhere else, where caves promised a better protection.'[24]

Many of the indigenous tribes of North America also speak of some distant epoch in their ancestral history when 'the waters rose to quench a Great Fire which raged in the world'.[25] According to one tradition recorded by the Sacs and Foxes – Indians of Algonkian stock who settled in Iowa and Oklahoma:

. . . long ago two powerful manitous felt themselves insulted by the hero Wisaka. This put them into a fearful passion, and, intending to kill their enemy, they raged and roared over the Earth which heaved and shook under their angry steps. They threw fire everywhere where they thought Wisaka was hidden. Then they sent a great rain. The waters rose and Wisaka had to leave his hiding-place. He climbed a high peak, and then a high tree on the top of that peak, and at last, when all the Earth had disappeared under the waters, he saved himself in a canoe.[26]

Yet for me the most convincing story is that preserved by the Yurucaré of Bolivia. They remember a time:

When, long ago, the demon Aymasune destroyed plants, animals and man, by causing fire to fall from heaven, one man, who had foreseen the catastrophe, had richly victualled a cave to which he withdrew when the fire-hail started. To see if the fire was still raging he now and then held a long rod out of the mouth of the cave. Twice he found it charred, but the third time it was cool. He waited another four days before he left his shelter.[27]

There is a certain realism about this legend from the Yurucaré that somehow struck a nerve. Who would want to make up such a peculiar story if it had no basis in truth? Sticking a long rod out of a cave entrance to find out whether or not the 'fire-hail' had diminished is a very strange tale to interpret in a mythological context alone. Might it have been aerial bombardments of this sort that the peoples of eastern Anatolia had been attempting to escape when they built their underground cities? If so, then were they volcanic in origin? Might this link with the veneration of the volcano among the protoneolithic peoples of Çatal Hüyük?

Memories of fire and flood in primordial times were not confined to the Americas either. They could also be traced in myths and legends belonging to the ancient races of Brazil, Mexico, New Zealand and India. Furthermore, there were clear stories from Hebraic tradition concerning a fiery conflagration that apparently accompanied the traditional Great Flood of Noah, as the following passage demonstrates:

When men saw the waters well forth from the fountains of the deep they took their children, of whom they had many, and pressed them to the mouths of the fountains without mercy. Then the Lord let a deluge descend from above. But they were strong and tall. When the Lord saw that neither the fountains of the deep nor the deluge of heaven could undo them he caused a rain of fire to fall from heaven which annihilated them all.[28]

This Jewish story about God's attempt to purge the earth of its antediluvian inhabitants, who are portrayed here as sinful giants, brought me back to the alleged destruction of the Watchers and Nephilim by fire and flood. Was it possible that the Watchers of Kurdistan had existed during the final phases of the last Ice Age? Enochian literature, particularly that found among the Dead Sea Scrolls, states quite clearly that 'those two hundred demons (Watchers) fought a hard battle with the four [arch]angels, until the angels used fire, naphtha, and brimstone . . .',[29] during which 'four hundred thousand Righteous' people were killed.[30] Elsewhere it states that, in the dream experienced by the two Nephilim sons of Shemyaza, they see the terrestrial Garden of Paradise – which contained the two hundred 'trees', or Watchers – destroyed by 'all the waters; and the fire burned all'.[31]

It seems very possible that these references to a heavenly fire, referred to in connection with the Great Flood, must relate to the global cataclysms that heralded the end of the last Ice Age.

The Fires of Hell

For some reason the punishment of heavenly fire sent by the archangels to destroy the wickedness of the Watchers and their Nephilim offspring is not found in the biblical account of the Flood. Academics would argue that the Book of Enoch, as well as the other Enochian and Dead Sea material, is of a much later date than the Pentateuch of Moses, implying that these accounts of heavenly conflagrations are simply much later embellishments of an original theme. I disagree entirely with this view, for there seems every good reason to argue that it was the Book of Genesis that was heavily influenced by the stories found in the earliest Enochian literature, not the other way around.

The idea of punishment by fire, however, was not ignored by the Jewish faith. It seems to have lingered on in the imaginations of the Jewish race until it finally reappeared in the guise of Gehenna, the Valley of Fire, in which the wicked would writhe tormented in flames. Here, too, the two hundred fallen angels had been cast following their expulsion from heaven.

Although Gehenna was geographically linked with a place of this name just outside Jerusalem where the city's rubbish was incinerated, the concept itself is much older. Moreover, Gehenna was linked with the Jewish belief in a great 'pit' or 'walled city' referred to as Sheol.[32] Also known as 'the land of forgetfulness'[33] and the 'land of silence', it was said that no god rules Sheol and the dead are forgotten by Yahweh.

In early Christian times the Jewish belief in Gehenna and Sheol was fused together with the Greek concept of an underworld realm named Hades, or Tartarus, before being transformed into the idea of hell – the place of eternal punishment. As has tended to be rammed into every good Christian from an early age, hell is a gloomy realm of devilish flames and burning brimstone, where fiery heat is the only illumination and the wicked live on in perpetual torment. Somehow the fusion of all these different ideas led to the belief that the fallen angels also now reside in hell. Here, under the command of Lucifer, they are in charge of punishing the sinners and unbelievers once they have departed this world.

The concept of hell became very popular in Christian beliefs from the fourth century onwards, when it was seized upon and used to instil the fear of God among church-goers. Anyone who turned their back on the Church of Rome would be cast into the fiery abyss to suffer eternal damnation. In medieval times hell gained its greatest popularity, especially in art and literature – Dante's *Inferno* being a prime example. So vivid a picture of the fiery domains did he paint that simple-minded folk actually believed he must have visited hell himself! Strange, then, that among the various torments and tortures portrayed in Dante's *Inferno* is a fiery hail that rains down upon the wicked.

Hell is the creation of the Christian Church, based on earlier beliefs adopted from both Jewish and Greek sources. The only hell that has ever existed is the one created by our own minds. Its true origin would seem to have stemmed from the bastardized memories of a time long ago when our most distant ancestors spent long periods of time in darkened underground citadels, sheltering from severe climatic conditions and fierce geological upheavals, including aerial bombardments of fiery hail expelled from the mouths of violent volcanoes.

Far-fetched? Maybe. Yet the only alternative is to assume that hell exists, and this solution has, in my view, no real evidence in its favour.

Two Floods?

There were certain unanswered questions that needed to be addressed before I could leave behind the subject of global cataclysms and move on to find the true homeland of the Watchers. If the story of the Anannage presented in the Kharsag tablets really did reflect events that had taken place in the highlands of Kurdistan (or, indeed, anywhere else in the Near East), then how was I to explain the apparent sequence of severe climatic changes, including periods of darkness, arctic-like conditions and severe flooding, that had supposedly occurred towards the end of the settlement's long history (see Chapter Fifteen)? When might these have taken place?

If the events at Kharsag were linked in some way with the geological upheavals and climatic changes taking place around the end of the last Ice Age, it suggests that this advanced community must have been established long before the eleventh millenium BC, which makes no sense at all.

The Ice Age solution also fails to account for the universal flood preserved in the Sumerian, Assyrian and Babylonian literature of the second and first millennia BC. Like their biblical counterpart, they place an emphasis on water raining down from the heavens as opposed to water levels simply rising steadily upwards, as would have been the case with the melting of the polar caps. The Ice Age explanation also fails to explain why the Yezidi tribes of Kurdistan, who emphasize their descent from the flood hero, seem certain that there were *two* deluges – the last of these being the Flood of Noah, which they say occurred seven thousand years ago.[34]

How on earth was I to reconcile these clear contradictions? The only logical explanation is to suggest there were in fact *two* quite distinct periods of climatic upheaval in the Near East – the first around the end of the last Ice Age, say between 10,500–9000 BC, and the second around 5000 BC, the date preserved quite specifically by the Yezidi. Unfortunately, there is very little evidence that any such climatic changes took place around this second date, although there *is* one possible solution, and this is Woolley's flood.

Between 1929 and 1934, Sir Leonard Woolley, while excavating a series of 'test-pits' on the site of the ancient city of Ur in Lower Iraq, dug through several occupational levels before unexpectedly coming across 'eleven feet of clean, water-laid silt', virtually clear of any obvious remains.[35] Immediately above *and* below this level were identifiable traces of the ʿUbaid culture who inhabited Lower Iraq between 4500 and 4000 BC. This suggested that at some point between these two dates, possibly slightly earlier (the ʿUbaid people were in northern Iraq as early as 5000 BC), some kind of localized deluge overran the region. Then, once the waters had receded, the land was left covered with a thick deposit of silt, which on hardening was reoccupied by the ʿUbaid people.

Perhaps inevitably, Woolley became somewhat excited by this tantalizing discovery and concluded that it constituted firm evidence of the Great Flood, which had in itself been heavily influenced by its earlier Mesopotamian counterparts. Sadly, this was not to be the case, for at other test-pits made on the site of the city of Eridu, just fifteen miles from Ur, no trace of any silt deposit was to be found, despite the land being even lower in this area.[36] Confusing the issue even further was the fact that in test-pits dug at the city of Kish, a 'flood level' of silt *was* found, although this time it appeared in a much later historical context, perhaps as late as the first half of the third millennium BC. Much thinner alluvial deposits were also found at the cities of Uruk, Lagash and Shuruppak, Utnapishtim's own home city.[37] This contradictory evidence of inundations from all over Lower Iraq therefore implied that the plains had been subject to localized flooding at various stages in their history, suggesting that the collective memory of these individual events had somehow been impressed upon flood myths from a much earlier date, perhaps around the end of the last Ice Age.

Such a solution has its shortcomings, and it may well be that more extensive evidence of major flooding during the ʿUbaid period lies waiting to be discovered beneath the sun-scorched sands of Iraq. This hypothesis does, however, make better sense of our knowledge of the Anannage's settlement in the mountains of Kurdistan. The introduction of a second period of climatic changes, including mass flooding, might therefore explain why Kharsag would appear to have suffered from severe climatic conditions towards the *end* of its recorded history – the period between 6000–5000 BC being suggested by Christian O'Brien.

This same confusion, I believe, is behind the Yezidi belief in two floods having taken place. It also explains how the Watchers of Hebraic tradition were able to establish themselves in Eden and then, after an unspecified period of time, suffer destruction at the time of the second flood, the Flood of Noah, plausibly around 5000 BC. It is also possible that great numbers of their Nephilim offspring were killed during the localized flooding, which would appear to have engulfed the low-lying plains of ancient Iraq in the middle of the ʿUbaid period.

Even if the extent of the second flood has been grossly exaggerated in myth and legend, it now provides us with workable dates for both the rise and fall of the Watchers. It would appear that the settlement of Eden/Kharsag had been established sometime towards the end of the last Ice Age, say 9500–9000 BC. It had then continued in relative isolation until some kind of split appears to have taken place among its inhabitants. This led to a large number of the Watchers/Anannage – two hundred in the Hebrew accounts, six hundred in the Sumerian texts – descending on to the surrounding plains and living among humanity. The chances are that this occurred around the time of the establishment of the first pre-Sumerian city-state of Eridu, *c.* 5500 BC. This would then seem to have been followed by a series of more localized climatic catastrophes, *c.* 5000–4500 BC. From then onwards there would seem to have been two opposing camps of Anannage, or Watchers – one in the mountainous 'heaven of Anu' and the other 'in the earth', i.e. on the plains of Mesopotamia. This last faction would appear to have provided the impetus for the later Assyrian and Babylonian legends concerning the underground race of great stature and vampiric tendencies known as the *Edimmu*.

Should this chronology prove correct, then we may also conclude that, if biblical patriarchs such as Jared, Enoch, Methuselah, Lamech and Noah really had existed as historical personages, they could well have lived any time between 5500 and 4500 BC, when the split or 'fall' among the Anannage, or Watchers, is thought to have taken place, and the second 'Flood of Noah' may well have occurred.

I was now pretty confident that the angels of heaven, and the Watchers of the Enochian and Dead Sea literature, had been a unique culture which had seriously influenced the foundation of civilization in the Near East from its earliest phases right down until the third millennium BC. The evidence was, I felt, too strong simply to dismiss out of hand. I knew what they looked like, where they had lived, the effect they had left on humanity, and how they had been perceived by the other developing cultures of the age. Yet still I had no idea of who they were, or where they might have come from. Had their ancestors constructed the underground cities of Cappadocia? Had they afterwards followed the course of the Euphrates as it curves through eastern Anatolia, before finally turning eastwards towards its headwaters close to Lake Van in Turkish Kurdistan? Or had they come from somewhere else – somewhere not yet in the picture?

It was time to reach even further back in time to find out whether there was any evidence which might suggest that the Watchers had been a remnant of a much more significant race that existed *before* the cessation of the last Ice Age. It was a clue from a most unlikely source which finally pointed me in the right direction.

Twenty-one

EGYPTIAN GENESIS

Where do you begin looking for a lost civilization – assuming, of course, that one existed in the first place? If the ancestors of the Watchers had migrated to Kurdistan from another land, rather than simply evolving on the spot, then somebody, somewhere must have preserved this fact. Perhaps I should start by asking the Kurds – the Watchers' most likely modern-day descendants – where exactly they believed their most distant ancestors had come from.

Pose the question to a Yezidi priest of the angel-worshipping tribes of the Iraqi-Kurdish foothills and he, or she, would say that their earliest ancestor was Noah himself, whose Ark had come to rest on Al Judi seven thousand years ago. In other words, they would see their race as wholly indigenous to the region. Pose the same question to the Christians of the Armenian and Nestorian Churches, and they would deliver a pretty similar answer, as would the Shi'ite and Sunni Muslims.

The more Iranian-influenced tribes, such as the Yaresan and Alevi priesthoods, might well claim descendency from those individuals rescued from the clutches of Azhi Dahâka, the demon king of Media. They might also see themselves as having come originally from the *Airyana Vaejah*, the Iranian Expanse, home of both the mystical kings of Iran and the Indo-Iranian race as a whole.

Only the Kurdish Jews would throw any possible light on the origin of the Watchers. Their claim that the gentile Kurds were the Children of the Djinn, the product of the union between five hundred djinn (a hundred genies in another version) from the court of Solomon and five hundred virgins (or a hundred maidens) from Europe (see Chapter Fourteen), was perhaps more relevant than I at first imagined. The link between the virgins and Europe was, perhaps, to explain the clear white Caucasian features of at least some of the Kurdish race. Their more inexplicable devilish features, which probably included recognizable Watcher traits, had been attributed to djinn, the fallen companions of the angels in Arabic and Yaresan lore. Yet why suggest that these djinn had originally come from the court of Solomon in Jerusalem? There was no obvious answer, and on its own this whimsical folk-tale meant very little at all.

Roots of the Mandai

Turning away from the indigenous cultures of Kurdistan, I found myself looking through the works of the Mandaeans, the religion of the Marsh Arabs of southern Iraq. Scholars have suggested that they are the direct descendents of the 'Ubaid culture, who moved down on to the plains of ancient Iraq from the Zagros mountains around 5000 BC. This view of the Mandaeans' migrational homeland makes perfect sense of their belief that the race's earliest ancestors came from the Mountain of the Madai, which was located somewhere in the mountains of eastern Kurdistan. Yet the Mandaeans also say that this was not the *true* place of origin of their race. Their most distant ancestors had, they say, migrated to the Mountain of the Madai, i.e. Kurdistan, from a *foreign* kingdom.

That foreign kingdom was Egypt, the land of the Pharaohs.[1] Admittedly the Mandaeans associate this migration with the Exodus of Moses, *c.* 1300 BC, but the mythological time-frames suggested by their religious traditions cannot be taken literally. Like so many other races of the Middle East, the Mandaeans have attempted to fit their own tribal history into the framework of biblical chronology, and this has often produced a distorted hotchpotch of legends and folk-tales, which are further confused by the introduction of Babylonian, classical and Persian mythology into their cultural backgrounds. It is therefore enough to accept that Mandaean lore insists that their most distant ancestors had come from Egypt.

As in the case of the Jewish folk-tale which says that the Kurds are descended from djinn who came originally from Palestine, this

Mandaean legend meant very little on its own. Yet taken together these archaic stories appeared to conjure up a huge imaginary arrow that seemed to point south-westwards through Syria, Israel and Palestine into Egypt. Clear as this directional marker appeared to be, it served only as an interesting indicator, and no more; for the myths and legends of Kurdistan, Iraq and Iran could throw no further light on the possible origins of the Watchers.

If the Watchers really had constituted the 'uncertain forces' spoken of by the Kurdish scholar Mehrdad Izady as instigating the Near East's neolithic explosion from around 8000 BC onwards, then their advanced technological skills must have included the knowledge of agriculture, cereal cultivation, animal domestication, plant lore, metallurgy, pottery, as well as more esoteric subjects such as astronomy, creation myths and time cycles.

To find evidence of the Watchers' existence outside of the Near East, I would therefore need to look for hard evidence of such technological capabilities existing in western Asia before the final cessation of the last Ice Age in the ninth millennium BC. The underground cities of Cappadocia could well constitute evidence of such advanced capabilities, if indeed they *were* constructed during the later stages of the palaeolithic age, *c.* 10,500–8500 BC. Yet what if I were to spread the net a little further to encompass, not just the Middle East, but also northern Africa; what evidence of advanced culture would I find then?

Such speculations immediately raised the question of exactly how old is community life, organized society and primitive technology? Turning to standard encyclopaedias on the origins of humanity, I traced the development of civilization in the Old World back from the foundations of the earliest Mesopotamian city-states, *c.* 5500 BC, to one of the earliest and most important settlements in the Middle East – that of Jericho.

And Then Jericho

The town of Jericho is thought to have been founded around a spring-head by early Natufian settlers, *c.* 8500 BC. Because of its extreme age, archaeologists have been forced to refer to this little-known epoch of human evolution as 'protoneolithic', in other words, those who came just before the start of the neolithic explosion.

So who were the protoneolithic people of Jericho?

All we know is that they made and used notched arrowheads, probably with bows. They did not have pottery of any sort, but instead used plates and dishes beautifully fashioned from flint. Their augers, knives, saws and scrapers were also either carefully carved from flint or made of black obsidian. Analysis of this volcanic glass has suggested that it was imported from central Anatolia, possibly as early as 8300 BC.[2] This statement is made despite the fact that almost *nothing* at all is known about the protoneolithic inhabitants of Anatolia until the rise of the Çatal Hüyük culture some 1,800 years *later*. So what culture could have been behind the exportation of obsidian at such an early stage in humanity's development? Might there have been some connection with the underground cities of Cappadocia?

Perhaps.

Over the next thousand years Jericho grew to become a major citadel of an extraordinarily advanced nature. Its half-egg-shaped, mud-brick houses were protected by three enormous superimposed town walls sixteen feet high, which were themselves encircled by a deep ditch gouged out of the hard bedrock. Dominating the fortress' soaring defences was a colossal stone tower thirty feet in diameter, complete with an internal staircase, which would seem more in keeping with a Crusader castle of the Middle Ages than a protoneolithic township of 7500 BC. Why did this very earliest of cultures need to construct such monumental defences, which must have required the long-term cooperation of many hundreds of individuals under a very strong hierarchical leadership? Just who, or what, were the people of Jericho trying to keep out? What possible culture could have wanted to oppose them so early on in the history of our civilized world?

Throughout the eighth millennium BC, Jericho continued to receive consignments of black obsidian from the unknown source in central Anatolia. Volcanic glass would appear to have been one of the trades linked with the Watchers of Lake Van, so might they have traded with Jericho?

No one knows.

During the age between the foundations of Jericho, *c.* 8300 BC, and the final phases of the palaeolithic age, *c.* 10,500–8500 BC, very little is known about human life in the Middle East. One or two examples of animal domestication have been found at archaeological sites in the Near East. There are a few burials attributed to the protoneolithic Natufian culture of Palestine, while the presence of the odd grinding-stone, mortar, sickle and storage-pit in the same areas would appear to imply 'the beginnings of agriculture', as James Mellaart has referred to it.[3] There is also the evidence of animal domestication and primitive agriculture from the mound named Tell Abu Hureya on the Upper Euphrates in northern Syria. Radiocarbon testing has thrown up dates as early as 9500 BC for communal life here. If these readings are correct, this extraordinarily early example of an organized settlement appears to be out on its own in relation to date, and cannot be explained in terms of the gradual evolution taking place in the Middle East prior to the commencement of the neolithic explosion around 8000 BC.[4]

So is that it? Had the foundations of civilized society, with some form of primitive technology, begun in a humble and fairly modest manner in the Old World sometime between 9000 and 8500 BC?

About to shut the large-format encyclopaedia, I noticed a minor reference in a different section to something about 'experiments' in protoagriculture as early as the thirteenth millennium BC in, of all places, *Egypt*.

What did this mean – 'experiments'?

What on earth had been going on in Egypt during the thirteenth millennium BC? I needed to know, and after some searching came across an authoritative book on Predynastic Egypt entitled *Egypt before the Pharaohs* by Michael A. Hoffman. This introduced me to a whole new ball-game unanticipated in my quest to find the origins of the fallen race.

Down by the Water

Of the palaeolithic tribal cultures in Egypt, it was the Isnan that had taken my interest right from the start. Their curious activities had finally convinced me that something highly unusual really did take place in Egypt sometime between 13,000 and 12,000 BC. At four Isnan sites on the Upper Nile – at Isna (from which the culture takes its name), at Naqada, at Dishna, and at Tushka, 125 miles up river from Aswan – palaeontologists have unearthed clear evidence that these ancient peoples selected and grew their own cereal crops. Stone sickle blades were used to reap the harvests, while grinding-stones were employed to extract the maximum amount of grain.[5] Not only did the Isnan possess a primitive form of agriculture, they would also appear to have mastered animal domestication and to have possessed a highly advanced microblade technology.

It was, however, the sudden decline of the Isnan's technological skills that really began to capture my imagination, for around 10,500 BC the grinding-stones and sickle blades used in the production of cereals suddenly disappear without trace, only to be replaced by much cruder stone implements of the sort used by the other, less advanced cultures of the Nile valley.[6] Agriculture then totally disappears from Egypt until it is finally reintroduced, possibly from Palestine, around 5500 BC, some five thousand years *after* the Isnan lost their advanced capabilities. Even stranger is the fact that, after 10,500 BC, agriculture appears nowhere else in the Old World for at least another thousand years.

Why?

Human evolution deems that, once you have invented something, you don't go back to older, more primitive ways of life. So what ever happened to the Isnan?

Palaeontologists attribute this change in lifestyle to the increased aridity and high floods that began to encroach on Egypt around 10,500 BC. But was this correct? As I had established, this precise date corresponded very well with the global cataclysms and climatic changes that pre-empted the cessation of the last Ice Age, and which may well have been caused by Professor Hapgood's so-called earth crust displacement. Yet if, as I believed, these catastrophes had been anticipated by certain cultures, then there seemed every likelihood that they had made provisions for this eventuality, and this could well have included relocation to what were considered to be safer territories.

An Egyptian Elder Culture?

This was, of course, possible, although the only way of solving the enigma was to try and understand why the Isnan started evolving so rapidly between 13,000 and 12,000 BC. In one way, it almost seemed as if their tribal culture had constituted an early genesis of the protoneolithic age. Yet how was it possible that the Isnan started evolving more quickly than anyone else in the Middle East? The easy answer is to suggest that they belonged to a mentally superior culture with the intellectual capacity to evolve faster than their rivals. This is certainly a plausible theory, but it is just possible there was an altogether different solution. Instead of simply having the intellectual capacity to learn faster than everyone else, perhaps the Isnan had been given their technological capabilities by an even more advanced culture. If so, then who might this have been? Was it possible that around the same time there existed in Egypt a superior race who began disseminating some of their basic skills and technology to more primitive communities in exactly the same manner as the Watchers appear to have done in Kurdistan? Perhaps the Nilotic peoples of late palaeolithic times had actually collaborated with this highly evolved culture for purposes of mutual benefit.

If such a theory was in any way correct, then it implied that the cessation of the Isnan communities' use of agriculture and microblade technology had been caused, not because they themselves had dropped their tools and relocated, but because those who were instructing them had upped and left Egypt sometime around 10,500 BC. Unable to continue their communal farming without the encouragement of their superior tutors, the Isnan had simply reverted to their former hunter-gathering lifestyles, like those shared by the other contemporary cultures of that age.

At this stage such suggestions were purely hypothetical. There were, however, certain similarities between the way in which agriculture had suddenly appeared in palaeolithic Egypt and the way in which it had re-emerged in the highlands of Kurdistan sometime after 8000 BC. Might there be a link somewhere? Could the remnants of this proposed Egyptian elder culture have also been the 'uncertain forces' behind the sudden neolithic explosion in Kurdistan?

Who might this unknown culture have been? Were they the ancestors of the Watchers? Were they also behind the legends that spoke of the earliest ancestors of the Mandaeans arriving at the Mountain of the Madai from Egypt? If so, then there had to be a very real possibility that this culture was also behind the legends of the five hundred djinn who settled with five hundred 'European' virgins amid the inaccessible mountains of Kurdistan. Only by looking deeper into the mysteries of ancient Egypt would I be able to find any convincing answers to this mystery.

The Long-headed Folk

Following the turbulent period of global upheavals and climatic changes that signalled the end of the last Ice Age, everything seems to have gone quiet in Egypt. All that is known from palaeo-climatological research is that between 8000 and 5000 BC the country suffered heavily from intensely long periods of rain – a time known to scholars as the neolithic subpluvial (a pluvial being a period of constant rain). Little is known about the peoples who inhabited Egypt during this age.

The next notable period of human activity began with the arrival in Egypt of the neolithic peoples, who, unlike their palaeolithic predecessors, set up permanent communities and towns, formed organized societies, domesticated animals, produced their own crops, established primitive industries and traded with cultures in foreign lands. The two final phases that preceded the coming of the Pharaohs were known as Amratian, after the village of El Amrah, near Luxor in Upper Egypt, and Gerzean, after the village of El Gerzeh, forty-five miles south of Cairo. The Amratian peoples lived *c.* 4000–3500 BC and are significant in that they were the first people to introduce the use of totemic imagery on pottery. Their graves were also notable in that they lined them with mud walls. The Gerzeans were their successors, and among their achievements were the building of more substantial houses from materials such as reeds, mud and straw, as well as the construction of papyrus rowing-boats, complete with cabins. They also discovered the art of making faience, a form of blue-green glazed earthenware, and of casting copper tools and weapons, such as hand-axes, daggers and knives. In addition to this, the Gerzeans imported lead and silver from south-west Asia and lapis lazuli from as far away as Afghanistan. Craftsmen and artists in different trades began appearing and intercourse with other cultures in south-west Asia, including ancient Iraq, became more frequent.[7] This is the period in Egyptian history known as Predynastic times.

The Gerzean culture came to an end *c.* 3100 BC, just as Egypt was making its final transformation into the mainly arid desert we know today. At the same time, various chieftains or kings, each using different totemic emblems and signs of recognition, began establishing themselves as war-lords in both Upper or Lower Egypt. It was the suppression of these petty kings, and the eventual unification of their individual territories by early Pharaohs such as Narmer and Hor-aha, that established the foundations of Dynastic Egypt, just a hundred years before the rise of the Sumerian civilization.

There were no references anywhere in Egyptian archaeology to a highly advanced race having existed in these parts during the period of the neolithic subpluvial. I did, however, find tantalizing evidence to suggest that such a race had been present in Egypt towards the end of the fourth millennium BC. It would seem that a number of late Predynastic graves in the northern part of Upper Egypt have yielded up 'anatomical remains of a people whose skulls were of a greater size and whose bodies were larger than those of the natives'.[8] Walter Bryan Emery, an eminent and very respected Egyptologist, made a detailed study of Predynastic and early Dynastic society in Egypt, and was so moved by these important discoveries that, in his 1961 book, *Archaic Egypt*, he concluded that:

. . . *any suggestion that these people derived from the earlier stock is impossible. The fusion of the two races must have been considerable, but it was not so rapid that by the time of the Unification it could be considered in any way accomplished, for throughout the whole of the Archaic Period (i.e. the first two pharaonic dynasties, c. 3100–2700* BC) *the distinction between the civilized aristocracy and the mass of the natives is very marked, particularly in regard to their burial customs. Only with the close of the Second Dynasty do we find evidence of the lower orders adopting the funerary architecture and mode of burial of their masters.*[9]

So who were these 'masters', this race of great stature believed to have founded the royal line of Egypt and to have introduced new burial customs to the local population? Emery identified them with the *Shemsu-Hor*, the Companions, or Followers, of the hawk-headed god Horus, who, according to one very ancient king-list preserved in Turin, dominated Egypt for an incredible 13,420 years *before* the ascent of Narmer and Hor-aha (the Greek Menes), the first recognized Pharaohs.[10]

Emery must have been aware of this fact when writing *Archaic Egypt*, so he was therefore implying that the most distant ancestors of the Egyptians had been tall in stature with large craniums. Emery also made it clear that: 'The racial origin of these invaders is not known and the route they took in their penetration of Egypt is equally obscure.'[11] His book goes on to compare the unique architecture of this culture with that of ancient Iraq, hinting at a common origin for both civilizations.

Further evidence of this clear relationship between the most ancient inhabitants of Egypt and the earliest city-states of Mesopotamia has come from the study of human skulls found in the Predynastic cemeteries excavated at Abydos in Upper Egypt during 1897 by the flamboyant French archaeologist, Jacques de Morgan. Each cranium was examined by an anthropologist named D. Fouquet, who reported that among them was a racial type entirely unlike any ancient or modern inhabitant of Egypt. These skulls were 'big-headed' and of a so-called dolichocephalic shape, that is long and narrow.[12]

Adding weight to this argument is the knowledge that 'people allied in type to the big-headed Predynastic Egyptians are to be found buried in the early Sumerian graves of Mesopotamia'.[13] For example, long-headed skulls, entirely unlike the rest of the Sumerian race, are known to have been found during excavations at Kish and Jemdet Nasr in Iraq.[14] They were found at the lowest occupational levels, indicating that they are at least five thousand years old. In an important article written on this subject for the *American Anthropologist* in 1933, its author, Henry Field, concluded that these outsized skulls represented evidence of a 'proto-Semitic' culture, who were the original founders of the pre-Sumerian city-states before they were overrun by an indigenous culture with a quite different skull shape sometime around 3000 BC.[15]

Just who were these long-headed individuals? Might they have been the descendants of a culture who inhabited Egypt during its earliest stages of development? Might some remnant of this culture have been responsible for the foundation of Sumer, a role both Christian O'Brien and I had already assigned to the Watchers of Eden? The viper-like faces recorded in connection with the fallen race would undoubtedly be seen by anthropologists as a classic feature of a long-headed individual, such as those found in the most ancient graves of both Egypt and Sumer.

The Watch Gods

If the ancestors of the Watchers really were linked with the long-headed, aristocratic race of Predynastic Egypt, then what more was there to learn about this unknown culture? Could they really have been the *Shemsu-Hor*, the Companions of Horus, who had supposedly ruled Egypt for a staggering 13,420 years before the reign of its first Pharaoh? I found it intriguing that even before these mythical personages supposedly ruled the country, the Turin king-list speaks of Egypt as being the domain of the *ntr*, a term meaning, quite literally, the 'gods'. Furthermore, acting as intermediaries between the *ntr*-gods and mortal kind had been the Urshu, or 'Watchers', a race of supposedly 'divine beings' comparable to the *Shemsu-Hor*.[16]

Was the Turin king-list, and others like it, pure fantasy? Or had there been an age when the *ntr*-gods and other 'divine beings' inhabited Egypt in physical form? One tentative link between this mythical age and the origins of the Watchers concerned the term *ntr*.

According to Mandaean tradition, after physical death the soul of the deceased goes 'like a bullet' towards the heavenly realm of Pthahil, who is a god of the dead. It first flies over a great white mountain named Sur, beyond which is the Mataratha, or place of judgement. Here they will find the *ntr*, or watch-houses, from which beings of light watch over each individual *matarta*, or realm.[17] If the soul is pious, it is allowed after forty-five (sometimes forty) days to journey on to the Pole Star. If the evil it has committed during its lifetime outweighs, or is equal to, the good it has done, the soul remains in the Mataratha to receive purification and punishment. If the soul is inherently evil, it is received into the belly of a giant serpent named 'Ur, where it suffers alternately fire and ice until the Day of Judgement.[18] By virtue of its directional position to the Pole Star, the Mataratha is located to the north of the Mandaean's homeland. This places both the heavenly realm, which has similarities to the purgatory of Christian tradition, and the 'great white' mountain of Sur, firmly in the direction of the highlands of Kurdistan.

That the Mandaeans should believe in an ethereal realm located in the north and controlled by 'beings of light', who 'watch', *ntr*, from heavenly towers is highly significant. Indeed, I understand that in certain Near Eastern languages the root *ntr*, the Egyptian word for 'god', or 'gods', relates to the verb 'watch' and the noun 'watcher'.[19] A further link with Egyptian mythology is the root of the name Pthahil, the Mandaean spirit of the dead. It bears so close a similarity to Ptah, the Egyptian god who created humanity on a potter's wheel, that the two very similar names almost certainly derive from the same primary source. This supposition is supported by the fact that the suffix *il* on Pthahil is simply an appended term meaning 'god',[20] leaving the actual name of the deity as Pthah. Since the Mandaeans have always claimed that their roots lay in Egypt, these etymological comparisons should come as no surprise.

There really did appear to be some justification to link the Egyptian *ntr*-gods with the Watchers of Kurdistan. Yet, despite this conclusion, it seemed absurd even to contemplate the idea that organized society, controlled by a succession of god-kings, could have existed in Egypt for tens of thousands of years before the first civilized society appeared in the Near East. Yet the ancient Egyptians also spoke of something known as *Zep tepi*, or the First Time, a kind of Golden Age that began at the point of First Creation and was ruled over by the *ntr*-gods, such as Osiris and his son Horus. According to the noted Egyptian language scholar, R. T. Rundle Clark, this Golden Age was viewed by the Egyptians as a time of 'absolute perfection – "before rage or clamour or strife or uproar had come about". No death, disease or disaster occurred in this blissful epoch, known variously as "the time of Re", "the time of Osiris", or "the time of Horus"'.[21]

Not only were the Egyptians sure of the immense antiquity of their race, but Greek philosophers were as well. For example, Plato (429–347 BC), in his *Timaeus*, tells the story of 'a relative and great friend of my great-grandfather', whose name was Solon. This man had apparently travelled to Egypt and engaged the priests at the temple of the goddess Neith, located within the Nile delta town of Sais, in a rather enlightening conversation that had supposedly taken place some six hundred years before the Christian era. On the subject of the antiquity of the Hellenes, one very ancient priest had lectured Solon, saying:

'O Solon, Solon, you Hellenes are but children, and there is never an old man who is an Hellene.' Solon, hearing this, said, 'What do you mean?' 'I mean to say,' he replied, 'that in mind you are all young; there is no old opinion handed down among you by ancient tradition, nor any science which is hoary with age. And I will tell you the reason of this: there have been, and there will be again, many destructions of mankind arising out of many causes . . . [which include] *a great conflagration of things upon the earth recurring at long intervals of time; when this happens, those who live upon the mountains and in dry and lofty places are more liable to destruction than those who dwell by rivers or on the sea-shore; and from this calamity the Nile, who is our never-failing savior, saves and delivers us. When, on the other hand, the gods purge the earth with a deluge of water, among you herdsmen and shepherds on the mountains are the survivors, whereas those of you who live in cities are carried by the rivers into the sea; but in this country neither at that time nor at any other does the water come from above on the fields, having always a tendency to come up from below, for which reason the things preserved here are said to be the oldest.'*[22]

The old priest at Sais goes on to tell Solon about 'the fairest and noblest race of men which ever lived', before he recounts the story of how the fabled 'islands of Atlantis', beyond the 'Pillars of Heracles', were destroyed by devastating earthquakes and floods '9,000 years' before their age, giving an approximate date of around 9600 BC, exactly the time-frame of the global cataclysms and climatic changes that apparently heralded the end of the last Ice Age. He also tells Solon that according to the 'sacred registers' the Egyptian race was founded '8,000 years' ago, in other words 1,000 years after the submergence of Atlantis and the foundation of the Hellenic race by the survivors of this 'noblest' race.[23]

These dates have often been dismissed by academics, who attempt to demonstrate that Plato must have got it wrong, meaning instead either 900 years or 9,000 lunar cycles. Despite this criticism, other Graeco-Egyptian scholars have contested these views, stating that if Plato wrote 9,000 years, then he meant 9,000 solar years, no more and no less.[24] If correct, then it suggests that each time extensive global cataclysms occur, the world has the habit of losing its memory. Meanwhile we prefer to think of ourselves as the first and only human race that God has placed in this world.

The orthodox anthropology and archaeology of Egypt from late palaeolithic times right down to the age of the Pharaohs could take me only so far along the path of rediscovery of this lost memory. The heady myths and legends of ancient Egypt are filled with prominent references to an epoch when the gods ruled Egypt, but this was not enough. I was not going to find any hardcore evidence of Egypt's elder culture by wallowing in ancient fables. I needed something more tangible to work with, and right from the start it was clear that one monument held virtually all the keys to unlocking Egypt's final secrets. This was the Great Sphinx – the next destination in my quest to find the roots of the fallen race.

Twenty-Two

FATHER OF TERRORS

Beyond the city lights of Cairo, the bus navigated its way through exhaust-drenched streets, packed with hooting cars, beaten donkeys, Coca-Cola signboards and young Egyptians on mopeds. It was dark, and somewhere well beyond the run-down suburbs the crowded vehicle came to a halt in a busy road, alive with nocturnal activity.

Not knowing where on earth I ought to be heading, I passed along a narrow street filled with a selection of low-key souvenir shops. The path seemed to climb higher and higher – the rising plateau now visible before me. Reaching a certain point, I glanced up to see one of the most breathtaking sights of my life – the Great Pyramid and its two accompanying neighbours soaring upwards like colossal giants, higher than anyone could ever have prepared me for. Bright lights illuminated their awesome, silhouetted forms, while all around the trackway leading to their base were literally hundreds of stallholders, camel handlers, street peddlers and security men. It was a sight I shall never forget.

The Pyramids of Giza symbolize everything that ancient Egypt stands for in the minds of the world today: advanced technology, immense building capabilities, exact geodesy, precision geometry and astronomical knowledge far exceeding that of any other contemporary culture. Egypt's history alone is enough to conjure up some of the most vivid and romantic images the world has known. Cleopatra, Nefertiti and the boy king Tutankhamun – this is how almost everybody imagines this ancient kingdom, but what of its reality? Where does the romance stop and the truth begin?

The World's Greatest Wonders

The age of the Pharaohs began in earnest around 3100 BC[1] with the unification of Upper and Lower Egypt, and the rule of a joint kingdom by one king. Narmer and his successor Hor-aha established what is known to Egyptologists as the Archaic Period – that is, Dynasties One and Two. With the commencement of the Third Dynasty, *c.* 2700 BC, there came an era known as the Old Kingdom, an age marked by the sudden urge among the Egyptians to begin building pyramids – an idea inspired by the necessity to find a way of preserving the physical body of a dead Pharaoh, and thus ensuring the immortality of his soul in the afterlife. The mighty step pyramid of Sakkara, built for the Pharaoh Djoser, or Zoser, was the first to be undertaken around 2650 BC.

Ever grander pyramids were built along the western banks of the river Nile, until the construction during the Fourth Dynasty, *c.* 2620–2481 BC, of the Old Kingdom's greatest ever achievement – the Great Pyramid. At 756 feet across each baseline, 481 feet in height, and covering an area of just over 13 acres,[2] it is probably the finest piece of workmanship human hands have ever produced, yet, despite this, its history and ownership are contradictory and vague. When the hired workmen of the Arab Caliph Al-Ma'moun finally broke into the Great Pyramid after weeks of tunnelling through its solid limestone blocks in AD 820, they came across its famous granite sarcophagus in the King's Chamber. This lidless stone box was said to have contained 'a statue like a man (i.e. a body-shaped coffin), and within it a man, upon whom was a breast-plate of gold set with jewels', while 'a sword of inestimable price' and 'a carbuncle (a precious red stone, probably a ruby) of the bigness of an egg' lay beside the corpse.[3]

Despite the fact that this account was first recorded during Al-Ma'moun's own lifetime,[4] archaeologists and pyramidologists alike tend to dismiss these discoveries as complete fantasy. So what might Ma'moun's workmen have actually discovered? The body of its builder? Or the remains of some much later interment?

In ancient times many theories were put forward as to the designer of the Great Pyramid, but only Herodotus appears to have got it right. He spoke of its builder as one Cheops, the Greek rendering of a Fourth Dynasty Pharaoh named Khufu, who reigned for twenty-three years from *c.* 2596 BC onwards. This ancient tradition, repeated by later authors, remained unconfirmed until the mid nineteenth century when an English treasure hunter and self-proclaimed Egyptologist, Colonel Richard Howard-Vyse, announced the discovery of quarry marks bearing the cartouche (i.e. the oval-encased signature) of Khufu in a previously unknown relieving chamber, situated above the King's Chamber. Although these marks are generally believed to have been left by quarrymen in around 2590 BC, some people now firmly believe that they were faked on the instructions of Vyse so as to boost his credibility as an Egyptologist.[5]

No one really knows for sure why the Great Pyramid – or its two neighbouring pyramids, one assigned to Khufu's son, Khafre, the Greek Chephren, *c.* 2550 BC, and the other attributed to Khafre's own successor, Menkeure, the Greek Mycerinos, *c.* 2500 BC – was actually built. Hundreds, if not thousands, of books have voiced their often conflicting opinions as to its true purpose. Although it might well have acted as a tomb for its founder, it also probably played a major role as a place of funerary rites and rituals associated with the journey of the soul of the Pharaoh in the afterlife. Other theories have suggested that the Great Pyramid acts as a giant celestial clock highlighting the actions of the sun's yearly course, and that its angles, measurements and geometry bear a geodesic relationship to the actual size, movements and axis of the earth. All theories are at least partially correct.

It was not, however, just the Pyramids that I wanted to see tonight. Hiding among the broken temples and tomb structures, off to the left of the Second Pyramid, was Giza's other great prize. It was not the most easy monument to find in the dark, but away from the path, beyond the low fences, I confronted the deeply scarred, noseless face of the Great Sphinx. The eerie overhead glow made by the street-lights of nearby Cairo only partially illuminated its visible head and long flat back. Its long front paws, its belly and curled tail remained under a blanket of darkness that covered the deep rectangular enclosure hewn out when the monument was constructed by ancient hands.

For too long I gazed up at its motionless visage that extended from the huge *nemes*-headdress. According to all orthodox sources, this mysterious edifice had been carved from the living rock on the eastern edge of the Giza plateau, sometime around 2550 BC. It is said to be 240 feet long, 66 feet high, and some 36 feet broad at the shoulders. The Sphinx was made at the request of Khafre, the believed builder of the nearby Second Pyramid. The monument's face, they say, is the likeness of Khafre. A life-size statue of this Pharaoh, with a visage that bears a close resemblance to that of the Sphinx, was discovered hidden in the nearby ruins of the so-called Valley Temple, constructed from the huge white limestone blocks extracted from the deeply cut enclosure.

The Egyptologists say that the Sphinx has been battered by sandstorms throughout its long history. These have effectively weathered its features and buried it up to its neck on many occasions. A curious tale is told of how a young prince named Thutmose experienced a very strange dream after falling asleep against its towering head, the only part exposed above the desert sands. In his slumber the spirit of the Sphinx told him that if he cleared away the sand that was choking it to death, then it would ensure that one day he would become Pharaoh. Enthused by this loaded offer, the prince respectfully did what was asked of him and, as a consequence, the Sphinx kept its side of the bargain, enabling the prince to ascend to the throne as Thutmose IV in *c.* 1413 BC. To commemorate this event, the Pharaoh had an inscribed stone slab, or stela, erected between the Sphinx's long paws, and here it has remained to this day.

In time the Sphinx was once more covered up to its neck in sand, and even though the Romans dug it out again during their own age, the body was to remain hidden by the desert almost permanently, thus preserving its carved features for future generations. It was said that in 1380 a Muslim fanatic named Saim el-Dahr became so incensed by the attention being paid to this pagan monument that he deliberately cut off its nose![6] Adding to its misery is the knowledge that European travellers chipped off fragments from the Sphinx's carved face and lips, which they took away and used as lucky charms. Worse still, the Mameluke Turkish guards are alleged to have used the Sphinx's head for target practice!

Only in 1816, when excavations were conducted around its base for the first time, was it realized that the Sphinx had once borne both a stone crown and a beard, and that its face had at one time been painted red. Even so, it was not until the 1930s that an Egyptologist, Dr Selim Hassan, undertook to rescue the stone monument completely from the sands for the first time since Roman times. Hassan made many important discoveries during his excavations, including the fact that the Sphinx had been the subject of a special cult and royal pilgrimages throughout the New Kingdom period, *c.* 1308–1087 BC. What, then, did this huge recumbent stone monument *mean* to the ancient Egyptians?

Horus and the Horizon

The Great Sphinx faces directly towards the eastern horizon where the sun rises at the spring and autumn equinoxes – the midway markers in the solar cycle which currently fall around 21 March and 22 September each year. Mythically speaking, the leonine monument has many identities and functions, although first and foremost is its association with *Hor-em-akhet*, Horus-in-the-Horizon, and *Hor-akhty*, Horus-of-the-Horizon, both forms of the sun god Horus. In this capacity the Sphinx was equated with a leonine beast called Aker, which was said to guard the entrance and exit of the underworld tunnels through which the sun god travelled each night in the form of a divine falcon after setting on the western horizon. The role played by Horus in this myth cycle was originally assigned to the sun god Re, in his form as Atum, 'the Complete One',[7] or *Atum-re*, who, as the setting sun, journeys as a bird through the dark caverns of the underworld, only to re-emerge at dawn on the eastern horizon as the god *Re-harakhty*. This original myth was undoubtedly the work of the astronomer-priests of Annu, or Heliopolis, the Old Kingdom's cult centre for the worship of Re, situated in what is today just another fume-filled suburb of Cairo.

The Greek rendering of *Hor-em-akhet*, Horus-in-the-Horizon, is Harmakhis, the name by which the Sphinx was more commonly known in classical times, and this blatant geomythic connection between the equinoctial sunrise, the double horizon and the Great

Sphinx probably accounts for why the Giza plateau was once known as *Akhet Khufu*, Khufu's Horizon. Other names for the Sphinx were *hu*, meaning 'the protector'; Khepera, a form of Re as the scarab beetle, and *Rwty*, or *Ruty*, 'the Leonine One', who is the fierce guardian and protector 'on the far north of the underworld'.[8] In around the year AD 1200, a noted Arab named el-Latif claimed that the great carved lion was known to his people as *Abou'l Hôl*, the 'Father of Terrors', a connection perhaps with its role as the omnipotent guardian of the Giza plateau.[9]

Such was the known, accepted story of the Sphinx, but it seemed that certain more left-field scholars had other ideas on its origin – ideas which, if proved to be correct, would mean the world was going to have to rethink everything it had ever been taught about the foundations of the Egyptian civilization.

The Greatest Riddle

Over the years many open-minded individuals have pointed out clear anomalies in respect of the traditionally held views concerning the origins and dating of the Sphinx. For instance, just by looking at the carved face one can see how out of proportion it is to the rest of the head, while the head itself is quite obviously too small when compared against the rest of the body. Another problem has been identifying the Sphinx. Detective Frank Domingo, a New York Police Department senior forensic expert, made a detailed profile study of the monument's face and concluded that it barely resembled Khafre's known features, showing more an African or Nubian Negroid face than an Egyptian Pharaoh.[10] Might the monument's present face have replaced a much earlier one of, say, a lion, a god or a goddess perhaps? Remember how in Greek myth the Theban Sphinx that posed the famous riddle possessed a female gender.

A further anomaly regarding the date of the Great Sphinx is the stone stela recording the dream of Thutmose IV, which still rests up against the monument's breast, between its great paws. Towards the bottom of the stela, the lines have eroded heavily, but just visible is Thutmose's praise 'to Un-nefer . . . Khaf[re] . . . the statue made for Atum and *Hor-em-akhet*'.[11] Interpretation of this line has led to much speculation in Egyptological circles, for it is possible that Thutmose is not praising Khafre for building the Sphinx, but for *clearing away the sand* from around its body, exactly as he himself had done 1,100 years later. Respected Egyptologists such as J. H. Breasted and Gaston Maspero endorsed this controversial interpretation.[12]

Adding further weight to this curious enigma is the so-called Inventory Stela found during the mid nineteenth century by the French Egyptologist Auguste Mariette (1821–81) in a minor temple dedicated to the goddess Isis, east of the Great Pyramid. It records how Khufu had apparently discovered a temple dedicated to Isis (probably not the same one) 'by the side of the cavity of the Sphinx, or on the northwest of the House of Osiris, Lord of Rosta'. Here the Sphinx is given the name 'Horemakhet . . . Guardian of the Atmosphere, who guides the winds with his gaze'.[13] Further on, the text states that the king went on a tour to see the Sphinx and a nearby great sycamore tree struck by lightning – the same bolt that had supposedly severed part of the monument's *nemes*-headdress (i.e. the back of its head). Since Khufu was Khafre's father, this clearly implies that the leonine monument had already been in place during Khufu's reign. There is, however, a problem, for the white limestone stela – currently in the Cairo Museum – dates only to the Twenty-sixth Dynasty, *c.* 664–525 BC, i.e. during the Late Dynastic Period, yet it *is* thought to be a copy of an original Old Kingdom inscription. It should also be remembered that the Egyptians meticulously copied original royal inscriptions and texts, translating them into the textual grammar of the period.

By far the most convincing evidence for the monument's enormous antiquity is the severe erosion clearly visible on the Sphinx's worn body, as well as on the walls of the surrounding enclosure, and on the remains of the Temple of the Sphinx and the nearby Valley Temple. This distinctive weathering shows a subjection to the elements far beyond many of the neighbouring monuments, temples and tombs supposedly constructed at the same time as the Sphinx and its accompanying temples, using the same white limestone.

By Wind or Water?

John Anthony West, a maverick Egyptologist and successful author, was the first person publicly to draw attention to these uncharacteristic weathering effects with the publication in 1979 of his essential work *Serpent in the Sky: The High Wisdom of Ancient Egypt*. His theory, inspired originally by various observations made by the French mathematician and philosopher, R. A. Schwaller de Lubicz, was that the deep horizontal scars found along the Sphinx's body were caused not by wind and sand erosion, as had always been assumed, but by water.

His arguments for this conclusion were simple.[14] For almost all of the past 4,500 years the Sphinx and its accompanying temples have been covered by sand. This means that they would have been protected from the *khamsin*, or desert wind, which periodically gusts from the south. If the erosion *had* been caused by wind and sand, then one should expect to find heavier erosion on the south side of the Sphinx. This is simply not the case; the horizontal gullies are evenly placed around the whole of the body. Similar rock erosion can be recognized on cliff faces at Abydos, Luxor and at other exposed locations along the Nile. These effects have been unanimously attributed by geologists to water erosion, caused at a time when heavy rains persisted in ancient Egypt.

Why, then, were almost identical signs of erosion found on the Sphinx?

John Anthony West championed this new interpretation of the weathering on the Sphinx for ten years, although he would have to wait until 1989 before being given the chance to put his water erosion theory to the test. It was in this year that West managed to secure the services of a qualified geologist named Dr Robert Schoch, Associate Professor of Science at Boston University. He holds a doctorate in geology and geophysics, attained at Yale University, and is a specialist in the effects of weather erosion on rocks. Dr Schoch, working under the auspices of West, began an in-depth study of not only the Sphinx but also its rectangular enclosure and the limestone blocks used in the construction of the nearby Sphinx and Valley Temples. After only a relatively short time, the geologist became convinced that the deep horizontal gouges and vertical fissures seen on all these rock-faces, especially the Sphinx itself, were indeed 'classic textbook' examples of water erosion induced by rain precipitation. Evidence of more obvious wind erosion could be seen on nearby Old Kingdom tombs that were dated by conventional Egyptologists to the very same age as the Sphinx, yet this weathering was entirely different. Sand carried by harsh winds scours out softer layers of rock, leaving much harder layers intact. This gives a distinct, sharp profile with evenly spaced pitted areas, entirely unlike heavy rain erosion, which creates a smooth, undulating profile that curves into the rock's softer layers, and also leaves deep vertical fissures as the water flows down the rock surface.

In argument against Schoch's claims, first published in an edition of the speculative Egyptological magazine *KMT* in the summer of 1992,[15] an archaeologist, Mark Lehner, who is considered to be an authority on the Sphinx, argued one major point. He claimed that although the weathering of the Sphinx might well have been caused by water, it had occurred in Old Kingdom times and was simply the result of poor-quality rock being used to carve the monument. He drew attention to the nearby Old Kingdom tombs that had clearly been weathered by wind and sand, and pointed out that these were carved from much harder white limestone. If this were so, then it brought Schoch's theory into serious disrepute. Seizing the opportunity to prove whether Lehner's views were indeed correct, a BBC-backed *Timewatch* team, who were collaborating at the time with an American production company to screen a documentary on Schoch and West's findings, conducted their own independent survey of the geology around the Sphinx enclosure. They discovered that the sand-beaten tombs of the Old Kingdom were carved from exactly the same rock as the body of the nearby Sphinx.[16]

Schoch was right and Lehner wrong.

Few Egyptologists have taken up the gauntlet and attempted to shoot down Schoch's discoveries, since very few of them are qualified in the field of geology. Those who *have* looked into the matter have so far been unable to come up with a suitable explanation for the presence of water erosion on monuments found on the Giza plateau. Furthermore, Schoch received a major boost of confidence when he presented his findings at the 1991 Geological Society of America's convention held in San Diego. This event is a forum to air new ideas in geology, and the delegates are always quick to express their opinions on the lectures presented. Yet not only could they find no obvious flaw in Schoch's thesis, but no less that 275 of the attending geologists offered help with the on-going project![17]

So for the moment it was game, set and match to Schoch.

In his published report, Schoch concluded that the Sphinx, its surrounding enclosure, along with the Sphinx and Valley Temples, must have been carved from the limestone bedrock during a period in history when there were sufficient rains to cause such adverse water erosion, and these had not been present for at least five thousand years. After due assessment of the available evidence, Schoch had placed the construction of the Sphinx between 7000 and 5000 BC, during the so-called neolithic subpluvial when it rained almost constantly in the eastern Sahara. In support of his proposals, Schoch pointed out that during this same time-frame protoneolithic communities, such as those at Çatal Hüyük in central Anatolia and Jericho in Palestine, were engaged in sophisticated building projects. These would have necessitated not just individual skills, but communal leadership similar to that which must have been necessary first to remove the huge stone blocks from the enclosure, then to carve the Sphinx as the extracted stone blocks were used to construct the Sphinx and Valley Temples.

Made in the Age of Leo

More recent research has pushed back the age of the Sphinx to at least 10,500 BC, some 2,500 years earlier than the estimations of Schoch and West. A construction engineer and Egyptologist, Robert Bauval, working alongside the investigative journalist and author Graham Hancock, has recently published details of an extensive survey concerning the complex astro-archaeology of the Giza plateau. In their important book, *Keeper of Genesis*, Bauval and Hancock convincingly demonstrate that the Sphinx's easterly orientation towards the equinoctial sunrise hints at an importance far greater than Egyptologists could previously ever have

Fig. 17. Nineteenth-century illustration showing the Great Pyramid, the Sphinx and the still half-buried Valley Temple. Does the Giza plateau conform to a precise ground-plan incorporating astro-mythic and geomythic data that preserves the date 10,500 BC? If so, then what do we know about the people who lived during this lost age of humanity?

imagined. They argue that the leonine monument was connected directly with the ancient Egyptians' understanding of precession, a celestial effect produced by the earth as it gently wobbles around its polar axis in a manner quite similar to the way a child's gyroscope or spinning top is seen slowly to sway when revolving at high speed.

This gentle wobble of the earth produces various visual effects, the most important of which is the phenomenon known to astronomers as precession. This is where the starry canopy, or firmament, appears to shift its position relative to the path of the sun at a rate of 1° of a 360° circle every seventy-two years. Since prehistoric times, this astronomical cycle has been observed and recorded by noting which constellation rises just before the sun each spring (or vernal) equinox. Twelve major constellations, corresponding to what we know today as the signs of the zodiac, mark this 25,920-year celestial merry-go-round, each one taking a period of 2,160 years to cross the equinoctial sunrise line before being replaced by the next sign, and so on until all twelve have completed a full 360° circle in reverse order – hence the term 'precession', or backwards motion.[18] So instead of Capricorn following Sagittarius, or Aquarius following Capricorn, as they do in the conventional yearly zodiac – Capricorn follows Aquarius, Sagittarius follows Capricorn, and so forth. During our current age it is the constellation of Pisces that rises with the sun at the vernal equinox, and soon this will have shifted enough to make way for the constellation of Aquarius to guide us through the next period of 2,160 years; hence the well-known phase 'the age of Aquarius'.

With all this in mind, Bauval and Hancock felt it beyond coincidence that the Great Sphinx should face directly towards the point on the eastern horizon where the current precessional sign appears each spring equinox, just before the sun itself rises. Since the Egyptian astronomer-priests were meticulous in their use of celestial alignments and star-related symbolism, the presence of a leonine creature marking the equinoctial sunrise line would appear to suggest that the Sphinx was constructed at a time when the constellation of Leo rose with the sun on the spring equinox – in other words, during 'the age of Leo'. There is a slight problem to this, however, for the last age of Leo took place between 10,970 and 8810 BC.[19]

It was an extraordinary theory, and to prove it correct it would be necessary to establish whether or not the ancient Egyptians really were aware of precession, most astronomers assuming that the Greeks developed the idea in the second century BC, through a combination of long-term observations of the celestial sphere and a few, fairly simple mathematical calculations. This may indeed have been the case, but research by an American Egyptologist, Jane B. Sellers, in addition to new findings by Bauval and Hancock, has made it clear that the Egyptians were not merely *aware* of precession, they also acknowledged its presence in mythical events[20] and incorporated its slowly shifting cycle into the design and orientation of the pyramids.[21] Furthermore, a connection between the

Great Pyramid and the precessional cycle had been suspected as early as the mid nineteenth century,[22] while in 1907 an Egyptian scholar and astro-mythologist named Gerald Massey concluded in an extraordinary work entitled *Ancient Egypt the Light of the World* that the Sphinx's association with the age of Leo had given rise to the monument's mythical connection with both the Aker and *Hor-em-akhet*, Horus-in-the-Horizon.[23] Indeed, Massey had no qualms in asserting that: '. . . we may date the Sphinx as a monument which was reared by these great (Egyptian) builders and thinkers, who lived so largely out of themselves, some thirteen thousand years ago.'[24]

If the Great Sphinx really was built by an unknown culture during the age of Leo, as Bauval and Hancock assert, then it had been accomplished by a race which possessed an acute knowledge of astronomy and saw an incredible significance in marking out great cycles of time. And as if this were not enough to contend with, then the fact that the huge cyclopean blocks removed from its rectangular enclosure had been used to construct the nearby Sphinx and Valley Temples meant that these people possessed the skill and ability to build colossal edifices at a time when the rest of the Old World was striving to learn the very basics of civilized society. Moreover, if we were to accept this, then these two temples were almost certainly not their only architectural achievements. At the Predynastic cult centre at Abydos in Upper Egypt there is another cyclopean monument sunk deep into the earth and built in exactly the same style as the Giza temples.

Here I am referring to the enigmatic Osireion constructed of massive granite monoliths lined on top with enormous stone lintels. At the base of its central hall is a spring that permits the water-table to flood its lower levels, obviously to give the site an aquatic aspect that was carefully incorporated into its design.[25] In this capacity, the Osireion must have functioned very much like the Abzu pool found beneath the pre-Sumerian temple at Eridu in Lower Iraq. The Osireion's presence was remarked upon by the Greek geographer Strabo (60 BC–AD 20), following a visit to Abydos in the first century BC, although confirmation of its existence did not come until excavations began at the nearby temple complex of the Pharaoh Seti I (1309–1291 BC) during 1903. It was

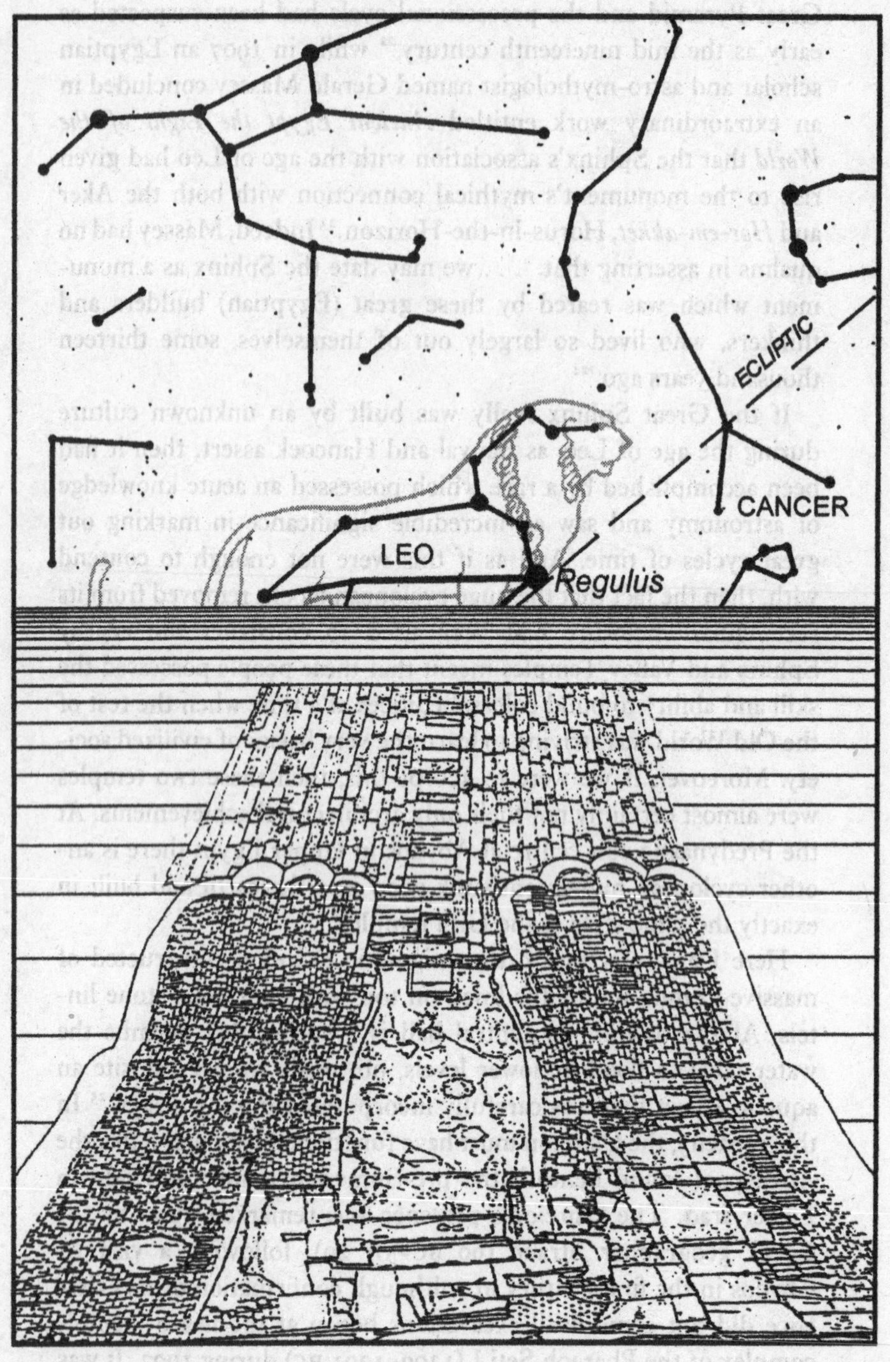
ECLIPTIC
CANCER
LEO
Regulus

not, however, fully exposed until work was resumed at Abydos between 1912 and 1914 by Professor Naville of the Egypt Exploration Fund. Only then did the full extent of this 'gigantic construction of about 100 feet in length and 60 in width' become apparent.[26]

Naville compared the structure's architectural style with that of Giza's Valley Temple, which showed 'it to be of the same epoch when building was made with enormous stones without any ornament'.[27] This led him to conclude that it was 'characteristic of the oldest architecture in Egypt. I should even say that we may call it the most ancient stone building in Egypt.'[28] Yet the Egyptological community back-tracked on their earlier announcements after excavations recommenced at Abydos under the leadership of Henry Frankfurt between 1925 and 1930. Among the minor finds he made in connection with the Osireion was a cartouche of Seti I on a granite dovetail above the main entrance into the central hall, as well as a few minor finds which linked the Pharaoh's name to the interior of the building. As a consequence, the building was henceforth seen as contemporary with Seti's reign.[29]

The likelihood that Seti I had incorporated this archaic structure, devoid of any other inscriptions, into his own temple complex, probably because of its immense antiquity and sanctity, was never even considered by the Egyptological community. Only Margaret Murray, the anthropologist and Egyptologist who helped to uncover the Osireion during the early stages, remained convinced that its great stone blocks were 'of the style of the Old Kingdom', *c.* 2700–2159 BC, and that the decoration was added later by Seti. In her opinion, this strange structure with its own reservoir was built 'for the celebration of the mysteries of Osiris', who is probably Egypt's oldest deity.[30]

Fig. 18. Conceptual view from the head of the Great Sphinx along the line of the paws to the eastern horizon as it would have looked shortly before the sun rose on the vernal equinox 9220 BC – the date suggested for a universal deluge by the ninth-century Coptic manuscript entitled *Abou Hormeis*. The presence of the Sphinx's leonine imagery makes sense *only* if it was constructed during the precessional age of Leo.

A similar controversy has surrounded the dating of the enigmatic Valley Temple. Because a single statue of Khafre and a lone cartouche were discovered within its enormous granite interior, it has been credited to the reign of Khafre, *c.* 2550 BC, and is therefore seen as contemporary with the construction of the Second Pyramid. Yet there seemed every good reason to place the limestone outer walls (but not the granite interior) of this weather-beaten structure in exactly the same time-frame as the Sphinx itself – in other words, it was at least 10,000 years old. A similar age would therefore have to be attributed to the Osireion at Abydos.

Quite naturally the Egyptologists can never accept such an immense antiquity for any man-made structure, for to do so would mean disregarding everything they have stood for in respect of Egyptian history. This is despite the fact that some of their pioneering predecessors were far more open-minded in this respect.[31]

Yet such distant dates are not so incredible as they may at first seem. By 7500 BC the protoneolithic inhabitants of Jericho had constructed a huge stone tower amid colossal fortifications that included a deep, rock-cut ditch. Jericho, it should be noted, is only three hundred miles from Giza.

Personally, I have no problem with accepting the possibility that the Sphinx, as well as the Sphinx and Valley Temples and the Osireion at Abydos, might well constitute the last remaining evidence of an elder culture that had thrived in Egypt sometime between 10,970 and 8810 BC, during the last age of Leo. Yet just accepting this proposal still told me little about the people behind these monuments. Neither did it tell me whether this mysterious race could have had any tangible link with the underground cities of Cappadocia, or the proposed Watcher culture of Kurdistan. All I had established so far was that evidence of long-headed individuals of great stature, who had belonged to an aristocratic group, had been found among the Predynastic cemeteries excavated at Abydos by Jacques de Morgan in 1897, and that these matched anatomical remains unearthed at the earliest Sumerian grave-sites. Could it be possible that representatives of this elite race had been responsible, not only for the construction of Giza's leonine time-marker, as well as the country's cyclopean stone structures, but also for the initiation of the much later neolithic explosion in Kurdistan and the foundation of the earliest city-states of Mesopotamia?

Whoever the Sphinx builders were, they undoubtedly possessed architectural and engineering skills far beyond the capabilities of almost every culture that came afterwards, save perhaps the builders of the Fourth Dynasty pyramids (the construction date for which must remain fixed in this time-frame unless any new evidence suggests otherwise). Some of the stone blocks used in the building of the Valley Temple are 200 tons apiece,[32] and if it is borne in mind that there is hardly a crane today that could lift such a weight, then some idea of the effort needed to move extraordinary blocks of this size suddenly becomes apparent. This does not, of course, mean that such feats of engineering were impossible, only that this style of building construction was highly unusual for any period of Egyptian history.

What more could I learn about the ultimate destiny of this lost culture? There were very few strands to work with, other than the overt astronomical data that these people had evidently encoded into the Giza plateau itself, and this conspicuously proclaimed one specific time-frame – the age of Leo. What made this epoch so important to them, and why construct such an obviously leonine structure to mark a particular precessional age? Surely this advanced culture had not simply sculpted the Sphinx for devotional or ritualistic purposes alone. Why leave such a legacy to future humanity?

Egypt's elder culture was no longer around to provide me with any answers. It was possible, however, that they had passed on the real significance of the age of Leo and the true purpose of the Sphinx in allegorical stories that had been told around camp-fires until they were finally set down in written form during ancient times. Of course, they would by then have become highly abstract and distorted, yet a kernel of truth must have remained within them, and it was this that I needed to extract to discover the ultimate fate of those who had built the Great Sphinx.

Twenty-Three

KOSMOKRATOR

When the earth was a little younger, Saurid Ibn Salhouk, the king of Egypt – who lived three hundred years before the Great Flood – found that his slumber was constantly being disturbed by terrible nightmares. He saw that 'the whole earth was turned over', its inhabitants too. He saw men and women falling upon their faces and 'stars falling down and striking one another with a terrible noise'.[1] As a consequence, 'all mankind took refuge in terror'.[2]

These nightmares continued to trouble the good king, but for some time he concealed them, without telling another soul what he had seen. Finally, after one further night of misery, he summoned his chief priests, who came from all the provinces of Egypt. No less than 130 of them stood before him, the chief among them being the learned Almamon, or Aclimon.[3]

King Saurid related every detail of his curious nightmare, and before they offered their own opinions concerning this strange portent, each one consulted the altitude of the stars.[4] Upon returning they unanimously announced to the worried king that his nightmare foretold that first a great flood would cover the earth. Then a great fire would 'come from the direction of the constellation Leo'.[5] They assured him, however, that after these disasters 'the firmament would return to its former site'.[6]

'Will it come to our country?' the king asked.

They answered him honestly. 'Yes,' they said, 'and it will destroy it.'

Having accepted the future fate of his kingdom, Saurid decided that he would command the building of three wondrous pyramids as well as a very strong vault. All these were to be filled with 'the knowledge of the secret sciences', which included everything they had learned of astronomy, mathematics and geometry.[7] All this knowledge would remain concealed for those who would one day come and find these secret places.

This was the story recorded by various Arab and Coptic historians, including Ibn Abd Alhokm, who lived in the ninth century, and Al Masoudi, who died around AD 943; the latter having included it in his book *Fields of Gold – Mines of Gems*.[8] These accounts have no obvious equivalents in ancient Egyptian literature, while the king, Saurid Ibn Salhouk, has proved impossible to trace. He is not one of the Pharaohs accredited with having built the Pyramids of Giza during the Fourth Dynasty of Egyptian history.

The statement implying that 'the whole earth was turned over' – 'twisted around'[9] in one version – is teasingly significant. If the story does preserve some kind of allegorical representation of actual events, then these words clearly bore out Hapgood's idea of a shift in the earth's axis, leading to global catastrophes of the sort described in the tale. More intriguing, however, was the reference to the final cataclysm coming from 'the direction of the constellation of Leo.'

What could this possibly mean?

On an initial reading of this statement, one is tempted to imagine some kind of astronomical body, an asteroid or comet perhaps, breaking up on entry into the earth's atmosphere before raining down a shower of gaseous fireballs that consume everything in their path and leave a trail of death and destruction in their wake. Perhaps this is indeed what happened. More likely, however, is that this reference to a great fire coming specifically from the constellation of Leo relates, not to the area of the firmament where the constellation is placed in the sky, but to the time-period *in which these events took place* – in other words, during the age of Leo. This deduction would be completely in keeping with the geological upheavals and climatic changes now believed to have occurred during the eleventh, and possibly even right down to the tenth millennium BC.

There is also further tantalizing evidence of this specific link between the era of cataclysms and the precessional age of Leo. In a Coptic Christian manuscript translated into Arabic during the ninth century, entitled *Abou Hormeis*, it records that: 'The deluge was to take place when the heart of the Lion entered into the first minute of the head of Cancer.'[10] The 'heart of the Lion' was the name given in classical times to the star Regulus, Leo's 'royal star', which lies exactly on the ecliptic, the sun's perceived daily path through the sky. Since the constellation of Cancer follows Leo *only* in the precessional cycle (Leo *follows* Cancer in the yearly cycle), then this appears to confirm that these legends preserved, not just the memory of actual historical events, but also the time-frame in which they occurred.

At my request, electronics engineer Rodney Hale punched the astronomical information contained in the *Abou Hormeis* account into a computer using a Skyglobe 3.5 programme. With some degree of accuracy, he discovered that the last time Leo's 'royal star' would have risen and been visible on the eastern horizon just prior to the equinoctial sunrise was around 9220 BC.[11] When the star Regulus, the 'heart of the lion', no longer rose with the sun on the vernal equinox, this would have been seen by the astronomer-priests of Egypt as a signal that the age of Leo had come to an end, and that the age of Cancer was either about to commence or that it had already entered its 'first minute' of arc across the sky.[12] This information therefore suggested that the ninth-century Coptic manuscript was implying that a major deluge had occurred in the Middle East, either around or shortly after this date.

If all this was correct, then it seemed likely that Egypt's elder culture had come to associate the age of Leo with the aforementioned global catastrophes. Was it possible, therefore, that besides acting as a marker and guardian of the Giza complex, the Sphinx had been carved by these people as a firm reminder of the great cataclysms that took place during this troublesome epoch of human history? Might this also account for why the leonine guardian of the Giza plateau gained the title 'Father of Terrors'?

The Terrible Eye

Another possible insight into this perplexing mystery may be found in the myth cycles associated with the Egyptian goddess Sekhmet. She is described as 'the Mighty Lady, Mistress of Flame', and is depicted in Egyptian art with the head of a lion and the body of a woman. According to legend, Sekhmet is said to have had the power of the 'fierce scorching, and destroying heat of the sun's rays'. In one account she

took up her position on the head of her father Ra (or Re), and poured out from herself the blazing fire which scorched and consumed his enemies who came near, whilst at those who were some distance away she shot forth swift fiery darts which pierced through and through the fiends whom they struck.[13]

These passages are taken from the account of how Ra the sun god attempted to destroy humanity, because it saw him as 'too old', and as a consequence turned its back on his faith. In vengeance, the sun god summoned all the gods and asked them to assemble at the place where he 'performed creations'. He also told them to bring with them his terrible 'Eye', who was the goddess Sekhmet (sometimes named as Hathor). He then addressed Nu, the leader of the assembled gods, saying:

'O thou firstborn god, from whom I came into being, O ye gods [my] *ancestors, behold ye what mankind is doing, they who were created by thine Eye are uttering murmurs against me. Give me your attention, and seek ye out a plan for me, and I will not slay them until ye shall say* [what I am to do] *concerning it.'*[14]

Nu had then praised Ra, suggesting that his Eye destroy those who have 'uttered blasphemies against thee'. Yet in response Ra had exclaimed that mankind had already 'taken flight into the mountain'. In due course the Eye 'went forth and slew the people on the mountain'. Yet this slaughter became so terrible that Ra himself had been forced to intervene before the goddess caused the destruction of the entire human race. Sekhmet, however, would not listen, so Ra deposited a mixture of beer, blood and crushed mandrakes all over the earth. The lioness quickly became intoxicated by this powerful brew and as a consequence was unable to complete her mass genocide.[15]

Later on in the text, Ra summons Geb, the earth god, and tells him to keep watch over the 'snakes' (or worms) who have caused him strife and are in his territory, and that Geb's 'light' should find them in their 'holes', a reference to those who have taken flight and are now seeking refuge in caves and underground caverns. Ra then 'promises that he will give the men who have knowledge of words of power, dominion over them (the snakes), and that he will furnish them with spells and charms which shall draw them from their holes'.[16]

The idea of the fierce lioness's heavenly fire that consumes the earth is so similar to the events recorded by the Arab and Coptic writers concerning the great fire that came from the constellation of Leo, that the two quite separate traditions may once have shared a common origin. It must also be remembered that the Great Sphinx probably possessed a female gender, bringing these accounts even closer together.

Ra's destruction of the human race might well preserve in highly symbolic form the events which led to the close of the age of Leo. It also suggests that Egypt's elder culture was scattered far and wide as the fiery cataclysms were taking place. The story of how some of these people had first ascended a mountain, only to be blasted by fire, while others had hidden themselves in 'holes', seems to parallel the efforts made by the human race to escape these global cataclysms in folk-tales from other parts of the world. The intoxicating brew that prevented Sekhmet from destroying any more of the human race is surely a reference to some kind of subsequent deluge, perhaps the one that the Coptic *Abou Hormeis* manuscript said had occurred 'when the heart of the Lion entered into the first minute of the head of Cancer'.

Snakes in the Holes

Those who are said to have hidden away from the burning might of the terrible Eye by taking refuge in 'holes' are described as 'snakes'. After the fire has ceased, these individuals are hunted out by the light of Geb and the 'men who have knowledge of words of power', implying that these 'snakes' were not popular in certain quarters for having turned their backs on the cult of Ra. That they attempted to survive, and maybe succeeded in surviving, the onslaught of the devastating Eye by hiding in what would seem to have been underground places is very revealing. Could it be possible that these mixed-up tales are trying to say that at least some of

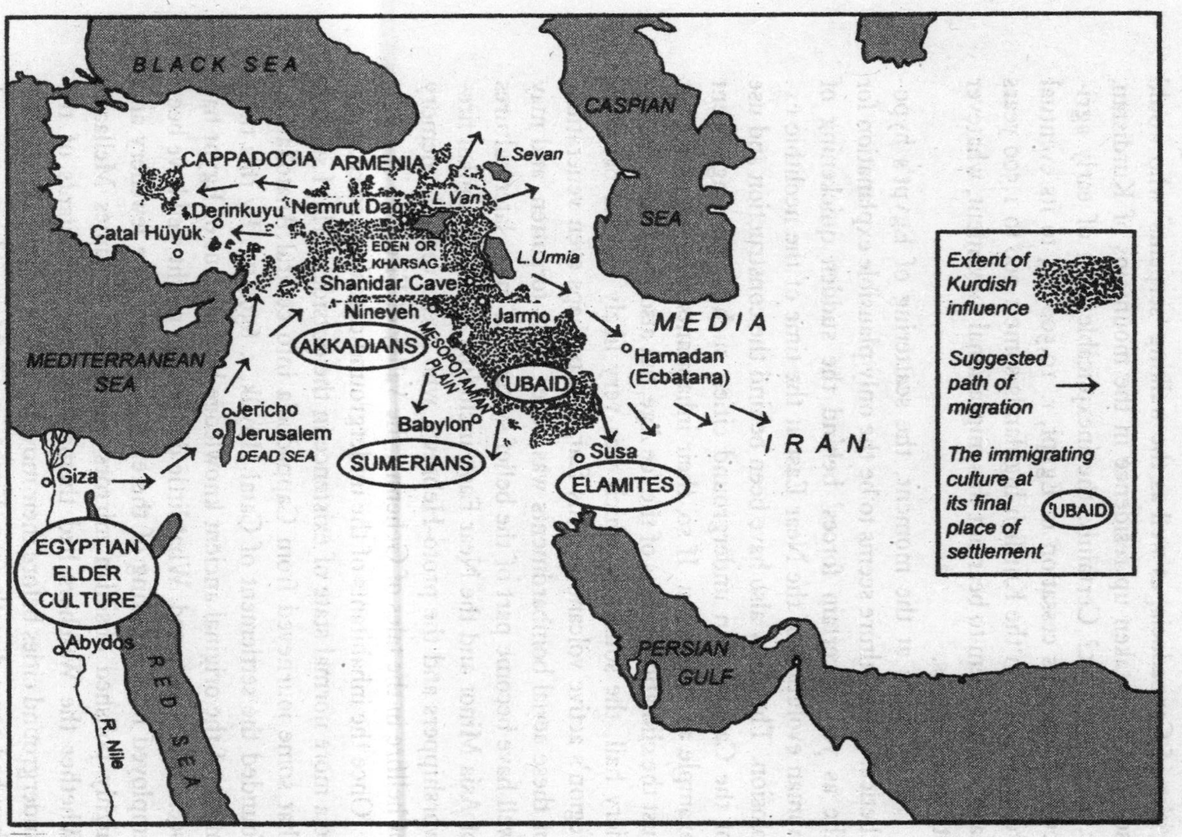
BLACK SEA
CAPPADOCIA
ARMENIA
L.Sevan
Derinkuyu
Nemrut Dağ
L.Van
Çatal Hüyük
EDEN OR KHARSAG
L.Urmia
Shanidar Cave
Nineveh
Jarmo
CASPIAN SEA
MEDIA
Hamadan (Ecbatana)
MEDITERRANEAN SEA
AKKADIANS
MESOPOTAMIAN PLAIN
'UBAID
Jericho
Jerusalem
DEAD SEA
Babylon
SUMERIANS
Susa
ELAMITES
IRAN
Giza
EGYPTIAN ELDER CULTURE
Abydos
RED SEA
R. Nile
PERSIAN GULF
Extent of Kurdish influence
Suggested path of migration
The immigrating culture at its final place of settlement
'UBAID

the former inhabitants of Egypt had escaped the global cataclysms by either going underground or ascending mountains? Might some of these 'snakes' have been the inhabitants of the underground cities of Cappadocia, as well as the walking 'serpents' who would seem to have taken up residence in the mountains of Kurdistan, *c.* 9500–9000 BC? Certainly, the inexplicable shift of early agriculture from its cessation in Egypt, *c.* 10,500 BC, to its eventual re-emergence in the Kurdish highlands some 1,000 to 1,500 years later, would seem to bear out this migrational movement, whatever its actual causes.

As it stands at the moment, the scattering of Egypt's hypothetical elder culture seems to be the only plausible explanation for the as yet 'uncertain forces' behind the sudden quickening of human evolution in the Near East at the time of the neolithic explosion. They may also have been behind the construction and use of the Cappadocian underground cities, such as the magnificent example at Derinkuyu. If so, their inhabitants were escaping, not just the climatic excesses of the Ice Age, but also the deadly rains of fiery hail, the source of which was very likely to have been the region's active volcanoes. This fear, and perhaps even veneration, of these aerial bombardments was never quite forgotten, and may well have become part of the belief systems of many later cultures of Asia Minor and the Near East, including the Indo-Iranian fire-worshippers and the proto-Hebrews, who preserved this memory of hellfire in the tales of Gehenna, the Valley of Fire.

Once the inhabitants of the underground domains had returned to a more normal state of existence in the outside world, I suspect that some journeyed from Cappadocia into central Anatolia and founded the settlement of Çatal Hüyük, *c.* 6500 BC. By this time much of the original ancient knowledge brought out of Egypt had been lost or distorted. What little did remain might well have been employed in the making of the extraordinary stone jewellery and highly polished obsidian mirrors unearthed by James Mellaart. Whether the Watchers had themselves been inhabitants of the underground cities before their move to higher ground, or whether they had come directly from Egypt, is uncertain. The memory of Yima's *var* in Iranian mythology points towards the first solution, which I am personally happy to accept.

Chart 3. SUGGESTED CHRONOLOGY OF EGYPT'S ELDER CULTURE AND THE PROPOSED WATCHER CULTURE OF KURDISTAN. *The dates are approximate only.*

c. 10,500–9500 BC
Decline of Egypt's elder culture during the age of Leo. The construction on the elevated plateau at Giza of the Sphinx monument, the Temple of the Sphinx and the Valley Temple before their eventual abandonment. The cessation of early agriculture by the Isnan Nilotic communities.

c. 9,500–9000 BC
Geological and climatic upheavals accompany the cessation of the Ice Age, including severe volcanic activity and mass flooding; diaspora of Egypt's elder culture to Asia Minor and Kurdistan. Construction of underground cities in Cappadocia to escape the final excesses of the Ice Age.

c. 9000 BC
Establishment of Dilman/Eden/Kharsag settlement around Lake Van in the Kurdish Highlands. This advanced shamanistic culture becomes the angels and Watchers of Judaic tradition, the *ahuras* of Iranian legend, and the Anannage of Sumero-Akkadian myth and legend.

c. 9000–8500 BC
The Shanidar cave on the Greater Zab is used for shamanistic practices involving goats' skulls, and the wings of bustards, eagles and vultures. Establishment of earliest protoneolithic settlements in Palestine and Syria, particularly at Jericho.

c. 8500–5500 BC
High-point of Watcher culture, which remains in virtual isolation in northern Kurdistan.

c. 6500–6000 BC
Height of Çatal Hüyük culture on the Anatolian plain, practising excarnation and an advanced form of death-trance shamanism that features the vulture. The Jarmo community flourishes in Upper Iraq, its direct contact with the fallen race being preserved as abstract serpentine art.

c. 5500–5000 BC

Gradual fragmentation of the Watcher colony into two opposing camps. One remains in isolation within the Kurdish highlands, while the other emerges on to the surrounding plains of Armenia, Iran and Mesopotamia. This new subculture is variously remembered as the Nephilim of Enochian and Dead Sea literature, the *daevas* in Iranian mythology and the *Edimmu* in Assyrio-Babylonian myth and legend. Foundation of first settled communities on the Mesopotamian plains, the earliest being Eridu in *c.* 5500 BC. Possible time-frame of biblical patriarchs.

c. 5000–4000 BC

The 'Ubaid culture come down off the Zagros mountains of Iraq and Iran to establish themselves at various sites in Upper and Lower Iraq. They inherit the serpentine art of the Jarmo people and, like the Watchers, their totems include the goat, the serpent and the vulture. A 'second' flood strikes the Mesopotamian plains in the form of a series of localized inundations. The memory of these events is confused with much earlier traditions concerning a deluge accompanying the cessation of the last Ice Age, *c.* 9500–9000 BC. They are remembered as the 'Flood of Noah' by the Yezidis of Kurdistan.

c. 4000–3000 BC

The gradual emergence of city-states on the Mesopotamian plains, perhaps under the influence of the Anannage, the Sumero-Akkadian name given to the Watchers.

c. 3000–2000 BC

Continued influence of Anannage/Watchers over the Sumero-Akkadian city-states. This was recorded either as contact with gods and goddesses, generally through the Sacred Marriage ceremony, or through battles with demonic bird-men, like those encountered in the Kutha tablet. Kings descended from the Anannage/Watchers are granted deification, or are looked upon as part-demon. A similar contact takes place in Media and Iran. Final fragmentation of the fallen race.

Guardian of Infinite Time

The Egyptian elder culture's apparent obsession with the measurement of great cycles of time, from the point of First Creation right down to their own epoch, would seem to have been inherited by the Watchers. If the accounts of Enoch's visits to the seven heavens are in any way based on actual fact, then it would appear that the Watchers possessed an acute understanding of astronomical time-cycles. Tentative evidence can also be found in Enochian literature for astro-mythology and precessional data.[17] The Watchers would seem to have passed on this complex astronomical information to the various cultures that eventually developed across western and central Asia. This included highly symbolic myths relating directly to the precessional time-cycle and the significance of the age of Leo, as is very possibly evidenced in Persia.

During the Sassanian, or second empire, period (AD 226–651) of Persian history, there existed a very dominant form of Zoroastrianism known as Zurvanism, or fatalism. It revolved around a great god named Zurvan, a word meaning 'fate' or 'fortune', who was seen as the *genius*, or intelligence, of *Zrvan Akarana* (Pahlavi *Zurvan i Akanarak*), 'infinite time'.[18]

The principal creation myth of Zurvanism ran as follows:

In the beginning, only Zurvan existed. Then for a period of a thousand years he sacrificed *barsom*-twigs in the hope of achieving a son who would rule heaven and earth. At the end of this time he mixed together fire of the air and water of the earth[19] to produce twins – Ormuzd (Ahura Mazda) and Ahriman (Angra Mainyu), who represented light and darkness, or good and evil. To the first to be born the great father promised dominion over the earth for 9,000 years.[20]

On learning of Zurvan's promise, Ahriman immediately broke free of the cosmic womb and approached his father. Yet on seeing that the child was dark and stinking, the great god realized that he was not the rightful heir. Ormuzd then was born, and on seeing that he was radiant with light, Zurvan knew that he was to be the true ruler of both heaven and earth. Yet because of his earlier pact with the first-born, he would have to grant Ahriman dominion over the earth for 9,000 years. During this time, Ormuzd was made high priest in heaven alone – and only afterwards was he able to reign supreme.

It is a simple story, but one that encodes extremely important cosmological data. The reference to 9,000 years appears to denote the period of time the Zurvanites believed that the dark forces – personified as Ahriman and his *daevic* offspring – ruled the world before the light of Ormuzd took control of both heaven and earth. If this archaic tradition dealt with actual and not simply metaphorical time, then when were these mythical events considered to have taken place?

The answer is simple.

The 9,000 years undoubtedly referred to the time-period immediately *prior* to the coming of Zoroaster, who was, of course, seen as having vanquished the rule of Angra Mainyu, his *daevic* race and, of course, the *daeva*-worshippers during his lifetime. Since we know that a figure of 258 years before the fall of the Persian empire in 330 BC was generally given as the date for the coming of Zoroaster, i.e. 588 BC, the Zurvanite time-frame implied that Ahriman had begun his dominion over the earth in 9588 BC.

This same approximate time-frame is confirmed by the chronology given in the ninth-century *Bundahishn* text, which states that the first millennium had begun on a date calculated by Zoroastrian scholars as 9630 BC.[21] In Avestan literature dating to the Sassanian period, a figure of 9,000 years is *also* given as the amount of time (3 × 3,000 years) that Ahura Mazda and Angra Mainyu struggled for supremacy over the world.[22]

The coincidence of these dates to the time-scale of the global cataclysms that accompanied the end of the last Ice Age, as well as Plato's reference to 9600 BC as the date when Atlantis submerged, and, of course, the suggested time-frame of 9500–9000 BC for the establishment of the Watcher culture in Kurdistan, cannot be overlooked.

Had the Zoroastrians and Zurvanites been privy to a hidden tradition preserving the approximate foundation date of Iranian chronology – perhaps the point of genesis of the Iranian race in the *Airyana Vaejah*, their mythical homeland? More importantly, did the Zurvanite creation myth preserve the fact that the *daevic* race – in other words, the Watchers – had entered the scene around 9600 BC?

Ormuzd and his twin brother Ahriman are said to have been created out of fire of the air and water of the earth. Surely this is an abstract reference to the conflagration and flood that supposedly accompanied the cessation of the last Ice Age. If so, then it implied that the twin deities of the Zurvan myth had been born out of this age of global catastrophes, just as the Phoenix of Graeco-Egyptian legend was supposed to have risen anew from the ashes of its funeral pyre at the commencement of each new age. The necessity for two opposing forces, one ruling heaven and the other ruling earth, is perhaps yet another allegory concerning the clear split in the ranks between those Watchers, or *ahuras*, who remained loyal to heaven, and those, i.e. the *daevas*, who decided to take their chances among the developing peoples of the Near East.

The Lion-headed God

There is an even closer link between Iranian myth and the global events surrounding the age of Leo. One of the principal animal forms of Angra Mainyu is the lion, and this association is personified no better than in the mysterious lion-headed figure once venerated in the dark subterranean temples dedicated to the god Mithras. Life-sized statues of this winged deity show it with the body of a human male, a pair of keys in one hand and either the earth or the cosmic egg beneath its feet. Coiled around its torso is a snake – its head rising up over the top of the mane (or sometimes shown entering the mouth of the lion), while studded either on to its chest or carved in an arc above its head are the twelve signs of the zodiac.

Mithraism emerged into the limelight of classical history during the first century BC. According to Plutarch (50–120 AD), the pirates of Cilicia, a country in Asia Minor, conducted 'secret mysteries' to Mithra on Mount Olympus. He added that these strange rites had been 'originally instituted by them'.[23] The cult's rise to prominence during this era may well have been influenced by the alliance forged between the Cilician pirates and Mithridates IV, the king of Pontus, a country in north-eastern Asia Minor, whose personal name meant 'given by Mithra' – Mithra being the deity who judged the souls after death in the Magian religion.[24] Mithridates' greatest ally, however, had been his son-in-law Tigran the Great, the king of Armenia, with whom he had driven the Romans out of Cappadocia and Phrygia in 88 BC. A great number of Cilicians had been persuaded by Tigran to live in the fortress of Tigranakert, south of Lake Van, and it is extremely likely that these people introduced Mithraism into the city (see Chapter Fourteen).

The roots of Mithraism are obscure, but it is thought to have been a revitalized form of a mystery cult involving the Greek god Perseus, which had thrived in the Cilician city of Tarsus during the first century BC.[25] Perseus' attributes had been combined with those of the Iranian god Mithra, and through this merging of the two deities a hybrid god named Mith*ras* had been born.[26] Both Perseus and Mithras were depicted in classical art wearing the Phrygian cap, or the cap of Hades, which had been adopted as an important symbol of the Mithraic faith. Perseus, it must be remembered, was said to have founded the Magi priesthood as guardians of the 'sacred immortal fire', and was also looked upon by the Persian race as its progenitor.[27] Scholars are in no doubt that the development of Mithraism was influenced both by the Magi and Zoroastrian priesthoods, while the Kurdish scholar Mehrdad Izady is convinced that the cult owes much to the angel-worshipping religions of Kurdistan.[28]

Who, or what, did the cult's lion-headed god actually represent? The worshippers of Mithras have left us with very few clues in this respect, although a Mithraic scholar named Howard Jackson managed to sum up the figure's place in the cult by observing that:

> *The most common attributes which the* [lion-headed] *deity possesses suffice to identify it as what late antique texts often term a* kosmokrator, *an astrologically conditioned embodiment of the world-engendering and world-ruling Power generated by the endless revolution of all the wheels of the celestial dynamo.*[29]

In other words the lion-headed deity played exactly the same role as Zurvan – it was seen as the controller of infinite time. Furthermore, another Mithraic scholar named David Ulansey made an in-depth study of this deity and came to the conclusion that it was looked upon by cult worshippers as the 'personification of the force responsible for the precession of the equinoxes'.[30] This leonine form was therefore believed to regulate the movement of the stars during the 25,920-year precessional cycle, immediately linking it with the Great Sphinx, which had apparently acted in a very similar capacity on the elevated plateau at Giza.

Franz Cumont, a well-known nineteenth-century scholar of Mithraism, linked the lion-headed deity of Mithraism directly with the great god Zurvan, the *genius* of infinite time.[31] This association, however, has been seriously contested by modern-day academics, and instead the leonine figure is now thought to represent Ahriman – the evil principle of Zurvanism.[32] Should this prove to be the case, then it would conform perfectly with the Zurvanite view that Ahriman had been given dominion over the earth around 9600 BC, i.e. during the precessional age of Leo. This, of course, is also the approximate time-frame in which the apparent survivors of the Egyptian elder race had established their colony in the Near East – an event which had perhaps inspired the commencement of the first millennium in Iranian chronology.

Could it possibly be that, because the inheritors of this astromythology provided by the Egyptian settlers somehow misunderstood the nature of cosmic precession, they had continued to see the lion as the *kosmokrator*, or regulator of time, even after the age of Leo gave way to the age of Cancer? So instead of evolving their mythological data to include the symbols of the subsequent precessional ages, these people had remained stuck in a groove that preserved the significance of the age of Leo right down until the emergence of Zoroastrianism in the first millennium BC. After this date, the leonine *kosmokrator* would appear to have been downgraded from its role as controller of fate and regulator of infinite time to the evil principle of the Iranian religion, its place being taken by Zurvan himself.

Could this be the true origin behind the creation myth of Zurvan tradition?

If it was, then it pointed towards a direct connection between the Egyptian elder culture's obsession with the precessional cycle during the age of Leo, and the most distant ancestors of the Iranian race. Yet the fact that knowledge of the lion-headed *kosmokrator* had been best preserved by the cult of Mithras hinted at the probability that they must have been privy to a hidden tradition unavailable to the Magi and Zoroastrian priesthoods of the first millennium BC. So from where might this secret knowledge have come?

The mystery cult surrounding the god Perseus, the wearer of the conical-shaped Phrygian cap, may well provide an answer. As I had already discovered, when E. S. Drower visited the Yezidi's secret cavern at Ras al-'Ain, close to the Iraqi-Syrian border, during 1940, her guide, Sitt Gulé, had pointed out strange carvings on the walls. They showed bearded personages wearing conical caps, who sat in concave frames, similar to the lotus thrones of Tibetan tradition (see Chapter Thirteen). Could it be that these wall-carvings depicted the true givers of knowledge and wisdom to the first Kurdish races? Might they show direct descendants of the original colony of Egyptian elders who had established themselves in the region sometime between *c.* 9500 and 9000 BC? Were they also the creators not only of the Magian and Zurvan faiths of Persia, but also of the angel-worshipping cults? Certainly, we know that the Yaresan revere the lion and the dragon (or serpent) as the key-holders and guardians of the first and fifth heavens, through which the human soul has to pass on its way to the heavenly abode.[33] Had these mysterious conical-cap people gone on to provide the worshippers of the god Perseus, the traditional founder both of the Magi priesthoods and the Persian race, with intimate knowledge concerning the leonine keeper of infinite time?

On the floor of the hidden cavern shown to Mrs Drower at Ras al-'Ain were deep grooves carved into the polished stone floor. They were arranged to form 'an oblong with twelve small round depressions, placed six a side'. Mrs Drower identified the design as some kind of 'gaming board', but in my opinion the round depressions represented the twelve signs of the zodiac and, by virtue of this, the precessional cycle of 25,920 years. If so, then what type of ritual practices might the conical-cap people have conducted in this secluded cave of immense antiquity? Did they observe the movement of the precessional cycle from this place of great retreat? What other cultures did they influence?

And what was their ultimate fate? Perhaps we can never know the answers.

The Theft of Fate

In Zurvanism, Ahriman differs from the evil principle in orthodox Zoroastrianism in that he is not considered to have been inherently evil. He chooses to be this way, and as an example of his wicked powers he immediately creates the peacock.[34] This seemed like an absurd example of his apparent abilities. Why should he have wanted to create the peacock over and above anything else? The Yezidi revere the peacock as the symbol of *Melek Taus*, or *Melek el Kout*, the Greatest Angel, although this faith did not take its final form until the thirteenth century. The Zurvan religion had been established at least several hundred years beforehand. Since the Peacock Angel would appear to have been an abstract personification of the Watchers' influence in Kurdistan, this once again hinted at the enormous antiquity of these obscure myths and legends.

The leonine *kosmokrator* and its association with the Watchers of Kurdistan may also be preserved in the shape of the Simurgh, which was said to have been half lion, half eagle (or vulture). In Zoroastrian literature of the Sassanian period it was said to have sat upon the Tree of All Remedies, also known as the Tree of All Seeds, which was located in the middle of the mythical Vourukasha Sea (see Chapter Eleven). When it 'alights upon the branches of the tree it breaks off the thorns and twigs and sheds the seed therefrom. And when it soars aloft a thousand twigs shoot from the trees.'[35] Imagery of this type refers quite specifically to the passage of time and the movement of the starry firmament around the cosmic axis – the thousand twigs symbolizing a thousand years, the seeds representing stars, and so on.[36] Did the legends surrounding this mythical bird therefore also preserve knowledge of the precessional cycle and the age of Leo?

And if we include the Simurgh in this formula, we cannot forget that other half lion, half eagle – the Imdugud, or Anzu, of Mesopotamian myth and legend (see Chapter Sixteen). This monstrous creature was said to have stolen the Tablets of Destiny from the god Enlil (Ellil in Akkadian), which, when in its possession, gave 'him power over the Universe as controller of the fates of all',[37] enough to endanger 'the stability of civilization'.[38] Saying that the Imdugud had become 'controller of the fates of all', aligned it directly with the figure of Zurvan, who was also the controller of 'fate' or 'fortune'. So, in addition to its proposed connection with the Watchers, might the story of the Imdugud refer to the 'theft', or revealment, of hidden knowledge concerning the precessional time-cycle, which was seen by the Zurvanites as ruling over earthly 'destiny'?

Starry Numbers

The Imdugud's Indian counterpart, the half giant, half eagle named Garuda, was said to have stolen not the Tablets of Destiny but the moon goblet containing the Ambrosia, Amrita or nectar of the gods. Did this theft relate to astro-mythology in some way? It is difficult to say; however, it *is* known that the Brahmans of India possessed an age-old system of measuring extremely long periods of time spanning millions of years. This system would appear to have been based on a profound knowledge of the precessional cycle.[39] Immensely long time-cycles, matching those of the Brahminic system, are also found in the writings of the Babylonian priest and scribe Berossus, *c.* 260 BC, as well as in a fragment of text accredited to the Greek writer Hesiod, *c.* 907 BC, where they are symbolized by the mythical Phoenix.[40]

Had all this knowledge been gained from the Watchers of Kurdistan, or had it come from Egyptian elders who may well have settled elsewhere in the world after the cataclysmic events of the eleventh and tenth millennia BC?

Allusions to the 25,920-year precessional cycle can also be detected in the heavenly architecture outlined in a Manichaean gospel of the third century entitled 'The Myth of the Soul'. Chapter Eleven, for example, reads as follows:

Now for every sky he made twelve Gates with their Porches high and wide, every one of the Gates opposite its pair, and over every one of the

Porches wrestlers in front of it. Then in those Porches in every one of its Gates he made six Lintels, and in every one of the Lintels thirty Corners, and twelve Stones in every Corner. Then he erected the Lintels and Corners and Stones with their tops in the height of the heavens: and he connected the air at the bottom of the earths with the skies.[41]

Multiply the 12 Gates with the six Lintels to each Porch and you get 72 – the number of years it takes for the earth to move 1° of a precessional cycle. Multiply this number with the 30 Corners of each Lintel and you get 2,160 – the number of years in one complete precessional age. Multiply this figure with the 12 Stones in every Corner and you arrive at 25,920 – the number of years in one complete precessional cycle.

Since the passage in question concerns the ethereal architecture of the heavens, I find it difficult to see this numerology in terms of pure coincidence, suggesting therefore that the Manichaeans were carriers of precessional information that was of extreme age even in their own day.

In addition to these examples, clear knowledge of the precessional cycle can be detected within the Yezidi belief in the 72 Adams who each lived 10,000 years, between which were further periods of 10,000 years when no one had lived in the world. Simplistic as this time-cycle may seem, the 72 Adams refer to the 72 years it takes for the starry firmament to move 1° of a precessional cycle, while 1,440,000 – the total number of years alluded to by adding together these amounts – is another important figure in the precessional canon of numbers.[42]

How had the Yezidis come into possession of this complex system? Had it been from the Watchers? Or had this knowledge come from the conical-cap wearing people depicted on the walls of the hidden cavern at Ras al-'Ain in the Kurdish foothills?

Universal Language

The presence of age-old precessional data is not, however, confined to the mythologies and religious traditions of western and central Asia. It has also been detected in myths and legends all around the world. Giorgio de Santillana, a professor of the History of Science at the Massachusetts Institute of Technology, made an in-depth study of these legends and traditions and published the results in an important work entitled *Hamlet's Mill*, co-authored with Hertha von Dechend, a professor of the history of science at Frankfurt University. They put this universal knowledge of precession down to 'some almost unbelievable ancestor civilization' that 'first dared to understand the world as created according to number, measure and weight'.[43]

The Egyptian elders were almost certainly that 'unbelievable ancestor civilization', who had paved the way for the genesis of our own world civilization in the mountains of Kurdistan sometime around 5000 BC. As I also now realized, they were very probably the true source behind the traditions concerning the angels and Watchers of the Book of Enoch, as well as the gods, goddesses and demons of ancient Mesopotamia; the Shining Ones of Iranian tradition; the giants and Titans of Greek and Armenian mythology; and the fire djinn and Cabiri of Asia Minor. These were powerful realizations, yet they left me feeling just a little uneasy. Why *had* these people been so insistent on leaving us timeless legacies in the form of the geo-mythic data encoded into the Giza plateau and the universal language of astro-mythology preserved by so many cultures relevant to this debate? What were they trying to tell us? And just what do these legacies mean to the world as it blindly embraces the new millennium?

Twenty-Four

TRAGEDY OF THE FALL

I met a traveller from an antique land,
Who said: Two vast and trunkless legs of stone
Stand in the desert . . . Near them, on the sand,
Half sunk, a shattered visage lies, whose frown
And wrinkled lip and sneer of cold command,
Tell that its sculptor well those passions read,
Which yet survive stamped on these lifeless things
The hand that mocked them, and the heart that fed:
And on the pedestal these words appear:
'My name is Ozymandias, King of Kings:
Look on my works, ye Mighty, and despair!'
Nothing beside remains. Round the decay
Of that colossal wreck, boundless and bare
The lone and level sands stretch far away.

This is the tale of the mighty Ozymandias as portrayed by the romantic poet Percy Bysshe Shelley (1792–1822). The poem demonstrates how an empire that has fallen may quickly be forgotten by the world. To those who come afterwards without any awareness of the former greatness of this once powerful kingdom, any fragments of monuments and inscriptions left for posterity will seem merely nonsensical and absurd. The moral of the story is plain enough. No matter how powerful a civilization becomes, or what achievements it attains, it can one day sink without trace.

From the evidence presented in this book, I now feel better placed to review the possible significance a knowledge of the fall of the Egyptian elder culture holds for our present world race. To begin with, there seem to be firm grounds to doubt what the academics and scholars have always told us about the origins of civilization. Their perception of the growth of humanity, from a state of barbarism to one of advanced sophistication and technology in the present age, is questionable. If the evidence for high civilizations in past world epochs is correct, then the academics are deluding and deceiving not only themselves but also us, the public.

Egypt's elder culture would appear to have possessed a high state of civilization as early as 10,500 BC. The achievements of these people included the construction of vast cyclopean structures such as the Valley Temple and Osireion, the carving of the Great Sphinx to mark the precessional age of Leo, as well as an intimate knowledge of cosmic time-cycles perhaps spanning tens of thousands of years. They would also appear to have been a civilized society with an extensive knowledge of agriculture, architecture, astronomy, diplomacy, education, engineering, land irrigation and centralized rule. This is what the evidence suggests – and almost certainly there was much more.

Yet the climatic changes and global upheavals which accompanied the cessation of the last Ice Age, it seemed, effectively stopped them in their tracks. This was not because of any Great Flood, or because of an all-encompassing conflagration, but through the fragmentation of their race.

The Egyptian elders who settled in the remote regions of Kurdistan, *c.* 9000 BC, managed to transform themselves into an advanced shamanistic culture that had a profound influence on the developing races of the surrounding foothills and plains. Despite this continuation of the original knowledge of their race, they were unable to preserve much of the scientific and technological capabilities displayed in the cyclopean monuments of Egypt and the great cities beneath the plains of Cappadocia. It could even be that they possessed too much mental sophistication and not enough practical capability and manpower to establish the same type of high civilization they had previously been accustomed to in their former homeland.

The ultimate tragedy of this surviving colony, recognized today as the Watchers of the Book of Enoch, is that they survived fire and flood as well as unknown personal catastrophes merely to have the glories of their race and the wonders of their civilization erased from world history. Their survival into mythology is a hollow victory. We can only guess at the sense of loss they must have felt coming into the age of neolithic man. To see the knowledge they had preserved, the achievements they had made and the struggles behind their survival all being reduced to grossly distorted folktales must have been a painful blow. Maybe it was this sense of loss at the passing of their own world that inspired some of them to seek meaning by attempting to enlighten the races and cultures that followed in their footsteps.

There is ample evidence to suggest that these Egyptian colonists were responsible for the neolithic explosion that eventually led to the gradual emergence of civilization in the Near East around 5000 BC. Some of this slow release of information had, I feel, been carefully calculated, but knowledge concerning the fall of the Watchers would imply that some of those involved took matters into their own hands and decided, for their own gain, to reveal further wisdom and knowledge to humanity. Why some Watchers should have wanted to rebel remains a matter of conjecture. It is possible that the old values their ancestors had stood for no longer meant anything. There would also have been bitterness and resentment at what they had lost, and with this at the forefront of their minds they no doubt decided to exploit what little antediluvian knowledge they still possessed. This created a situation of too much, too soon, pushing the evolution of human society on to a level that has almost certainly had far-reaching consequences for the carefully balanced status quo of this world.

The events surrounding the revealment of this superior knowledge to the human species is remembered by us as the transgressions of the fallen angels, the descent of the gods, as well as the actions of *daevas*, demons and giants of the various Middle Eastern religions. Yet these transgressions of the fallen race have been preserved only in a mythological context, without any trace of a memory of the high civilization that originally attained this wisdom and knowledge through thousands of years of evolution. Moreover, the real legacies this culture left to the world have been totally misunderstood. Battered cyclopean ruins are accredited to much later kings who put claim to these monuments *because* of their immense antiquity and sanctity, while age-old legends and tales containing coded information on astro-mythology, precessional data and cyclic cataclysms are dismissed by academics as 'primitive creation myths'.

As the old priest of Sais was at pains to point out to Solon, civilizations rise and fall in accordance with cyclic factors – and to see your own race as unique is arrogant in the extreme. We have been given a false image of our past heritage through the arrogance of the world's academics, but in comparison with the way in which we have been deceived by theologians, their actions are almost excusable. The leaders of religions have told us that knowledge and wisdom is wholly divine, and was revealed to humanity by supernatural beings who transgressed the heavenly laws. The act of receiving this knowledge and wisdom from these supernatural beings, be it Angra Mainyu, the Devil, the Serpent, fallen angels, *daevas*, or whatever, was considered to be the original sin, and because of this disobedience humanity possesses an inherent tendency towards corruption and evil. It was these tendencies that caused mankind to establish civilization.

This is the basic tenet preached by many Western religions, including Christianity, Islam, Judaism and, of course, Zoroastrianism, which have each persecuted those who dared to question their authority on the matter. The myths associated with these supernatural beings appear to be no more than the bastardized memories of the way in which survivors of a previous high civilization passed on their skills and capabilities to our own ancestors. If this is so, then we are dealing with neither the divine nor the supernatural, but with physical beings of flesh and blood communicating on a one-to-one basis with human kind. The X-factor is effectively removed from the argument.

The theologians have in effect created their entire mythology out of the distorted memory of humanity's contact with the remnants of a previous civilization. This is the root behind the genesis of our current race, not the transgressions of supernatural beings of a divine nature. The consequences of the revelation are immense, for it means that the fundamental tenets of nearly all world religions are based on mythological events that never took place.

So, in effect, we have been double-crossed and fed false beliefs. Our religious leaders have tricked us into believing in divine beings and heavenly abodes that never existed (even if they *do* exist in people's beliefs today). Christianity, Islam, Judaism and Zoroastrianism – they have all been guilty of this crime. Indeed, it could be argued that they are the *real* teachers of the Lie, not Magianism or Manichaeanism. And if there were never any supernatural beings or any divine knowledge and wisdom, then perhaps there was never any God to create these things.

Newtonian science has led us to believe that there is a natural order and progression to life in the universe. We like to think of ourselves as knowing more today than at any time in the past. There is an immense pride in this knowledge. Yet, from the mass of evidence now freely available on Egypt's antediluvian civilization, the truth is that we have absolutely no idea where we come from and know far less about our roots than we could think possible. We see our own culture as technologically competent, reaching for the stars with space rockets, yet we have no concept of the fact that our ancestors of 10,500 BC knew more about astronomical precession and cyclic cataclysms than we care to imagine. With this knowledge, I feel that in many ways the human race is blindly feeling its way into the future, completely unaware that the reason why previous civilizations left us so many mythological clues concerning cycles of time, aerial conflagrations and universal floods is that they are trying to tell us it could all happen again.

Why, then, cannot we simply accept that we are not the first advanced race to have inhabited this planet? The answer is clear. To do so, with our current understanding of life on earth, would frighten us to death.

We fear that one day we, too, may fall.

One of the best-remembered cult movies of the 1960s is *Planet of the Apes*. Everyone who has seen this film remembers it almost exclusively for one chilling scene at the end. The hero, a marooned astronaut played by Charlton Heston, rides along a beach and sees before him the reason why apes and not human beings rule on this hostile planet. Exposed above the sands is the sunken head and raised arm of the Statue of Liberty. He realizes he is on earth many hundreds of years beyond his own time, and that, before the apes took control of the world, human beings had raised a mighty civilization that had crumbled to dust long ago – its history and achievements having been almost entirely erased from the memory of the planet. The shock factor of this film lies in the realization that it gives an apocalyptic vision of our own possible future.

In the legacies handed down to us, both by Egypt's elder culture and by the Watchers of Kurdistan, there is a clear message. They are telling us that, if we want to progress as a race, we must begin by looking back at the past and piecing together everything hitherto denied us by the academics and religious leaders of this world. We need to know the truth about ourselves as a race, and we will not find it by blindly accepting what we are being told about the origins of our civilization. If we fail to recognize the significance of the elder culture in our own times, then we will have compounded the tragedy behind the fall of the Watchers by denying the fact that their fate serves as a warning to us all.

At the moment the human race is like a child without a teacher. We seem to be going through an identity crisis, with no sense of place or responsibility in relation either to our past heritage or to the planet as a whole. Until we understand exactly who we are and where we have come from, we will continue to blunder forwards in a state of uncontrollable nihilism, destroying the world around us without realizing that the light could be switched off at any time. For unless our species can open its eyes and realize the past for what it really is, then we, too, are destined to end our days as Ozymandias – our achievements and history nothing but crumbling remains scattered across an antique land. Our future is our past. This knowledge can help us to avoid the same fate as the elder culture and their descendants, the Watchers. Only by accepting their place in world history will we come to realize that our true spiritual teacher is not some supernatural creation of God, but the forbidden legacy of a now fallen race.

Twenty-Five

AMNESIA OF THE MASSES

Time has dealt the Watchers a cruel blow. From being seen as extraordinarily advanced teachers of humanity, like those encountered by Enoch on his visit to the seven heavens, they quickly degenerated from angels of light into loathsome devils and demons of the underworld.

Very few people ever realized how the roots of civilization had arisen from the ashes of angels, and only religious literature such as the Book of Enoch preserved a distorted memory of this race's former trafficking with mortal kind. Some enlightened individuals, however, did manage to realize the significance this ancient culture had played in the shaping of humanity's later destiny, even though they could view such information only through their own blinkered perceptions of world history.

Yet there were, even at this early stage in the development of religion, those who also realized just how dangerous such heretical knowledge could be if broadcast to a much wider audience. If people actually believed that civilization had arisen from the wisdom imparted to humanity, not by God, but by walking serpents and fallen angels, then it would undermine the very foundations of a stable society built on religious fear. As a consequence, those who taught such blasphemies were to be treated both as liars and as *worshippers* of the Evil One. Furthermore, in the cause of stamping out such beliefs, these heretics were to be publicly denounced before being put to death, in the hope this would deter others from accepting such unholy doctrines. The Zoroastrians were perhaps among the first of the religions to instigate this cruel regime. They were followed by the Jews, the Christians and the Muslims. Not only did these religions condemn the 'heretics' for believing in the Lie, but they also made sure that any ancient work which alluded to such matters was promptly withdrawn from open circulation.

Quite naturally, such dogmatic views on forbidden knowledge simply draws it to the attention of the curious. Perhaps for this reason many of the gnostic cults of the early Christian era adopted the Serpent of Eden as their symbol of divinity, the Ophites being a particular example. Just how much these religious groups in fact knew about the fall of the Watchers is difficult to determine, although the Book of Enoch had certainly been in open circulation during this age. The gnostics practised different forms of dualism, which gave equal precedence to both the good and evil principles of religion, seen in terms of God and the demiurge, the great architect who created the physical world. Yet by far the best example of an individual who came very close to realizing the shocking truth about humanity's dark past was, of course, the prophet Mani. Having read and absorbed the Book of Enoch, he created his own rather pessimistic religious teachings on the basic tenet that humanity had been rotten to the core since the conception of Adam.

Mani realized that everything humanity stood for was as a direct result of the Powers of Darkness. *God had nothing to do with it*. The effect of the Watchers permeated everything we did, everything we thought, everything we made and everything we destroyed. Their evil ran through our veins, and in Mani's opinion the only way to escape their influence was in the release of the soul after death. The prophet's own horrific demise at the hands of fanatical Zoroastrians is a textbook example of how society has treated those who have dared to preach this dangerous view of humanity's past history.

Those dualists who followed in Mani's footsteps were treated in a similar vein. The Albigensians, or Cathars, who flourished in the south of France during the twelfth and thirteenth centuries, inherited many of Mani's religious ideals.[1] They attempted to change the face of religion by explaining the correctness of dualism, and by pointing out that the true heretics were those who now propagated the corruption of *Rex Mundi*, the King of the Earth, the greatest worshipper of this demon being in their minds the Church of Rome.[2] The hideous fate that befell the Cathars during the so-called Albigensian Crusade of the thirteenth century provides another perfect example of how Christian totalitarianism has attempted to obliterate any idea that the world as we know it is the work not of God but the gift of Satan or 'the Devil'.

Rosslyn's Fallen Angel

There were, however, those who appear to have understood the true role that the fallen angels played in providing humanity with its earthly knowledge and wisdom. One such person was William de St Clair, the architect of Rosslyn Chapel, a late fifteenth-century unfinished Scottish collegiate church, situated close to Edinburgh. Its interior and exterior are filled with mystifying imagery in sculpted stone and carved relief. Among the more obvious religious themes portrayed in this house of God are an assortment of plants, flowers and fruits, all interconnected with vines that either issue from or are gobbled up by the mouths of so-called Green Man heads. The whole place has been described as a herbal or physic garden in stone[3] – an imitation of that first paradisical garden planted eastwards, in Eden, by God himself. This idea is strengthened by the knowledge that the St Clair (modern Sinclair) family's heraldic device is the engrailed cross, which, while primarily an emblem of the True and Living Cross of Christ, also signifies the four rivers of paradise.

Rosslyn Chapel has many other fascinating themes running through its abundance of carvings. There are, for instance, a large number of statues that depict heavenly angels. Those with a cross above their heads appear to represent archangels, while among the parade of angelic carvings supporting the now empty stone plinths in the chapel's retro-choir are an altogether different collective of winged angels. These are covered either in body hair or feathers and each makes a different sign with its hands. Their individual poses bear a striking resemblance to the secret signs of Freemasonry, suggesting that the figures may therefore be interpreted as the rebel angels revealing the heavenly secrets to humanity.

By their side is an angel hanging upside down, its body tied and bound with rope. A round, pudding-basin haircut confirms the heavenly being's male gender and, like the other angels in the same group, he possesses wings. Both his hands are bound before him by a thick rope that winds twice around the body and trails away as raised relief to form the letter Z (like an S transposed) on each wing. The figure wears a long flowing garment and, unlike the other angels, there is what seems to be a beaded necklace or chain horizontally fastened above his inverted body.

The specific symbolism displayed in this figure leaves no doubt as to its identity. It is not Lucifer, Satan or the Devil, but the fallen angel Shemyaza, who was tied and bound before being made to hang perpetually upside down in the constellation of Orion as punishment for allowing the 'fall' of the angels to take place.[4] As in the story of Shemyaza (in his guise as Azza), the statue has one eye shut and the other eye open so that he may 'see his plight and suffer the more'.[5] The beaded necklace signifies the pearls of wisdom given up to humanity by the fallen angels.

This is perhaps the only remaining statue of Shemyaza in Europe. Its presence here, amid a veritable Garden of Eden carved in stone, points to the fact that the St Clair family (whose Latin name *sancto claro* means 'holy light') clearly understood the true significance of the fallen angels.[6] Yet it is also clear from the presence of this inverted figure that the St Clairs were only too aware of the consequences of being caught, either adhering to or passing on the forbidden knowledge about our lost heritage.

The St Clairs were the hereditary guardians of Scottish Freemasonry, from its earliest beginnings during the reign of Robert the Bruce in the fourteenth century, through till the first free election of a Grand Master in the eighteenth century. It was into this environment that James Bruce of Kinnaird became a prominent Freemason before embarking in 1768 on his famous travels to Ethiopia in search of the Book of Enoch (see Chapter Two). Was this Scotsman therefore influenced by the St Clairs' knowledge of the fallen angels and the role both Enoch and Noah played in the preservation of this heavenly wisdom? I feel the answer must be yes, and in my opinion it is highly likely that, had it not been for the St Clairs' intuitive understanding of this delicate matter, the world would have been deprived of the Book of Enoch for a great many years.

Paradise Lost

It was the publication in 1667 of John Milton's *Paradise Lost* that changed the way in which the world perceived fallen angels. He saw them as very human individuals with similar virtues and failings – a revolutionary approach that hit a nerve with many of the book's early readers. During the Victorian era the French artist Gustave Doré was asked to prepare illustrations for a new edition of Milton's classic. The result was a series of compelling images that, for the first time, showed Satan and his legions as beautiful male individuals. Each bore wings and shining armour like that displayed by the archangel Michael and his angelic host, leaving the reader with a much more romantic vision of heaven's fallen inhabitants.

When the Book of Enoch was finally published in 1821, the world was at last able to read for itself the transgressions of the fallen angels. It provided the motivation for romantics such as Lord Byron and Thomas Moore to write passionate stories about the forbidden loves of the angels,[7] while also inspiring artists, like the Pre-Raphaelite Simeon Solomon, to depict the 'Sons of God' on canvas.[8]

In other areas of society the release of the Book of Enoch seemed to have more disturbing effects. The Methodist Church, for instance – which held many liberal views on matters relating to spiritualism, witchcraft and the existence of supernatural beings[9] – unofficially saw Enoch as its new guardian light in the eternal struggle against Satan and his fallen angels. An example of the noncomformists' almost unhealthy interest in the Book of Enoch can be detected on the Lizard peninsular in the county of Cornwall, which has remained a stronghold of Methodism ever since John Wesley preached locally during the eighteenth century. Here, among the crashing waves and lingering sea-mists, we find place-names such as Enoch's Rock, Mount Hermon and Paradise Farm, reflecting the powerful local belief in Cornish 'giants', who were undoubtedly seen in terms of the Anakim, the offspring of the Nephilim.

The Re-emergence of Atlantis

Hand in hand with the increased popularity in fallen angels during the nineteenth century was the interest shown in the myths and legends surrounding the fabled islands of Atlantis, as presented by Plato in his works *Critias* and *Timaeus*. The idea of an advanced civilization having once existed in what seemed to have been the Atlantic Ocean appealed to many, especially since the old priest of Sais had informed Solon that Atlantis was lost during violent cataclysms 9,000 years before their own day.

Among those who became convinced that Atlantis really had existed was an American named Ignatius Donnelly (1831–1901), author of a bestselling book entitled *Atlantis: The Antediluvian World*, first published in 1882. In spite of its popularity, Donnelly went beyond simply trying to answer the question of whether or not Atlantis was fact or fantasy, reviewing – in addition to the evidence concerning this lost continent – literally hundreds of unexplained mysteries from both sides of the Atlantic. These included everything from a comparison of different flood myths to the study of elongated skulls, the discovery of anomalous artefacts and the mysteries of the Great Pyramid.

The following year, Donnelly's next book appeared. Entitled *Ragnarok: The Age of Fire and Gravel*, it was not such a hit with the public and quickly faded into obscurity. Yet its extraordinary contents, inspired by the extensive archive research Donnelly had already completed in connection with the myths of Atlantis, were explosive in their implications and testified to the fact that a series of truly terrifying cataclysms had shattered the relative calm of the last glacial age, a subject eventually taken up and explained by Professor Charles Hapgood in the 1950s.

The Hidden Masters

At the same time as Ignatius Donnelly was pushing the mysteries of Atlantis into the popular consciousness, the influence of Eastern mysticism from India and Nepal was also beginning to introduce the idea that previously unknown human races had once existed. One person deeply influenced by such thoughts was the Russian medium, Helena Petrovna Blavatsky. She returned from the East claiming to be in psychic communication with what she described as the Mahatmas, or Hidden Masters, who allegedly provided her with written accounts of primordial 'root' races that existed on earth long before the rise of modern civilization. On the basis of this information, she went on to found the Theosophical Society in 1875. This organization was welcomed in many countries, including Britain, India and the United States, and within a very short time its membership list ran to many thousands.

Madame Blavatsky's critics said the Mahatmas existed in her mind alone and that she had written the books alone. Despite these claims, which were never substantiated, her controversial views inspired many more individuals to investigate not only the mysteries of Atlantis, but also other lost civilizations, such as Mu and Lemuria, which had supposedly existed in the southern hemisphere during antediluvian times.

The Sleeping Prophet

With the popularity of Atlantis riding at an all-time high during the 1930s, an influential figure emerged on to the scene who was to ultimately inspire a whole new generation of academic research into lost civilizations. His name was Edgar Cayce, the so-called 'sleeping prophet' – an American psychic of some repute born on 18 March 1877 at a farm near Hopkinsville, Kentucky. From an early age he had been gifted with the power of second sight – a talent that apparently proliferated after a psychosomatic illness during his youth. In his early years, Cayce had apparently been able to self-induce a form of hypnotic trance which he then used to absorb great volumes of school-work. He went on to use this same form of altered state to 'diagnose' the illnesses of patients, during which time he would speak openly about the alleged previous lives of those patients. Cayce died on 3 January 1945, leaving behind no less than 14,000 documented 'psychic readings' given to over 8,000 people during a period of forty-three years.

A great many of these 'readings' included past-life material on supposed lives in Atlantis, and many of them painted a colourful and extremely vivid picture of the peoples, cities and environment of this lost continent before it apparently became submerged beneath the waves. Evidence of those who survived this massive natural cataclysm would be found, Cayce stated, as far apart as British Honduras, Morocco, the Pyrenees, the Yucatán, the Pacific coast of South America and the Mississippi basin.

More importantly, Cayce tied in the Atlantis myth with his supposedly unconscious belief that Egypt had once been a fertile region and that survivors of the Atlantean race established a community there after the continent's final submergence in 10,450 BC.[10] Survivors of this dying race are alleged to have built the Pyramids of Giza between 10,490 and 10,390 BC.[11] Many of Cayce's prophecies regarding Atlantis and Egypt are believed to have come to pass in recent years, prompting a lot of front-line researchers to assume that much more of his revealed information may eventually also prove accurate.

Ancient Astronauts

The study of lost civilizations took an unexpected turn in 1947, with the advent of the flying-saucer craze which swept across the United States in June that year. A commercial pilot named Kenneth Arnold saw nine 'wingless aircraft' flying over the Cascade Mountains of Washington State – the movement of which he later described as 'like a saucer if you skip it across water'.[12] His words were misunderstood, and in a subsequent news story it was reported that Arnold had described the objects, not their movement, as 'saucer-like',[13] so beginning the popular misconception that he was the first person to see a 'flying saucer'. Almost immediately after Arnold's 'sighting', many more reports of what later became known as UFOs (unidentified flying objects) began occurring all over the world. The frequency of these sightings increased dramatically during the 1950s and 1960s, with some people even claiming to have encountered the alleged occupants of the strange aerial craft.

Books began to appear on the subject of UFOs, and many pertinent questions were inevitably asked by their puzzled authors. Where did flying saucers come from? Who piloted them? Why were they appearing in our skies? Just how long had they been around? More importantly, people began to ask whether their existence might hold important clues regarding the mysteries of the past, such as the various obscure passages in the Bible which seemed to refer to unidentified aerial phenomena of some sort. From these well-meaning, though mostly fruitless, inquiries emerged a body of literature that eventually became known as the 'ancient astronaut' hypothesis.

With the publication in 1968 of Erich von Däniken's classic *Chariots of the Gods*, the banner headline 'Was God an astronaut?' began appearing in newspapers throughout the world. The book outlined the author's belief, already voiced by UFO authors such as Desmond Leslie, Paul Thomas and Brinsley le Poer Trench, that extraterrestrial beings from another world had supplied our most distant ancestors with the knowledge and technology to initiate the birth of civilization.

Von Däniken, and the many other ancient astronaut theorists who followed in his footsteps, would recite mysteries of our past that had no logical solution, planting seeds of doubt in the minds of many open-minded people. It was perhaps inevitable that a number of these authors should start to question the nature of angels against a backdrop of the UFO phenomenon. Some had ventured to examine Hebraic material concerning the fall of the angels, and this, of course, led them to the Book of Enoch. Reading this unique religious work gave many a field-day, as they dissected its contents and concluded that the Watchers had undoubtedly been a physical race of extraterrestrial origin who had divulged their universal knowledge to human kind. Best among the attempts to make a serious study of the extraordinary material of the Book of Enoch were those of the French author, Robert Charroux, in his 1964 book, *Legacy of the Gods*, and the American author, W. Raymond Drake, in his 1976 work, *Gods and Spacemen in Ancient Israel*.

The significance of these books lay in the fact that they brought together fallen angels and ancient civilizations for the very first time. Unfortunately, however, these authors invariably reached the conclusion that the Watchers *could only* have been extraterrestrial beings. Only Christian O'Brien, in his 1985 milestone work, *The Genius of the Few*, thankfully held back from exactly this conclusion.

Colony Earth

By the late 1970s, Erich von Däniken's ancient-astronaut crown had been forcibly removed in the wake of allegations that he had falsified the evidence featured in some of his half-dozen or so best-selling books. In the United States this crown passed to an author named Zecharia Sitchin, who, in a complex book entitled *The 12th Planet*, first published in 1976, put forward the theory that the 'Nefilim' of the Book of Enoch were extraterrestrials who arrived on earth from a distant '12th' planet, which, he said, orbits the sun. Using genetic technology, these tall aliens had created a creature called 'man' to perform mining operations deep below the earth's surface. Humanity eventually rebelled and broke free of its masters, who finally returned to their home planet, named Marduk or 'Nibiru', sometime during ancient times.

Clearly Sitchin had simply created another unprovable and highly unlikely extraterrestrial hypothesis; however, the difference between this ancient-astronaut theorist and previous authors was that Sitchin understood Near Eastern mythology better than most. Indeed, he is one of only a few hundred people in the world today who can read and translate the Sumerian written language.

In *The 12th Planet*, as well as in the subsequent volumes of his 'Earth Chronicles' series, Sitchin introduced the reader to extraordinary evidence that pointed towards the conclusion that the 'Nefilim' had been a race of physical beings who once had open contact with the earliest Old World civilizations, such as Egypt and Sumeria. After that, however, his books rather frustratingly revert back to the von Däniken-style school of thinking by all too often suggesting, for instance, that many representations of conical pillars and pyramidions in ancient art actually depict rockets in silos. Maybe he is right, but, in my opinion, such presumptions have been made purely on a basis of our own modern-day, mechanistic view of the world, and cannot be cited as evidence of alien technology in prehistoric times.

The Watchers' Return

Zecharia Sitchin's wild theories about fallen angels inadvertently influenced a whole generation of youth culture during the 1980s. Popular music is probably one of the quickest ways to influence a sympathetic audience, especially if a particular subject is promoted by individual singers or groups of musicians. The growth of interest in Eastern mysticism among the hippy generation following George Harrison's much-publicized visits to the Maharishi Mahesh Yogi, or even the extraordinary increase in Mormon convertees among teenage girls following the international success of the Osmond brothers during the early 1970s, are both prime examples of this diffusion at work.

In a similar way, the sudden rise, initially in Britain, of all things black and gothic during the mid 1980s, brought with it a whole new interest in the reality of fallen angels and the affiliated subjects of vampires and the occult. Spearheading the more serious side of the 'gothic' movement was an influential rock group called Fields of the Nephilim, who first achieved international success with their extraordinary single 'Moonchild' in 1988. A succession of hit singles and hit albums through till 1991 made them the new gods of the gothic scene across the world.

The front man of Fields of the Nephilim, now known just as The Nefilim (with an 'f' instead of a 'ph'), is 'goth' icon Carl McCoy, who holds a personal interest in fallen angels. During his childhood he was subjected to a strict religious upbringing, his parents and family being practising Jehovah's Witnesses. As in the case of early Methodism, this religion holds strong views on the corruption of humanity by the Watchers and Nephilim at the time of the fall of the angels. This connection had a deep and lasting impact on McCoy, who claims to have experienced dreams and visions concerning the Nephilim from an early age. Finding further inspiration on the subject of the 'Nefilim' in Zecharia Sitchin's *The 12th Planet*, McCoy introduced the concept of fallen angels into many of his songs, which bear titles such as 'Return to Gehenna', 'Sumerland' and 'The Wail of Sumer'. In these mostly long, moody pieces, powerful lyrics blend with deep evocative musical arrangements to conjure dark, foreboding visions of a cyclopean age when fallen angels walked freely among humanity.

As a direct result of McCoy's fundamental interest in the Watchers and Nephilim, black-dressed goths world-wide began buying books on angels, fallen angels and related topics, such as the works of infamous English occultist Aleister Crowley and the Enochian magic of the Elizabethan magus Dr John Dee. Most important was the effect this revitalization of interest in fallen angels has had on the literary world. Various young authors of fiction began swapping the more clichéd anti-heroes, such as vampires, for fallen angels of the type portrayed in the Book of Enoch. By far the most historically accurate and conceptually original of this new breed of books have been those penned by the British novelist Storm Constantine. In works with titles such as *Burying the Shadow*, *Stalking Tender Prey* and *Scenting Hallowed Blood*, she has portrayed the Watchers as an ancient race whose descendants still live on among humanity today.

In the art world it has been the modern sculpture of Essex-born artist John Day that has captured the true spirit of the historical Watchers. Since 1979 he has created a series of evocative images that represent this ancient race, which Day firmly believes once inhabited the earth. The most extraordinary of these is a sculpture entitled 'Kether', a Hebrew word meaning 'crown', which shows a huge bird-man with enormous wooden fan-like wings. Day claims the piece was inspired by an out-of-the-body experience involving contact with Watcher-like beings.

And, indeed, the Watchers are fast becoming a religious cult in their own right. Inspired perhaps by the books that have linked them with extraterrestrial intelligences, various UFO groups now claim psychic communication with this ancient race. They include the so-called Raelian Movement, founded in France by a strange figure named Claude Vorilhon (who bears an uncanny physical resemblance to the 1960s cult leader Charles Manson), following an alleged UFO encounter in December 1973.[14] Among the deepest beliefs of the Raelians is one that the Sons of God, seen by them as 'the Elohim', seeded this earth long ago, and that open communication should be gained in readiness for their planned 'return' to earth. During meetings held behind closed doors, they invite the Elohim into their presence through the use of psychics.

Fingerprints of the Gods

By far the most important and influential book on lost civilizations to have appeared in recent years is *Fingerprints of the Gods* by the investigative journalist and author Graham Hancock. Riding on the storm of controversy which followed the announcement that the Great Sphinx is almost certainly many thousands of years older than was previously imagined, the book pulled together in a no-nonsense, straightforward manner, evidence of an advanced civilization in primordial times. It also showed that Charles Hapgood's crustal displacement theory is the only workable solution for explaining the reported cataclysms that brought the last Ice Age to a dramatic close during the tenth millennium BC.

In 1995 *Fingerprints of the Gods* became a bestseller in many countries of the world, selling to date a staggering 3.5 million copies. Its sequel, *Keeper of Genesis*, co-written with Robert Bauval and first published in 1996, focuses on Egypt's Giza plateau. It demonstrates in a sober, academic manner, quite inconceivable just a few short years ago, that Giza's ancient monuments conform to an astronomical star-clock preserving the date 10,500 BC.

Yet, if we now accept the existence of such an advanced culture in our past history, we must also ask ourselves who exactly were these people? Did they simply develop in Egypt? Or had they themselves come from distant shores? *Fingerprints of the Gods* speaks of them only as tall, white and bearded. Hancock does, however, lend open support to a revolutionary new theory put forward in 1995 by a Canadian couple, Rand and Rose Flem-Ath, in an essential book entitled *When the Sky Fell – In Search of Atlantis*. After many years of examining the available evidence on the Atlantis myth, the authors came to the unique conclusion that this lost continent could be identified with Antarctica. It may not seem the most obvious answer to an age-old enigma that has so long baffled the world; however, as the Flem-Aths point out, large parts of this continent were completely free from ice in the eleventh and tenth millennia BC, when the global cataclysms that accompanied the cessation of the last Ice Age appear to have taken place.

Like Hancock in *Fingerprints of the Gods*, the Flem-Aths also reconfirm something that many earlier Atlantean and ancient-astronaut theorists have been at pains to point out. This is the undeniable fact that certain sea-maps of ancient mariners – like, for example, the Piri Re'is map of 1513 – not only show Antarctica, which was only 'discovered' in 1818, but also depict the continent as free of ice! Even more incredible is the knowledge that some of these maps show Antarctica as two separate land-masses, a fact completely unknown in modern times until 1958.[15]

The only logical explanation for this baffling mystery is to suppose that the sea-maps were copies of much older charts, which had themselves been copied from earlier versions, and so on and so forth, back to a time when Antarctica was last free of ice, which is estimated to have been around six thousand years ago.[16]

Tracing the Elders

Could any of these theories explain the presence in Egypt of a highly advanced elder culture from the thirteenth millennium BC through till around 9500–9000 BC? Might I be able to pin down the true genesis of this lost race by further assessing what little evidence is available?

Early Judaic literature gives the Watchers, the elder culture's apparent descendants, specific physiological characteristics, and these appear to define the striking contrasts between these individuals and those who came into contact with them. To define them one last time, these human angels are described as extremely tall with white skin, white woolly hair, ruddied complexions, piercing eyes and serpent-like faces. Mesopotamian texts, as well as other tales of giant races from the Near East, appear to confirm that the gods, goddesses and ancestors of their own races were also of 'giant' stature. More importantly, anatomical remains unearthed both in Iraq and in the Predynastic graves of Egypt, have shown that individuals of great size with long heads represented the aristocratic, or ruling, class of the countries' earliest cultures during the fourth millennium BC. It is therefore possible that Egypt's elder culture also bore the same characteristics as their Near Eastern counterparts.

This is all the evidence we have so far, and even if the Judaic texts can be taken at face value, then there is no reason whatsoever to assume that these distinctive physiological traits were borne by all the race. Indeed, it is far more likely that only a few individuals were exceptionally tall, or possessed white hair or viper-like faces. Yet for obvious reasons it was encounters with these particular individuals that were more readily preserved by the story-tellers of subsequent cultures. If this is correct, then it is also probable that only a very few of Egypt's elder culture ever bore extreme physiological traits like those of the Watchers and Nephilim described in Enochian and Dead Sea literature.

Beyond this, everything is pure speculation. In similar with its Kurdish descendants of post-9000 BC, the antediluvian elder culture has left us with just a few tantalizing clues as to its former glory. The Great Sphinx and the other cyclopean monuments of Egypt, as well as the glimpses of extraordinarily advanced technology possessed by the Near East's very earliest cultures, the astro-mythology encoded in creation epics found throughout Egypt and Asia, and perhaps even the maps of the ancient sea-kings, are all faint echoes of their presence in this world. Yet simply to admit this would be to end the book on a frustrating cliff-hanger. We all want to know exactly who these people were and where they came from. Did they just evolve as a race in Egypt? or did they migrate to this region from somewhere else?

Perhaps the elder culture developed in southern Africa before migrating northwards into Egypt sometime before the thirteenth millennium BC. Sophisticated mining operations dating back to at least 80,000 to 70,000 BC have been found in southern Swaziland, demonstrating the level of technological advancement among the supposedly primitive ancestors of mankind, even at this very early stage in human evolution.[17] It would be easy to suggest that the level of evolution achieved by these mining communities increased gradually and finally culminated with the rise of Egypt's elder culture. Yet such words would ring blatantly hollow without even the slightest corroborative evidence to support them.

Authors such as Erich von Däniken and Zecharia Sitchin would have us believe that both the elder culture and its Near Eastern off-shoots, the Watchers, Nephilim and Anannage, were extraterrestrial in origin. This, however, must remain a completely unsupported claim, unless hard evidence of alien contact with the human species, either in the past or in this present age, should ever come to light. As I do not see this as a likelihood in the forseeable future, I am unwilling to entertain this wild hypothesis at the present time.

In stark contrast to the ancient-astronaut theorists, the Flem-Aths, Graham Hancock and others are promoting the more realistic hypothesis that the elder culture developed in Antarctica – in my estimation the only plausible candidate for the fabled Atlantis of Plato's writings. Then, during the long period of cataclysms that accompanied a proposed crustal displacement between 15,000 and 9500 BC, the race abandoned Antarctica and migrated to different parts of the world, including Egypt. Certainly, legends found both in Egypt and in the Near East speak of the respective cultures' earliest ancestors as having originated in a mythical land, seen sometimes as situated in the south.[18] Furthermore, there is compelling evidence preserved by ancient cultures world-wide, particularly in Meso-America, which speak of tall white men with beards, or even anthropomorphic serpents, who were the original bringers of knowledge and wisdom.[19] These are tantalizing clues to the presence in the world of a universal culture responsible for the rise of organized society after the cessation of the last Ice Age.

Adding weight to this argument are the findings of Professor Charles Hapgood. He concluded that those who had made the maps of the ancient sea-kings must have been '*one culture*' with maritime connections all over the globe.[20] This makes sense of Giorgio de Santillana and Hertha von Dechend's observations in *Hamlet's Mill* regarding the original sources behind the astro-mythology and precessional information contained in myths and legends world-wide. In similar with the nineteenth-century mythologist, Gerald Massey, they concluded that this complex data must have originated with 'some almost unbelievable ancestor civilization'.[21] In addition, Massey came to realize that this same high civilization must also have been responsible for the carving of the Great Sphinx during the age of Leo some 'thirteen thousand years ago'.[22]

It is therefore quite conceivable that before the end of the last Ice Age there existed in different parts of the world an ocean-going, high civilization with international cities and ports, thus implying that the Egyptian elder culture had simply been one of its many foreign colonies. There is another possibility, however; and this is that the elder culture *did* develop in Egypt, or north Africa at least, and that after its apparent fragmentation in the tenth millennium BC, remnants of the race not only entered and settled in the Near East, but also travelled to other parts of the world searching for safe havens where they could escape the on-going series of cataclysms. Some of these isolated colonies would certainly have disappeared without trace. Yet others may well have been responsible for the rise of civilizations – the Watchers of Kurdistan being a prime example.

I favour the second solution, but do not discount the first. All that can be ascertained with any certainty is that the Egyptian elder culture may be seen as an evolutionary tributary in the development of the human species, especially in respect of the development of the Eurasian neolithic age. The actual place of origin of this culture, some members of whom would appear to have been extremely tall with white skin and white hair, must for the time being remain a complete mystery.

Maybe we will have an answer in the not too distant future.

In the past no one believed in dinosaurs, and the first ever evidence of their former glory on earth was greeted with much derision among the academic and literary communities of the world. Yet once knowledge of their awesome presence had become more widely accepted, overwhelming evidence of their existence poured in from all over the globe. Now there are very few people who would deny their existence.

Maybe in time the same will be said both of Egypt's elder culture and their Near Eastern descendants – the Watchers of Kurdistan. Now that the scene has been set, there is no reason why our knowledge of this lost world will not increase accordingly. The angels of the Bible are coming back to life and there seems no way we can prevent it happening, for they now exist not only in our minds, but also in the pages of human history. For some reason I feel they are with us to stay this time, and no one should deny them their lost heritage.

Towards the New Millennium

Modern supporters of an advanced civilization in primordial times are turning more and more to psychics for revealed information on how best to investigate this subject further. Many realize that the only way forward is to combine intuitive processes alongside sound, objective research. If this proves to have been the correct decision, then great discoveries are likely to be made in the coming years, especially as all eyes will be on the Great Pyramid as the world sees in the new millennium.

One compelling prophecy suggests that there are, beneath the Giza plateau, twelve rock-hewn chambers positioned in a double-hexagonal arrangement, each representing one of the precessional signs of the zodiac. All chambers are linked via a series of interconnecting corridors with a large central chamber containing a huge multi-faceted crystal that symbolizes the cosmic egg, the point of first creation in the physical universe.[23]

Ancient myths and legends preserved by many different cultures have all alluded to the existence of such chambers, referred to by Edgar Cayce as the Hall of Records. Judaic tradition asserts that these underground chambers were constructed by the patriarch Enoch, with the help of his son Methuselah, to contain the ancient sciences at the time of the Great Flood – a theme still preserved in European Masonic tradition (see Chapter Two).

Until recently, no one knew whether or not such a hidden legacy might lay undiscovered beneath the drifting sands of the Giza plateau. Then, in 1993 seismic soundings of the hard bedrock below the Sphinx enclosure revealed the presence, some sixteen feet down, of a large, rectangular room. This hollowed-out area was quickly identified as a hewn-out chamber some thirty feet by forty feet in size. The geophysicist in charge of the operation, Dr Thomas Dobecki, is a former professor at the Colorado School of Mines who now works in the commercial sector. Naturally he has been somewhat cautious about the significance of this discovery, but is willing to admit that: 'The regular, rectangular shape of this (chamber) is inconsistent with naturally occurring cavities, so there is some suggestion that it could be man-made.'[24]

If this chamber does constitute the entrance into an underground complex constructed by Egypt's elder culture, either before or during the age of Leo, then the impact of such a discovery on our understanding of religion and world history cannot be underestimated. Once and for all the human race will be obliged to realize that the collective amnesia from which it seems to have been suffering over the past 11,000 years, is no longer a valid excuse to deny the fact that we were never the first.

Perhaps, deep inside, each of us knows the truth about humanity's dark past, the cataclysms that befell Egypt's elder culture, and the fall of the Watchers.

Maybe it is this that has made us so want to obliterate it from our conscious memory for so long.

Yet, inside ourselves, we *know*.

Somehow fallen angels are important to our past, and at some point we will have to address the problem they pose once and for all.

In my view there are only three choices.

Either the Watchers were incorporeal beings – divine messengers in the service of God who fell from grace. Or they were simply the creation of our ancestors' deep psychological needs, fears and desires. Or they really did once walk the earth as beings of flesh and blood.

The evidence is there. The choice is yours.

Postscript

Research continues into the origins and lost history of the elder culture of Egypt and the Watchers of Kurdistan. Many talented authors, researchers and specialists in their own particular fields of study, be it anthropology, archaeology, astronomy, engineering, geology, linguistics, mythology, palaeontology, parapsychology, or any other related subject, are now coming forward in an attempt to take on orthodoxy and demonstrate the existence of advanced civilizations in prehistoric times.

From the Ashes of Angels is just one among a number of books that are challenging our accepted views on world history and religion. If, by reading it, this work has inspired you to begin your own investigations into the ancient mysteries of our past, or if it has simply made you question our current understanding of prehistory, then it has achieved its aim. May I suggest that you review the titles included in the recommended booklist at the start of the bibliography. I would suggest these are essential reading if you intend to pursue this subject in any greater detail. Almost all of the titles listed in the bibliography can be obtained through the library system.

Should you feel you can add to our knowledge and understanding regarding any of the topics under discussion, and/or you wish to be kept informed of future books, developments, events and projects in respect of the author's own on-going research into Watcher-related matters, then please write to Andrew Collins at PO Box 189, Leigh-on-Sea, Essex SS9 1NF.

Notes and References

Chapter 1: I HAVE BEGOTTEN A STRANGE SON

1. Charlesworth, *The Old Testament Pseudepigrapha, Apocalyptic Literature and Testaments*, vol. 1, note g to 1En. 106, p. 86.
2. ibid., trans. of 1 Enoch by E. Izaac, 1En. 106:1–6.
3. ibid., p. 7.
4. See, for instance, Easton, *The Illustrated Bible Dictionary*, s.v. 'Angels', pp. 42–3.
5. Avigad and Yadin, *A Genesis Apocryphon, A Scroll from the Wilderness of Judaea*.
6. Vermes, *The Dead Sea Scrolls in English*, p. 252. The spelling of Bathenosh's name is taken from this translation of 1QapGen.
7. ibid., 1QapGen, II:1.
8. ibid., 1QapGen, II:9–16.
9. Charlesworth, *The Old Testament Pseudepigrapha, Apocalyptic Literature and Testaments*, vol. 1, 1En. 106:6.
10. 1En. 106:13–8.
11. Gen. 6:1–2. All biblical quotations are taken from the 1884 Revised Version of the Authorized Version of the Bible.
12. Gen. 6:4.
13. Drake, *Gods and Spacemen in Ancient Israel*, pp. 79–80.
14. Hooke, *Middle Eastern Mythology*, p. 132.
15. Legge, *Forerunners and Rivals of Christianity*, vol. 1, pp. 158–60.
16. See Milik, *The Books of Enoch – Aramaic Fragments of Qumrân Cave 4*.
17. Eisenman, *Maccabees, Zadokites, Christians and Qumran*, pp. xiv, 54–5 n. 82, 54–5 n. 82; *Zohar* 1:55a–55b; *Forerunners and Rivals of Christianity*, vol. 1, pp. 159–60, p. 159 n. 1.
18. Charlesworth, *The Old Testament Pseudepigrapha, Apocalyptic Literature and Testaments*, vol. 1, p. 8.
19. Tertullian, 'On the Veiling of Virgins', *Ante-Nicene Christian Library*, i:196; iii:163–4; cf. 1 Cor. 11:10.

20. Lactantius (AD 260–330) and Tatian (AD 110–172), for instance, fully accepted the corporeal existence of fallen angels in their works. See Schneweis, *Angels and Demons According to Lactantius*, pp. 103, 127.
21. Augustine, St, *De Civitate Dei*, xv, 23.
22. Alexander, 'The Targumim and Early Exegesis of "Sons of God" in Genesis 6', *Journal of Jewish Studies*, No. 23, 1972, pp. 60–61.
23. Prophet, *Forbidden Mysteries of Enoch – Fallen Angels and the Origins of Evil*, p. 59.
24. *New Catholic Encyclopaedia*, 1967, s.v. 'Devil'.

Chapter 2: THE SEARCH FOR THE SOURCE

1. See Bruce, *Travels to Discover the Source of the Nile in the Years 1768, 1769, 1770, 1771, 1772 and 1773*.
2. Hancock, *The Sign and the Seal*, p. 191.
3. Mackenzie, *The Royal Masonic Cyclopaedia*, p. 328.
4. Jackson, *Beyond the Craft*, p. 61.
5. Its antiquity cannot be doubted, for it is known to have played a major part in the formation of the Scottish Grand Lodge in 1736. (From a personal communication with Robert Bryden, a leading authority on Scottish Knight Templarism and Freemasonry.)
6. Mackenzie, *The Royal Masonic Cyclopaedia*, pp. 201–2.
7. Hall, *An Encyclopedic Outline of Masonic, Hermetic, Qabbalistic and Rosicrucian Symbolic Philosophy*, p. 173.
8. Horne, *King Solomon's Temple in the Masonic Tradition*, p. 233.
9. Hall, *An Encyclopedic Outline of Masonic, Hermetic, Qabbalistic and Rosicrucian Symbolic Philosophy*, p. 173.
10. 1 Kings 7:21. The Solomonic aspects of this legend, along with the subsequent loss and rediscovery of the hidden vaults at the time of the Babylonian Captivity of the Jews, still form a major role in the archaic rites of what is known today as the Royal Arch degree, a side-order entered only once the candidate has passed through the three basic grades of Craft Freemasonry. In contrast, the Enochian elements within speculative Masonry finally disappeared almost without trace for reasons that have never been made clear. Despite the loss of the association between Enoch and early speculative Masonry, the thirteenth degree of the Ancient and Accepted Rite is still known as the Royal Arch of Enoch, suggesting a long-forgotten connection with the original rendering of the legend concerning the Antediluvian Pillars. See Jones, *Freemason's Book of the Royal Arch*, p. 130.

Although the construction of the Antediluvian Pillars has been variously ascribed in Judaic and Masonic writings to Seth, the son of Adam, to Jabal, Jubal and Tubal-cain, the sons of Lamech; and even to Enoch's great-grandson, Noah, Dr James Anderson, whose revised constitutions of Freemasonry were published in 1738, stated quite clearly that 'the old Masons always call'd them Enoch's Pillars, and firmly believ'd this Tradition' (i.e. the legend attached to their ancient origin). See Horne, *King Solomon's Temple in the Masonic Tradition*, p. 233. More importantly, according to the Masonic historian, E.W. Donovan, the legend of the Pillars of Enoch was, to his knowledge, preserved alone in the degrees of the Royal Order of Scotland, the very order instituted by James Bruce of Kinnaird's distant ancestor, Robert I of Scotland (Robert the Bruce), at the dawn of the fourteenth century. See Donovan, *British Masonic Miscellany*, viii, p. 73, quoted in *King Solomon's Temple in the Masonic Tradition*, p. 233 n.1.

11. Gen. 5:22, 24.

12. Davidson, *A Dictionary of Angels*, s.v. 'Enoch-Metatron', p. 106.

13. ibid., s.v. 'Azza', p. 65.

14. Bruce, *Travels*, abridged edition, Introduction, p. 14. As quoted by Fanny Burney after her 'lively' meeting with Bruce in 1775.

15. See ibid., Introduction, pp. 1–19, for a good résumé of Bruce's life and his travels in Ethiopia.

16. See Budge, *The Queen of Sheba and her Only Son Menelik – being the 'Book of the Glory of Kings' (Kebra Nagast)*.

17. For a full account of the Ark's apparent journey to Ethiopia, see Hancock, *The Sign and the Seal*, 1992.

18. 'The real reason he came was to steal our treasures,' claimed an Addis Ababa historian, Belai Gedai, to Hancock, 'our cultural treasures. He took many precious manuscripts back to Europe.' See *The Sign and the Seal*, p. 181. Hancock also shows that Bruce's journey to Axum in January 1770 was timed to coincide with the celebration of Timkat, a major festival in the calendar of the Ethiopian Orthodox Church. It was believed that the Ark, which was kept in a chapel at Axum, was paraded through the streets during these celebrations. See ibid., p. 180.

19. Charlesworth, *The Old Testament Pseudepigrapha, Apocalyptic Literature and Testaments*, vol. 1, p. 8.

20. Dee's communication with angels on 25 June 1584 in Cracow reads: 'And after 50 days Enoch had written: and this was the Title of his books, let those that fear God and are worthy read. But behold, the people waxed wicked . . . And they began to counterfeit the doings of God and his power . . . so that the memory of Enoch washed away: and the spirits of Errour began to teach them Doctrines . . . Now hath it pleased God to deliver this Doctrine again out to darknesse: and to fulfill his promise with thee,

for, the books of Enoch.' See Casaubon, *A True and Faithful Relation* . . ., Cotton appendix XLVI, p. 174.

These words clearly imply that Dee was actually given the 'books of Enoch', as is further suggested in the 7 July 1584 entry, where it states: 'My brother, I see thou dost not understand the mystery of this Book, or work thou hast in hand. But I told thee, it was the knowledge that God delivered unto Enoch.' See ibid., p. 196.

That *a* 'Book of Enoch' was transcribed to Dee and Kelly seems indisputable. It is named among the books and papers allegedly burnt at the request of the angels on 10 April 1586 in Prague and later returned without harm on 29 April. See ibid., p. 418; G. Suster, *John Dee Essential Readings*, pp. 77–81. Furthermore, there is some evidence that Dee's 'books of Enoch' refer to MS. Sloane 3189 in the British Library. Entitled *Liber Mysteriorum, Sextus et Sanctus*, one of the few flyleaves accompanying the text describes it as 'The Book of Enoch revealed to Dr John Dee by the Angels'. This entry is not, however, contemporary with the original manuscript and was probably added by one of its subsequent owners. Sloane 2599 consists of angelic tables extracted from Sloane 3189 by an unknown hand around the close of the seventeenth century. Towards the end is the statement: 'These Tables follow the Book of Enoch.' It goes without saying that these interesting angelic tracts bear no relation whatsoever with the actual Book of Enoch.

(I would like to thank London researcher Gareth J. Medway for extracting this material from the British Library on my behalf.)

21. Suster, *John Dee Essential Readings*, pp. 137–46; Turner, R. (ed.), *The Heptarchia Mystica of John Dee*.

22. *Thesaurus Temporum Eusebii Pamphili, Caesareae Palaestinae episcopi Chronicorum Canonum omnimodae Historiae libri duo*, Lugduni Batavorum, 1606, 'Animadversiones in Chronologica Eusebii', pp. 244*a*–245*b*; Scaliger, *Chronicus Canon of Eusebius*, Amsterdam, 1658, pp. 404–5.

23. Syncellus, *Chronographia*, quoted by J. A. Fabricius in his *Codex Pseudepigraphus Veteris Testamenti*, vol. 1, pp. 179–98.

24. The first of these copies appears to have been procured for Bruce by a Greek servant of the governor of Tigre, named Janni, during his visit to its capital Adowa in early 1770. See *Travels*, abridged edition, p. 48.

25. ibid., vol. 2, p. 422. (Unabridged edition only.)

26. ibid., vol. 2, pp. 425–6.

27. Laurence, *The Book of Enoch the Prophet – An Apocryphal Production, Supposed for Ages to Have Been Lost; but Discovered at the Close of Last Century in Abysinnia; now First Translated from an Ethiopic* MS. *in the Bodleian Library*.

28. Byron, 'Heaven and Earth – A Mystery', 1821, included in *The Poetic Works of Lord Byron*, 1823.
29. Moore, *The Loves of the Angels – A Poem, with Memoir*, 1823.
30. See, for example, Simeon Solomon's 'And the sons of God saw the daughters of men that they were fair', a water- and body-colour dated 1863.
31. Leatherdale, *Dracula – the Novel and the Legend*, pp. 192–3.
32. Personal communication from Robert Bryden.
33. See Charles, *The Book of Enoch or 1 Enoch*.
34. Morfill and Charles, *The Book of the Secrets of Enoch, or 2 Enoch*, pp. vii, xii. All references to 2 Enoch have been taken from this edition, unless otherwise specified.
35. See Milik, *The Books of Enoch – Aramaic Fragments of Qumrân Cave 4*.
36. Charlesworth, *The Old Testament Pseudepigrapha, Apocalyptic Literature and Testaments*, vol. 1, p. 8. E. Izaac, the translator here of 1 Enoch, places an upper limit on this date as AD 650, although this seems far too late, especially as the Book of Enoch fell out of favour with the Christian Church Fathers during the first half of the fourth century AD.

Chapter 3: DEMONIC DOCTRINE

1. Charlesworth, *The Old Testament Pseudepigrapha, Apocalyptic Literature and Testaments*, vol. 1, p. 7.
2. ibid.
3. See Matt. 17:1–8; Mark 9:2–8; Luke 9:28–36 for accounts of the Transfiguration of Christ.
4. 1En 6:4–5. All quotations from 1 Enoch are taken from Charles, *The Book of Enoch*, 1912, unless otherwise indicated.
5. 1En. 6:6–8.
6. 1En. 7:2–6.
7. Although the terms *gibborim* and *nephilim* are used quite separately in Enochian literature to describe the offspring of the Watchers, out of personal preference I mainly use the term 'Nephilim', as it seems to convey the dark, brooding nature of these people far better than the terms 'giants' or 'mighty men'.
8. 1En. 8:1.
9. 1En. 8:3.
10. 1En. 69:8–9.
11. 1En. 69:12.
12. 1En. 10:9.
13. 1En. 10:4–6, 8.

14. 1En. 10:12–13.
15. Graves, and Patai, *Hebrew Myths – the Book of Genesis*, pp. 101–2.
16. 1En. 13:3.
17. 1En. 13:7.
18. Charles, *The Book of Enoch*, 1912, p. 31.
19. 1En. 10:2.
20. See Henning, 'The Book of the Giants', *Bulletin of the School of Oriental and African Studies*, vol. 11, pt 1, pp. 52–74; Milik, *The Books of Enoch.*
21. Henning, 'The Book of the Giants', p. 69.
22. 1En. 10:3.
23. 1En. 15:9, 11–12.
24. Charles, *The Book of Enoch*, 1912, p. 37.
25. ibid., p. xxxviii.
26. ibid., p. xi.
27. Eisenman, *Maccabees, Zadokites, Christians and Qumrân*, pp. xiv, 54–5 n. 82.
28. ibid., p. 74 n. 138.
29. ibid., pp. xiv, 54–5 n. 82.

Chapter 4: INSANE BLASPHEMY

1. Gen. 4:16.
2. The figure 520 is a very important number in cosmological numerology. It relates to the astronomical phenomenon of precession, known to the ancients as the Great Year. Certain 'canonical' numbers relating to this celestial system of time keeping crop up again and again in mythologies across the world. See Chapter 23.
3. For a concise résumé of the Cave of Treasures story, consult Graves and Patai, *Hebrew Myths*, pp. 105–6.
4. Morgenstern, 'The Mythological Background of Psalm 82', *Hebrew Union College Annual*, vol. 16 (1939).
5. Budge, *Kebra Nagast*, p. 188.
6. Budge, *The Cave of Treasures*, p. 92.
7. St Jerome, Homily 45 on Psalm 132 (133), trans. Ewald, *Fathers of the Church*, No. 48, 1964, pp. 338–9.
8. Greenlees, *The Gospel of the Prophet Mani*, pp. xxii-xxiii.
9. Commonitorium, PL. 42: 1154–5, quoted in Greenlees, *The Gospel of the Prophet Mani*, p. 337.
10. ibid., p. li.
11. ibid., pp. lxxvi–lxxix.
12. Jean Chrysostom, 'Homelies sur la Genèse', *Saint Jean Chrysostome*

Oeuvres Complètes, trans. M. Jeannin and ed. L. Guerin, Paris, 1865, 5:136–7, quoted in Prophet, E. C., *Forbidden Mysteries of Enoch – Fallen Angels and the Origins of Evil*, p. 54.
13. Gen. 3:4.
14. Gen. 3:5.
15. Gen. 3:14–15.
16. Gen. 3:16–17.
17. Gen. 3:22–3.
18. Easton, *The Illustrated Bible Dictionary*, s.v. 'Fall of Man', p. 251.
19. See, for instance, John 8:44; Rom. 16:20; 2 Cor. 11:3, 14; Rev. 12:9; 20:2.
20. Mundkur, *The Cult of the Serpent – An Interdisciplinary Survey of Its Manifestations and Origins*, p. 70.
21. Graves and Patai, *Hebrew Myths*, p. 100. Through the union of Eve's daughter and Shemyaza came Hiwa and Hiya, two of the leaders of the Nephilim. This legend is quoted in various midrashic texts (*Yalqut Gen.* 44; *Bereshit Rabbati*, 29–30) and almost certainly stems from the partially reconstructed Book of Giants written during the second century BC.
22. Easton, *The Illustrated Bible Dictionary*, s.v. 'Seraphim', p. 615.
23. Graves and Patai, *Hebrew Myths*, p. 106.
24. 1En. 69:12.
25. 1En. 69:6.
26. Davidson, *A Dictionary of Angels*, s.v. 'Satan', p. 261.

Chapter 5: VISAGE LIKE A VIPER

1. Gen. 18:8.
2. Gen. 19:3.
3. Gen. 19:5.
4. Gen. 32:24–5.
5. Gen. 28:12.
6. Eisenman and Wise, 4Q543, 'Testament of Amram', *The Dead Sea Scrolls Uncovered*, Manuscript B, Fragment 1, pp. 153–6.
7. 2En 1:4–5.
8. Davidson, *A Dictionary of Angels*, s.v. 'Cherubim', pp. 86–7.
9. Milik, *The Books of Enoch – Aramaic Fragments of Qumrân Cave 4*, p. 306; Henning, 'The Book of the Giants', p. 66; see also 'The Midrash of Semhazai and 'Aza'el' quoted in Milik, *The Books of Enoch – Aramaic Fragments of Qumrân Cave 4*, p. 327.
10. 1En. 87:2.
11. 1En. 106:2. (E. Izaac trans.)

12. 2En. 22:8–10.
13. 1En. 106:2 (E. Izaac trans.).
14. 4En. 5i:106:2, quoted in Milik, *The Books of Enoch – Aramaic Fragments of Qumrân Cave 4*, p. 207.
15. Charlesworth, *The Old Testament Pseudepigrapha, Apocalyptic Literature and Testaments*, vol. 1, n. g to 1En. 106, p. 86.
16. Written communication dated 18 September 1995, following a lecture at Leigh-on-Sea, Essex, on the origins of the fallen race, during which Margaret Norman first notified me of this fascinating account of an 'angel child'.
17. I refer here to the text entitled the Book of Giants, the existence of which had always been known to Hebrew and Middle Eastern scholars, although up until the 1970s our only knowledge of its contents came from the few fragments collected together and reconstructed by literary scholar W. B. Henning, from quotes traced in various Manichaean and anti-Manichaean works dating from the fourth century onwards. During his own lifetime, the prophet Mani is thought to have studied an Aramaic copy of this text and subsequently to have initiated its translation into six, possibly even seven, different Asian languages, including Middle Persian, Parthian, Sogdian and Uighur, as well as Egyptian Coptic. The Manichaean Book of Giants was known and used not only in central Asia and the Middle East, but also as far afield as North Africa and Chinese Turkestan. There is even evidence to indicate that it was translated into Latin.

Where exactly Mani obtained an original Aramaic rendition of this little-known text, and how it corresponded to the extant Book of Enoch, was unknown until the 1970s, when it became apparent to the Hebrew scholar J. T. Milik that textual fragments of no less than twelve copies of the Book of Giants, some corresponding to those already reconstructed by Henning, existed among the corpus of Qumrân literature found in Cave 4 on the Dead Sea from 1947 onwards. This startling discovery not only confirmed that the Essene community had possessed, used and probably even written the Book of Giants, but that it had once been placed alongside the other books or sections making up the original Book of Enoch.

From the surviving Aramaic and Manichaean fragments of the Book of Giants, we know that its contents were contemporary with, if not older than, the surviving sections of the now lost Book of Noah; indeed, there is some indication that either the two books once went hand in hand, or that the Book of Giants was the original source material for the Noahic fragments contained in 1 Enoch. Just how old this archaic religious tract might be, or in what language it was originally written, is uncertain; although it is at least as old as the very earliest parts of the Book of Enoch.

As Milik himself admits, the Book of Giants – which he believes once

formed one of the five books in an Enochian pentateuch – adds greatly to our knowledge and understanding of the fall of the Watchers and, more importantly, the plight of their Nephilim offspring, who give the book its title. Indeed, from the few small fragments gleaned from both the Aramaic and Manichaean versions of the text, it appears to show the Nephilim as real-life characters with very human feelings and failings, quite unlike the way in which both the rebel Watchers and their giant offspring are portrayed in the Book of Enoch. See Henning, 'The Book of the Giants', pp. 52–74, and *The Books of Enoch – Aramaic Fragments of Qumrân Cave 4*, 'The Book of Giants', pp. 298–329.
18. For a résumé of this story of the two hundred trees, see 'The Midrash of Semhazai and 'Aza'el' quoted in Milik, *The Books of Enoch – Aramaic Fragments of Qumrân Cave 4*, p. 327.
19. 4EnGiants, in ibid., p. 306.
20. ibid., pp. 306–7.
21. Henning, 'The Book of the Giants', p. 61.
22. Milik, *The Books of Enoch – Aramaic Fragments of Qumrân Cave 4*, p. 313, l. 6.
23. Bailey, *The God-Kings and the Titans*, p. 186.
24. 1En. 69:12.

Chapter 6: WHEN GIANTS WALKED THE EARTH

1. Hebrew scholars demonstrate that the Book of Genesis was written by two main authors, codenamed J and E. J stands for Jahweh, the name of God used by an author from the southern kingdom of Judah, and E stands for Elohim, the name of the Jewish god used by an author belonging to the northern tribe of Israel. The editors of the Old Testament utilized stories collected from both kingdoms, often placing quite different variations of the same account side by side, so creating considerable confusion and contradiction in many of its books, particularly in Genesis. There are many other subdivisions of alleged authorship of the Bible, though space does not permit me to go into these within the present work.
2. Gen. 14:5.
3. Deut. 2:20.
4. Num. 13:33.
5. Num. 13:32.
6. Num. 13:22.
7. Jos. 14:14.
8. Jos. 15:13–4.

9. Easton, *The Illustrated Bible Dictionary*, s.v. 'Anak', p. 40.
10. Odelain and Séguineau, *Dictionary of Proper Names and Places in the Bible*, s. v. 'Anak', p. 27.
11. Jos. 12:4.
12. Deut. 1:4.
13. Norvill, *Giants*, p. 40.
14. Deut. 3:13.
15. Easton, *The Illustrated Bible Dictionary*, s. v. 'Bashan', p. 83.
16. Gen. 14:5.
17. Jos. 13:11.
18. Babylonian Talmud, Nidda 61 a (ix, 5).
19. Graves and Patai, *Hebrew Myths – the Book of Genesis*, p. 112.
20. Green, 'Chronology of the Bible', *The Illustrated Bible Treasury*, ed. Wright, p. 169.
21. 1 Sam. 17:4–7. The imperial weights of Goliath's spear and armour are given in Norvill, *Giants*, p. 43.
22. See ibid. for various instances of giant bones being discovered in both ancient and more modern times. See also Wood, *Giants and Dwarves*, 1868, for an exhaustive study of this subject that gives countless stories of giant remains found throughout the world. See also the article by Hall, 'Giant Bones'.
23. Morgenstern, 'The Mythological Background of Psalm 82', *Hebrew Union College Annual*, No. 14, 1939, p. 107.
24. Lev. 16:10.
25. Lev. 16:21.
26. Isaiah 1:18.
27. Cavendish, *The Black Arts*, p. 314.
28. ibid., p. 34.
29. Nigosian, *Judaism – The Way of Holiness*, p. 186.
30. ibid., p. 187.
31. Blair, *The Word Illustrated Bible Handbook*, p. 168.
32. Foakes-Jackson, *The Biblical History of the Hebrews*, p. xx.
33. Blair, *The Word Illustrated Bible Handbook*, p. 30.
34. The existence of this silver amulet, which was only discovered during the 1990s, was made known to me by the Hebrew scholar, Professor Philip Alexander, during a conversation on 8 June 1995.
35. The Priestly Blessing is found in Num. 6:24–6.

Chapter 7: ANGELS IN EXILE

1. Jer. 4:16.
2. Blair, *The Word Illustrated Bible Handbook*, pp. 178–83.
3. Dan. 4:10–12.
4. Dan. 4:13–15.
5. Dan. 4:17.
6. Dan. 4:22.
7. Dan. 4:23.
8. 4EnGiants in Milik, *The Books of Enoch – Aramaic Fragments of Qumrân Cave 4*, pp. 306–7.
9. Dan. 7:9.
10. 1En. 106:2.
11. Dan. 6:26.
12. Dan. 10:5–6.
13. 2En. 1:4.
14. Dan. 10:13.
15. Dan. 12:1.
16. Easton, *The Illustrated Bible Dictionary*, s. v. 'Captivity', pp. 125–6.
17. Dan. 8:16.
18. Luke 1:11–19, 26–38.
19. Easton, *The Illustrated Bible Dictionary*, s. v. 'Captivity', pp. 125–6.
20. 2 Kings 17:6, 18:9; Chr. 5:26.
21. Tobit 5–8.
22. Tobit 6:4, 8.
23. Tobit 9.
24. Tobit 12:15.
25. Easton, *The Illustrated Bible Dictionary*, s. v. 'Daniel', pp. 178–9.
26. Lempriere, J., *A Classical Dictionary*, s. v. 'Medes', p. 355.
27. Matheson, *Persia – An Archaeological Guide*, p. 217.
28. According to Herodotus, Cyrus' grandfather was the Median king Astyages, whose daughter, Mandane, married a Persian vassal named Cambyses. To them was born a son named Kurush, who rose to become Cyrus the Great, the founder of the Persian Empire. See Herodotus, *History*, I, 107–8.
29. Matt. 2:7.
30. Herodotus, III, 61–78.
31. ibid., III, 79.
32. Josephus, *Antiquities of the Jews*, X, xi, 7.
33. Herodotus, I, 98.
34. In one form, the seven Indo-Iranian gods are mentioned in an

inscription commemorating the signing of a treaty between the Hittite peoples of Anatolia, modern-day Turkey, and the Mitanni culture of Syria, at a place named Boghagköy. Dating to around 1500 BC, they include Mitra, the Vedic form of the Zoroastrian Mithra, Varuna, Indra and two Nasatyas. The first two, Mitra and Varuna, are preceded by a word meaning 'two gods', showing some form of dualistic relationship between them, similar to that found in Iranian mythology between Ahura Mazda and Angra Mainyu. In the *Rig Veda* they often appear together under the compound name of Mitra-Varuna.

35. For instance, see Graves (ed.), *New Larousse Encyclopaedia of Mythology* p. 317. Others, however, such as W. O. E. Oesterley, have suggested that the seven archangels derive from the seven planetary influences of both Akkadian and Babylonian mythology. See 'Angelology and Demonology in Early Judaism' in Manson (ed.), *A Companion to the Bible*. It is far more likely that the Jews identified the *Amesha Spentas* as symbolic aspects of their own God, yet in so doing inadvertently added an extra angel, making seven archangels and the godhead itself.

36. 1En. 20.

37. Strugnell, 'The Angelic Liturgy', in *Congress Volume Oxford*, Supplements to Vetus Testamentum, vii, Leiden, 1960, pp. 318–45. See also Vermes, 'Songs for the Holocaust of the Sabbath', 4Q400–7, *The Dead Sea Scrolls in English*, pp. 220–30.

38. Oesterley and Robinson, *Hebrew Religion – Its Origin and Development*, pp. 312–14, 386–400.

39. Frye, *The Heritage of Persia*, p. 154.

40. Charles, *The Book of Enoch*, 1912, p. 16 n. 1En. 6:2.

41. Alexander, 'Targumim and Early Exegesis of "Sons of God" in Genesis 6', pp. 60–61.

42. Eisenman and Wise, 4Q543, 'Testament of Amram', *The Dead Sea Scrolls Uncovered*, p. 153.

43. ibid, pp. 30–31, 151–2.

44. Zaehner, *The Dawn and Twilight of Zoroastrianism*, pp. 36–7.

45. 4Q543 'Testament of Amram', *The Dead Sea Scrolls Uncovered*, p. 156.

46. Zaehner, *The Dawn and Twilight of Zoroastrianism*, pp. 34–6.

47. Laurence, *The Book of Enoch*, xlv–xlvi.

Chapter 8: TERRIBLE LIE

1. Zaehner, *The Dawn and Twilight of Zoroastrianism*, p. 33.

2. ibid.

3. Mehr, *The Zoroastrian Tradition*, p. 5.

4. Graves, *New Larousse Encyclopaedia of Mythology*, p. 317.
5. Ulansey, *The Origins of the Mithraic Mysteries*, pp. 29–30, citing Charles Dupuis, *Origine de tous les cultes*, H. Agasse, Paris, 1795, vol. 1, Part 1, p. 78.
6. Lempriere, *A Classical Dictionary*, s. v. 'Zoroaster', p. 659.
7. Davidson, *A Dictionary of Angels*, s. v. 'Tir', p. 290.
8. ibid., s. v. 'Tiriel', p. 290.
9. Graves, *New Larousse Encyclopaedia of Mythology*, p. 317.
10. Boyce, *A History of Zoroastrianism*, vol. 1, p. 201.
11. Churchward, *Signs and Symbols of Primordial Man*, p. 234.
12. Davidson, *A Dictionary of Angels*, s. v. 'Azazel', p. 63; ibid., s. v. 'Eblis', p. 101.
13. ibid., s. v. 'Peri', pp. 222–3.
14. Atkinson, *The Shah Nameh of the Persian Poet Firdausi*, p. 1.
15. ibid., p. 2.
16. Snesarev, G. P., 'Remnants of pre-Islamic Beliefs and Rituals Among the Khorezm Uzbeks', trans. from the Russian, in *Soviet Anthropology and Archaeology*, New York, Spring 1971, p. 339, quoted in Scott, 'Zoroastrian Traces Along the Upper Amu Darya (Oxus)', p. 218.
17. Snesarev, G. P., trans. from the Russian, in *Soviet Anthropology and Archaeology*, New York, Summer 1971, p. 34 n. 44, quoted in Scott, art. cit., p. 218.
18. Delitzsch, *A New Commentary on Genesis*, vol. 1, p. 225.
19. In Hindu mythology, which derives its pantheon of heavenly and earthly deities from the same primary source as Iran, the roles are reversed, with the *ahuras – asuras* in their language – being seen as evil, destructive spirits and the *daevas* – referred to as *devas* or *suryas* – being looked upon as shining deities of light. The *Rig Veda* contains approximately the same number of *asuras* as it does *devas*, although there is often no clear distinction between the two opposing groups of deities. See Graves, *New Larousse Encyclopaedia of Mythology*, pp. 336–7; Davidson, *A Dictionary of Angels*, s.v. 'Asuras', p. 60.
20. Davidson, *A Dictionary of Angels*, s.v. 'Surya', p. 281.
21. Milik, *The Books of Enoch – Aramaic Fragments of Qumrân Cave 4*, p. 172, n. L. 7.
22. Mehr, *The Zoroastrian Tradition*, p. 3.
23. Account and spellings taken from Boyce, *A History of Zoroastrianism*, p. 96.
24. Staniland Wake, *Serpent-Worship and Other Essays*, p. 38.
25. Boyce, *A History of Zoroastrianism*, vol. 1, p. 96.
26. Staniland Wake, *Serpent-Worship and Other Essays*, pp. 39–40, n. 4.
27. ibid., p. 39.
28. ibid.

29. Zaehner, *The Dawn and Twilight of Zoroastrianism*, p. 100.
30. ibid., p. 37; Boyce, *A History of Zoroastrianism*, vol. 1, p. 12.
31. Zaehner, *The Dawn and Twilight of Zoroastrianism*, p. 163, citing an account of the *daeva*-worshippers described by Plutarch.
32. ibid., p. 40; citing Yasht 47.4.
33. ibid.; citing Yasht 46.6.
34. There seems good evidence to indicate that the Magi heavily influenced the final form of the *Bundahishn* by removing the legendary place-names mentioned in Avestan material from their traditional sites in eastern Iran to new locations in their homeland of Media. Scholars have seen these alterations as deliberate falsifications by the Magi; in my opinion, however, all that this demonstrates is the fierce mythological rivalry which existed between the Magi of Media and the Avestan priests of eastern Iran, both of whom laid claim to Zoroaster's legendary ancestry. See *A History of Zoroastrianism*, vol. 1, p. 278; Izady, *The Kurds – A Concise Handbook*, p. 44.

Chapter 9: BORN OF THE DEMON RACE

1. Firdowsi, *The Shah Nameh of the Persian Poet Firdausi*, trans. Atkinson, pp. 1–2.
2. ibid., pp. 3–4.
3. ibid., pp. 35–41.
4. Curtis, *Persian Myths*, p. 37.
5. Ferdowsi, *The Epic of the Kings – Shah-Nama*, trans. Levy, p. 35.
6. ibid.
7. ibid.
8. Firdowsi, *The Shah Nameh of the Persian Poet Firdausi*, trans. Atkinson, p. 49.
9. Katrak, *Who Are the Parsees?*, p. 6.
10. ibid.
11. Firdowsi, *The Shah Nameh of the Persian Poet Firdausi*, trans. Atkinson, p. 49.
12. Ferdowsi, *The Epic of the Kings – Shah-Nama*, trans. Levy, p. 36.
13. Charlesworth, *The Old Testament Pseudepigrapha, Apocalyptic Literature and Testaments*, trans. of 1 Enoch by E. Izaac, 1En. 106:2.
14. ibid.
15. ibid.
16. Vermes, *The Dead Sea Scrolls in English*, 1QapGen, II:1, p. 252.
17. Curtis, *Persian Myths*, p. 31.
18. Graves, *New Larousse Encyclopaedia of Mythology*, p. 322.

19. Firdowsi, *The Shah Nameh of the Persian Poet Firdausi*, trans. Atkinson, p. 50.
20. Curtis, *Persian Myths*, p. 37.
21. Firdowsi, *The Shah Nameh of the Persian Poet Firdausi*, trans. Atkinson, p. 51.
22. Katrak, *Who Are the Parsees?*, p. 7.
23. Firdowsi, *The Shah Nameh of the Persian Poet Firdausi*, trans. Atkinson, p. 52.
24. Ferdowsi, *The Epic of the Kings – Shah-Nama*, trans. Levy, p. 42.
25. ibid., p. 39.
26. ibid., p. 41.
27. Curtis, *Persian Myths*, p. 38.
28. Firdowsi, *The Shah Nameh of the Persian Poet Firdausi*, trans. Atkinson, p. 64.
29. ibid., p. 65.
30. Katrak, *Who Are the Parsees?*, p. 7.
31. Curtis, *Persian Myths*, pp. 38–9.
32. Katrak, *Who Are the Parsees?*, p. 7; citing J. Malcolm, *History of Persia*, vol. 1.
33. Ferdowsi, *The Epic of the Kings – Shah-Nama*, trans. Levy, pp. 47–8.
34. Katrak, *Who Are the Parsees?*, p. 7, cf. 'Sanjana'.
35. Brown, in *Pears Medical Encyclopaedia*, pp. 88–9.
36. Firdowsi, *The Shah Nameh of the Persian Poet Firdausi*, trans. Atkinson, p. 313.
37. Henning, 'The Book of the Giants', p. 55.
38. ibid.
39. Ferdowsi, *The Epic of the Kings – Shah-Nama*, trans. Levy, p. 5.
40. Curtis, *Persian Myths*, p. 34; Ferdowsi, *The Epic of the Kings – Shah-Nama*, trans. Levy, p. 17.
41. Curtis, *Persian Myths*, p. 32.
42. Hamzeh'ee, *The Yaresan – A Sociological, Historical and Religio-Historical Study of a Kurdish Community*, p. 92.
43. Ferdowsi, *The Epic of the Kings – Shah-Nama*, trans. Levy, p. 37.
44. ibid.
45. Curtis, *Persian Myths*, p. 32.
46. ibid., p. 26; citing Yasht 19,34.
47. Ferdowsi, *The Epic of the Kings – Shah-Nama*, trans. Levy, p. 17.
48. Inman, *Ancient Faiths Embodied in Ancient Names*, vol. 2, p. 460 n. 88, citing Malcolm, *History of Persia*, pp. 192–3.
49. For an account of Enoch and Elijah, with 'faces that were bright' and eyes that 'shone brighter than the morning star', see Sir E. A. Wallis Budge, *The Life and Exploits of Alexander the Great*, 1896, quoted in

Sitchin, *The Stairway to Heaven*, p. 23; an account of Noah's facial radiance is found in 1En. 106; for Abraham's facial radiance at birth, which 'lighted up the cave from end to end', see Graves and Patai, *Hebrew Myths – the Book of Genesis*, p. 136.
50. For an account of Enoch and Elijah's great height, see Budge, *The Life and Exploits of Alexander the Great*, quoted in Sitchin, *The Stairway to Heaven*, p. 23; for Abraham, see Graves and Patai, *Hebrew Myths – the Book of Genesis*, p. 137; also Talmud, Sophrim, Ch. 21.
51. Inman, *Ancient Faiths*, vol. 2, p. 460 n. 88.

Chapter 10: ON THE EDGE OF DEATH

1. Firdowsi, *The Shah Nameh of the Persian Poet Firdausi*, trans. Atkinson, p. 49.
2. Drower, *The Mandaeans of Iraq and Iran*, 'The Simurgh and Hirmiz Shah', pp. 393–9.
3. Firdowsi, *The Shah Nameh of the Persian Poet Firdausi*, trans. Atkinson, pp. 279–80.
4. ibid., p. 307.
5. ibid., p. 308.
6. ibid., pp. 308–9.
7. Boyce, *A History of Zoroastrianism*, p. 156.
8. Curtis, *Persian Myths*, p. 18.
9. Devereux, *Shamanism and the Mystery Lines*, pp. 148–9, quoting the pioneering work of R. Gordon Wasson and his wife, taken from Weston La Barre, 'Anthropological Perspective on Hallucinations and Hallucinogens', in R. K. Siegel and L. J. West (eds.), *Hallucinations*, John Wiley, 1975.
10. Hastings (ed.), *Encyclopaedia of Religion and Ethics*, s.v. 'Haoma', vol. 8, p. 294 col. B.
11. Mackenzie, *Indian Myth and Legend*, pp. 41, 145–6; Cotterell, *A Dictionary of World Mythology*, p. 90.
12. Curtis, *Persian Myths*, p. 53.
13. Gen. 3:22–4.
14. For example, in the early thirteenth-century Islamic classic, *The Conference of the Birds* (*Mantiq al-Tayr*), by the Persian poet Farid ud-Din Attar, a large group of birds, including the nightingale, the peacock, the hawk, and many more besides, set out on a hazardous journey under the leadership of the hoopoe (the bird which in legend guided King Solomon to the Queen of Sheba) in search of their mysterious king, the Simurgh. Having traversed seven different valleys signifying Search, Love, Know-

ledge, Detachment, Unity, Bewilderment and Self-noughting, the surviving thirty birds are finally admitted into the presence of their master, who, they realize, is a personification of themselves – a pun on the word *simorgh* which means thirty (*si*) birds (*morgh*) in the Persian language.

The story is really about the wisdom of Sufism, the mystical branch of Islam, and there is every indication not only that Attar was a Sufi himself, but that he was also an inheritor of pre-Islamic traditions borrowed from the Magi, who were an important influence on the development of the mostly Shi'ite Sufism in Attar's native Persia. This influence is clearly prominent in the book, which, like Magianism and Zoroastrianism, utilizes the image of fire to signify the divine illumination of God. See Farid ud-Din Attar, *The Conference of the Birds*.

15. Graves, *New Larousse Encyclopaedia of Mythology*, p. 315.

16. Boyce, *A History of Zoroastrianism*, vol. 1, p. 299 n. 28. Knowledge that the lion was an Ahrimanic creature makes sense of the story of Daniel being cast into the lions' den by Darius in Dan. 6:16–28, for it suggests that this account represents the symbolic struggles between the exiled Jewish priesthood and the Magi, seen as representatives of Angra Mainyu in the minds of Zoroastrians.

17. Cameron, *Symbols of Birth and of Death in the Neolithic Era*, p. 27.

18. Turner, *Vultures*, p. 61.

19. Herodotus, *Histories*, 1, 140.

20. Mehr, *The Zoroastrian Tradition*; cf. D. Dhalla, *History*, p. 135.

21. Katrak, *Who are the Parsees?*, p. 229.

22. ibid. p. 228.

23. Drower, *The Mandaeans of Iraq and Iran*, p. 200 n. 6 to p. 184.

24. ibid.

25. Childe, *New Light on the Most Ancient East*, pp. 232–3.

26. Drower, *The Mandaeans of Iraq and Iran*, p. 200 n. 6, cf. Dr Frankfurt, *Archaeology and the Sumerian Problem*, p. 27.

27. For vulture imagery from Susa phase 1, see Childe, *New Light on the Most Ancient East*, p. 234 pl. xxv, 245 pl. xxvii; from Tepeh Aly Abad, see ibid., p. 246 fig. 96; from central Asia, see Trubshaw, 'Bronze Age Rituals from Turkmenistan', p. 32.

28. Jackson, N., 'Bird's Way and Cow-Lane – the Starry Path of the Spirits', p. 30.

29. Haug, *Essays on the Sacred Language, Writings and Religion of the Parsis*, p. 240. The dog chosen is described as follows: 'It is called "the four-eyed dog", a yellow spot on each of its eyelids being considered an additional eye. He has yellow ears, and the colour of the rest of his body varies from yellow to white. To his eyes a kind of magnetic influence is ascribed.'

30. Drower, *The Mandaeans of Iraq and Iran*, p. 200 n. 6, citing the *Rivâyât Kama Bohra*.
31. Heinberg, *Memories and Visions of Paradise*, pp. 226–32.
32. ibid., p. 234; cf. Ring, *Heading toward Omega*, pp. 226–7.
33. See Mellaart, *Çatal Hüyük – A Neolithic Town in Anatolia*; Bacon, *Archaeology Discoveries in the 1960s*, pp. 110–26.
34. Cameron, *Symbols of Birth and of Death in the Neolithic Era*, p. 28; citing *Anatolian Studies*, vol. XIV, 1964, p. 64; Mellaart, *Çatal Hüyük – A Neolithic Town in Anatolia*, p. 168.
35. Gimbutas, *The Civilization of the Goddess*, p. 238 fig. 7–26:2.
36. ibid.; Cameron, *Symbols of Birth and of Death in the Neolithic Era*, pp. 27–33.
37. Gimbutas, *The Civilization of the Goddess*, p. 238 fig. 7–26:3.
38. Mellaart, *Çatal Hüyük – A Neolithic Town in Anatolia*, p. 84; Bacon, *Archaeology Discoveries in the 1960s*, p. 124.
39. ibid.
40. Mellaart, *Çatal Hüyük – A Neolithic Town in Anatolia*, p. 20.
41. ibid., p. 167; Bacon, *Archaeology Discoveries in the 1960s*, pp. 121–2.
42. Mellaart, *Çatal Hüyük – A Neolithic Town in Anatolia*, pp. 49–53.
43. ibid., pp. 211–2.
44. ibid., p. 213.

Chapter 11: IN THE REALM OF THE IMMORTALS

1. Turner, *Vultures*, pp. xi, 60–61.
2. ibid., p. 60.
3. Boyce, *A History of Zoroastrianism*, vol. 1, p. 299.
4. Turner, *Vultures*, p. 69.
5. Attar, *The Conference of the Birds*, l. 734.
6. ibid., ll. 744–5.
7. ibid., l. 737.
8. Curtis, *Persian Myths*, p. 13; citing Yasht 14: 35–6.
9. Jackson Coleman, S., 'Treasures of An Archangel'.
10. Davidson, *A Dictionary of Angels*, s.v. 'Sa'adiya'il', p. 251.
11. ibid., s.v. 'Sadayel', p. 252.
12. Boyce, *A History of Zoroastrianism*, vol. 1, pp. 76–8, 78 n. 375.
13. ibid., vol. 1, pp. 144–5.
14. Curtis, *Persian Myths*, p. 19.
15. Boyce, *A History of Zoroastrianism*, vol. 1, p. 145.
16. Hancock, *Fingerprints of the Gods*, pp. 200–202, 485. The author suggests that the climate of *Airyana Vaejah* hints at a polar region, like that

experienced by Antarctica, the proposed place of origin of a high civilization that perhaps existed on the continent before geological upheavals and a crustal displacement caused severe global cataclysms towards the end of the last Ice Age, *c.* 15,000–9500 BC. (See also Chapters 20 and 25 of the present work.)

17. Boyce, *A History of Zoroastrianism*, vol. 1, pp. 143–4.
18. ibid., vol. 1, p. 145; citing the Greater (or Iranian) *Bundahishn*, XXIX, 12 (BTA, 257).
19. Drower, *The Mandaeans of Iraq and Iran*, p. 385.
20. ibid., p. 6.
21. ibid., p. 9.
22. Staniland Wake, *Serpent-Worship and Other Essays*, p. 105.
23. Drower, *The Mandaeans of Iraq and Iran*, p. 9.
24. ibid. Drower's book gives dozens of correspondences between the beliefs and rituals of the Mandai and those of the Magians, Zoroastrians and Parsees of India. These include cleanliness, health of body and ritual obedience, p. xxi; ritual purity and impurity, p. 129; the similarity between the design of the Mandai ritual huts and Cyrus' tomb at Pasargadae, p. 142; ritual invocations, p. 144; ritual clothes and actions, p. 166; funerary practices, pp. 184, 186, 200; Magian sacrifices, p. 225; Parsee ritual meals, pp. 234, 238; fire worship, p. 300.
25. ibid., pp. 6–7.
26. ibid., p. xxiv n. 3. The reputed tomb of Idris, i.e. Enoch, called *Sayyid Idris*, is to be found in a village outside Baghdad. It is visited by Moslems on Sundays, particularly on Easter Sunday.
27. Charroux, *Legacy of the Gods*, p. 86.
28. Vermes, 1QapGenII, 'The Genesis Apocryphon', *The Dead Sea Scrolls in English*, p. 253.
29. Charlesworth, *The Old Testament Pseudepigrapha, Apocalyptic Literature and Testaments*, vol. 1, 1En. 106:6.
30. Drower, *The Mandaeans of Iraq and Iran*, pp. 6–7.
31. Frye, *The Heritage of Persia*, pp. 70–71.

Chapter 12: EASTWARD, IN EDEN

1. Gen. 2:8–10.
2. Odelain and Séguineau, *Dictionary of Proper Names and Places in the Bible*, s.v. 'Eden', p. 103.
3. Politeyan, *Biblical Discoveries in Egypt, Palestine and Mesopotamia*, p. 27.
4. Sinclair, *The Sword and the Grail*, p. 91.
5. O'Brien, *The Genius of the Few*, p. 28.

6. ibid.
7. Graves and Patai, *Hebrew Myths – The Book of Genesis*, p. 70.
8. 2En. 5:1.
9. 2En. 3:3.
10. 2En. 4:1.
11. 2En. 7:1.
12. 2En. 7:2.
13. 2En. 7:5.
14. 2En. 8:1–4.
15. 2En. 8:6.
16. 2En. 8:7–8.
17. Curtis, *Persian Myths*, p. 19.
18. 2En. 10.
19. 2En. 11:1.
20. 2En. 11:2.
21. 2En. 11:3.
22. 2En. 18:1.
23. 2En. 18:2.
24. 2En. 19:1.
25. 2En. 19:2–3.
26. 2En. 20.
27. 1En. 14:9.
28. 1En. 14:12.
29. 1En. 14:16–20.
30. 1En. 14:21.
31. 2En. 21:2.
32. Gen. 2:11–14.
33. Gen. 2:8.
34. Graves and Patai, *Hebrew Myths – The Book of Genesis*, p. 73 n. 2.
35. Gen. 11:2.
36. Gen. 11:1–9.
37. Eupolemus, citing Euseb. Praep. Evan 9 in Cory, *Ancient Fragments*, p. 51.
38. See, for instance, George Smith's attempts at equating Nimrod with Gilgamesh in his 1876 work, *The Chaldean Account of Genesis*.
39. Wigram and Wigram, *The Cradle of Mankind*, p. 26.
40. Graves and Patai, *Hebrew Myths – The Book of Genesis*, p. 74; Odelain and Séguineau, *Dictionary of Proper Names and Places in the Bible*, s.v. 'Eden', p. 104.
41. Chahin, *The Kingdom of Armenia*, p. 114.
42. See, for instance, Berlitz, *The Lost Ship of Noah – In Search of the Ark at Ararat*.
43. Wigram and Wigram, *The Cradle of Mankind*, p. 335.

44. ibid., pp. 335–6.
45. For example, the Armenian monastery of St Jacob in the town of Arghuri (Ahora), north-east of Greater Ararat, is reputed to contain pieces of wood from the Ark itself. See Berlitz, *The Lost Ship of Noah – In Search of the Ark at Ararat*, p. 24.
46. Graves and Patai, *Hebrew Myths – the Book of Genesis*, p. 117 n. 5.
47. Sabar, *The Folk Literature of the Kurdistani Jews – An Anthology*, p. xiii n. 5.
48. Wigram and Wigram, *The Cradle of Mankind*, p. 264.
49. ibid., p. 26.
50. Warren, *Paradise Found – The Cradle of the Human Race at the North Pole*, p. 24 n. 1; cf. Massey, *The Natural Genesis*, vol. 2, p. 231.
51. Moses Khorenats'i, *History of the Armenians*, p. 80.
52. ibid., p. 84.
53. ibid., pp. 85, 92.
54. ibid., p. 86.
55. ibid., pp. 87–8.
56. ibid., p. 88 n. 6.
57. Wigram and Wigram, *The Cradle of Mankind*, p. 249.
58. ibid., p. 26.
59. 1En. 24:1.
60. 1En. 17:5.
61. Charroux, *Legacy of the Gods*, p. 91.

Chapter 13: THE PEACOCK ANGEL

1. The entire account of Sir Austen Henry Layard's visit to the Yezidi shrine of Sheikh Adi has been taken from the 1851 edition of *Nineveh and Its Remains*.
2. Izady, *The Kurds – A Concise Handbook*, p. 154.
3. Empson, *The Cult of the Peacock Angel*, p. 25.
4. Hamzeh'ee, *The Yaresan*, p. 121.
5. Empson, *The Cult of the Peacock Angel*, p. 44.
6. Izady, *The Kurds – A Concise Handbook*, p. 153.
7. ibid., p. 155.
8. Empson, *The Cult of the Peacock Angel*, p. 86.
9. ibid., p. 43.
10. Wigram and Wigram, *The Cradle of Mankind*, p. 105.
11. Empson, *The Cult of the Peacock Angel*, pp. 32–3.
12. ibid., p. 122.
13. Guest, *The Yezidis*, p. 138.
14. Empson, *The Cult of the Peacock Angel*, p. 85.

15. ibid., p. 86.
16. Drower, *Peacock Angel*, p. 27; Empson, *The Cult of the Peacock Angel*, pp. 87, 101.
17. Empson, *The Cult of the Peacock Angel*, p. 87.
18. Drower, *Peacock Angel*, p. 27.
19. ibid.
20. ibid.
21. Empson, *The Cult of the Peacock Angel*, pp. 52–3.
22. Drower, *Peacock Angel*, p. 7.
23. Izady, *The Kurds – A Concise Handbook*, p. 154.
24. Layard, *Nineveh and Its Remains*, p. 195.
25. Izady, *The Kurds – A Concise Handbook*, p. 154.
26. Layard, *Nineveh and Its Remains*, p. 197; Empson, *The Cult of the Peacock Angel*, p. 141.
27. Cavendish (ed.), *Man, Myth and Magic*, s.v. 'Peacock', p. 2154.
28. ibid.
29. 'Wildlife on One with David Attenborough', BBC TV documentary, screened in UK, 18 May 1995.
30. ibid.
31. Cavendish (ed.), *Man, Myth and Magic*, s.v. 'Peacock', p. 2154.
32. ibid.
33. Empson, *The Cult of the Peacock Angel*, p. 45.
34. ibid., p. 85.
35. ibid., p. 83.
36. Wigram and Wigram, *The Cradle of Mankind*, p. 336.
37. ibid., p. 335.
38. ibid.
39. Empson, *The Cult of the Peacock Angel*, p. 148.
40. ibid., p. 100.
41. Drower, *Peacock Angel*, p. 55.
42. ibid.
43. ibid.
44. Ulansey, *The Origins of the Mithraic Mysteries – Cosmology and Salvation in the Ancient World*, pp. 27–8.
45. Empson, *The Cult of the Peacock Angel*, p. 46.

Chapter 14: CHILDREN OF THE DJINN

1. Izady, *The Kurds – A Concise Handbook*, p. 149.
2. Hamzeh'ee, *The Yaresan*, pp. 50–51.
3. Izady, *The Kurds – A Concise Handbook*, p. 146.

4. ibid.
5. ibid., p. 147.
6. ibid., p. 34.
7. Curtis, *Persian Myths*, pp. 35–6.
8. Hamzeh'ee, *The Yaresan*, p. 80.
9. ibid.
10. Izady, *The Kurds – A Concise Handbook*, p. 147.
11. Staniland Wake, *Serpent-Worship and Other Essays*, p. 112; cf. Sir Henry Rawlinson.
12. Moses Khorenats'i, *History of the Armenians*, p. 121.
13. Izady, *The Kurds – A Concise Handbook*, p. 139.
14. Black and Green, *Gods, Demons and Symbols of Ancient Mesopotamia – An Illustrated Dictionary*, s. v. 'Ningišzida', fig. 115.
15. ibid. pp. 138–9.
16. Moses Khorenats'i *History of the Armenians*, p. 121.
17. ibid., p. 121 n. 17.
18. Izady, *The Kurds – A Concise Handbook*, p. 241.
19. ibid., p. 147.
20. Ferdowsi, *The Epic of the Kings – Shah-Nama*, pp. 39, 42.
21. Moses Khorenats'i, *History of the Armenians*, p. 127.
22. ibid., pp. 83, 85.
23. Izady, *The Kurds – A Concise Handbook*, p. 38; Moses Khorenats'i, *History of the Armenians*, pp. 114–39. It is important to note that Moses of Khorenats'i confuses the later Tigran the Great with an earlier Tigran who ruled Armenia at the time of Cyrus the Great in the sixth century BC. This has led to much of the history of the latter being applied to the former in his work.
24. Chahin, *The Kingdom of Armenia*, pp. 227–8.
25. ibid., p. 229.
26. Izady, *The Kurds – A Concise Handbook*, p. 39.
27. Chahin, *The Kingdom of Armenia*, p. 229.
28. Plutarch, *Lives*, p. 356.
29. Chahin, *The Kingdom of Armenia*, p. 236.
30. Lenormant, *Chaldean Magic*, pp. 232–3; cf. the author's *Lettres Assyriologiques*, vol. 1, pp. 97–101.
31. Hamzeh'ee, *The Yaresan*, p. 74, citing *Haqq ol-haqayeq*, pp. 92–3, 101.
32. Sabar, *The Folk Literature of the Kurdistani Jews – An Anthology*, p. 6.
33. ibid., p. 4.
34. Hamzeh'ee *The Yaresan*, p. 79; cf. Buraka'i's *Doureh-ye haftavaneh*, pp. 78, 135–6.
35. ibid., p. 91, citing Jayhunabadi, *Haqq ol-haqayeq*, pp. 155–6, 540, 562, etc.

36. ibid., p. 93.
37. ibid., p. 91.
38. ibid., p. 87.
39. Sabar, *The Folk Literature of the Kurdistani Jews – An Anthology*, p. xv, citing Minorsky, p. 1134.
40. Izady, *The Kurds – A Concise Handbook*, p. 241.
41. ibid.
42. Drower, *Peacock Angel*, p. 25.
43. ibid., p. 32.
44. Chahin, *The Kingdom of Armenia*, p. 42.

Chapter 15: WHERE HEAVEN AND EARTH MEET

1. Black and Green, *Gods, Demons and Symbols of Ancient Mesopotamia – An Illustrated Dictionary*, s.v. 'E-kur', p. 74.
2. ibid.
3. Dates of reigns taken from Roux, *Ancient Iraq*, chronology chart, pp. 460–61.
4. Barton, *Miscellaneous Babylonian Inscriptions*, p. 1.
5. ibid., 'Introductory Note'.
6. ibid.
7. ibid., pp. 16–17.
8. ibid., p. 4.
9. O'Brien, *The Genius of the Few*, pp. 37–8. O'Brien includes the word *ge*, 'of', in the title of the *a-nun-na*, making *a-nun-na-(ge)*. This is not usual. I have decided to stick with this particular spelling so as not to break with the continuity of his translation of the Kharsag texts.
10. ibid., p. 43.
11. ibid., p. 37.
12. ibid., p. 66.
13. ibid.
14. ibid., pp. 44–5, 53.
15. ibid., pp. 45–6.
16. ibid., p. 54.
17. ibid., p. 46.
18. ibid., p. 59.
19. ibid., p. 47.
20. ibid., p. 48.
21. ibid., pp. 48–9.
22. ibid., pp. 62–3.
23. ibid., p. 69.

24. ibid., p. 70.
25. ibid.
26. ibid., p. 167.
27. ibid., p. 168.
28. ibid., p. 169.
29. ibid., p. 15.
30. ibid., pp. 108–9.
31. Hamzeh'ee, *The Yaresan*, p. 112, citing V. Justin Prásek, Darmstadt, 1968.
32. Black and Green, *Gods, Demons and Symbols of Ancient Mesopotamia – An Illustrated Dictionary*, s.v. 'Anuna (Anunnakku)', p. 34.
33. Dalley, *Myths from Mesopotamia*, 'Etana', Tablet I, p. 190.
34. Black and Green, *Gods, Demons and Symbols of Ancient Mesopotamia – An Illustrated Dictionary*, s.v. 'Anuna (Anunnakku)', p. 34.
35. Spence, *Myths and Legends of Babylonia and Assyria*, p. 90.
36. Black and Green, *Gods, Demons and Symbols of Ancient Mesopotamia – An Illustrated Dictionary*, s.v. 'Anuna (Anunnakku)', p. 34.
37. Roux, *Ancient Iraq*, pp. 70–71.
38. See O'Brien's argument in respect to the cuneiform *a - id - nun - bi - ir - ra*, translated by Barton as 'canal Nunbiira', a nonsensical name assumed to be the title of a canal at Nippur. O'Brien shows that the more direct translation should read 'river great the flowed swiftly' – *The Genius of the Few*, p. 57.
39. ibid., p. 45, 63.
40. ibid., p. 63.
41. Lenormant, *Chaldean Magic*, p. 154
42. Warren, *Paradise Found – The Cradle of the Human Race at the North Pole*, pp. 126–7, 170–71.
43. ibid., p. 170.
44. ibid., pp. 126–7, 126 n. 2; cf. Smith, *Assyrian Discoveries*, pp. 392–3; Massey, *The Natural Genesis*, vol. 2, p. 231.
45. Lenormant, *Chaldean Magic*, p. 154.
46. Warren, *Paradise Found – The Cradle of the Human Race at the North Pole*, p. 127; Roux, *Ancient Iraq*, p. 147.
47. Dalley, *Myths from Mesopotamia*, p. 40.
48. Jacobsen, *The Treasures of Darkness – A History of Mesopotamian Religion*, pp. 195–204.
49. Black and Green, *Gods, Demons and Symbols of Ancient Mesopotamia – An Illustrated Dictionary*, s. v. 'Huwawa (Hubaba)', p. 106.
50. Izady, *The Kurds – A Concise Handbook*, p. 19, citing *The Epic of Gilgamesh*, trans. and ed. Sanders, 1972.
51. O'Brien, *The Genius of the Few*, p. 38.

52. Izady, *The Kurds – A Concise Handbook*, p. 19.
53. ibid., pp. 23–4.
54. ibid., p. 18.
55. ibid., p. 19.
56. O'Brien, *The Genius of the Few*, p. 15.
57. ibid., p. 120.
58. Heinberg, *Memories and Visions of Paradise – Exploring the Universal Myth of a Lost Golden Age*, p. 42.
59. Roux, *Ancient Iraq*, p. 106.
60. ibid.
61. Bibby, *Looking for Dilmun*, p. 43.
62. Kramer, *Sumerian Mythology*, p. 81.
63. Izady, *The Kurds – A Concise Handbook*, p. 43.
64. ibid., p. 44.
65. ibid.
66. ibid.
67. ibid.
68. Jacobsen, *The Treasures of Darkness – A History of Mesopotamian Religion*, pp. 110–11.
69. Izady, *The Kurds – A Concise Handbook*, map showing the religious composition of Kurdistan, p. 134.
70. ibid.
71. ibid., p. 151.
72. Trowbridge, 'The Alevis, or Deifiers of Ali', p. 340.

Chapter 16: SLEEPING WITH GODS

1. Mackenzie, *Myths of Babylonia and Assyria*, p. 165.
2. Dalley, *Myths from Mesopotamia*, 'Etana III', pp. 189–200.
3. Black and Green, *Gods, Demons and Symbols of Ancient Mesopotamia – An Illustrated Dictionary*, s. v. 'Etana', p. 78.
4. ibid., s. v. 'Gilgamesh', p. 91.
5. Dalley, *Myths from Mesopotamia*, 'Gilgamesh', Tablet I, p. 51.
6. ibid.
7. Black and Green, *Gods, Demons and Symbols of Ancient Mesopotamia – An Illustrated Dictionary*, s. v. 'Sacred Marriage', pp. 157–8; Roux, *Ancient Iraq*, p. 93.
8. Black and Green, *Gods, Demons and Symbols of Ancient Mesopotamia – An Illustrated Dictionary*, s. v. 'Sacred Marriage', pp. 157–8.
9. ibid.; Roux, *Ancient Iraq*, p. 93.
10. Herodotus, *Histories*, I, 181.

11. ibid., I, 182.
12. Roux, *Ancient Iraq*, p. 150.
13. ibid., p. 145.
14. O'Brien, *The Genius of the Few*, p. 27.
15. Dalley, *Myths from Mesopotamia*, 'Etana III', p. 199.
16. Mackenzie, *Myths of Babylonia and Assyria*, p. 74.
17. Black and Green, *Gods, Demons and Symbols of Ancient Mesopotamia – An Illustrated Dictionary*, s. v. 'Ninurta', pp. 142–3.
18. Mackenzie, *Myths of Babylonia and Assyria*, p. 74.
19. Ibid.
20. Black and Green, *Gods, Demons and Symbols of Ancient Mesopotamia – An Illustrated Dictionary*, s. v. 'Imdugud (Anzu)', p. 107.
21. Spence, *Myths and Legends of Babylonia and Assyria*, p. 93.
22. Roux, *Ancient Iraq*, p. 137; Black and Green, *Gods, Demons and Symbols of Ancient Mesopotamia – An Illustrated Dictionary*, s. v. 'Imdugud (Anzu)', p. 107; Solecki and McGovern, 'Predatory Birds and Prehistoric Man', p. 89.
23. ibid., pp. 89–90.
24. Roux, *Ancient Iraq*, p. 328.
25. Sitchin, *The 12th Planet*, p. 22.
26. Smith, *The Chaldean Account of Genesis*, p. 105.
27. ibid., p. 103.
28. ibid., p. 227.
29. The entire account of the flood story is paraphrased and quoted from Dalley, *Myths from Mesopotamia*, 'Gilgamesh XI', i-iv, pp. 109–15.
30. Jacobsen, *The Treasures of Darkness – A History of Mesopotamian Religion*, pp. 206–7; Black and Green, *Gods, Demons and Symbols of Ancient Mesopotamia – An Illustrated Dictionary*, s. v. 'Gilgamesh', pp. 89–91; 'plant of life', pp. 148–9.
31. Campbell-Thompson, *Semitic Magic*, p. 2.
32. Summers, *The Vampire – His Kith and Kin*, p. 222.
33. ibid., p. 225.
34. Campbell-Thompson, *Semitic Magic*, p. 2.
35. ibid., p. 3.
36. Summers, *The Vampire – His Kith and Kin*, citing R. Campbell-Thompson, *The Devils and Evil Spirits of Babylonia*, vol. 1, pp. 69–71.
37. ibid.
38. ibid.
39. Roux, *Ancient Iraq*, p. 411, ch. 7 n. 11, citing E. A. Speiser, *Annual of the American Schools of Oriental Research*, New Haven, VIII (1928), pp. 18, 31.
40. Lambert and Millard, *Atra-Hasis – The Babylonian Story of the Flood*, p. 136.

41. Izady, *The Kurds – A Concise Handbook*, p. 35.
42. Sabar, *The Folk Literature of the Kurdistani Jews – An Anthology*, p. xiii n. 4, citing Ginzberg, 5, 186; 4, 269.
43. Roux, *Ancient Iraq*, p. 299.
44. Sabar, *The Folk Literature of the Kurdistani Jews – An Anthology*, p. xiii n. 4, citing Benjamin II, p. 94: 'I myself obtained several fragments of the ark (from the base of Al Judi) which appeared to be covered with a kind of substance resembling tar.'
45. ibid., citing Benjamin II, p. 94: 'At the base of the mountain stand four stone pillars, which, according to the people residing here, formerly belonged to an ancient altar. This altar is believed to be that which Noah built on coming out of the ark.'
46. Civil (ed.), 'The Sumerian Flood Story', CBS 10673: 254–60, in Lambert and Millard, *Atra–Hasis – The Babylonian Story of the Flood*, p. 145.
47. 1En. 10:3.
48. Lambert and Millard, *Atra-Hasis – The Babylonian Story of the Flood*, p. 135.
49. ibid., p. 136.

Chapter 17: IN THE FOOTSTEPS OF THE WATCHERS

1. Moore, 'A Pre-Neolithic Farmer's Village on the Euphrates', pp. 62–70.
2. Izady, *The Kurds – A Concise Handbook*, p. 24.
3. ibid.
4. Braidwood, R. J., 'Miscellaneous Analyses of Materials from Jarmo', in Braidwood (ed.), *Prehistoric Archaeology along the Zagros Flanks*, p. 542.
5. Braidwood, R. J., 'Jarmo Chronology', in ibid., p. 538.
6. Mellaart, *Çatal Hüyük – A Neolithic Town in Anatolia*, pp. 211–12.
7. Izady, *The Kurds – A Concise Handbook*, p. 24.
8. Roux, *Ancient Iraq*, p. 59.
9. ibid.
10. ibid.
11. ibid., p. 23.
12. Braidwood, R. J., 'Jarmo Chronology', in Braidwood (ed.), *Prehistoric Archaeology along the Zagros Flanks*, p. 539.
13. Roux, *Ancient Iraq*, p. 67.
14. ibid., p. 69; Braidwood, R. J. 'Miscellaneous Analyses of Materials from Jarmo', in Braidwood (ed.), *Prehistoric Archaeology along the Zagros Flanks*, p. 543.

15. See Solecki, *Shanidar – The Humanity of Neanderthal Man*, for a full account of excavations at Shanidar.
16. Mellaart, *Çatal Hüyük – A Neolithic Town in Anatolia*, pp. 19, 207.
17. Solecki, 'Predatory Bird Rituals at Zawi Chemi Shanidar', pp. 42–7.
18. ibid., p. 42, citing Reed, 1959.
19. ibid.
20. ibid.
21. ibid., p. 44.
22. ibid.
23. ibid.
24. ibid., p. 47.
25. ibid.
26. ibid., p. 45.
27. Izady, *The Kurds – A Concise Handbook*, p. 156.
28. ibid.
29. Lev. 17:7.
30. Milik, *The Books of Enoch – Aramaic Fragments of Qumrân Cave 4*, p. 313 n. L. 6.
31. Spence, *Myths and Legends of Babylonia and Assyria*, p. 292.
32. Wigram and Wigram, *The Cradle of Mankind*, p. 334.
33. ibid.
34. 1En. 15:11.
35. Charles, *The Book of Enoch*, p. 37, n. to 1En. 15:11.
36. Roux, *Ancient Iraq*, p. 58.
37. Braidwood, R. J. 'Miscellaneous Analyses of Materials', in Braidwood (ed.), *Prehistoric Archaeology along the Zagros Flanks*, p. 543.
38. Morales, V. B., 'Jarmo Figurines and Other Clay Objects', in ibid., pp. 369–83.
39. ibid., p. 383.
40. ibid., p. 384.
41. ibid., p. 386.
42. ibid., p. 383.

Chapter 18: SHAMAN-LIKE DEMON

1. Cottrell, *The Land of Shinar*, p. 81, citing Sir L. Woolley, *Excavations at Ur*.
2. ibid., citing Woolley.
3. ibid., pp. 82, 84 n. 1.
4. ibid., p. 82.
5. Roux, *Ancient Iraq*, p. 71.

6. ibid., p. 72.
7. Morales, V. B., 'Jarmo Figures and Other Clay Objects', in Braidwood (ed.), *Prehistoric Archaeology along the Zagros Flanks*, pp. 383–4.
8. Roux, *Ancient Iraq*, p. 72.
9. von Däniken, *In Search of Ancient Gods – My Pictorial Evidence for the Impossible*, p. 12 pl. 2, p. 16 pl. 9.
10. Mundkur, *The Cult of the Serpent – An Interdisciplinary Survey of Its Manifestations and Origins*, p. 187, citing Sir L. Woolley, *Ur Excavations*, vol. 4, 'The Early Periods', 1955, pp. 12–13.
11. Gen. 10:22.
12. Gen. 14:1.
13. Hinz, *The Lost World of Elam*, p. 14, citing the work of Frank Hole and Kent V. Flannery at Ali Kosh in 1961 and E. O. Negahban from the University of Tehran at Haft Tepeh, between Ahwaz and Susa, in 1966.
14. Curtis, J., 'Introduction' to Curtis (ed.), *Early Mesopotamia and Iran – Contact and Conflict 3500–1600 bc*, p. 18.
15. Porada, E., 'Seals and Related Objects from Early Mesopotamia and Iran', in Curtis (ed.), *Early Mesopotamia and Iran – Contact and Conflict 3500–1600 bc*, p. 47.
16. Curtis (ed.), *Early Mesopotamia and Iran – Contact and Conflict 3500–1600 bc*, pl. 25–17.
17. Childe, *New Light on the Most Ancient East*, pp. 232–3.
18. Drower, *The Mandaeans of Iraq and Iran*, p. 184, 200 n. 6.
19. For vulture imagery from Susa I, see Childe, *New Light on the Most Ancient East*, pl. xxv; for Susa II, see pl. xxvii.
20. Porada, E. 'Seals and Related Objects from Early Mesopotamia and Iran', in Curtis (ed.), *Early Mesopotamia and Iran – Contact and Conflict 3500–1600 bc*, p. 47.
21. Cameron, *Symbols of Birth and of Death in the Neolithic Era*, p. 34.
22. ibid., pp. 35–8.
23. ibid., p. 32.
24. ibid., p. 40.
25. ibid., p. 43.
26. Drower, *Peacock Angel*, p. 7.
27. Mundkur, *The Cult of the Serpent – An Interdisciplinary Survey of Its Manifestations and Origins*, p. 13.

Chapter 19: BORN OF FIRE

1. Mango, *Discovering Turkey*, p. 247.
2. *Born of Fire* was written, directed and co-produced by Jamil Dehlavi and featured the search by a London flutist for the 'master musician'.
3. The visit actually took place in May 1987.
4. Zaehner, *The Dawn and Twilight of Zoroastrianism*, p. 169.
5. Izady, *The Kurds – A Concise Handbook*, p. 38.
6. *Nagel's Encyclopaedia Guide – Turkey*, p. 574.
7. Roux, *Ancient Iraq*, p. 214.
8. *Nagel's Encyclopaedia Guide – Turkey*, p. 574.
9. Mellaart, *Çatal Hüyük – A Neolithic Town in Anatolia*, p. 213.
10. ibid., p. 222.
11. Bacon, *Archaeology Discoveries in the 1960s*, p. 116.
12. Smith, *The Chaldean Account of Genesis*, p. 227.
13. Mellaart, *Çatal Hüyük – A Neolithic Town in Anatolia*, pp. 176–7.
14. ibid., p. 212.
15. ibid., p. 104.
16. For instance a fire shrine, *c.* 1750 BC, was found at Margiana, on the delta of the Murgab river in the Karakum desert of Turkmenistan, and another, *c.* 2000 BC, was excavated in northern Bactria. See R. Trubshaw, 'Bronze Age Rituals in Turkmenistan', pp. 30–32, citing several original sources on the Bactrian-Margiana Archaeological Complex (BMAC).
17. Firdowsi, *The Shah Nameh of the Persian Poet Firdausi*, trans. Atkinson, pp. 3–4.
18. Plutarch, *Lives*, p. 351 and fn.
19. Graves, *New Larousse Encyclopaedia of Mythology*, p. 129.
20. ibid.
21. Boz, *Cappadocia*, p. 22.
22. Mellaart, *Çatal Hüyük – A Neolithic Town in Anatolia*, pls. 29, 37–8.
23. ibid., pp. 152–3.
24. ibid., p. 152.
25. Boz., *Cappadocia*, p. 59.
26. Demir, *Cappadocia – Cradle of History*, pp. 9, 14.
27. ibid., p. 15.
28. ibid., pp. 11–12.
29. ibid., pp. 13, 39–40.
30. ibid., pp. 15, 36–7.
31. ibid., p. 39.
32. ibid.
33. ibid., pp. 16–17.

34. ibid., p. 18.
35. von Däniken, *According to the Evidence*, pp. 317–18.

Chapter 20: HELL-FIRE AND FLOOD

1. Hancock, *Fingerprints of the Gods*, p. 201, citing Vendidad, Fargard I.
2. ibid.
3. ibid.
4. Graves, *New Larousse Encyclopaedia of Mythology*, p. 320.
5. The term Ark was applied to the citadel or fortress of Tabriz, the capital city of Azerbaijan. See Harnack, *Persian Lions, Persian Lambs*, pp. 3–4.
6. Mellaart, *Çatal Hüyük – A Neolithic Town in Anatolia*, p. 222.
7. Graves, *New Larousse Encyclopaedia of Mythology*, p. 320.
8. ibid.
9. ibid.
10. Izady, *The Kurds – A Concise History*, pp. 1, 3.
11. Tomas, *Atlantis – From Legend to Discovery*, p. 25.
12. Hapgood, *The Path of the Pole*, p. 277, citing F. C. Hibben, *The Lost Americans*, pp. 168–70.
13. ibid., p. 277, citing Hibben, *The Lost Americans*, pp. 176–8.
14. ibid.
15. ibid. pp. 275–6, citing Hibben, *The Lost Americans*, pp. 90–92.
16. ibid., p. 276, citing Hibben, *The Lost Americans*, pp. 168–70.
17. Tomas, *Atlantis – From Legend to Discovery*, p. 24.
18. For instance, a reindeer skull found in a rugged region of Russian Armenia, close to Lake Sevan, is a total enigma. Reindeer graze on the plains, not in highland country, and no other evidence of the presence of this species has been found in the region. There is every possibility it was deposited by humans, perhaps as part of some shamanistic practice; however, the fact that it has been dated to 10,000 BC throws a slightly different light on the matter. If the animal really had lived in this region, why was it so far outside its normal habitat? Could the altitude of the location have changed through some kind of cataclysmic upheaval? See Tomas, *Atlantis – From Legend to Discovery*, p. 25.
19. Hapgood, *The Path of the Pole*, pp. 280–86, citing J. B. Delair and E. F. Oppé, 'The Evidence of Violent Extinction in South America'.
20. Hapgood, *Maps of the Ancient Sea Kings*, pp. 174–5.
21. ibid., p. 178.
22. ibid., pp. 175–6.
23. Bellamy, *Moons, Myths and Man*, p. 59.

24. ibid., p. 105.
25. ibid., p. 95.
26. ibid., pp. 95–6.
27. ibid., pp. 105–6.
28. ibid., p. 107. Bellamy unfortunately fails to give an original reference source for this important Hebrew passage, although it is probably taken from one of the many midrashic texts of uncertain origin.
29. Henning, 'The Book of the Giants', p. 69.
30. ibid., p. 58.
31. 4QGiants in Milik, *The Books of Enoch – Aramaic Fragments of Qumrân Cave 4*, p. 304.
32. Cavendish (ed.), *Man, Myth and Magic*, s.v. 'Hell', p. 1260.
33. ibid.
34. Empson, *The Cult of the Peacock Angel*, pp. 83, 85.
35. Roux, *Ancient Iraq*, p. 113.
36. ibid.
37. ibid., p. 114.

Chapter 21: EGYPTIAN GENESIS

1. Drower, *The Mandaeans of Iraq and Iran*, p. 10: 'Still more inexplicable is the assertion that the Egyptians were co-religionists, and that the original ancestors of the Mandaean race went from Egypt to the Tura d Madai.'
2. Mellaart, *Çatal Hüyük – A Neolithic Town in Anatolia*, p. 20.
3. ibid., p.19.
4. Moore, 'A Pre-Neolithic Farmer's Village on the Euphrates', pp. 62–70.
5. Wendorf and Schild, *Prehistory of the Nile Valley*, p. 291.
6. Hoffman, *Egypt Before the Pharaohs*, pp. 89–90.
7. ibid., p. 140.
8. Emery, *Archaic Egypt*, p. 39.
9. ibid., p. 40.
10. Schwaller de Lubicz, *Sacred Science*, p. 86.
11. Emery, *Archaic Egypt*, p. 40.
12. Field, 'The Antiquity of Man in Southwestern Asia', p. 55.
13. ibid.
14. Field, 'The Cradle of Home Sapiens', p. 429, citing appendix by L. H. Dudley Buxton in S. Langdon's *Excavations at Kish*, vol. 1, pp. 115–25, and *Journal for the Asiatic Society*, 1932, pp. 967–70. The only complete example contemporaneous with painted pottery found at Jemdet Nasr was

hyper-dolicocephalic. See also Field, 'The Antiquity of Man in Southwestern Asia', p. 60.

15. Field, 'The Antiquity of Man in Southwestern Asia', pp. 59–60.

16. Budge, *The Gods of the Egyptians*, vol. 1, pp. 84, 161.

17. Drower, *The Mandaeans of Iraq and Iran*, p. 197.

18. ibid., p. 198.

19. Sitchin, *The Stairway to Heaven*, p. 77.

20. Drower, *The Mandaeans of Iraq and Iran*, p. 27.

21. Rundle Clark, *Myths and Symbols in Ancient Egypt*, pp. 263–4.

22. Donnelly, *Atlantis – The Antediluvian World*, p. 8, citing Plato's dialogues: *Timaeus*, ii, 517.

23. Donnelly, *Atlantis – The Antediluvian World*, p. 9.

24. Griffiths, 'Atlantis and Egypt', pp. 19–21.

Chapter 22: FATHER OF TERRORS

1. All dynastic dates according to the reckoning of Gardiner in *Egypt of the Pharaohs*.

2. Cole, *The Determination of the Exact Size and Orientation of the Great Pyramid of Giza*.

3. Bonwick, *Pyramid Facts and Fancies*, pp. 41–2.

4. 'The statement relating to Al Mamoon's discovery could hardly rest on a better authority than that of Ibn Abd Alhokm; for not only was he a contemporary writer, having died at Old Cairo, AH 269, that is, thirty-eight years after Al Mamoon's death, but he is certainly quoted by later writers, as an historian of the highest authority' – Dr Rieu of the British Museum, quoted in Bonwick, *Pyramid Facts and Fancies* pp. 41–2. Another Arab, Al-Raisi, claimed that the body-shaped case still stood at the Cairo palace door in the year AH 511, or AD 1133. See ibid.

5. Colonel R. W. Howard-Vyse left England in 1837, openly proclaiming that he was about to make a 'dramatic discovery' in respect to the Great Pyramid. He had his father's money and was able to hire workmen galore, but when, after several months, he had nothing to show for his activities, it has been said that he grew a little desperate. His digging concession from the Egyptian authorities was running out, and he knew that unless he came up with a stunning find, then his heavy-handed explorations would be at an end. Shortly afterwards he announced to the world that he had discovered the secret of the Great Pyramid – a sealed room containing quarry marks naming Khufu as its builder. He gained instant recognition and fame, and there the matter rested until certain diligent researchers

pointed out that the cartouches bearing Khufu's name were wrongly spelt – the first consonant was incorrect. More coincidentally, it was misspelt in exactly the same way as in the first edition of Sir John Gardner Wilkinson's *Materia Hieroglyphica*, published in Amsterdam by Heynis Books in 1806. Howard-Vyse is known to have had access to a copy of Wilkinson's book, so the question remains: did he discover the inscriptions or did he have them painted out of desperation for his own ruthless purposes? For a full account of this debate, see Jochmans, *The Hall of Records*, pp. 194–5.

6. Fakhry, *The Pyramids*, p. 159.
7. Rundle Clark, *Myth and Symbol in Ancient Egypt*, p. 37.
8. ibid., p. 151.
9. Bonwick, *Pyramid Facts and Fancies*, p. 109.
10. *The Mysteries of the Sphinx*, TV documentary, American edition, 1994.
11. Jochmans, *The Hall of Records*, p. 202.
12. Maspero, *The Dawn of Civilization, Egypt and Chaldea*, p. 366.
13. Hassan, *The Sphinx – Its History in Light of Recent Excavations*, pp. 222–4.
14. West, *Serpent in the Sky – The High Wisdom of Ancient Egypt*, pp. 196–232.
15. Schoch, 'Redating the Great Sphinx of Giza', pp. 52–9, 66–70.
16. *The Mysteries of the Sphinx*, TV documentary, English edition, BBC, *Timewatch* series, 1994.
17. *The Mysteries of the Sphinx*, TV documentary, American edition, 1994.
18. Modern astronomers have been able to calculate that the true period of one precessional cycle is, in fact, 25,773 years, this meaning that it takes each sign 2,148 years to cross the equinoctial line and 71.6 years to move one degree of a cycle. To save confusion, I have decided to remain with the ancient calculations.
19. Figures calculated from the Skyglobe 3.5 computer programme. (Thanks originally to Graham Hancock.)
20. See Sellers, *The Death of Gods in Ancient Egypt*.
21. Bauval and Gilbert, *The Orion Mystery*, pp. 242–9.
22. See Bonwick, *Pyramid Facts and Fancies*, pp. 166–8, for various theories linking the angles, dimensions and geometry of the Great Pyramid with both precession and the obliquity of the ecliptic.
23. Massey, *Ancient Egypt the Light of the World*, vol. 1, p. 339.
24. ibid.
25. For a full account of the Osireion, see Hancock, *Fingerprints of the Gods*, pp. 399–407.
26. ibid., p. 400, citing *The Times*, London, 17 March 1914.
27. ibid., p. 404, citing *The Times*, London, 17 March 1914.
28. ibid.

29. ibid., p. 404–5.
30. ibid., p. 406, citing Margaret Murray, *The Splendour That was Egypt*, pp. 160–61.
31. For example, on the matter of the Valley Temple, Bonwick records: 'Not even the pyramid itself excites more interest and wonder than this edifice recently discovered in the sands near the Sphinx. "It is," according to the learned Renan, "absolutely different from those known elsewhere." Whether temple or tomb, "not an ornament, not a sculpture, not a letter," appeared about it. The statue of King Cephren, with some other figures and tablets, rescued from the well of the building, were evidently thrust down there by the priests in some national struggle or disaster, without connection with the purposes of its erection. One has well characterized the structure as having "a beauty of repose, and an elegance of simplicity."

'Mariette Bey inclines to the opinion that it is the most ancient known sepulchre in the world . . . There can be but little doubt that the so-called temple of the Sphinx [i.e. the Valley Temple], and it may be the Sphinx itself, can claim the age of six thousand years.' (*Pyramid Facts and Fancies*, pp. 107–8.)
32. See, for instance, West, *Serpent of the Sky*, p. 242; Bauval and Hancock, *Keeper of Genesis*, p. 28.

Chapter 23: KOSMOKRATOR

1. Bonwick, *Pyramid Facts and Fancies*, p. 117, citing Ibn Abd Alhokm.
2. Fix, *Pyramid Odyssey*, p. 52, citing Masoudi, *Fields of Gold – Mines of Gems*.
3. Bonwick, *Pyramid Facts and Fancies*, p. 117, citing Ibn Abd Alhokm.
4. ibid.
5. Fix, *Pyramid Odyssey*, p. 52, citing Masoudi, *Fields of Gold – Mines of Gems*.
6. ibid.
7. ibid.
8. Masoudi's full name was Abd el Kadar ben Mohammed al Makrizi, and the Arabic work quoted was originally entitled *Akbar al Zamen – Noumadj al Zemel*. See Fix, *Pyramid Odyssey*, p. 271, ch. 6 n. 7.
9. Fix, *Pyramid Odyssey*, p. 52, citing Masoudi, *Fields of Gold – Mines of Gems*.
10. Tomas, *Atlantis – From Legend to Discovery*, p. 117.
11. A twenty-minute period prior to sunrise was used for the purpose of predicting the heliacal rising of Regulus at the time of the vernal equinox in the tenth millennium BC.
12. Critics will argue that the signs of the zodiac were only invented by the

Greeks around 600 BC, during the precessional age of Aries – hence the connection between this sign and the spring equinox in modern-day astrological zodiacs. Other early zodiacs begin with the star Aldebaran or the Bull's Eye in the sign of Taurus, clearly hinting that these were copied from earlier examples dating back to a time when Taurus rose with the equinoctial sun, sometime between 4490 and 2330 BC. See Parker and Parker, *A History of Astrology*, p. 12. More puzzling, however, are zodiacs that use Regulus, Leo's 'royal star', as their point of commencement. See Parker and Parker, *A History of Astrology*, p. 12. These examples must include the famous stone zodiac originally to be found in the roof of the Temple of Denderah in Upper Egypt, but now in the Louvre museum, Paris. Although it was only carved in around the first century BC, its hieroglyphics clearly record that it was fashioned 'according to the plan laid down in the time of the Companions of Horus', taking its original design back to Predynastic times. See Hope, *Atlantis – Myth or Reality?*, p. 141. In its spiralling circuit of celestial constellations, the sign of Leo stands upon a long serpent exactly on the point of the Vernal Equinox.

If the same precessional argument is applied to star maps showing representations of Leo at the vernal equinox, then this strongly suggests they are copies of much earlier star maps dating back to a time when Leo last rose with the equinoctial sun. Adding weight to this argument is the fact that the Denderah Zodiac, as well as those to be found at the temples of Esneh and E'Dayr, all place the equator at 180 degrees to its present position, indicating that they represent the heavens at a time when the equator did indeed cross the ecliptic at such a longitude, which last occurred around 12,500 years ago. See Smyth, *Our Inheritance in the Great Pyramid*, pp. 318, 321–2.

In the light of this knowledge, various non-academic researchers of prehistory, such as the mythologist H. S. Bellamy, have long attempted to demonstrate a clear relationship between the Denderah Zodiac and the last age of Leo. See Bellamy, *Moons, Myths and Man*, p. 238.

13. Budge, *The Gods of the Egyptians*, vol. 1, p. 515.
14. ibid., vol. 1, p. 364.
15. Carlyon, *A Guide to the Gods*, p. 293.
16. Budge, *The Gods of the Egyptians*, vol. 1, pp. 369–70.
17. By adding together the different angels, wings, measures, flying spirits and fabulous beasts found in the celestial data contained in 2 Enoch 12:1–2, we arrive at canonical figures familiar to the precessional cycle. See Morfill and Charles, *Book of the Secrets of Enoch*, pp. 13–14.
18. Zaehner, *The Dawn and Twilight of Zoroastrianism*, p. 181.
19. ibid., p. 215, citing *'Ulama-yi-Islam*.
20. ibid., pp. 207–8.

21. Williams Jackson, *Zoroaster – The Prophet of Ancient Iran*, p. 179, citing *Bundahishn*, I, 8, XXXIV, I.
22. Zaehner, *The Dawn and Twilight of Zoroastrianism*, p. 209.
23. Plutarch, *Lives*, p. 440.
24. Ulansey, *The Origins of the Mithraic Mysteries*, pp. 89–90.
25. ibid., pp. 40–45.
26. ibid., pp. 25–30.
27. ibid., p. 28.
28. Izady, *The Kurds – A Concise Handbook*, p. 138.
29. Ulansey, *The Origins of the Mithraic Mysteries*, p. 117, citing H. Jackson, 'The Leontocephaline in Roman Mithraism', *Numen*, 32, No. 1 (July 1985), p. 19.
30. ibid., pp. 47, 106.
31. ibid., pp. 11–12.
32. Zaehner, *The Dawn and Twilight of Zoroastrianism*, p. 129.
33. ibid., p. 130.
34. ibid., p. 213.
35. Massey, *The Natural Genesis*, p. 341, citing Minokhird, lxii, 37–9.
36. See ibid. For instance, *barsom* twigs were sacrificed by Zurvan for 1,000 years in the Zurvanite creation myth, while 1,000 is two 500-year periods linked with the myth-cycle of the Egyptian phoenix bird.
37. Mackenzie, *Myths of Babylonia and Assyria*, p. 74.
38. Black and Green, *Gods, Demons and Symbols of Ancient Mesopotamia – An Illustrated Dictionary*, s.v. 'Ninurta', pp. 142–3.
39. In precessional terms, 4,320 solar years represents 60° or two complete zodiacal houses of the great year of 25,920 years. In Indian Brahminic tradition, 4,320 solar years forms 12 divine years each of 360 years. Multiply 4,320 by 100 and you come to 432,000 solar years or 1,200 divine years. Multiply this by two and you get 864,000 years, which forms a subdivision of a Brahmic *yuga* or great age of 4,320,000 years. Finally, if you take 4,320 solar years and multiply it by 1 million, you come to 4,320 million years – a so-called day of Brahma and the alleged age of the earth in Vedic tradition. Finally, 4,320 million solar years is two complete houses or 60° of a grand precessional cycle lasting 1 million precessions, each of 25,920 years.
40. The integral relationship between these various great cycles of time and the myth cycle of the Egyptian phoenix, as portrayed by the Greek writer Hesiod, is outlined in Van Den Broek, *The Myth of the Phoenix – According to Classical and Early Christian Traditions*, pp. 88–99.
41. Greenlees, *The Gospel of the Prophet Mani*, Ch. 11, 'The Myth of the Soul', pp. 37–8.
42. The figure, 144, which is 1,440,000 divided by 10,000, is a major

canonical number in precessional numerology. The figure 12 is the square root of 144, while 1,440 (144 × 10) years constitutes exactly two thirds of one precessional sign of 2,160 years. The figure 144, and multiplications thereof, also relates to the circumference of a circle, and the perimeter of a squared cycle, based on precessional numerology. For a full account of the significance of the numbers 144 and 1,440, see Michell, *The City of Revelation*, pp. 45–7, 54.

43. Santillana, and von Dechend, *Hamlet's Mill*, p. 132.

Chapter 25: AMNESIA OF THE MASSES

1. Baigent, Leigh and Lincoln, *The Holy Blood and the Holy Grail*, pp. 344–5.
2. ibid., p. 28.
3. Sinclair, *The Sword and the Grail*, pp. 91–104.
4. See Collins, 'Rosslyn's Fallen Angel – A Commentary on the Fallen Angel Statue in the Retro-choir of Rosslyn Chapel', in Wallace-Murphy, *The Templar Legacy*.
5. Davidson, *A Dictionary of Angels*, s. v. 'Azza', p. 65.
6. Collins, *The Knights of Danbury*, p. 48.
7. Byron, 'Heaven and Earth – A Mystery', 1821, in *The Poetic Works of Lord Byron*; Moore, *The Loves of the Angels – A Poem, with Memoir*, 1823.
8. See, for instance, Simeon Solomon, 'And the sons of God saw the daughters of men that they were fair', a water- and body-colour dated 1863.
9. Morse (ed.), *News from the Invisible World*: Introductions by Rev. E. W. Sprague, 'Was he a Spiritualist?', and J. J. Morse, 'Experiences in the Family of Rev. John Wesley'.
10. See Cayce, E., in Cayce (ed.), *Edgar Cayce on Atlantis*, and Lehner, *The Egyptian Heritage – Based on the Edgar Cayce Readings*.
11. Fix, *Pyramid Odyssey*, p. 99.
12. Devereux, *Earth Lights Revelation*, p. 29.
13. Arnold, 'How It All Began', in *Proceedings of the First International UFO Congress* (1977).
14. Spencer, *The UFO Encyclopaedia*, pp. 318–19.
15. Flem-Ath and Flem-Ath, *When the Sky Fell*, p. 128.
16. Hapgood, *The Path of the Pole*, pp. 107–9.
17. Sitchin, *The 12th Planet*, p. 324, citing an unspecified article by South African scientists, Adrian Boshier and Peter Beaumont, in *Optima* magazine.
18. Hancock, *Fingerprints of the Gods*, pp. 438, 482–4; Flem-Ath and Flem-Ath, *When the Sky Fell*, pp. 53–71.

19. See Hancock, *Fingerprints of the Gods*, pp. 45–8, for descriptions of Viracocha and his variations as a tall, bearded, white-skinned individual who founded the earliest civilizations of Meso-America. See also Gilbert and Cotterell, *The Mayan Prophecies*, pp. 118–25, citing the work of Don José Diaz Bolio on the Mayan rattlesnake cult of Zamnaism. They speak of the wisdom bringer of the Mexican Maya tribes as Zamna, a god-form of *Ahau Can*, or the 'Great, lordly serpent', an early form of Quetzalcoatl, or Kukulcan, the 'feathered serpent'.

According to Don José, the Mayan priests were known as *chanes*, i.e. 'serpents', a title gained after initiation into the inner mysteries of their religion. Head flattening among the Maya was done to give a child what was known as a *polcan* – an elongated serpent-head, bringing to mind the viper-like faces attributed to the Watchers of Kurdistan. By deforming the infant's head at an early age, it was accepted into the family of *chanes*, or the people of the serpent. The *Ahau Can* also taught the Maya the knowledge of time and time cycles, while the rattlesnake became revered as an important totemic symbol, both in an animalistic and abstract form.

20. Hapgood, *Maps of the Ancient Sea Kings*, p. 221.

21. Santillana and Dechend, *Hamlet's Mill*, p. 132.

22. Massey, *Ancient Egypt the Light of the World*, vol. 1, p. 339.

23. Revealed information originally given to the author by the well-known British psychic, Bernard, in 1985.

24. Haigh, in *Psychic News*, pp. 1, 3. See also *Mysteries of the Sphinx*, TV documentary, American edition, 1994.

Bibliography

If two dates are given, the first relates to original publication and the second refers to the edition or impression used as reference for this work. Key: n. = footnote; nd = no date in work; npp = no place of publication.

(A) RECOMMENDED BOOKLIST

Bauval, Robert, and Adrian Gilbert, *The Orion Mystery*, Heinemann, London, 1994.

Bauval, Robert, and Graham Hancock, *Keeper of Genesis*, Heinemann, London, 1996.

Book of the Secrets of Enoch, The, trans. W. R. Morfill, edit. and intro. R. H. Charles, Oxford University Press, 1896.

Charles, R. H., *The Book of Enoch or 1 Enoch*, Oxford University Press, 1912.

Constantine, Storm, *Scenting Hallowed Blood*, Creed, London, 1996.

Constantine, Storm, *Stalking Tender Prey*, intro. by Andrew Collins, Creed, London, 1995.

Fix, William R., *Pyramid Odyssey*, Jonathan-James Books, Toronto, 1978.

Flem-Ath, Rand and Rose, *When the Sky Fell – In Search of Atlantis*, Weidenfeld & Nicolson, London, 1995.

Hancock, Graham, *Fingerprints of the Gods – A Quest for the Beginning and the End*, Heinemann, London, 1995.

Hapgood, Professor Charles, *The Path of the Pole*, Chilton, New York, 1970.

Hapgood, Professor Charles, *Maps of the Ancient Sea Kings* (1966), Turnstone Books, London, 1979.

Milik, J. T., *The Books of Enoch – Aramaic Fragments of Qumrân Cave 4*, Oxford University Press, 1976.

Norvill, Roy, *Giants – The Vanished Race of Mighty Men*, Aquarian Press, Wellingborough, 1979.

O'Brien, Christian, with Barbara Joy O'Brien, *The Genius of the Few – The Story of Those Who Founded the Garden in Eden*, Turnstone Press, Wellingborough, 1985.

Santillana, Giorgio de, and Hertha von Dechend, *Hamlet's Mill* (1969), Macmillan, London, 1970.

Tomas, Andrew, *Atlantis – From Legend to Discovery*, Robert Hale, London, 1972.

West, John Anthony, *Serpent in the Sky – The High Wisdom of Ancient Egypt*, Wildwood House, London, 1979.

Wilson, Colin, *From Atlantis to the Sphinx*, Virgin, London, 1996.

(B) GENERAL BACKGROUND

Alexander, Philip S., 'The Targumim and Early Exegesis of "Sons of God" in Genesis 6', *Journal of Jewish Studies*, Pt 23, 1972, pp. 60–71.

Arnold, K., 'How It All Began', *Proceedings of the First International UFO Congress* (1977), Warner Bros, New York, 1980.

Attar, Farid ud-Din, *The Conference of the Birds*, trans. and intro. by Afkham Darbandi and Dick Davis, Penguin Books, Harmondsworth, 1984.

Augustine, St, *De Civitate Dei* (The City of God) (AD 413–26), various editions in translation.

Avigad, Nahman, and Yigael Yadin, *A Genesis Apocryphon, A Scroll from the Wilderness of Judaea*, Hebrew University, Jerusalem, 1956.

Bacon, Edward, *Archaeology Discoveries in the 1960s*, Cassell, London, 1971.

Baigent, Michael, Richard Leigh and Henry Lincoln, *The Holy Blood and the Holy Grail*, Jonathan Cape, London, 1982.

Baigent, Michael, and Richard Leigh, *The Temple and the Lodge*, Jonathan Cape, London, 1989.

Bailey, James, *The God-Kings and the Titans*, Hodder & Stoughton, London, 1973.

Barton, George A., *Miscellaneous Babylonian Inscriptions*, Yale University Press, 1918.

Bellamy, H. S., *Moons, Myths and Man*, Faber & Faber, London, 1936.

Berlitz, Charles, *The Lost Ship of Noah – In Search of the Ark at Ararat* (1987), W. H. Allen, London, 1988.

Bibby, Geoffrey, *Looking for Dilmun*, Collins, London, 1970.

Bible, The, Revised Authorized Version (1884) Oxford University Press, 1905.

Black, Jeremy, and Anthony Green, *Gods, Demons and Symbols of Ancient*

Mesopotamia – An Illustrated Dictionary, British Museum Press, London, 1992.

Blair, Edward P., *The Word Illustrated Bible Handbook* (1975), Word Publishing, Milton Keynes, 1987.

Bonwick, James, *Pyramid Facts and Fancies*, Kegan Paul, London, 1877.

Boyce, Mary, *A History of Zoroastrianism* (1975), 3 vols., E. J. Brill, Leiden, 1989.

Boz, Muzaffer, *Cappadocia*, Dönmez Offset, Ankara, Turkey, nd (*c.* 1985).

Braidwood, Robert J. (ed.), *Prehistoric Archaeology Along the Zagros Flanks*, The Oriental Institute of the University of Chicago, 1983.

Brown, J. A. C., in *Pears' Medical Encyclopaedia*, Book Club Associates, London, nd (*c.* 1970).

Bruce, James, *Travels to Discover the Source of the Nile*, ed. C. F. Beckingham, Edinburgh University Press, 1964.

Budge, Sir E. A. Wallis, *The Book of the Cave of Treasures*, The Religious Tract Society, London, 1927.

Budge, Sir E. A. Wallis, *The Gods of the Egyptians*, 2 vols. (1904), Dover Publications, New York, 1969.

Budge, Sir E. A. Wallis, *The Queen of Sheba and her Only Son Menelik – being the 'Book of the Glory of Kings' (Kebra Nagast)*, Martin Hopkinson, London, 1922.

Byron, Lord, 'Heaven and Earth – A Mystery' (1821), included in *The Poetic Works of Lord Byron*, Longman, Hurst, Rees, Orme & Brown, London, 1823.

Cameron, D. O., *Symbols of Birth and of Death in the Neolithic Era*, Kenyon-Deane, London, 1981.

Campbell-Thompson, R., *Semitic Magic*, Luzac, London, 1908.

Carlyon, Richard, *A Guide to the Gods*, Quill, New York, 1982.

Casaubon, Meric, *A True and Faithful Relation of what passed for many Yeers Between Dr John Dee . . . and Some Spirits* (1659), Askin, London, 1974.

Cavendish, Richard, *The Black Arts* (1967), Routledge & Kegan Paul, London, 1974.

Cavendish, Richard (ed.), *Man, Myth and Magic*, 7 vols., Purnell, London, 1970.

Cayce, Edgar Evans, *Edgar Cayce on Atlantis*, ed. Hugh Lynn Cayce, Warner Books, New York, 1968.

Chahin, M., *The Kingdom of Armenia*, Croom Helm, Beckenham, 1987.

Charlesworth, James H., *The Old Testament Pseudepigrapha, Apocalyptic Literature and Testaments*, 2 vols., Darton, Longman & Todd, London, 1983.

Charroux, Robert, *Legacy of the Gods* (1964), Sphere, London, 1979.

Childe, V. Gordon, *New Light on the Most Ancient East*, Kegan Paul, Trench, Trübner, London, 1934.

Churchward, Albert, *Signs and Symbols of Primordial Man* (1910), Allen & Unwin, London, 1923.

Cole, J. H., *The Determination of the Exact Size and Orientation of the Great Pyramid of Giza*, Government Press, Cairo, 1925.

Collins, Andrew, *The Knights of Danbury*, Earthquest Books, Wickford, 1985.

Collins, Andrew, 'Rosslyn's Fallen Angel – A Commentary on the Fallen Angel Statue in the Retro-choir of Rosslyn Chapel', in Tim Wallace-Murphy, *The Templar Legacy*, Friends of Rosslyn, Rosslyn, 1994.

Cory, Isaac Preston, *Ancient Fragments, etc.* (1832), Wizard Bookshelf, Minneapolis, 1975.

Cotterell, Arthur, *A Dictionary of World Mythology* (1979), Oxford University Press, 1986.

Cottrell, Leonard, *The Concise Encyclopedia of Archaeology* (1960), Book Club Associates, London, 1972.

Cottrell, Leonard, *The Land of Shinar*, Souvenir Press, London, 1965.

Curtis, John (ed.), *Early Mesopotamia and Iran – Contact and Conflict 3500–1600 bc*, British Museum Press, London, 1993.

Curtis, Vesta Sarkhosh, *Persian Myths*, British Museum Press, London, 1993.

Dalley, Stephanie, *Myths from Mesopotamia – Creation, the Flood, Gilgamesh and Others* (1989), Oxford University Press, 1990.

Däniken, Erich von, *According to the Evidence*, Souvenir Press, London, 1977.

Däniken, Erich von, *In Search of Ancient Gods – My Pictorial Evidence for the Impossible*, (1973), Book Club Associates, London, 1974.

Davidson, Gustav, *A Dictionary of Angels* (1967), The Free Press, New York, 1971.

Delitzsch, Franz, *A New Commentary on Genesis*, trans. Sophia Taylor, 2 vols., T. & T. Clark, Edinburgh, 1888.

Demir, Ömer, *Cappadocia – Cradle of History*, International Society for the Investigation of Ancient Civilizations, Derinkuyu, Turkey, 1986.

Devereux, Paul, *Earth Lights Revelation*, Blandford, London, 1989.

Devereux, Paul, *Shamanism and the Mystery Lines*, Quantum, Slough, Berks., 1992.

Donnelly, Ignatius, *Atlantis: The Antediluvian World*, Harper & Brothers, New York and London, 1882.

Donnelly, Ignatius, *Ragnarok: The Age of Fire and Gravel*, Sampson Low, Marston, Searle & Rivington, London, 1888.

Drake, W. Raymond, *Gods and Spacemen in Ancient Israel*, Sphere Books, London, 1976.

Drower, E. S., *Peacock Angel – Being some Account of Votaries of a Secret Cult and Their Sanctuaries*, John Murray, London, 1941.

Drower, E. S., *The Mandaeans of Iraq and Iran*, Oxford University Press, 1937.

Easton, M. G., *The Illustrated Bible Dictionary* (1894), Bracken Books, London, 1989.

Eisenman, Robert H., *Maccabees, Zadokites, Christians and Qumrân*, E. J. Brill, Leiden, 1983.

Eisenman, Robert H., and Michael Wise, *The Dead Sea Scrolls Uncovered*, Element Books, Shaftesbury, Dorset, 1992.

Emery, Walter Bryan, *Archaic Egypt*, Penguin Books, Harmondsworth, 1961.

Empson, R. H. W., *The Cult of the Peacock Angel – A Short Account of the Yezîdî Tribes of Kurdistân*, H. F. & G. Witherby, London, 1928.

Fabricius, J. A., *Codex Pseudepigraphus Veteris Testamenti, collectus, castigatus, testimoniisque, censuris et animadversionibus illustratus*, Hamburg, 1722.

Fakhry, Ahmed, *The Pyramids* (1961), University of Chicago Press, 1970.

Ferdowsi [also Firdowsi], *The Epic of the Kings – Shah-Nama*, trans. Reuben Levy (1967), Arkana, London, 1990.

Field, Henry, 'The Antiquity of Man in Southwestern Asia', *American Anthropologist*, No. 35, 1933, pp. 51–62.

Field, Henry, 'The Cradle of Homo Sapiens', *American Journal of Archaeology*, V, XXXVI, The Archaeological Institute of America, 1932, pp. 426–30.

Firdowsi [also Ferdowsi], *The Shah Nameh of the Persian Poet Firdausi*, trans. James Atkinson, Frederick Warne, London, 1886.

Foakes-Jackson, F. J., *The Biblical History of the Hebrews*, Heffer, London, 1909.

Frye, Richard N., *The Heritage of Persia* (1963), Mentor, New York, 1966.

Gardiner, Sir Alan, *Egypt of the Pharaohs*, Oxford University Press, 1961.

Gilbert, Adrian, and Maurice M. Cotterell, *The Mayan Prophecies*, Element Books, Shaftesbury, Dorset, 1995.

Gimbutas, Marija, *The Civilization of the Goddess*, Harper, San Francisco, 1991.

Graves, Robert (ed.), *New Larousse Encyclopaedia of Mythology* (1959), Hamlyn, London, 1983.

Graves, Robert, and Raphael Patai, *Hebrew Myths – the Book of Genesis*, Cassell, London, 1964.

Greenlees, Duncan, *The Gospel of the Prophet Mani*, Theosophical Publishing House, Adyar, Madras, 1956.

Griffiths, J. Gwyn, 'Atlantis and Egypt', *Atlantis and Egypt with Other Selected Essays*, University of Wales Press, 1991, pp. 3–30.

Guest, John S., *The Yezidis – A Study in Survival*, KPI, London and New York, 1987.

Haigh, T., in *Psychic News*, 20 August 1994, No. 3245.

Hall, Manly P., *An Encyclopedic Outline of Masonic, Hermetic, Qabbalistic and Rosicrucian Symbolic Philosophy* (1901), Philosophical Research Society, Los Angeles, 1977.

Hall, Mark A., 'Giant Bones', *Wonders – Seeking the Truth in a Universe of Mysteries*, vol. 2, No. 1, Bloomington, Maryland, March 1993.

Hamze'ee, M. Reza, *The Yaresan – A Sociological, Historical and Religio-Historical Study of a Kurdish Community*, Klaus Schwarz, Berlin, 1990.

Hancock, Graham, *The Sign and the Seal – A Quest for the Lost Ark of the Covenant*, Heinemann, London, 1992.

Harnack, Curtis, *Persian Lions, Persian Lambs*, Gollancz, London, 1965.

Hassan, Selim, *The Sphinx – Its History in Light of Recent Excavations*, Government Press, Cairo, 1949.

Hastings, James (ed.), *Encyclopaedia of Religion and Ethics*, 13 vols. (1915), T. & T. Clark, Edinburgh, 1930.

Haug, M., *Essays on the Sacred Language, Writings and Religion of the Parsis*, Kegan Paul, Trench, Trübner, London, nd (*c.* 1880).

Heinberg, Richard, *Memories and Visions of Paradise* (1989), Aquarian Press, Wellingborough, Northants, 1990.

Henning, W. B., 'The Book of the Giants', *Bulletin of the School of Oriental and African Studies*, vol. 11, Pt 1, 1943, pp. 52–74.

Herodotus, *Histories*, trans. George Rawlinson, 2 vols. (1858), J. M. Dent, London, 1940.

Hibben, Frank C., *The Lost Americans*, Crowell, New York, 1946.

Hoffman, Michael A., *Egypt before the Pharaohs* (1979), Ark, London, 1984.

Holy Scriptures of the Old Testament – Hebrew and English, The British and Foreign Bible Society, London, 1925.

Hooke, S. H., *Middle Eastern Mythology*, Penguin, Harmondsworth, 1963.

Hope, Murray, *Atlantis – Myth or Reality?*, Arkana, London, 1991.

Horne, Alex, *King Solomon's Temple in the Masonic Tradition* (1972), Aquarian Press, Wellingborough, Northants, 1975.

Inman, Thomas, *Ancient Faiths Embodied in Ancient Names*, 2 vols., privately published, London and Liverpool, 1869.

Izady, Mehrdad R., *The Kurds – A Concise Handbook*, Crane Russak, London, 1992.

Jackson, Keith B., *Beyond the Craft* (1980), Lewis Masonic, London, 1982.

Jackson, Nigel, 'Bird's Way and Cow-Lane – the Starry Path of the Spirits', *The Ley Hunter*, No. 121, Summer 1994, p. 30.

Jackson Coleman, S., 'Treasures of an Archangel' in 'Folklore of Wiltshire', *Treasury of Folklore*, No. 23, nd (*c.* 1920).

Jacobsen, Thorkild, *The Treasures of Darkness – A History of Mesopotamian Religion*, Yale University Press, 1976.

Jean Chrysostom, 'Homelies sur la Genèse', *Saint Jean Chrysostome Oeuvres Complètes*, trans. M. Jeannin, ed. L. Guerin, Paris, 1865.

Jerome, St, 'Homily 45 on Psalm 132 (133)', trans. Marie Liguori Ewald, in *Fathers of the Church*, 48, 1964, pp. 338–9.

Jochmans, Joseph, *The Hall of Records*, Part One: *Revelations of the Great Pyramid and Sphinx*, Chapter II, 'A Glimmer at Giza – The Lost Hall and its Secret Brotherhood', privately published, 1985.

Jones, B. E., *Freemason's Book of the Royal Arch* (1957), Harrap, London, 1986.

Josephus, Flavius, *Antiquities of the Jews* and *Wars of the Jews*, in *The Works of Flavius Josephus*, trans. William Whiston, W. P. Nimmo, Edinburgh, nd (*c.* 1870).

Katrak, Sohrab K. H., *Who Are the Parsees?*, Herald Press, Karachi, 1958.

Kramer, S. N., *Sumerian Mythology*, Philadelphia, 1944.

Lambert, W. G., and A. R. Millard, *Atra-Hasis – The Babylonian Story of the Flood*, Oxford University Press, 1969.

Laurence, Richard, *The Book of Enoch the Prophet – An Apocryphal Production, etc., from an Ethiopic ms. in the Bodleian Library* (1821), John Henry Parker, Oxford, 1838.

Layard, Sir Austen Henry, *Nineveh and Its Remains* (1851), John Murray, London, 1891.

Leatherdale, Clive, *Dracula – the Novel and the Legend*, Desert Island Books, Brighton, Sussex, 1993.

Legge, F., *Forerunners and Rivals of Christianity, being Studies in Religious History from 330 bc to 330 ad*, 2 vols., Cambridge University Press, 1915.

Lehner, Mark, *The Egyptian Heritage* (1974), ARE Press, Virginia Beach, Va., 1976.

Lempriere, J., *A Classical Dictionary*, Routledge, London, 1919.

Lenormant, François, *Chaldean Magic – Its Origin and Development*, Samuel Bagster, London, 1877.

Mackenzie, Donald A., *Indian Myth and Legend*, Gresham Publishing, London, 1913.

Mackenzie, Donald A., *Myths of Babylonia and Assyria*, Gresham Publishing, London, nd (*c.* 1910).

Mackenzie, Kenneth, *The Royal Masonic Cyclopaedia* (1877), Aquarian Press, Wellingborough, Northants, 1987.

Mango, Andrew, *Discovering Turkey*, B. T. Batsford, London, 1971.

Manson, T. W. (ed.), *A Companion to the Bible*, T. & T. Clark, Edinburgh, 1956.

Maspero, Gaston, *The Dawn of Civilization, Egypt and Chaldea*, Society for Promoting Christian Knowledge, London, 1896.

Massey, Gerald, *Ancient Egypt the Light of the World*, 2 vols., T. Fisher Unwin, London, 1907.

Massey, Gerald, *The Natural Genesis*, 2 vols., Williams & Norgate, London, 1883.

Matheson, Sylvia A., *Persia – An Archaeological Guide*, 1972, Faber & Faber, London, 1979.

Mehr, Farhang, *The Zoroastrian Tradition – An Introduction to the Ancient Wisdom of Zarathustra*, Element Books, Shaftesbury, Dorset, 1991.

Mellaart, James, *Çatal Hüyük – A Neolithic Town in Anatolia*, Thames & Hudson, London, 1967.

Michell, John, *The City of Revelation*, Garnstone Press, London, 1972.

Moore, A. M. T., 'A Pre-Neolithic Farmer's Village on the Euphrates', *Scientific American*, No. 241, August 1979, pp. 62–70.

Moore, Thomas, *The Loves of the Angels – A Poem, with Memoir*, Frederick Warne, London, 1823.

Morgenstern, Julian, 'The Mythological Background of Psalm 82', *Hebrew Union College Annual*, vol. 16, 1939, pp. 29–126.

Morse, J. J. (ed.), *News from the Invisible World – From the Pen of Rev. John Wesley, with the Letters of the Wesley Family and the Diary of Mr Samuel Wesley, Sr., with Added Proof of John Wesley's Spiritualism*, Rev. E. W. Sprague, privately published, 1928.

Moses Khorenats'i, *History of the Armenians*, trans. and comm. Robert W. Thomson, Harvard University Press, 1978.

Mundkur, Balaji, *The Cult of the Serpent – An Interdisciplinary Survey of Its Manifestations and Origins*, State University of New York Press, Albany, NY, 1983.

Nagel's Encyclopedia Guide – Turkey, Nagel Publishers, Geneva, 1974.

Nigosian, Solomon A., *Judaism – The Way of Holiness*, Crucible, Wellingborough, Northants, 1986.

Odelain, O., and R. Séguineau, *Dictionary of Proper Names and Places in the Bible* (1978), Robert Hale, London, 1991.

Oesterley, W. O. E., and Theodore H. Robinson, *Hebrew Religion – Its*

Origin and Development, Society for Promoting Christian Knowledge, London, 1952.

Parker, Derek and Julia, *A History of Astrology*, André Deutsch, London, 1983.

Plato's *Timaeus*, various editions.

Plutarch, *Lives*, ed. John and William Langhorne, William Tegg, London, 1865.

Politeyan, Rev. J., *Biblical Discoveries in Egypt, Palestine and Mesopotamia*, Elliot Stock, London, 1915.

Prophet, Elizabeth Clara, *Forbidden Mysteries of Enoch – Fallen Angels and the Origins of Evil* (1983), Summit University Press, Livingston, Mont., 1992.

Ring, Kenneth, *Heading toward Omega*, Morrow, New York, 1985.

Roberts, James, and James Donaldson (eds.), *Ante-Nicene Christian Library – Translations of the Writings of the Fathers down to a d 325*, vol. XVIII: *The Writings of Tertullian*, 3 vols., T. & T. Clark, London, 1870.

Roux, Georges, *Ancient Iraq* (1966), Penguin Books, Harmondsworth, 1980.

Rundle Clark, R. T., *Myths and Symbols in Ancient Egypt* (1958), Thames & Hudson, London, 1978.

Sabar, Yona, *The Folk Literature of the Kurdistani Jews – An Anthology*, Yale University Press, New Haven, 1982.

Scaliger, J. J., *Chronicus Canon of Eusebius*, Amsterdam, 1658.

Schneweis, Emil, *Angels and Demons According to Lactantius*, Catholic University of America Press, Washington, DC, 1944.

Schoch, Dr Robert M., 'Redating the Great Sphinx of Giza', *KMT, A Modern Journal of Ancient Egypt*, San Francisco, 3:2, Summer 1992, pp. 52–9, 66–70.

Schwaller de Lubicz, R. A., *Sacred Science*, Inner Traditions, Rochester, Vermont, 1961.

Scott, D. A., 'Zoroastrian Traces along the Upper Amu Darya (Oxus)', *Journal of the Royal Asiatic Society*, No. 2, 1984.

Sellers, Jane B., *The Death of Gods in Ancient Egypt*, Penguin Books, Harmondsworth, 1992.

Sinclair, Andrew, *The Sword and the Grail* (1992), Century, London, 1993.

Sitchin, Zecharia, *The 12th Planet*, Avon Books, New York, 1976.

Sitchin, Zecharia, *The Stairway to Heaven* (1980), Avon Books, New York, 1983.

Smith, George, *The Chaldean Account of Genesis*, Sampson Low, Marston, Searle & Rivington, London, 1876.

Smyth, Professor Charles Piazzi, *Our Inheritance in the Great Pyramid*, Alexander Strahan, London, 1864.

Solecki, Ralph S., *Shanidar – The Humanity of Neanderthal Man*, Allen Lane The Penguin Press, London, 1972.

Solecki, Rose L., 'Predatory Bird Rituals at Zawi Chemi Shanidar', *Sumer*, XXXIII, Pt 1, 1977, pp. 42–7.

Solecki, Rose L., and Thomas H. McGovern, 'Predatory Birds and Prehistoric Man', *Theory and Practice – Essays Presented to Gene Weltfish Studies in Anthropology*, 1980, pp. 89–95.

Spence, Lewis, *Myths and Legends of Babylonia and Assyria*, Harrap, London, 1916.

Spencer, John, *The UFO Encyclopaedia*, Headline, London, 1991.

Staniland Wake, C., *Serpent-Worship and Other Essays, with a Chapter on Totemism* (1888), Banton Press, Largs, 1990.

Strugnell, J., 'The Angelic Liturgy', in *Congress Volume Oxford*, Supplements to Vetus Testamentum, vii, Leiden, 1960.

Summers, Montague, *The Vampire – His Kith and Kin* (1928), University Books, New York, 1960.

Suster, Gerald, *John Dee Essential Readings*, Crucible, Wellingborough, Northants, 1986.

Syncellus, *Chronographia*, in Fabricius, *Codex Pseudepigraphus Veteris Testamenti*, vol. 1, Paris, 1652.

Trowbridge, Stephen Van Rensselaer, 'The Alevis, or Deifiers of Ali', *Harvard Theological Review*, 1909, pp. 340–53.

Trubshaw, Robert, 'Bronze Age Rituals in Turkmenistan', *Mercian Mysteries*, No. 22, February 1995, pp. 30–32.

Turner, Ann Warren, *Vultures*, David McKay, New York, 1973.

Turner, Robert (ed.), *The Heptarchia Mystica of John Dee*, Aquarian, Wellingborough, Northants, 1986.

Ulansey, David, *The Origins of the Mithraic Mysteries – Cosmology and Salvation in the Ancient World*, Oxford University Press, 1989.

Van Den Broek, R., *The Myth of the Phoenix – According to Classical and Early Christian Traditions*, E. J. Brill, Leiden, 1972.

Vermes, Geza, *The Dead Sea Scrolls in English* (1962), Penguin Books, Harmondsworth, 1990.

Warren, William F., *Paradise Found – The Cradle of the Human Race at the North Pole*, Sampson Low, Marston, Searle & Rivington, London, 1885.

Wendorf, Fred, and Romuald Schild, *Prehistory of the Nile Valley*, Academic Press, New York, 1976.

Westwood, Jennifer, *The Atlas of Mysterious Places*, Weidenfeld & Nicolson, London, 1987.

Wigram, Rev. W. A., and Edgar T. A. Wigram, *The Cradle of Mankind – Life in Eastern Kurdistan*, Adam & Charles Black, London, 1914.

Williams Jackson, A. V., *Zoroaster – The Prophet of Ancient Iran*, Macmillan, London, 1899.

Wood, Edward J., *Giants and Dwarves*, Richard Bentley, London, 1868.

Woolley, Sir Leonard, *Excavations at Ur*, Ernest Benn, London, 1954.

Wright, William (ed.), *The Illustrated Bible Treasury*, Thomas Nelson, London, 1897.

Zaehner, R. C., *The Dawn and Twilight of Zoroastrianism*, Weidenfeld & Nicolson, London, 1961.

(C) TV DOCUMENTARIES

Mysteries of the Sphinx, Timewatch, British edition, screened in UK, November 1994.

Mysteries of the Sphinx, American edition, 1994.

Wildlife on One with David Attenborough, BBC, screened in UK, 18 May 1995.

Index

BOOKS OF RELATED INTEREST

Göbekli Tepe: Genesis of the Gods
The Temple of the Watchers and the Discovery of Eden
by Andrew Collins

The Cygnus Key
The Denisovan Legacy, Göbekli Tepe, and the Birth of Egypt
by Andrew Collins

Gods of Eden
Egypt's Lost Legacy and the Genesis of Civilization
by Andrew Collins

Atlantis in the Caribbean
And the Comet That Changed the World
by Andrew Collins

Slave Species of the Gods
The Secret History of the Anunnaki and Their Mission on Earth
by Michael Tellinger

DNA of the Gods
The Anunnaki Creation of Eve and the Alien Battle for Humanity
Chris H. Hardy, Ph.D.

There Were Giants Upon the Earth
Gods, Demigods, and Human Ancestry: The Evidence of Alien DNA
by Zecharia Sitchin

Black Genesis
The Prehistoric Origins of Ancient Egypt
by Robert Bauval and Thomas Brophy, Ph.D.

Inner Traditions • Bear & Company
P.O. Box 388
Rochester, VT 05767
1-800-246-8648
www.InnerTraditions.com

Or contact your local bookseller